Snow White with the Red Hair

Sorata Akiduki

11

The Tortoise and the Hare Version
FWOMP
Giddyap.
Umm?
THE END

THE STORY

Shirayuki was born with beautiful hair as red as apples, but when her rare hair earns her unwanted attention from the notorious prince Raj, she's forced to flee her home. A young man named Zen helps her in the forest of the neighboring kingdom, Clarines, and it turns out he is that kingdom's second prince! Shirayuki decides to accompany Zen back to Wistal, the capital city of Clarines.

Shirayuki has met all manner of people since becoming a court herbalist, and her relationship with Zen continues to grow, as the two have finally made their feelings known to each other.

SHIRAYUKI
"They say that red is the color of destiny."
PRINCE ZEN
The second prince of the kingdom of Clarines.
Working as a court herbalist. Has feelings for Zen—feelings that he shares.
MITSUHIDE & KIKI
PRINCE IZANA
OBI

Zen's aides. They're good friends who share a strong bond.

Zen's older brother and the crown prince of the kingdom. Keeping a close eye on Shirayuki and Zen's relationship...

Former assassin. Currently, Zen's underling. Served as Shirayuki's bodyguard for part of her stay in Lilias.

After being appointed a full-fledged court herbalist, Shirayuki travels to the northern checkpoint city of Lilias with her boss, Ryu. When a mysterious illness breaks out, it afflicts Shirayuki and Obi, but with the help of their new friends, they find the source of the outbreak and save the day!

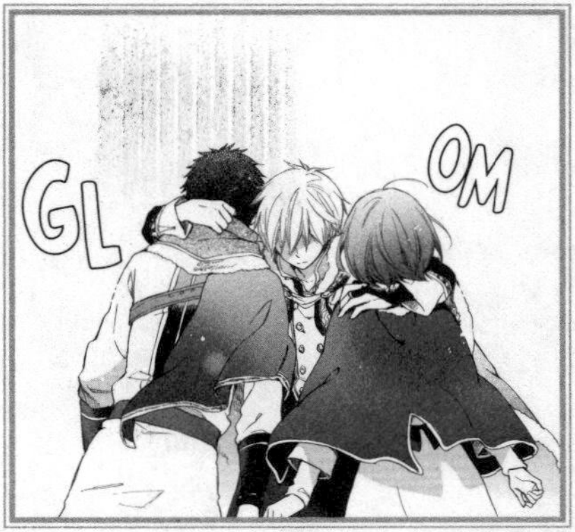
GL
OM

After making it back to Wistal, Shirayuki and Zen head into town for a day, in what is actually Zen's first-ever date.♡

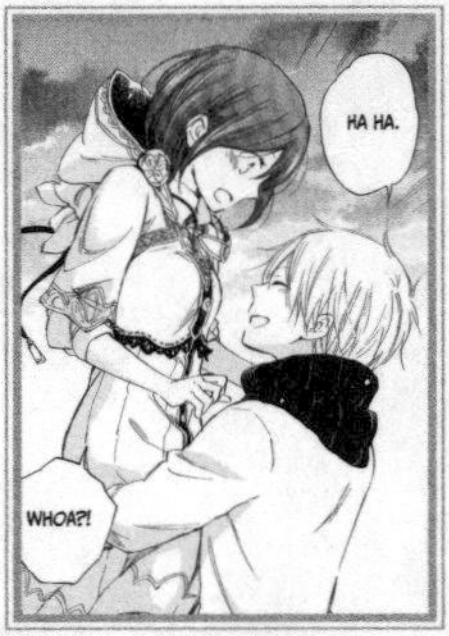
HA HA.
WHOA?!

Meanwhile, the deadline to fulfill the promise that Kiki made her father is approaching. In one year's time, she must leave Wistal Palace and return home to inherit her father's title and become Viscountess Seiran...
After recalling when she first met Zen and Mitsuhide, Kiki decides she wants to watch over Zen and Shirayuki for a while longer, prompting her to ask her father for an extension. When he responds by bringing up the matter of finding her a suitor, she says, "When the times comes, I will make a proposal myself."

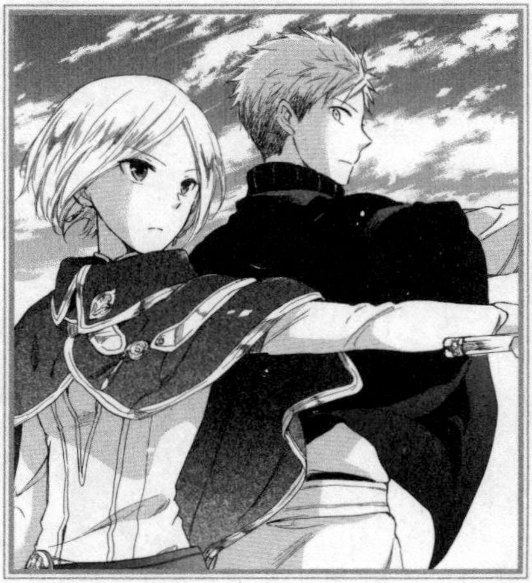

Snow White with the Red Hair

VOLUME 11
TABLE of CONTENTS

Chapter 45

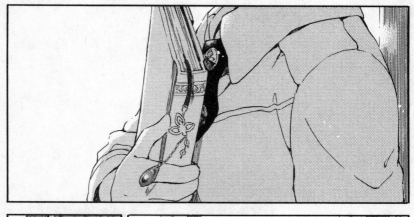

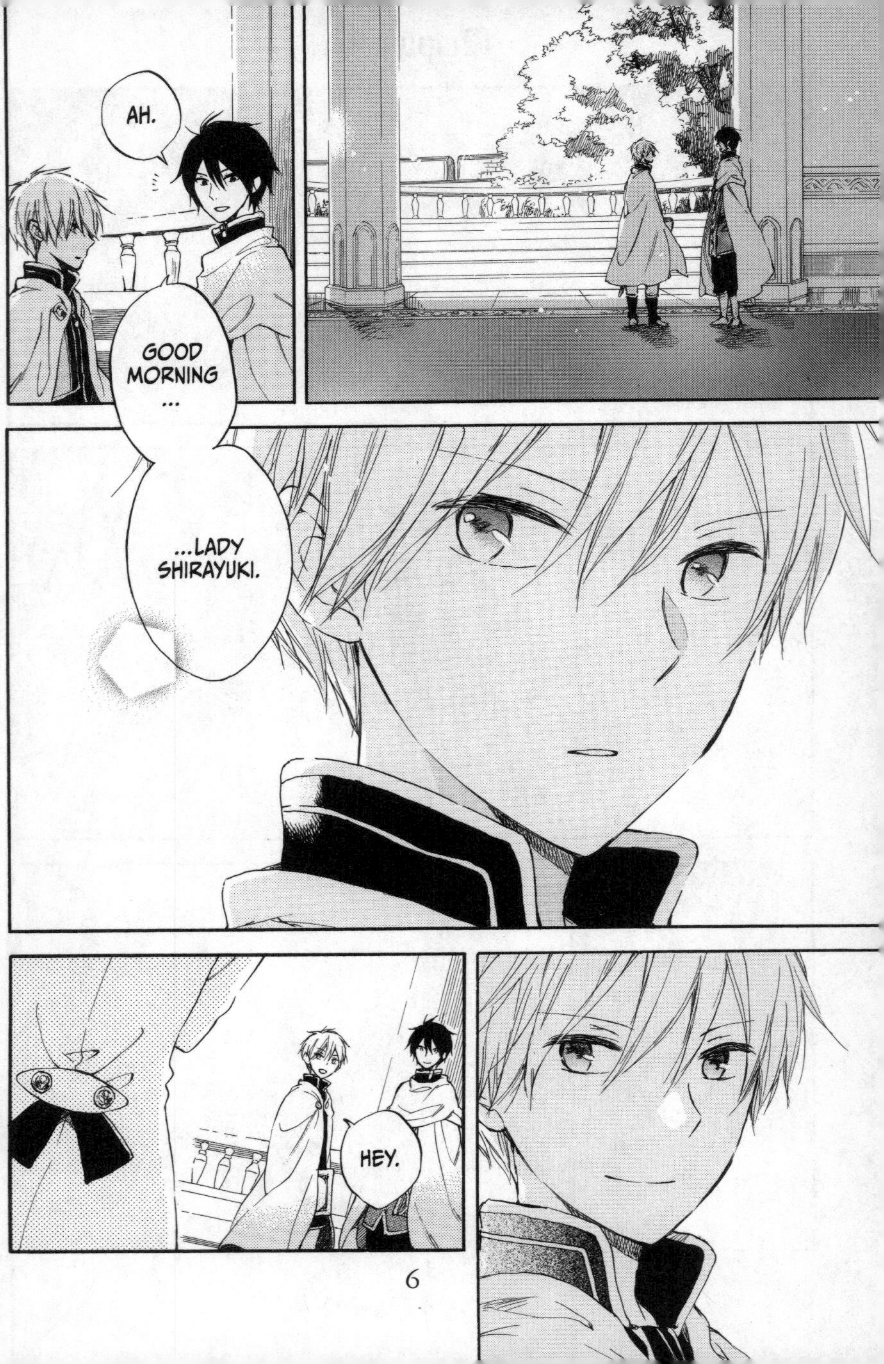
AH.
GOOD MORNING ...
...LADY SHIRAYUKI.
HEY.

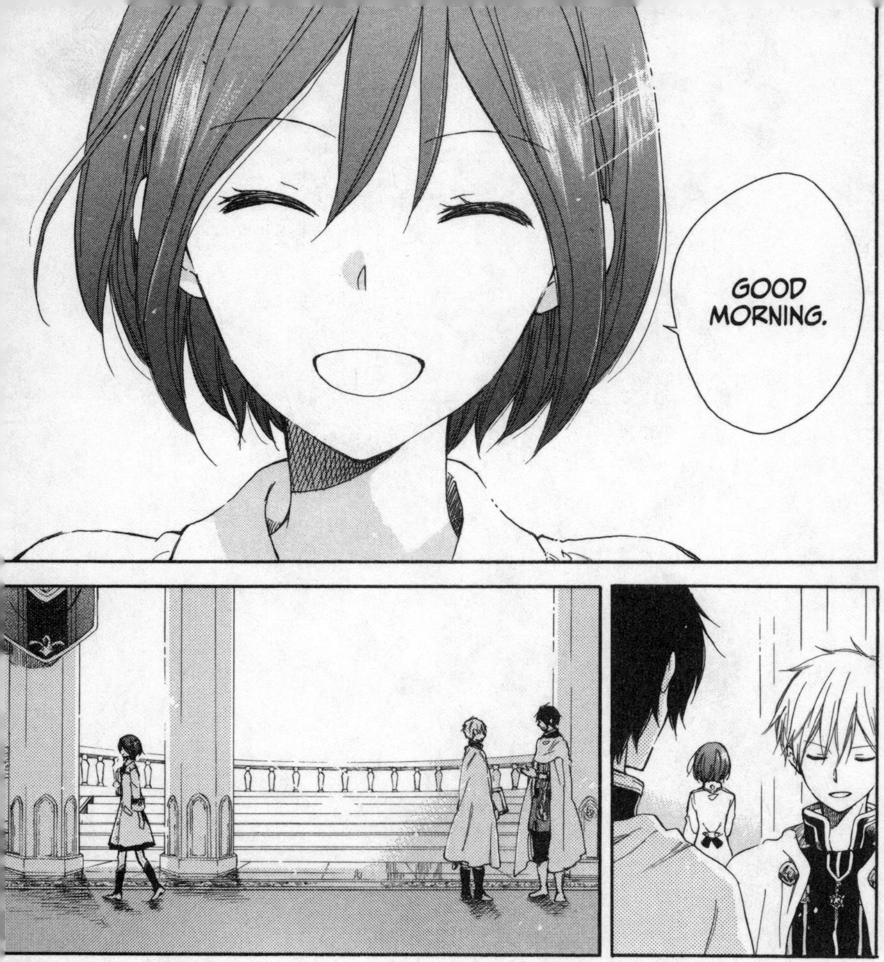
GOOD MORNING.

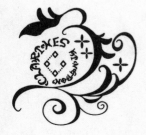

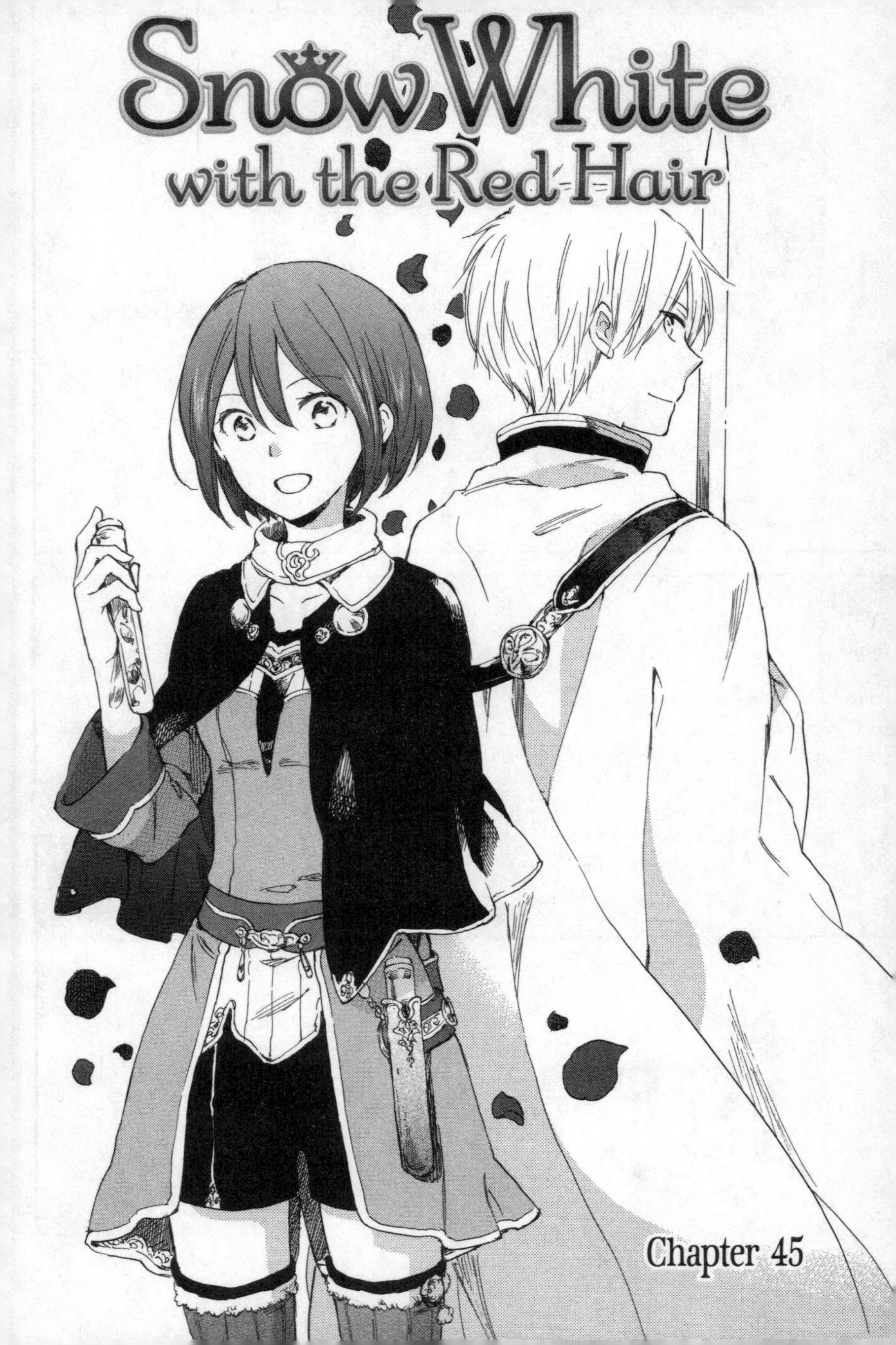
Snow White
with the Red Hair
Chapter 45

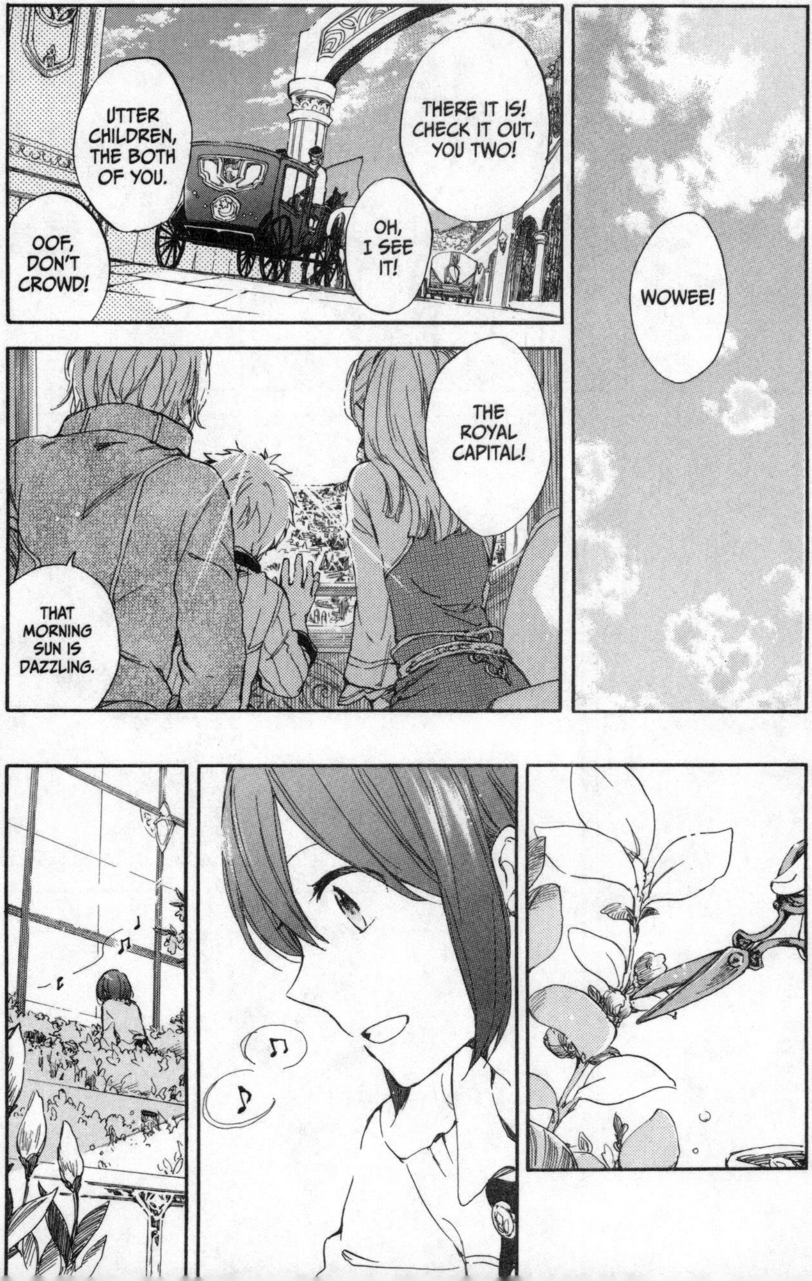
WOWEE!
THERE IT IS! CHECK IT OUT, YOU TWO!
OH, I SEE IT!
UTTER CHILDREN, THE BOTH OF YOU.
OOF, DON'T CROWD!
THE ROYAL CAPITAL!
THAT MORNING SUN IS DAZZLING.

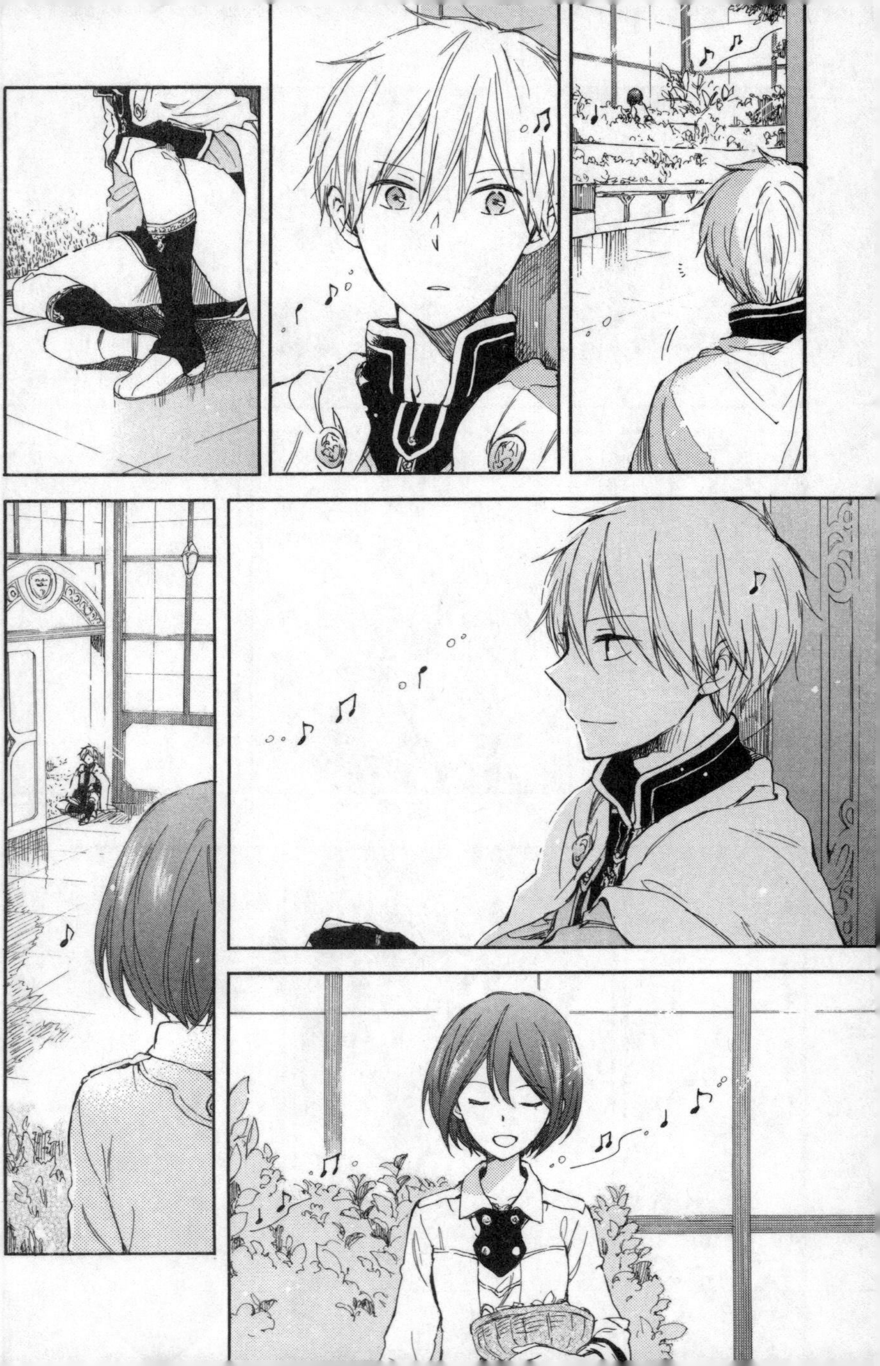

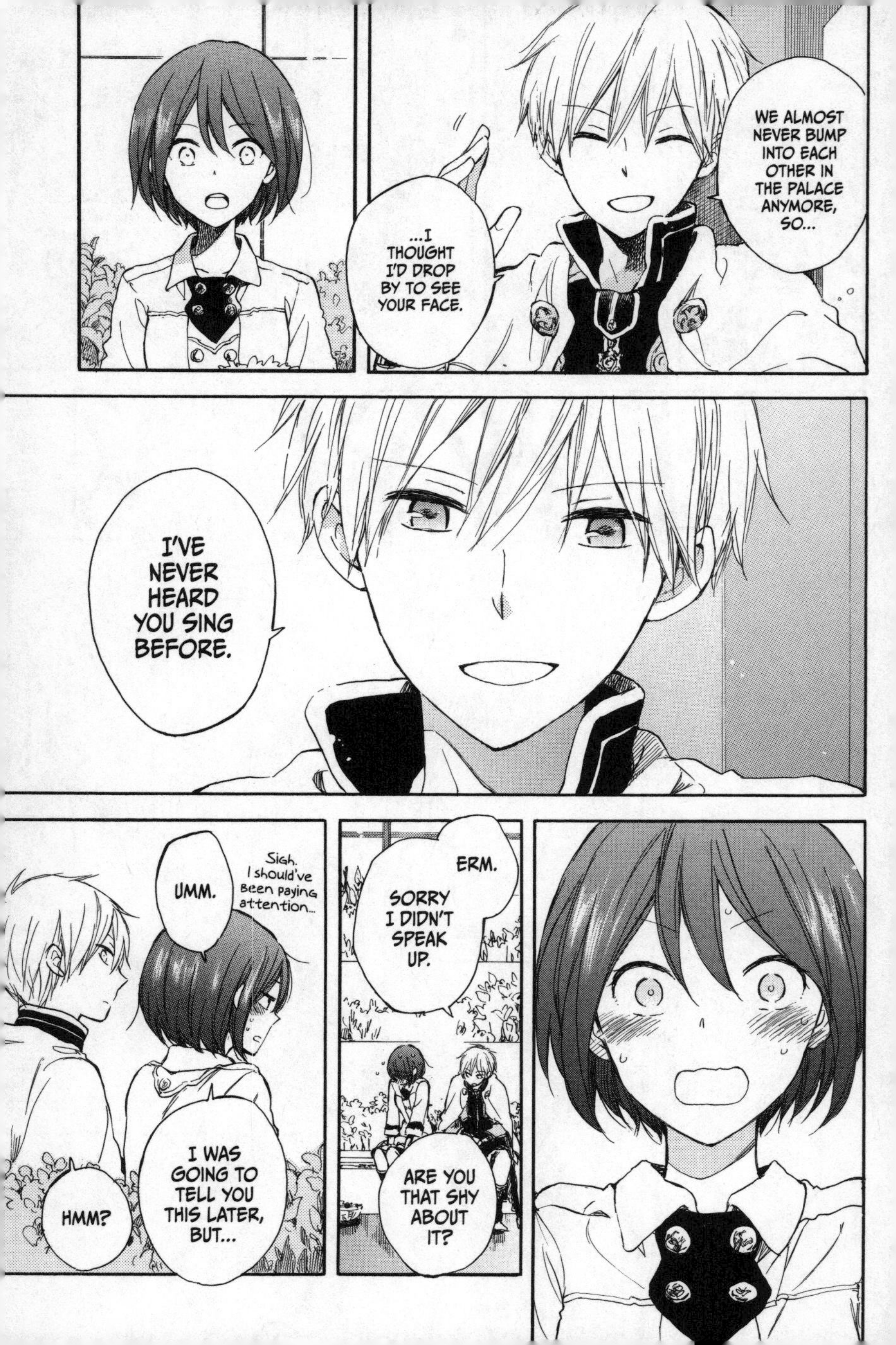
WE ALMOST NEVER BUMP INTO EACH OTHER IN THE PALACE ANYMORE, SO...
...I THOUGHT I'D DROP BY TO SEE YOUR FACE.
I'VE NEVER HEARD YOU SING BEFORE.
ERM.
SORRY I DIDN'T SPEAK UP.
ARE YOU THAT SHY ABOUT IT?
UMM.
Sigh. I should've been paying attention...
I WAS GOING TO TELL YOU THIS LATER, BUT...
HMM?

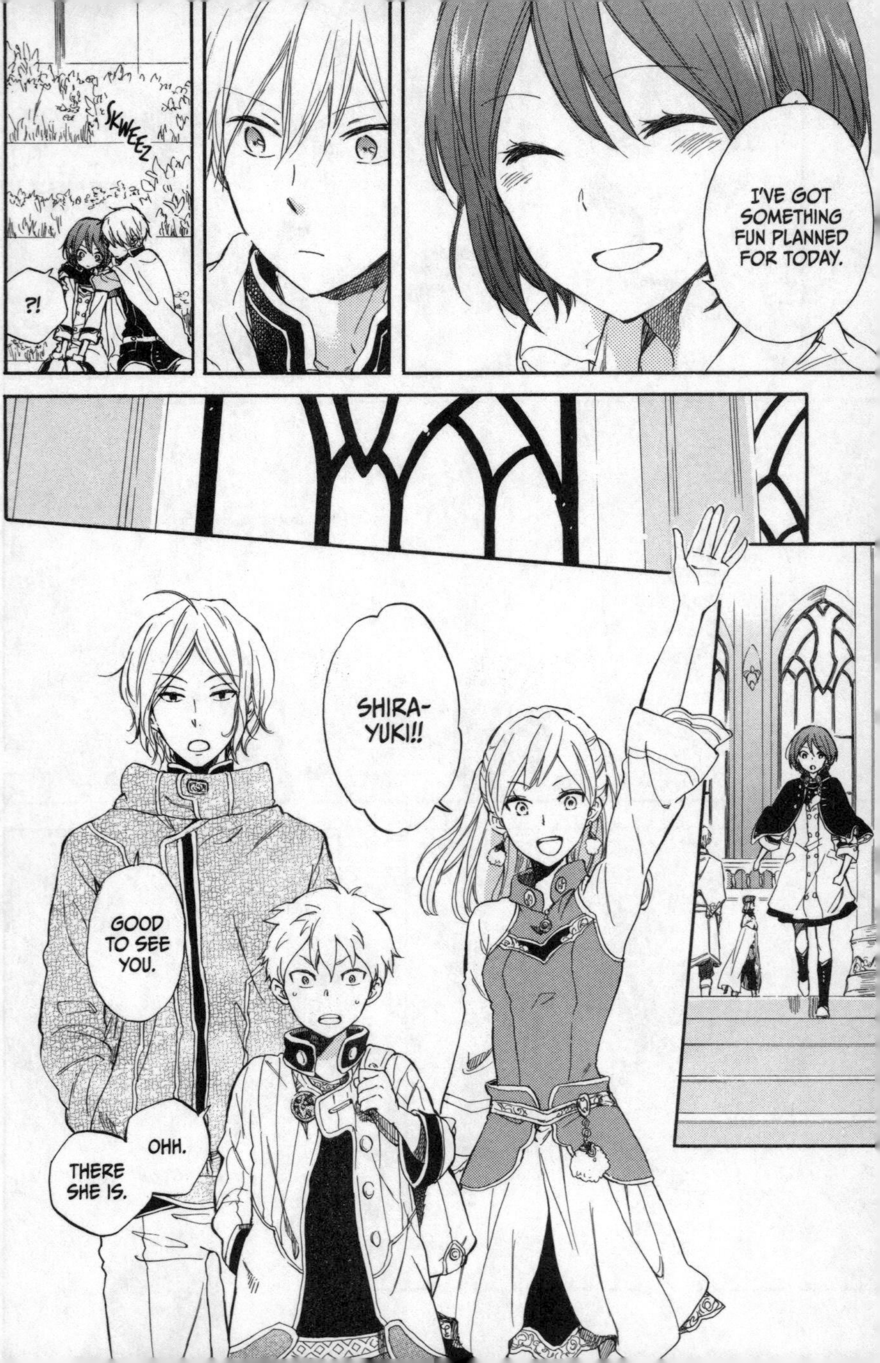
I'VE GOT SOMETHING FUN PLANNED FOR TODAY.
SKWEEZ
?!
SHIRA-YUKI!!
GOOD TO SEE YOU.
OHH. THERE SHE IS.

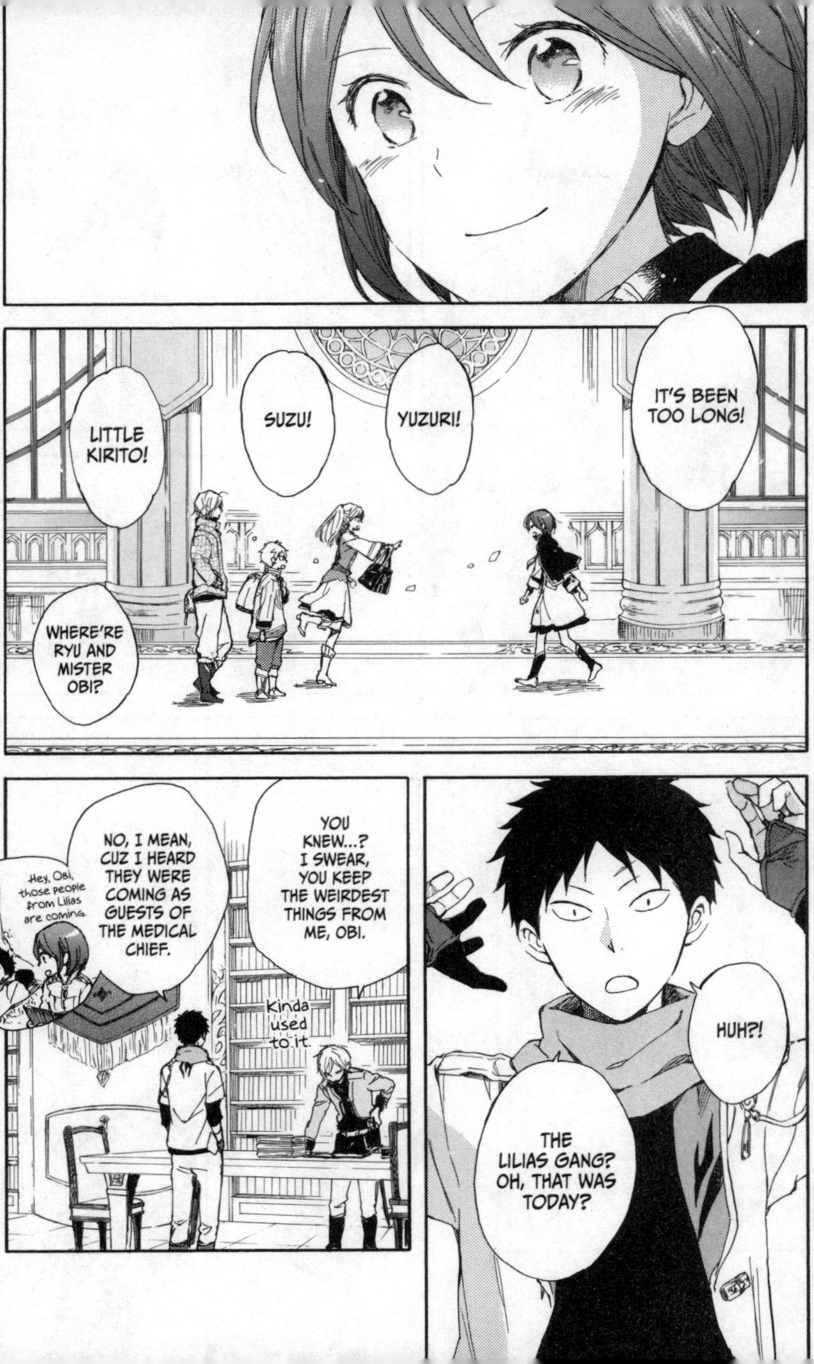
IT'S BEEN TOO LONG!
YUZURI!
SUZU!
LITTLE KIRITO!
WHERE'RE RYU AND MISTER OBI?
HUH?!
THE LILIAS GANG? OH, THAT WAS TODAY?
YOU KNEW...? I SWEAR, YOU KEEP THE WEIRDEST THINGS FROM ME, OBI.
Kinda used to it.
NO, I MEAN, CUZ I HEARD THEY WERE COMING AS GUESTS OF THE MEDICAL CHIEF.
Hey, Obi, those people from Lilias are coming.
Oh yeah?
Zzz

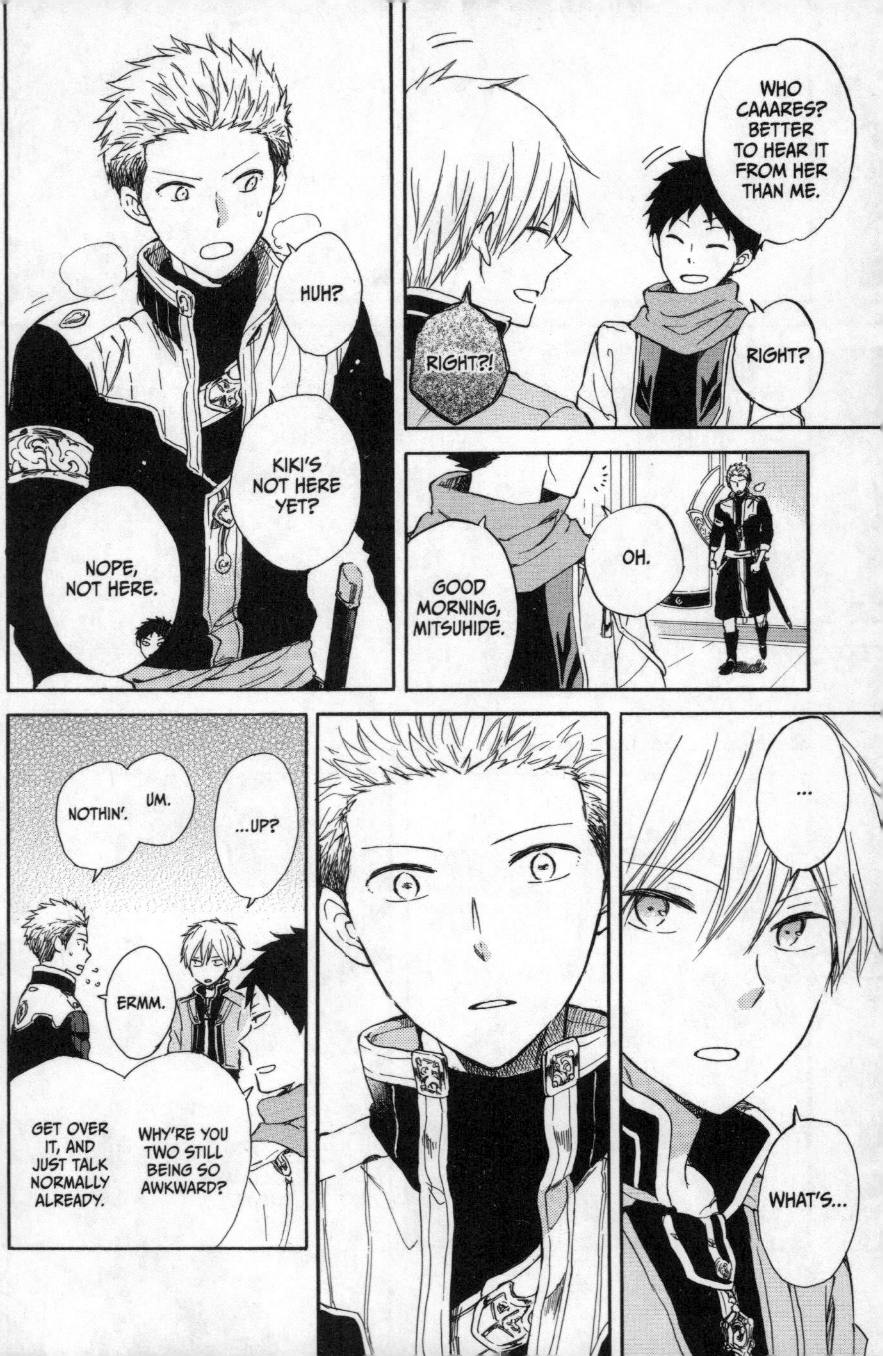
WHO CAAARES? BETTER TO HEAR IT FROM HER THAN ME.
RIGHT?
RIGHT?!
OH.
GOOD MORNING, MITSUHIDE.
HUH?
KIKI'S NOT HERE YET?
NOPE, NOT HERE.
...
WHAT'S...
...UP?
UM.
NOTHIN'.
ERMM.
WHY'RE YOU TWO STILL BEING SO AWKWARD?
GET OVER IT, AND JUST TALK NORMALLY ALREADY.

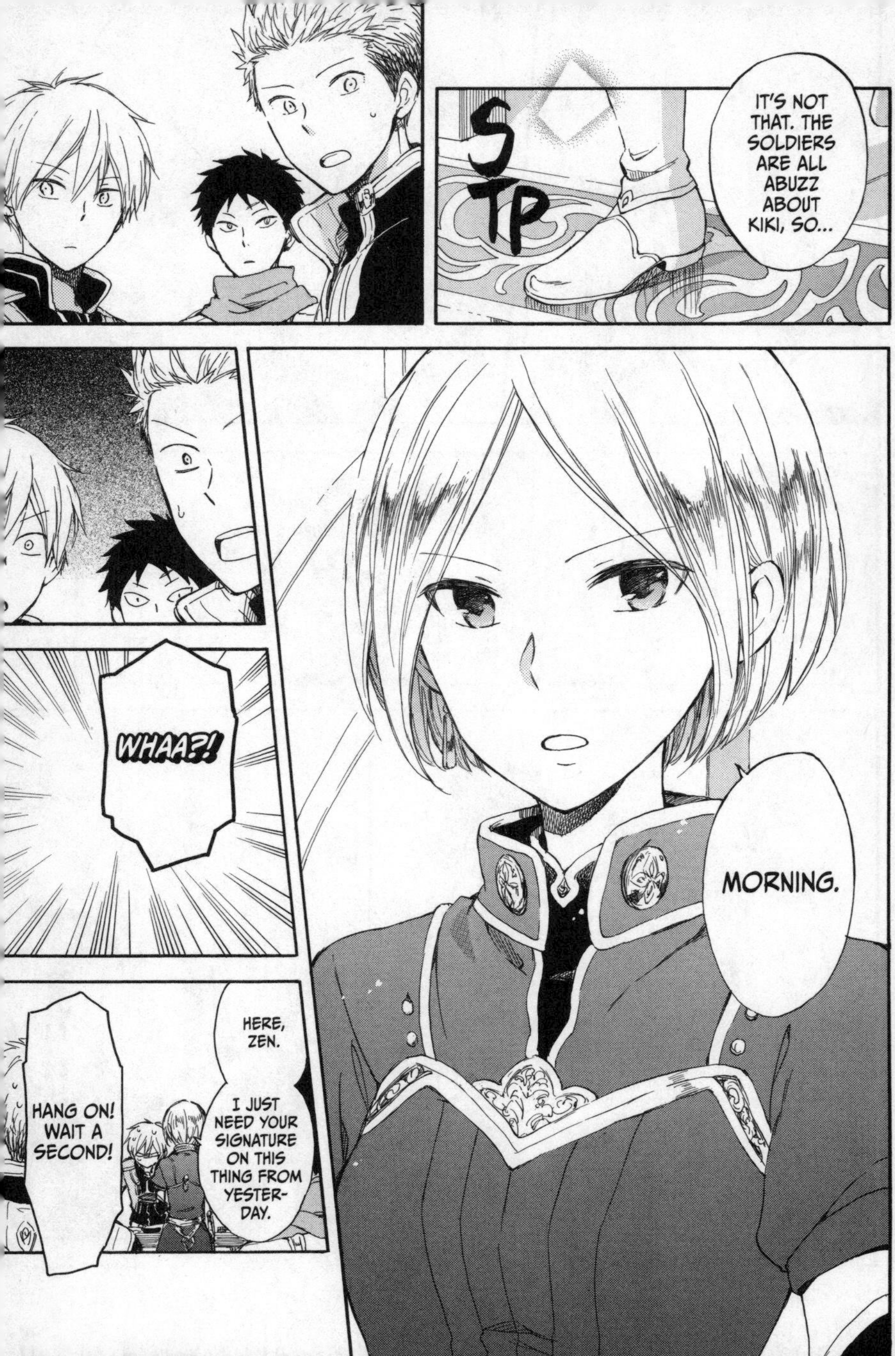
IT'S NOT THAT. THE SOLDIERS ARE ALL ABUZZ ABOUT KIKI, SO...
STP
MORNING.
WHAA?!
HERE, ZEN.
I JUST NEED YOUR SIGNATURE ON THIS THING FROM YESTER-DAY.
HANG ON! WAIT A SECOND!

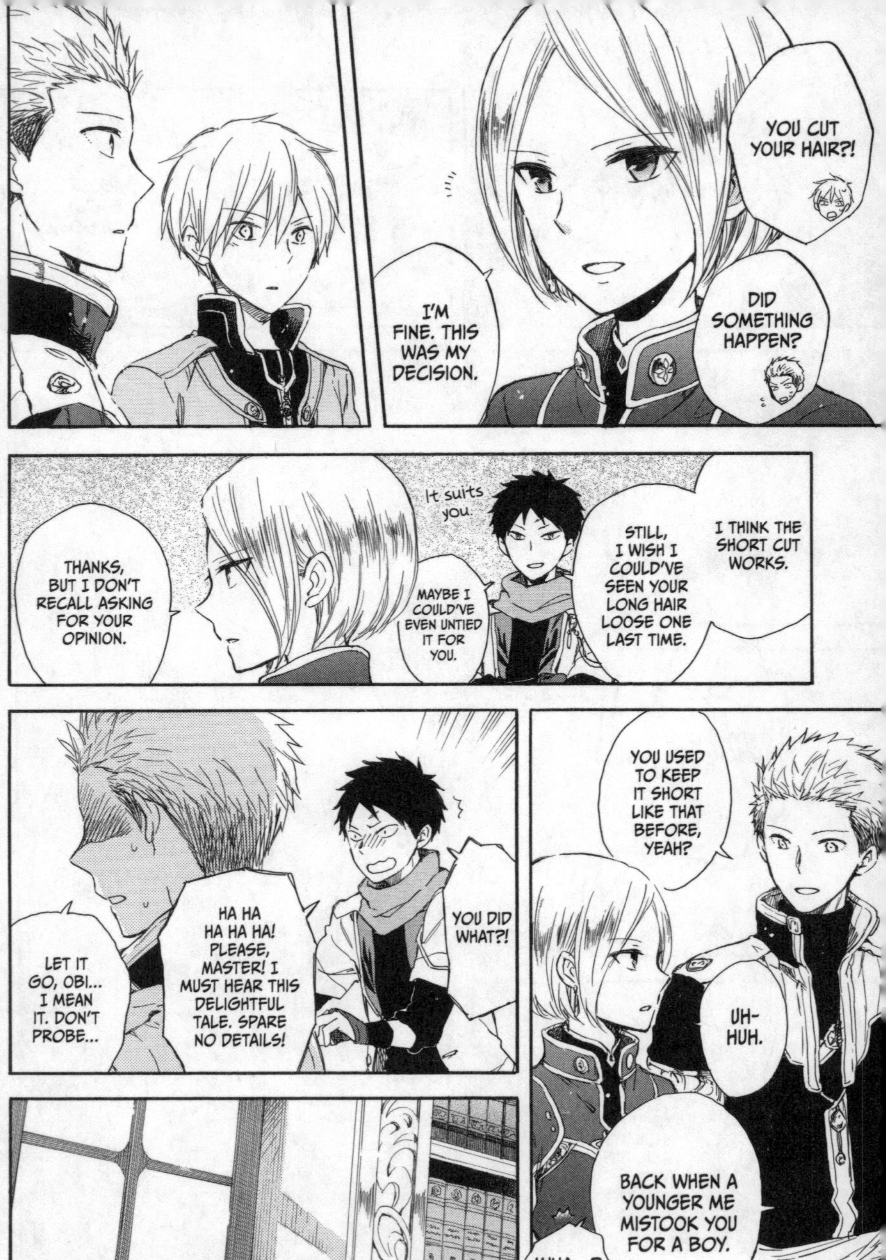
YOU CUT YOUR HAIR?!
DID SOMETHING HAPPEN?
I'M FINE. THIS WAS MY DECISION.
I THINK THE SHORT CUT WORKS.
STILL, I WISH I COULD'VE SEEN YOUR LONG HAIR LOOSE ONE LAST TIME.
It suits you.
MAYBE I COULD'VE EVEN UNTIED IT FOR YOU.
THANKS, BUT I DON'T RECALL ASKING FOR YOUR OPINION.
YOU USED TO KEEP IT SHORT LIKE THAT BEFORE, YEAH?
UH-HUH.
BACK WHEN A YOUNGER ME MISTOOK YOU FOR A BOY.
WHA...?
YOU DID WHAT?!
HA HA HA HA HA! PLEASE, MASTER! I MUST HEAR THIS DELIGHTFUL TALE. SPARE NO DETAILS!
LET IT GO, OBI... I MEAN IT. DON'T PROBE...

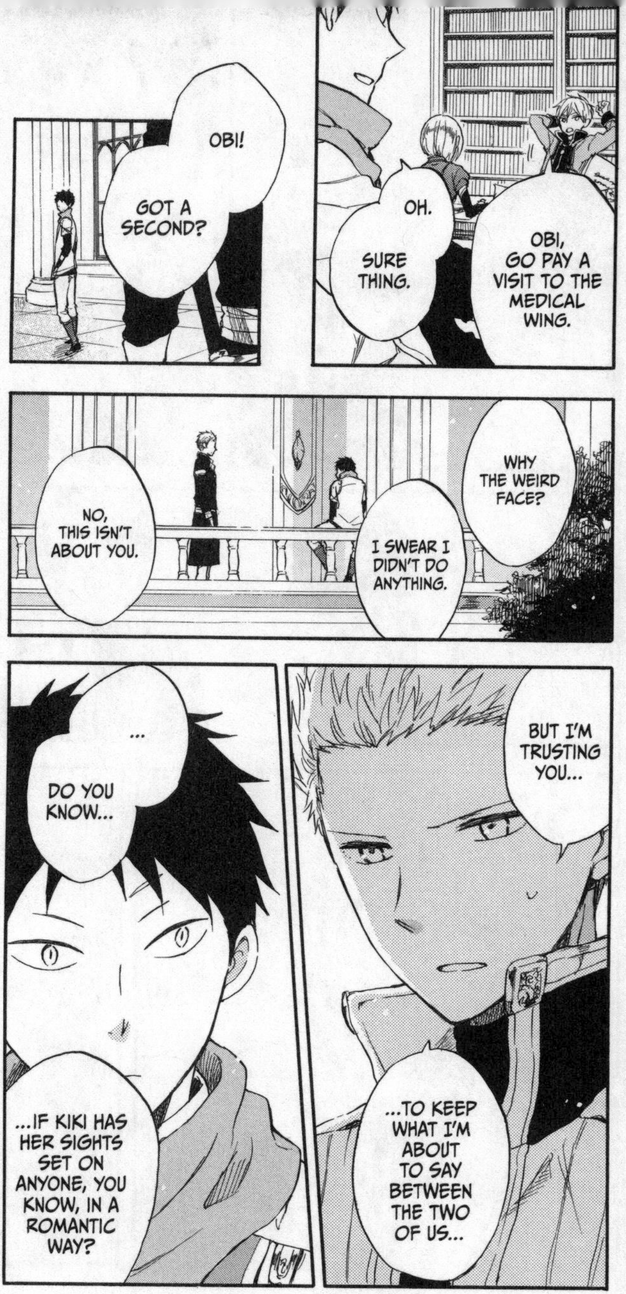
OBI, GO PAY A VISIT TO THE MEDICAL WING.
OH.
SURE THING.
OBI!
GOT A SECOND?
WHY THE WEIRD FACE?
I SWEAR I DIDN'T DO ANYTHING.
NO, THIS ISN'T ABOUT YOU.
BUT I'M TRUSTING YOU...
...TO KEEP WHAT I'M ABOUT TO SAY BETWEEN THE TWO OF US...
...
DO YOU KNOW...
...IF KIKI HAS HER SIGHTS SET ON ANYONE, YOU KNOW, IN A ROMANTIC WAY?

1

GREETINGS

Hello, Sorata Akiduki here.

Thank you for picking up volume 11 of Snow White with the Red Hair!!

This one takes us through chapter 49.

This is the perfect time for Obi and Shirayuki to grace a cover together.

Wouldn't you agree, Your Highness?!

Who's your fave, Your Highness?!

Anyhow, let's get back to volume 11.

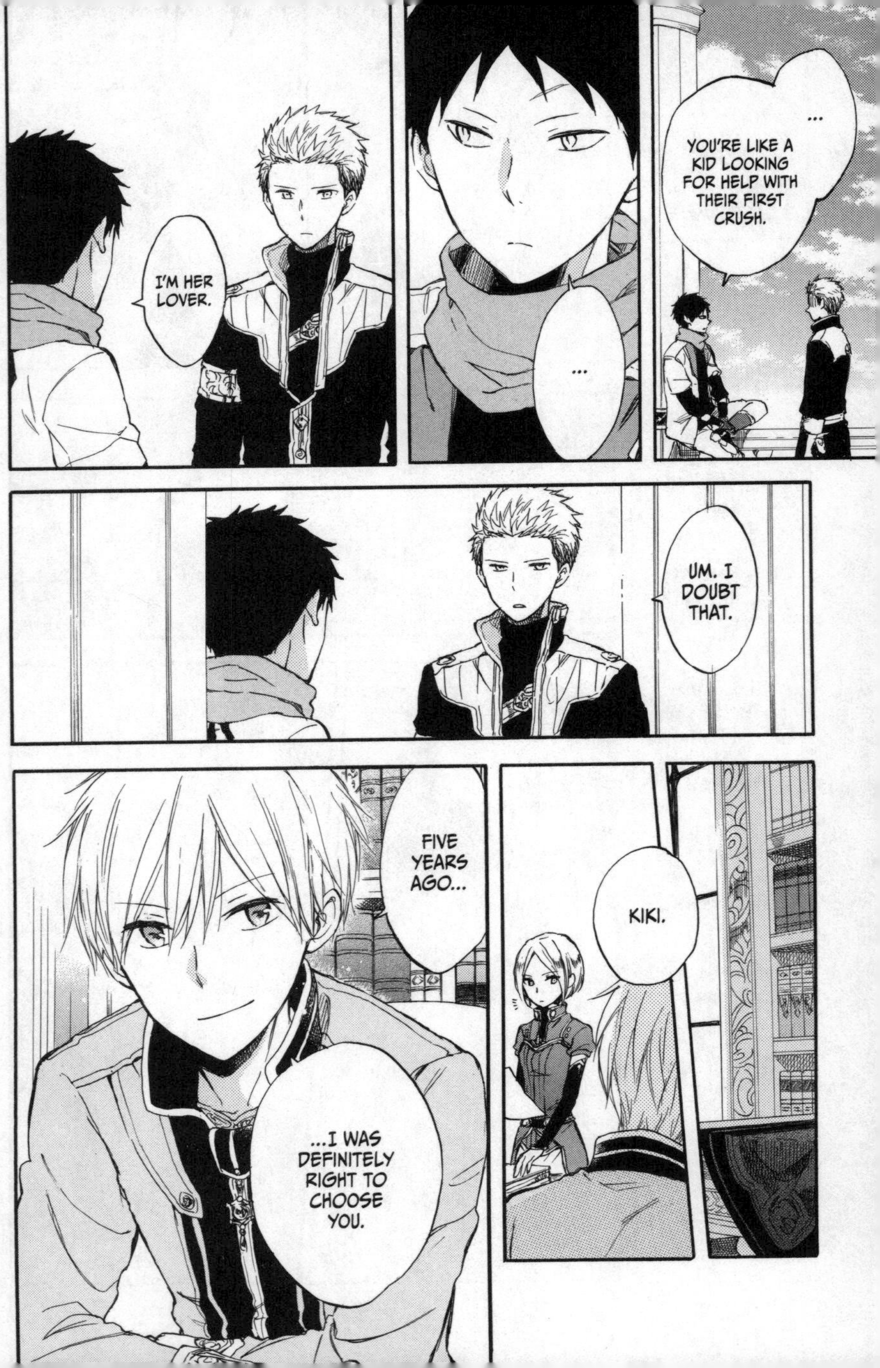
...
YOU'RE LIKE A KID LOOKING FOR HELP WITH THEIR FIRST CRUSH.
...
I'M HER LOVER.
UM. I DOUBT THAT.
KIKI.
FIVE YEARS AGO...
...I WAS DEFINITELY RIGHT TO CHOOSE YOU.

ACTUALLY, I'M THE ONE WHO CHOSE YOU GUYS.

Sheesh... SORRY, I'M BACK.

WHAT? WHAT IS IT?

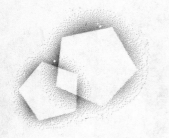

HA HA.

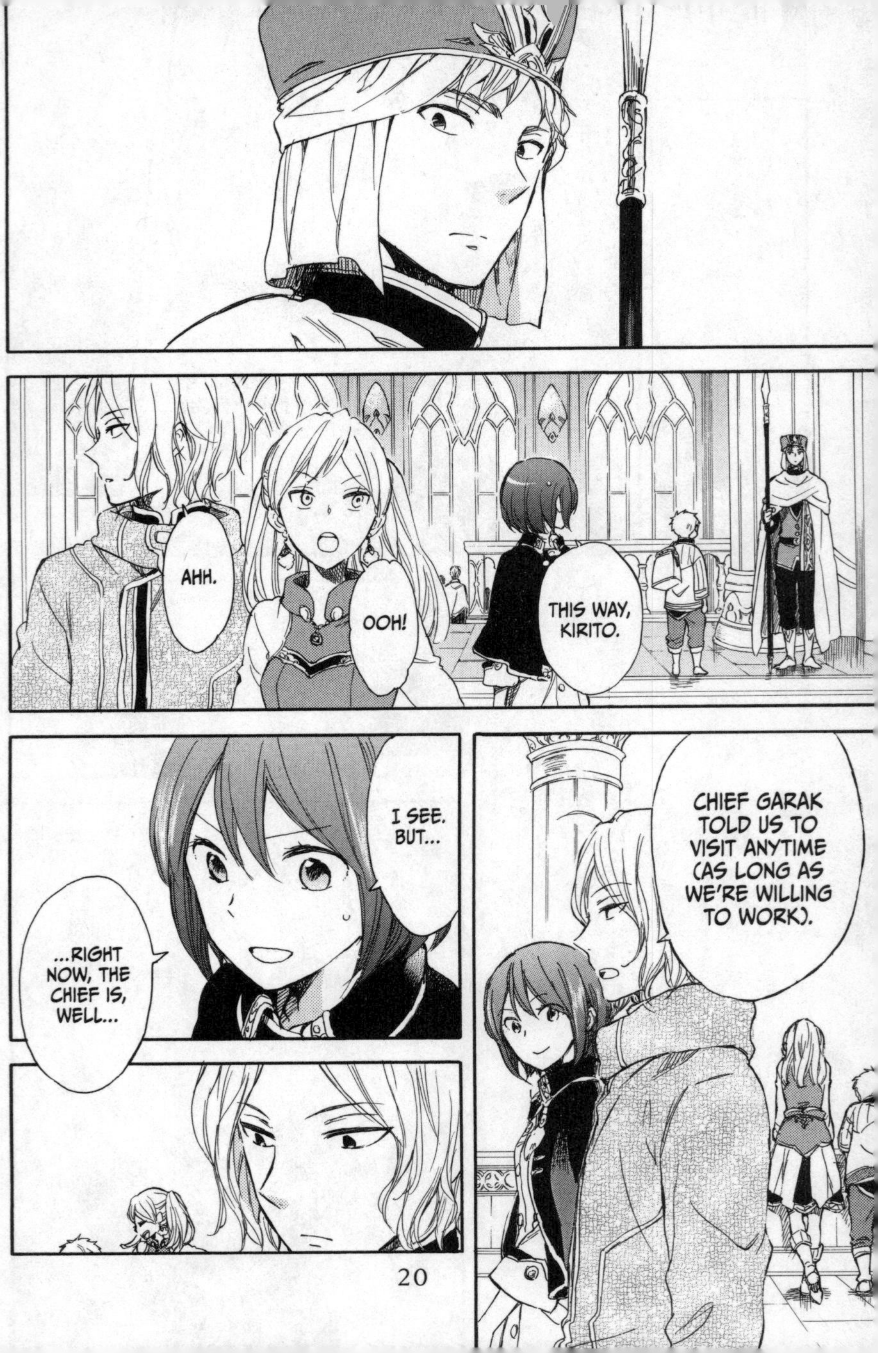
THIS WAY, KIRITO.
OOH!
AHH.
CHIEF GARAK TOLD US TO VISIT ANYTIME (AS LONG AS WE'RE WILLING TO WORK).
I SEE. BUT...
...RIGHT NOW, THE CHIEF IS, WELL...

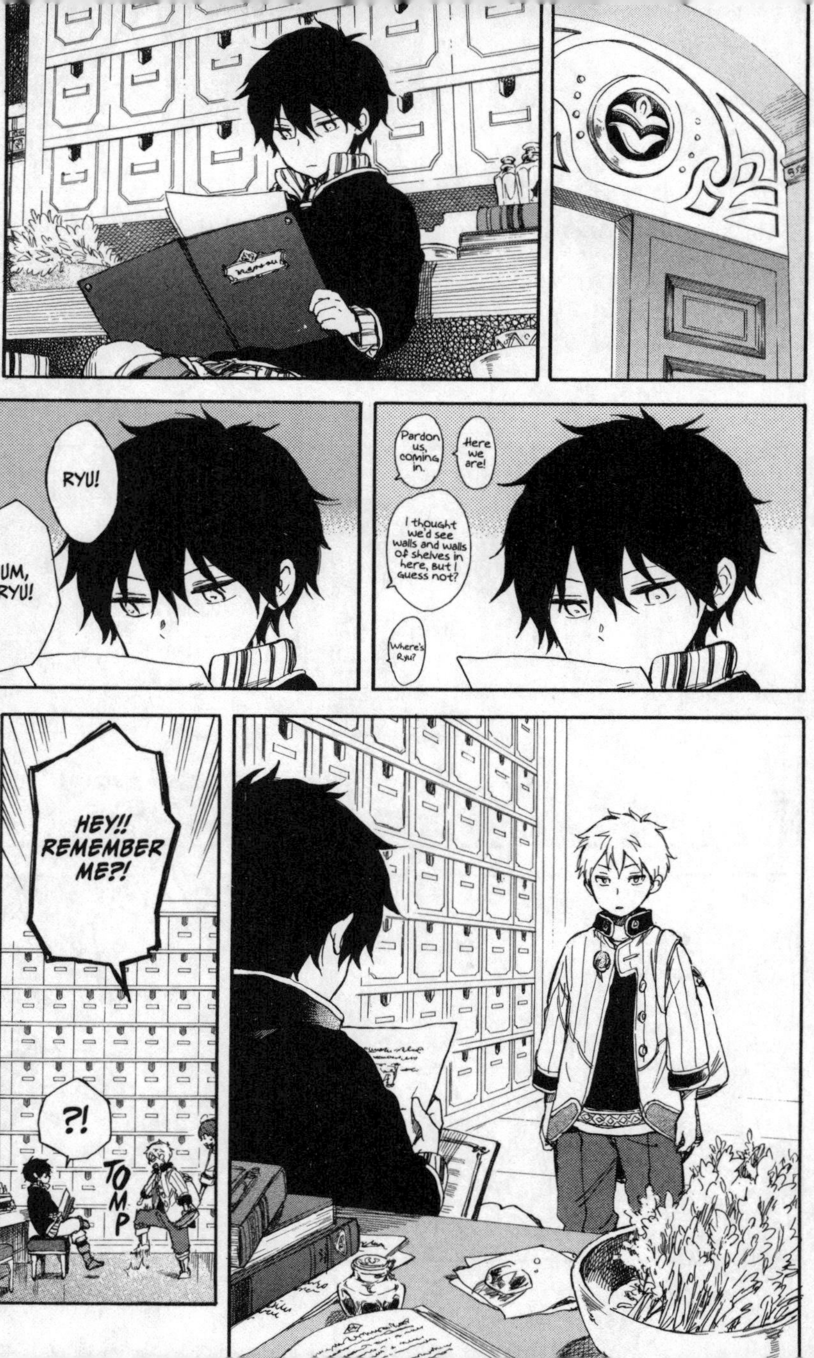
Here we are!
Pardon us, coming in.
I thought we'd see walls and walls of shelves in here, but I guess not?
Where's Ryu?
RYU!
UM, RYU!
HEY!! REMEMBER ME?!
?!
TOMP

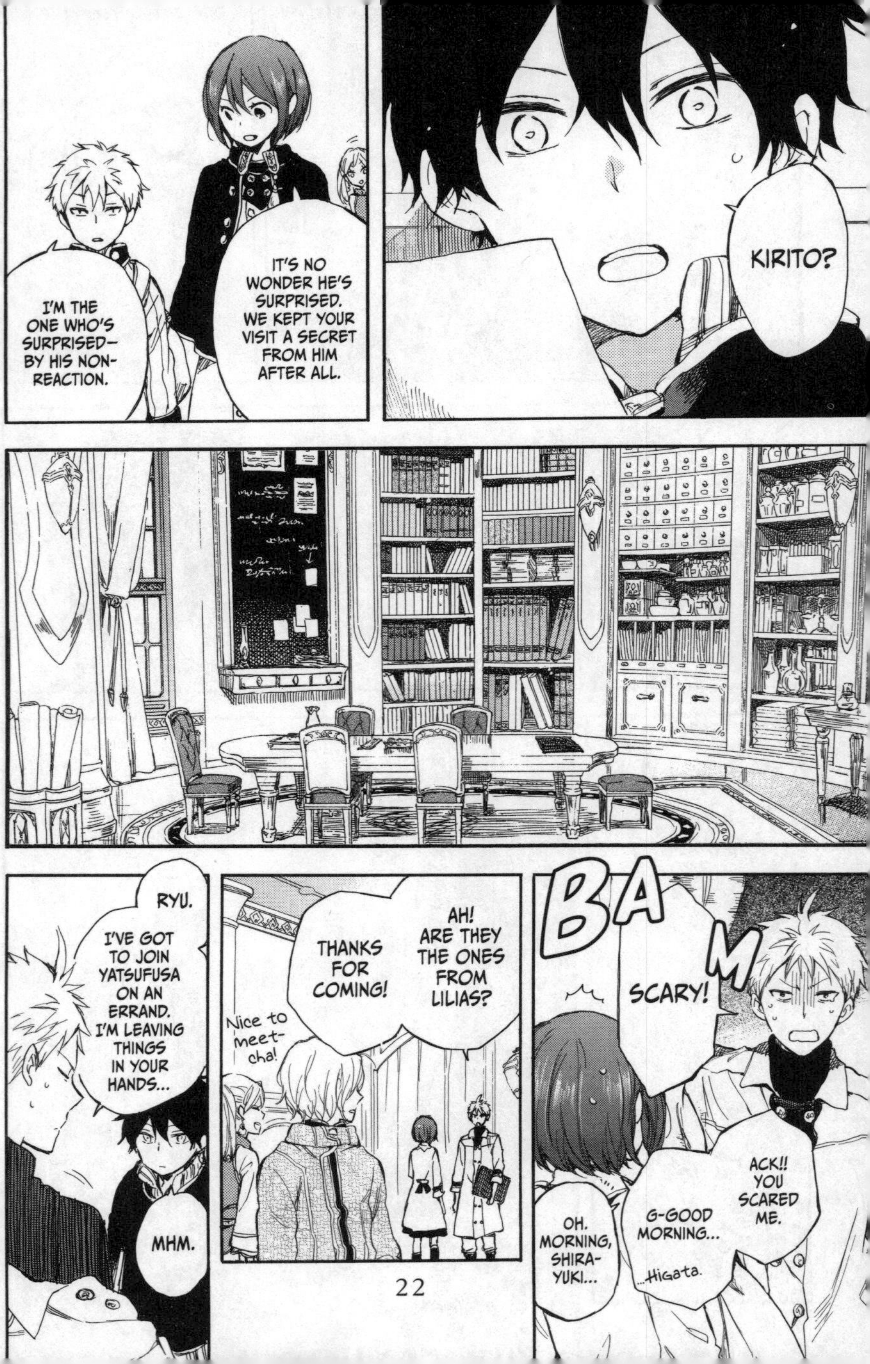
KIRITO?
IT'S NO WONDER HE'S SURPRISED. WE KEPT YOUR VISIT A SECRET FROM HIM AFTER ALL.
I'M THE ONE WHO'S SURPRISED— BY HIS NON-REACTION.
BAM
SCARY!
ACK!! YOU SCARED ME.
G-GOOD MORNING...
...Higata.
OH. MORNING, SHIRAYUKI...
AH! ARE THEY THE ONES FROM LILIAS?
THANKS FOR COMING!
Nice to meet-cha!
RYU.
I'VE GOT TO JOIN YATSUFUSA ON AN ERRAND. I'M LEAVING THINGS IN YOUR HANDS...
MHM.

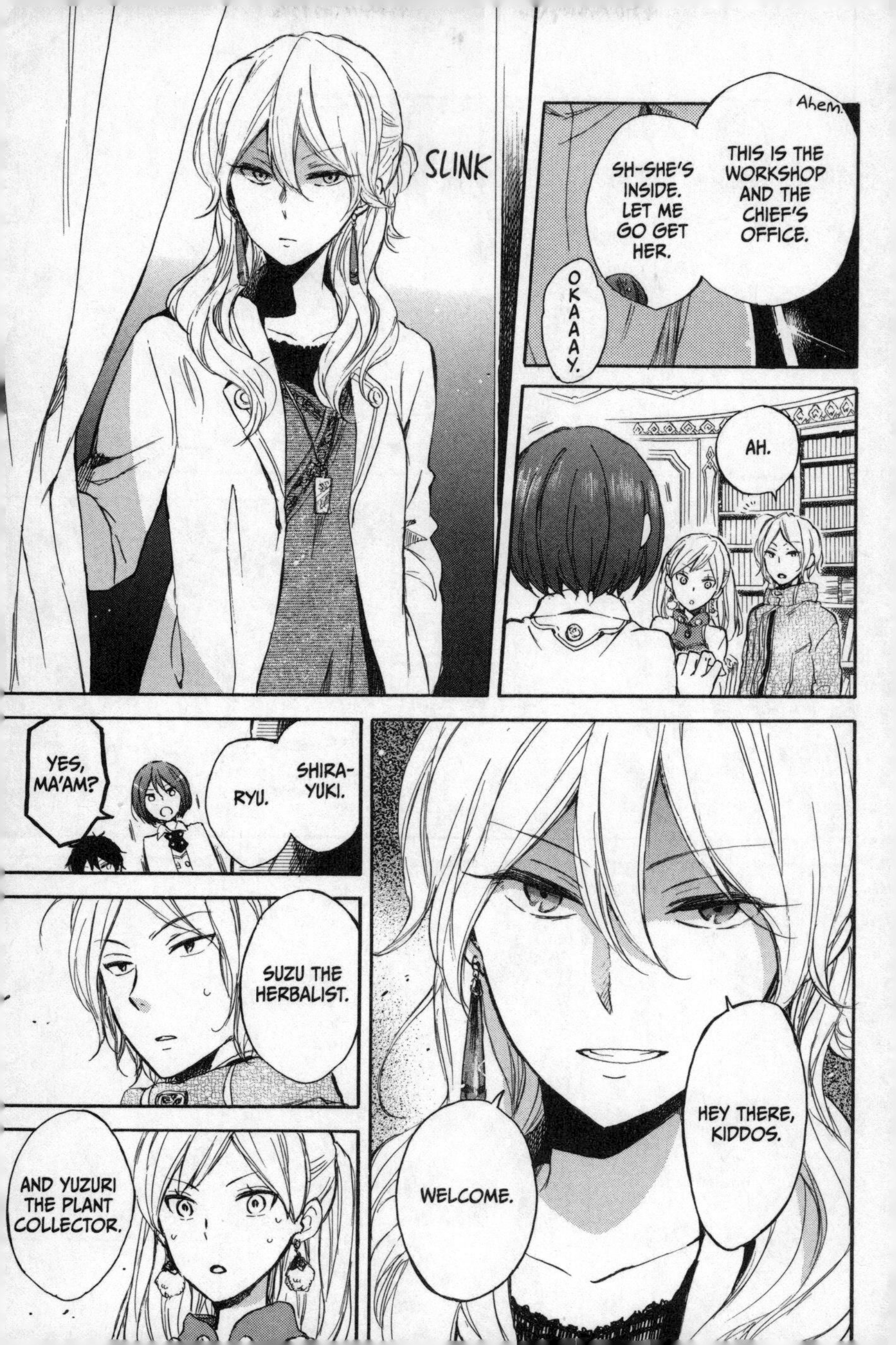
Ahem.
THIS IS THE WORKSHOP AND THE CHIEF'S OFFICE.
SH-SHE'S INSIDE. LET ME GO GET HER.
OKAAAAY.
AH.
SLINK
HEY THERE, KIDDOS.
WELCOME.
SHIRA-YUKI.
RYU.
YES, MA'AM?
SUZU THE HERBALIST.
AND YUZURI THE PLANT COLLECTOR.

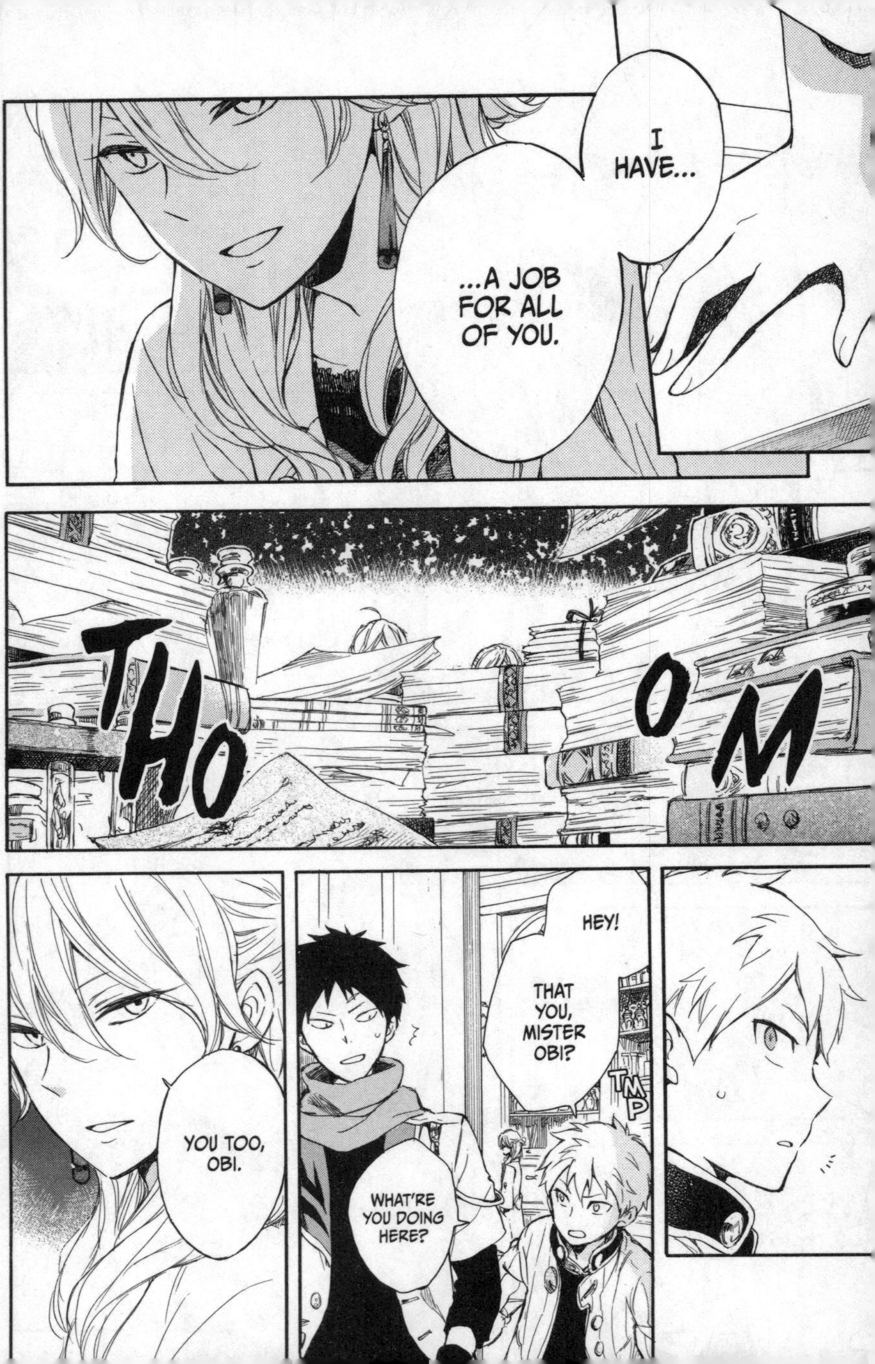
I HAVE...
...A JOB FOR ALL OF YOU.
THOOM
HEY!
THAT YOU, MISTER OBI?
TMP
WHAT'RE YOU DOING HERE?
YOU TOO, OBI.

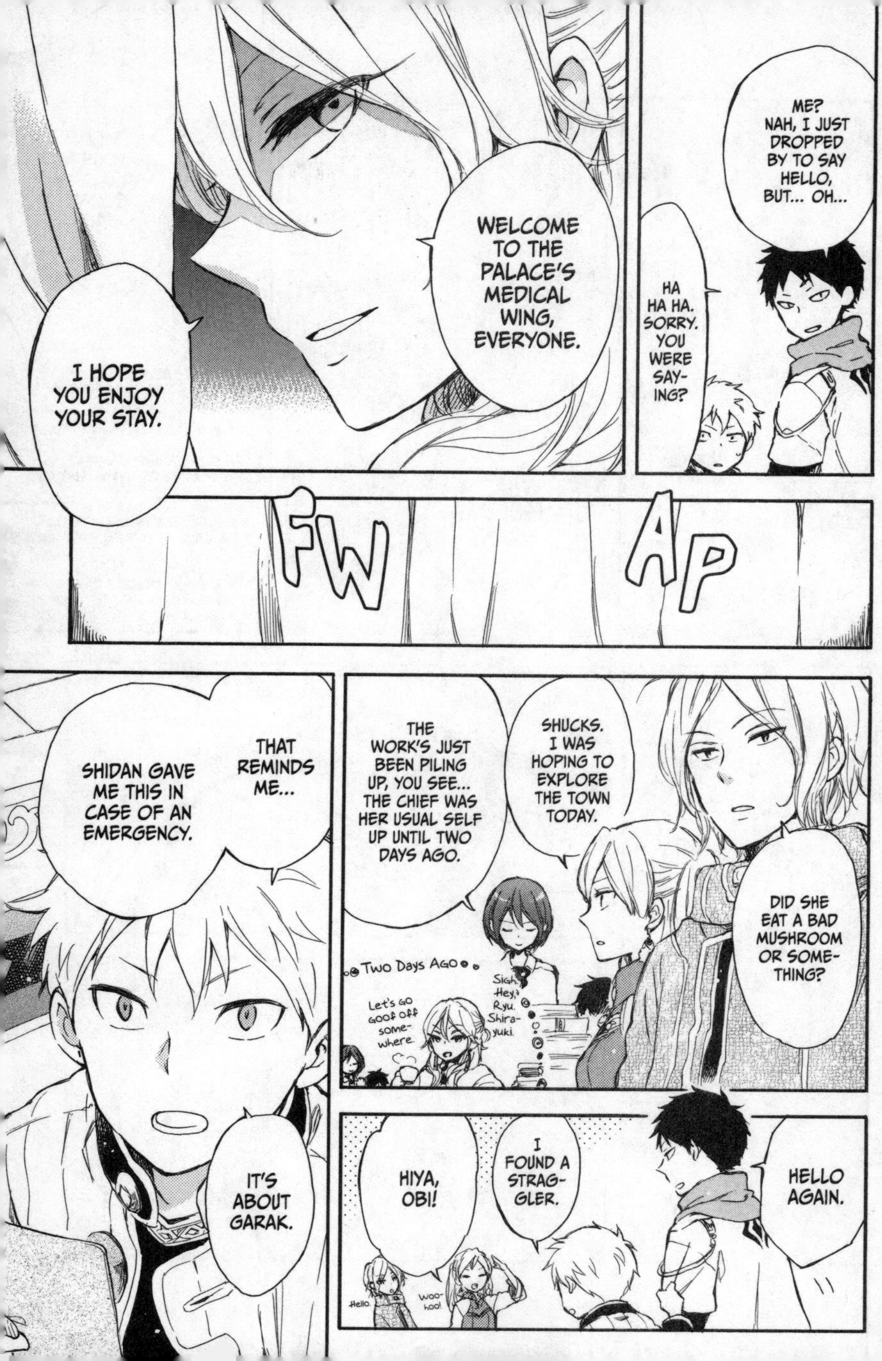

ME? NAH, I JUST DROPPED BY TO SAY HELLO, BUT... OH...
HA HA HA. SORRY. YOU WERE SAYING?
WELCOME TO THE PALACE'S MEDICAL WING, EVERYONE.
I HOPE YOU ENJOY YOUR STAY.
FWAP
SHUCKS. I WAS HOPING TO EXPLORE THE TOWN TODAY.
THE WORK'S JUST BEEN PILING UP, YOU SEE... THE CHIEF WAS HER USUAL SELF UP UNTIL TWO DAYS AGO.
DID SHE EAT A BAD MUSHROOM OR SOMETHING?
Two Days Ago
Sigh. Hey, Ryu. Shirayuki.
Let's go goof off somewhere.
HELLO AGAIN.
I FOUND A STRAGGLER.
HIYA, OBI!
Woo-hoo!
Hello.
THAT REMINDS ME...
SHIDAN GAVE ME THIS IN CASE OF AN EMERGENCY.
IT'S ABOUT GARAK.

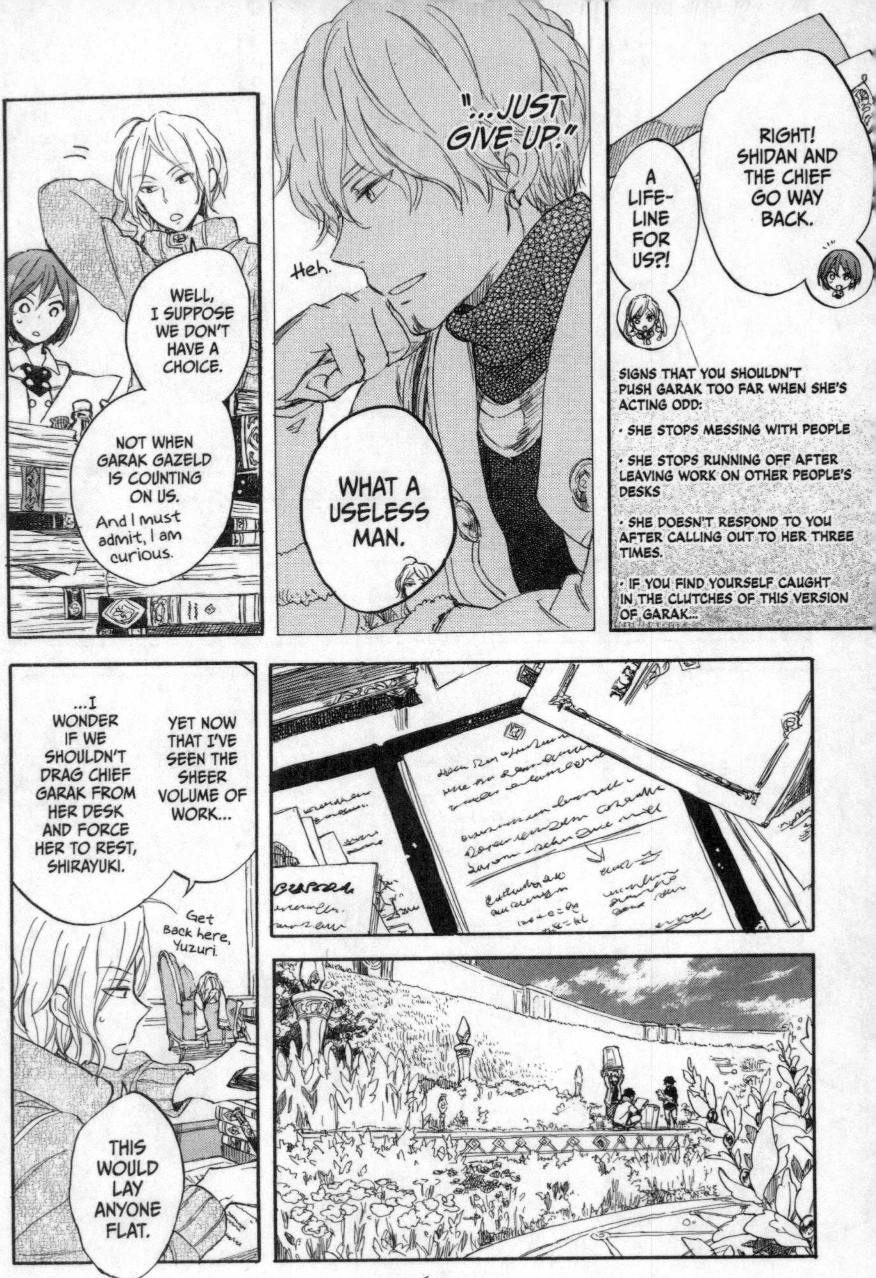
RIGHT! SHIDAN AND THE CHIEF GO WAY BACK.
A LIFE-LINE FOR US?!
SIGNS THAT YOU SHOULDN'T PUSH GARAK TOO FAR WHEN SHE'S ACTING ODD:
• SHE STOPS MESSING WITH PEOPLE
• SHE STOPS RUNNING OFF AFTER LEAVING WORK ON OTHER PEOPLE'S DESKS
• SHE DOESN'T RESPOND TO YOU AFTER CALLING OUT TO HER THREE TIMES.
• IF YOU FIND YOURSELF CAUGHT IN THE CLUTCHES OF THIS VERSION OF GARAK...
"...JUST GIVE UP."
Heh.
WHAT A USELESS MAN.
WELL, I SUPPOSE WE DON'T HAVE A CHOICE.
NOT WHEN GARAK GAZELD IS COUNTING ON US.
And I must admit, I am curious.
YET NOW THAT I'VE SEEN THE SHEER VOLUME OF WORK...
...I WONDER IF WE SHOULDN'T DRAG CHIEF GARAK FROM HER DESK AND FORCE HER TO REST, SHIRAYUKI.
Get Back here, Yuzuri.
THIS WOULD LAY ANYONE FLAT.

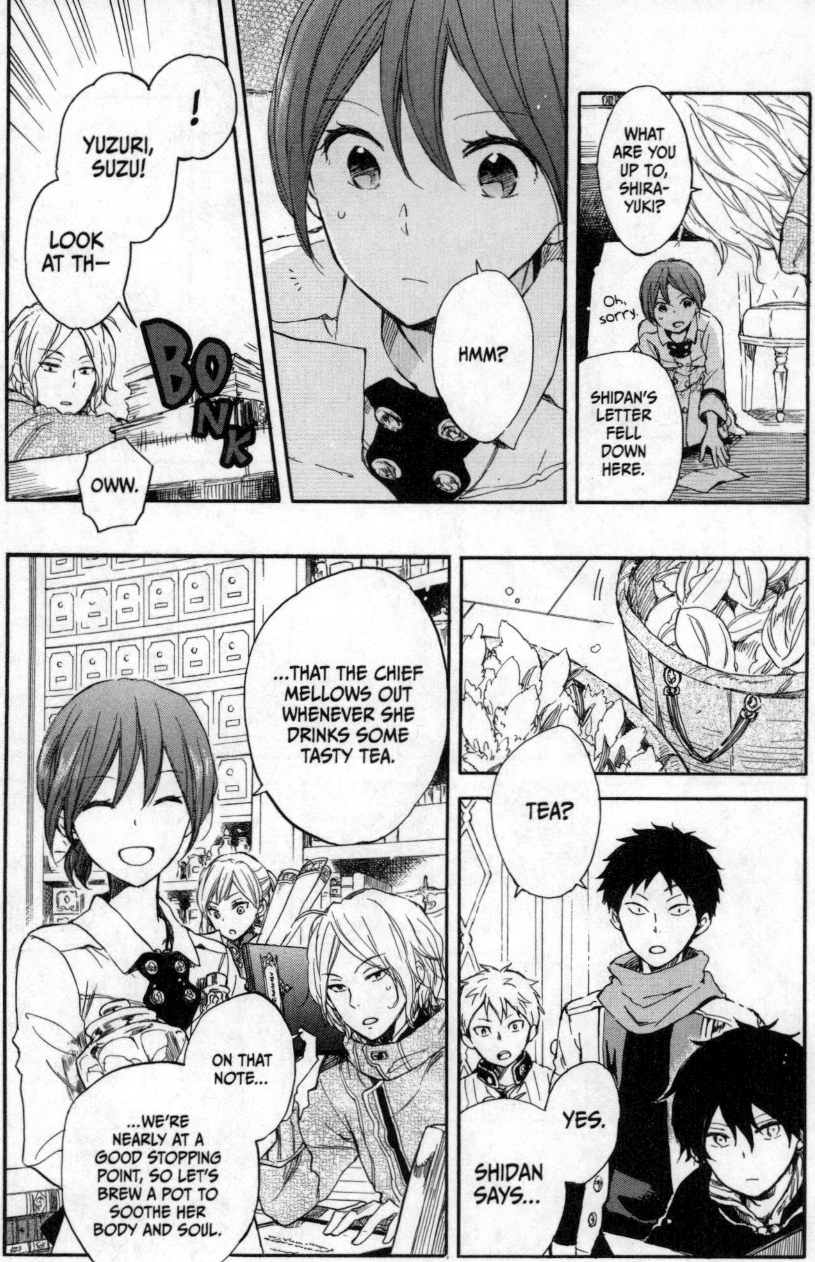
WHAT ARE YOU UP TO, SHIRAYUKI?
Oh, sorry.
SHIDAN'S LETTER FELL DOWN HERE.
HMM?
!
YUZURI, SUZU!
LOOK AT TH—
BONK
OWW.
TEA?
YES.
SHIDAN SAYS...
...THAT THE CHIEF MELLOWS OUT WHENEVER SHE DRINKS SOME TASTY TEA.
ON THAT NOTE...
...WE'RE NEARLY AT A GOOD STOPPING POINT, SO LET'S BREW A POT TO SOOTHE HER BODY AND SOUL.

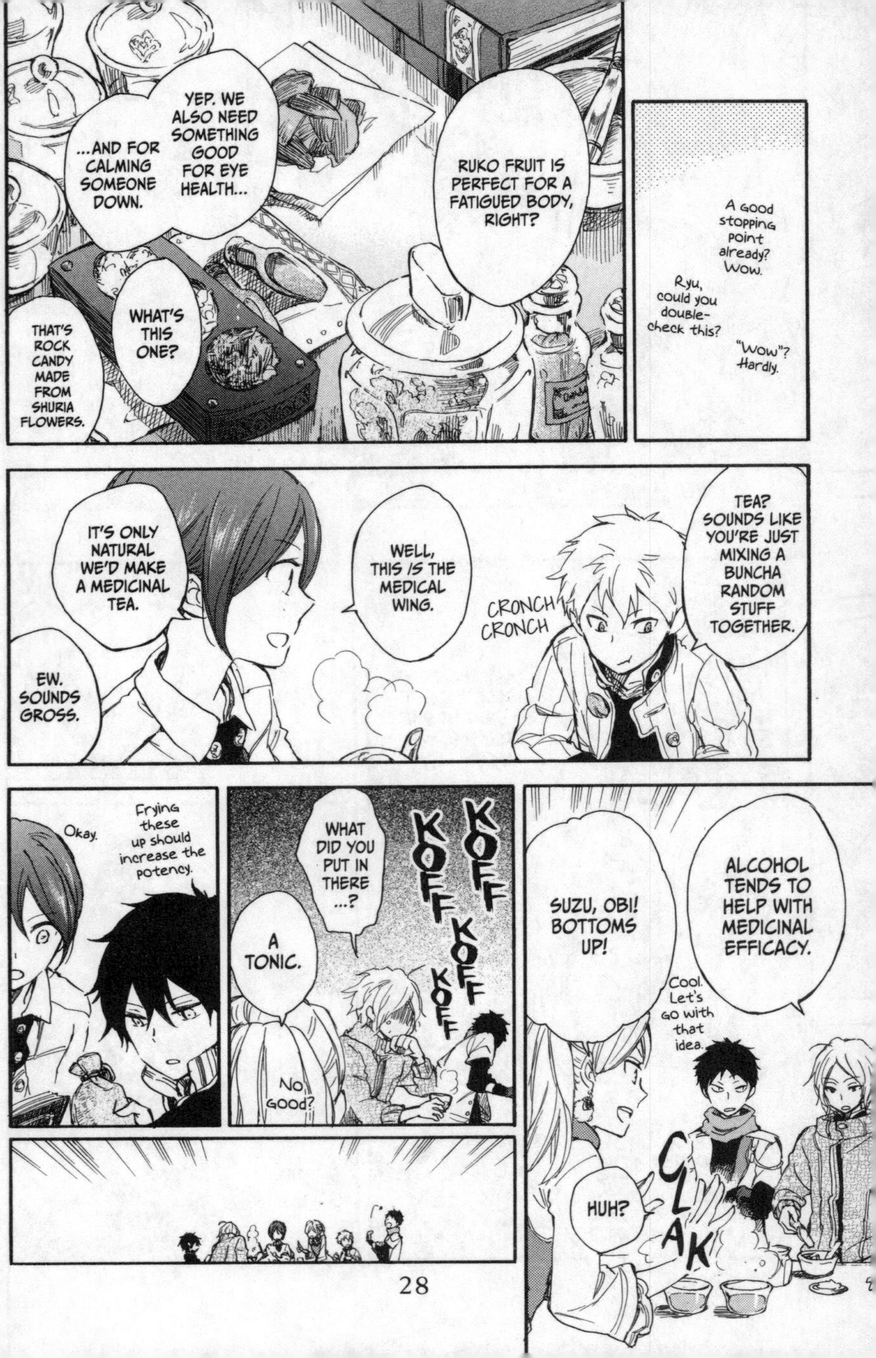
A good stopping point already? Wow.
Ryu, could you double-check this?
"Wow"? Hardly.
RUKO FRUIT IS PERFECT FOR A FATIGUED BODY, RIGHT?
YEP. WE ALSO NEED SOMETHING GOOD FOR EYE HEALTH...
...AND FOR CALMING SOMEONE DOWN.
WHAT'S THIS ONE?
THAT'S ROCK CANDY MADE FROM SHURIA FLOWERS.
TEA? SOUNDS LIKE YOU'RE JUST MIXING A BUNCHA RANDOM STUFF TOGETHER.
CRONCH CRONCH
WELL, THIS *IS* THE MEDICAL WING.
IT'S ONLY NATURAL WE'D MAKE A MEDICINAL TEA.
EW. SOUNDS GROSS.
ALCOHOL TENDS TO HELP WITH MEDICINAL EFFICACY.
SUZU, OBI! BOTTOMS UP!
Cool. Let's go with that idea.
CLAK
HUH?
KOFF KOFF KOFF KOFF
WHAT DID YOU PUT IN THERE ...?
A TONIC.
No good?
Frying these up should increase the potency.
Okay.

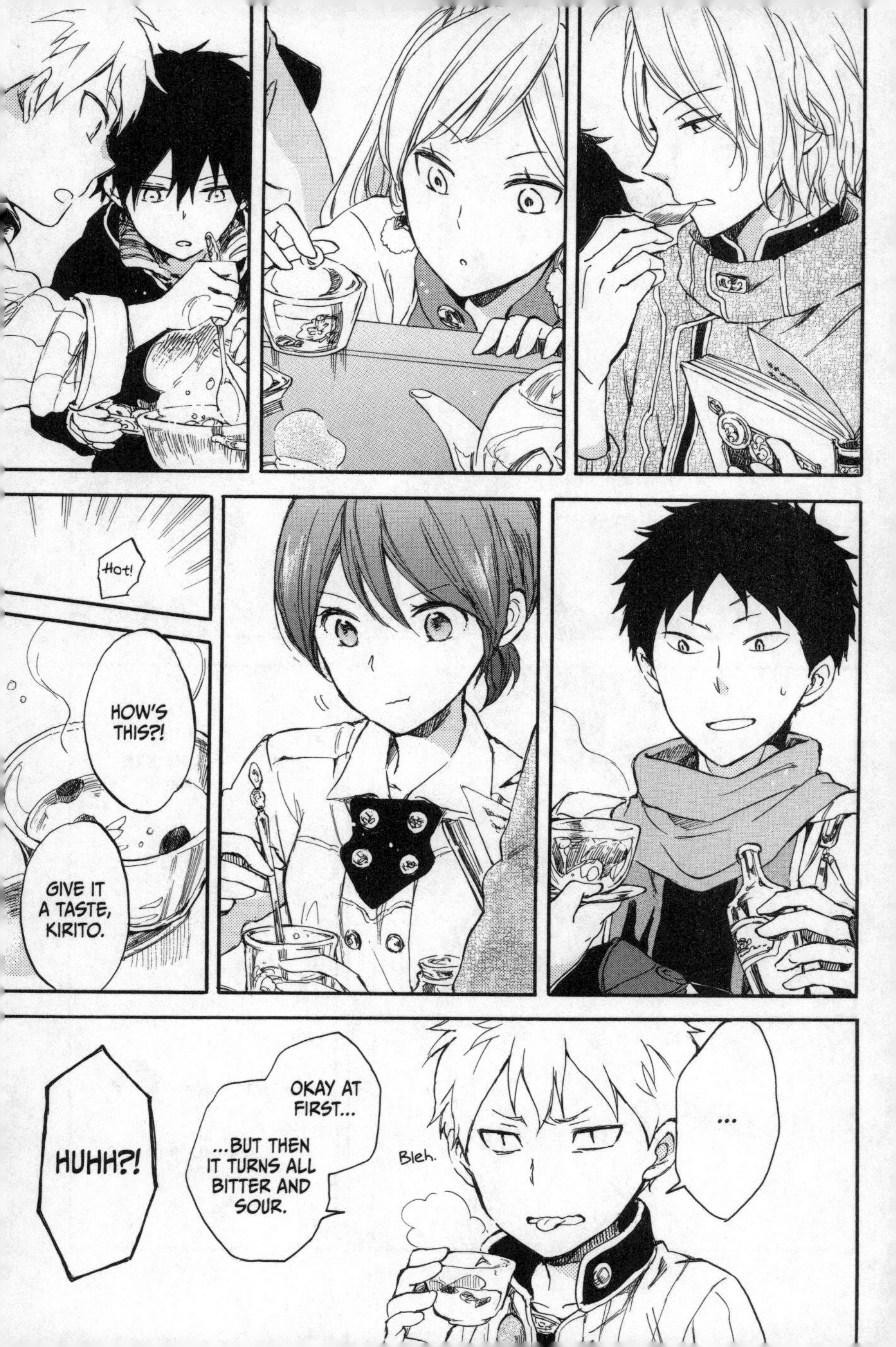
Hot!
HOW'S THIS?!
GIVE IT A TASTE, KIRITO.
...
Bleh.
OKAY AT FIRST...
...BUT THEN IT TURNS ALL BITTER AND SOUR.
HUHH?!

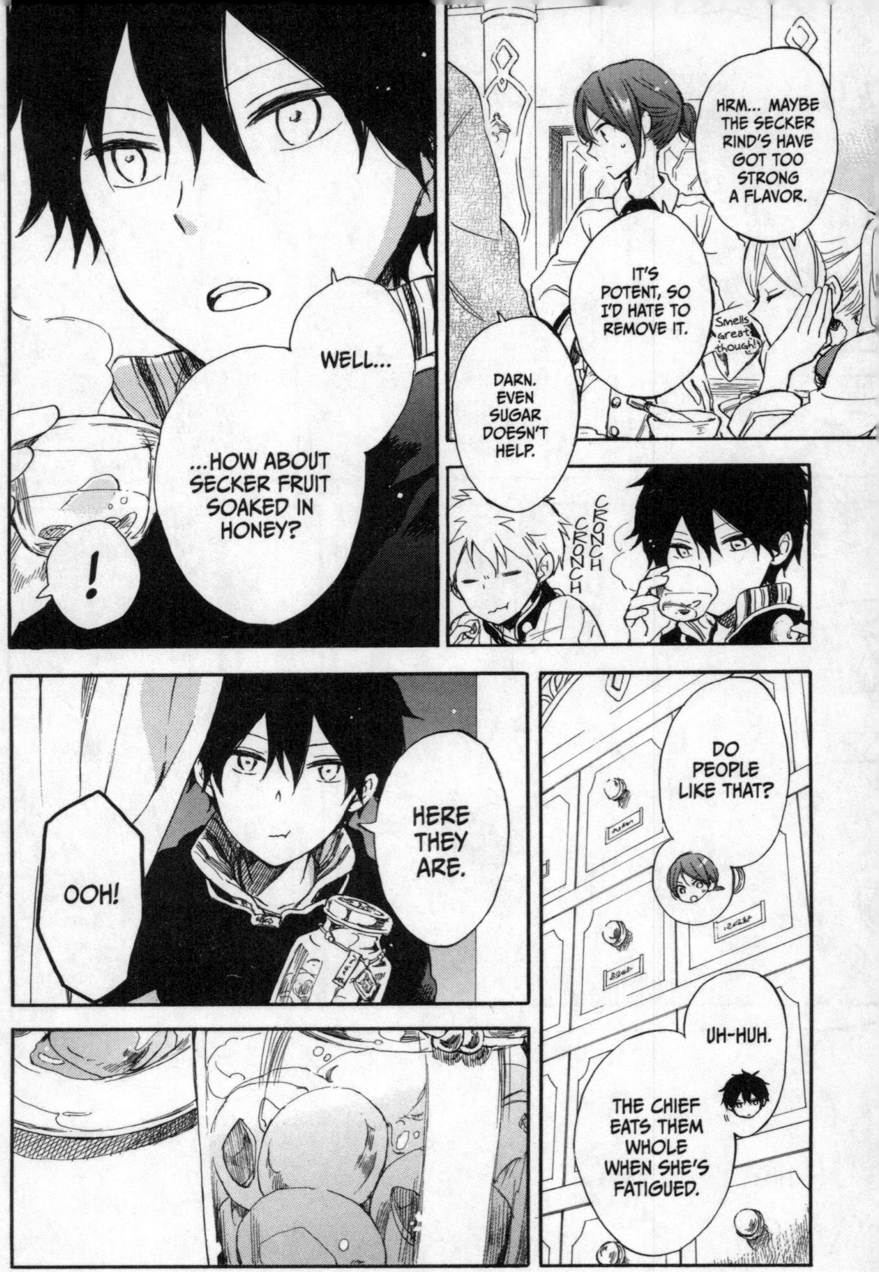
HRM... MAYBE THE SECKER RIND'S HAVE GOT TOO STRONG A FLAVOR.
IT'S POTENT, SO I'D HATE TO REMOVE IT.
Smells great though!
DARN. EVEN SUGAR DOESN'T HELP.
CRONCH CRONCH
WELL...
...HOW ABOUT SECKER FRUIT SOAKED IN HONEY?
!
DO PEOPLE LIKE THAT?
UH-HUH.
THE CHIEF EATS THEM WHOLE WHEN SHE'S FATIGUED.
HERE THEY ARE.
OOH!

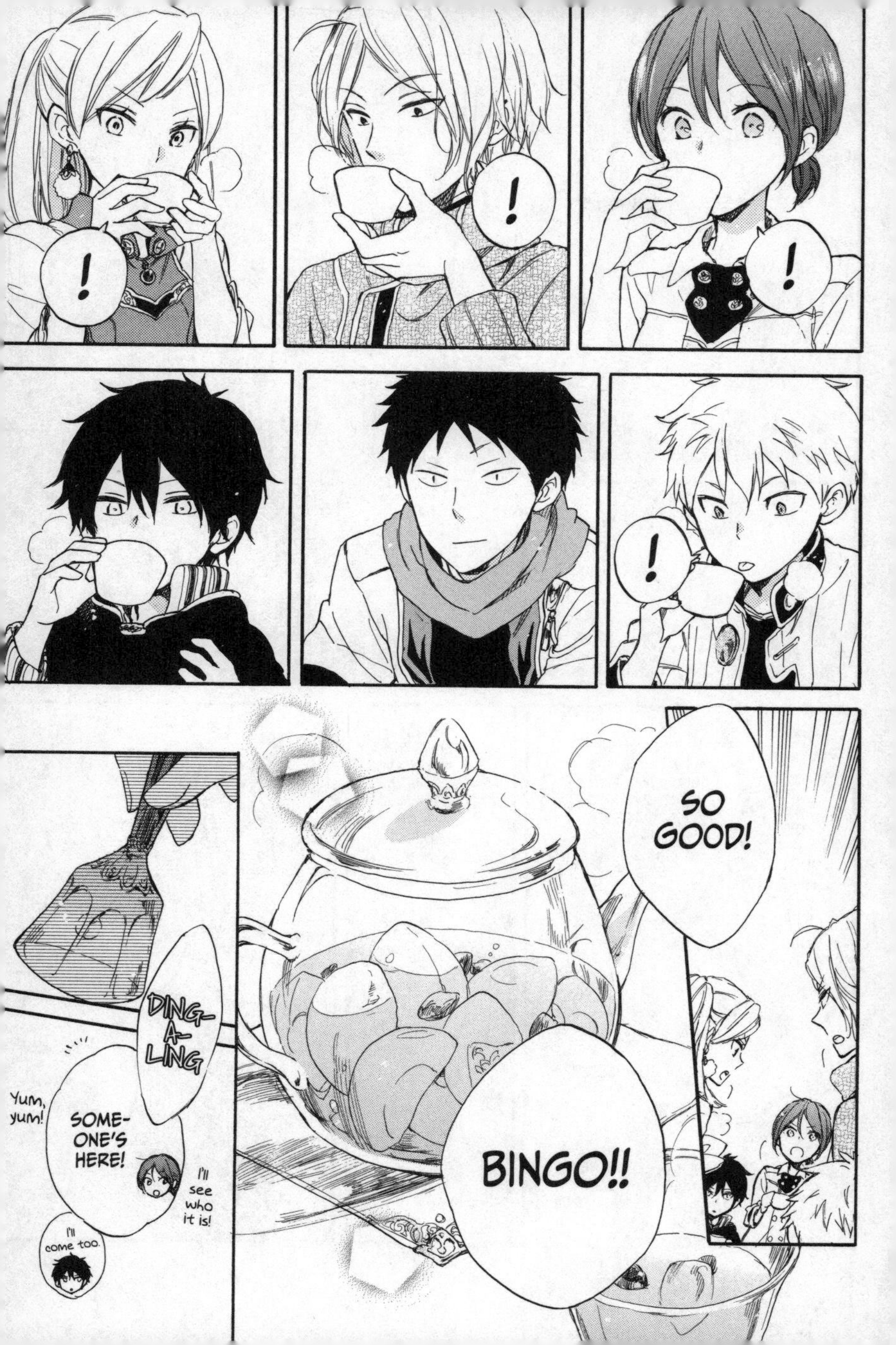
!
!
!
!
SO GOOD!
BINGO!!
DING-A-LING
SOME-ONE'S HERE!
I'll see who it is!
Yum, yum!
I'll come too.

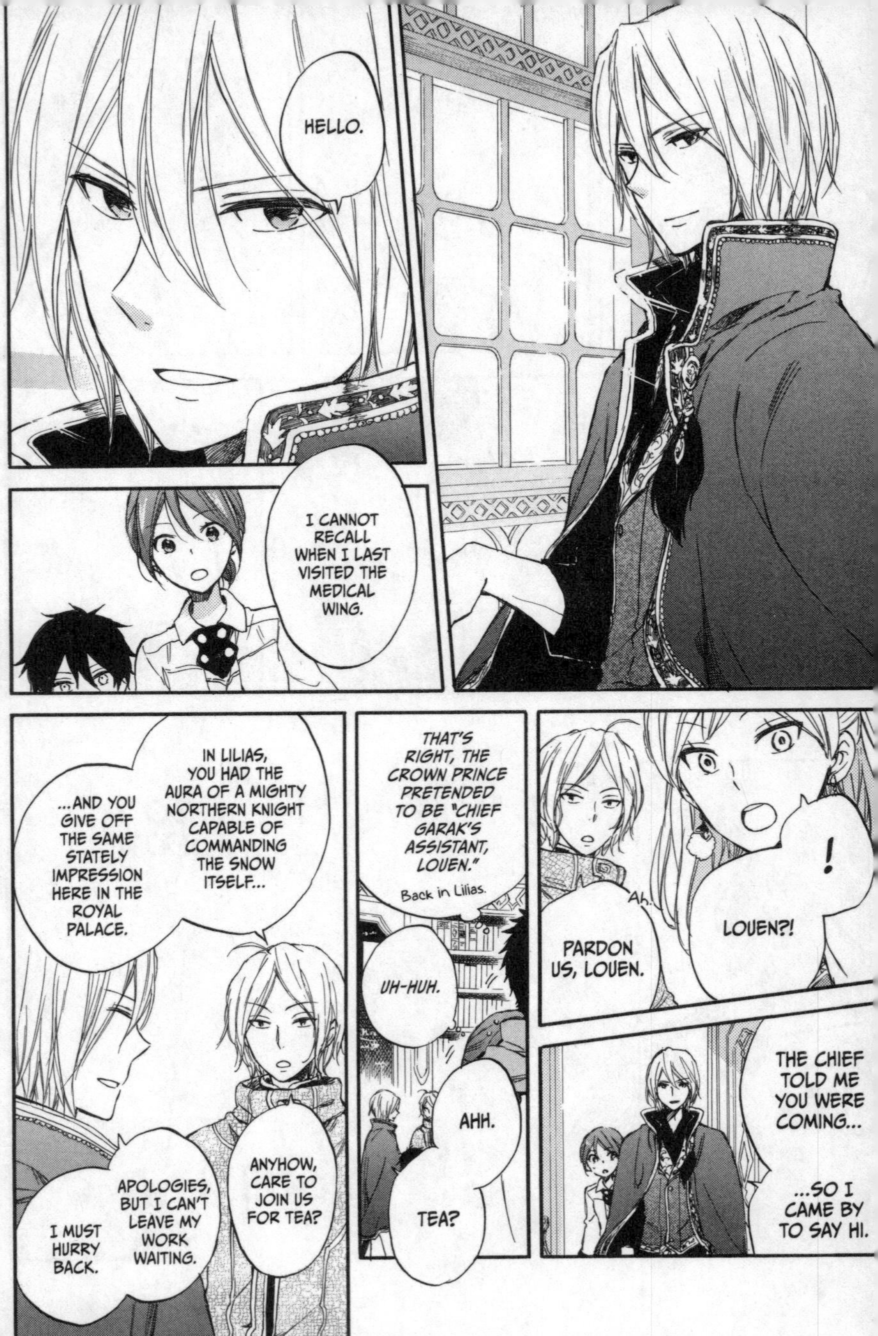
HELLO.
I CANNOT RECALL WHEN I LAST VISITED THE MEDICAL WING.
!
LOUEN?!
Ah.
PARDON US, LOUEN.
THE CHIEF TOLD ME YOU WERE COMING...
...SO I CAME BY TO SAY HI.
THAT'S RIGHT, THE CROWN PRINCE PRETENDED TO BE "CHIEF GARAK'S ASSISTANT, LOUEN."
Back in Lilias.
UH-HUH.
AHH.
TEA?
IN LILIAS, YOU HAD THE AURA OF A MIGHTY NORTHERN KNIGHT CAPABLE OF COMMANDING THE SNOW ITSELF...
...AND YOU GIVE OFF THE SAME STATELY IMPRESSION HERE IN THE ROYAL PALACE.
ANYHOW, CARE TO JOIN US FOR TEA?
APOLOGIES, BUT I CAN'T LEAVE MY WORK WAITING.
I MUST HURRY BACK.

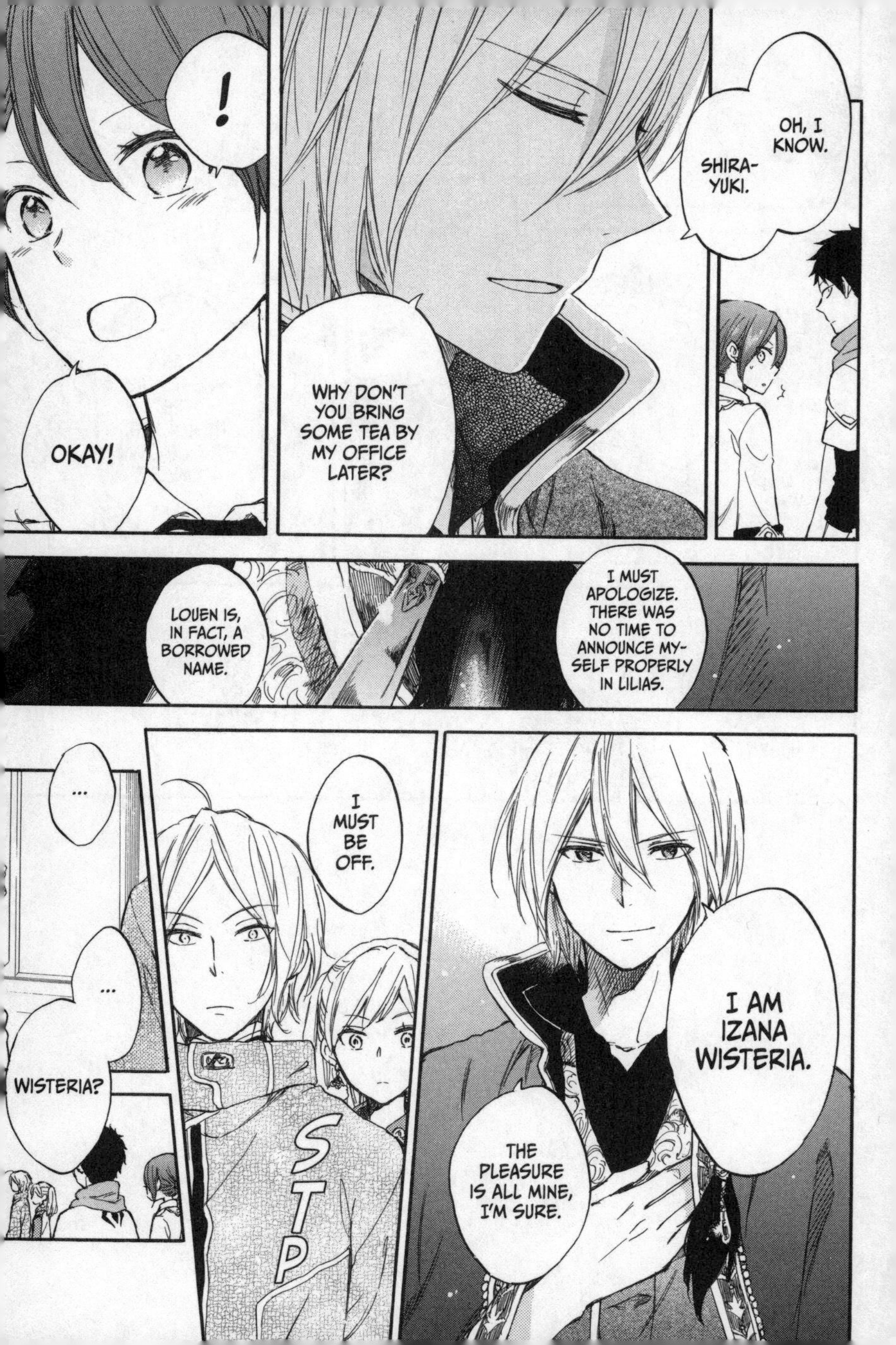
OH, I KNOW.
SHIRA-YUKI.
WHY DON'T YOU BRING SOME TEA BY MY OFFICE LATER?
!
OKAY!
I MUST APOLOGIZE. THERE WAS NO TIME TO ANNOUNCE MY-SELF PROPERLY IN LILIAS.
LOUEN IS, IN FACT, A BORROWED NAME.
I AM IZANA WISTERIA.
THE PLEASURE IS ALL MINE, I'M SURE.
I MUST BE OFF.
STP
...
...
WISTERIA?

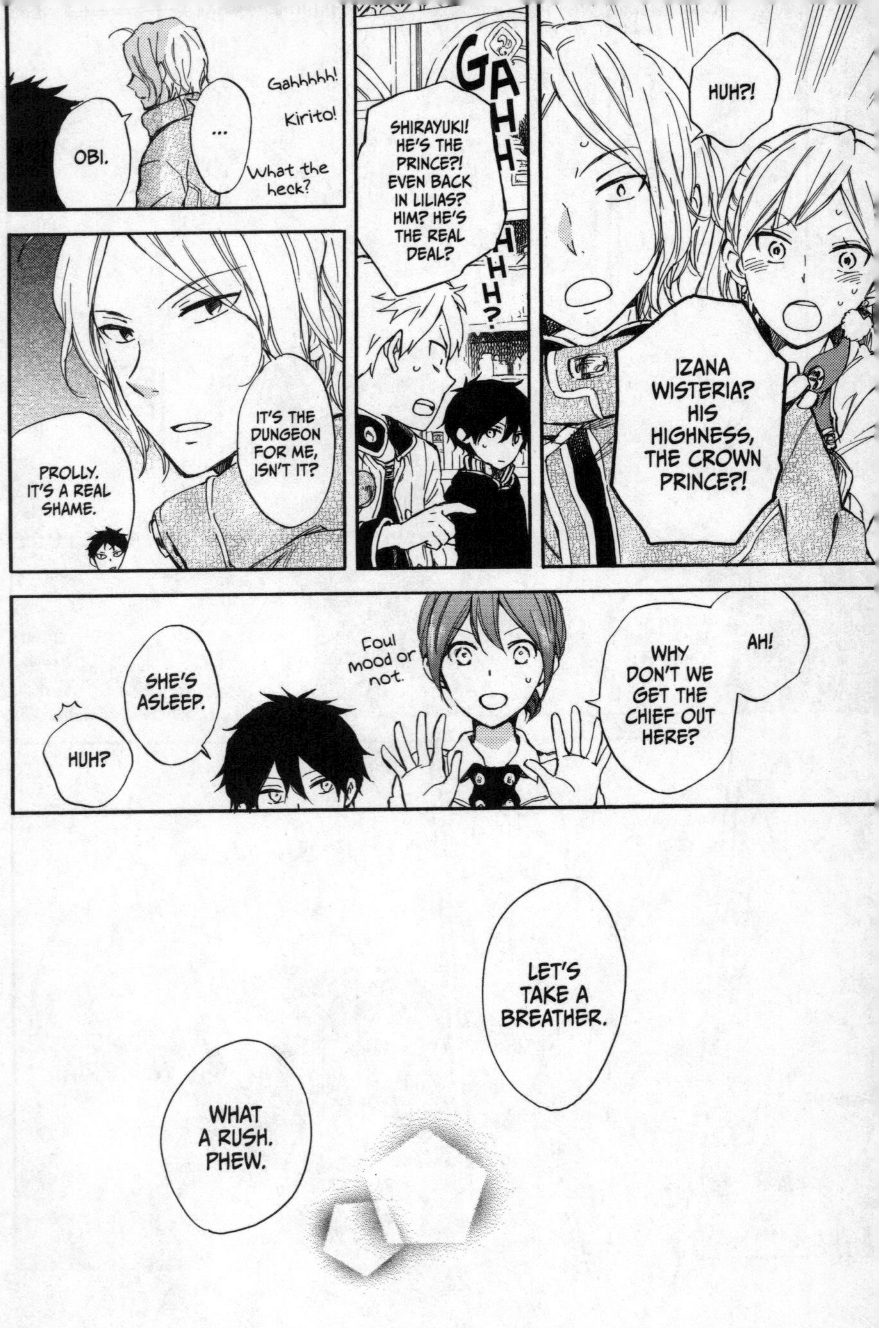
HUH?!
IZANA WISTERIA? HIS HIGHNESS, THE CROWN PRINCE?!
GAHHHHHH?
SHIRAYUKI! HE'S THE PRINCE?! EVEN BACK IN LILIAS? HIM? HE'S THE REAL DEAL?
Gahhhhh! Kirito! What the heck?
...
OBI.
IT'S THE DUNGEON FOR ME, ISN'T IT?
PROLLY. IT'S A REAL SHAME.
AH!
WHY DON'T WE GET THE CHIEF OUT HERE?
Foul mood or not.
SHE'S ASLEEP.
HUH?
LET'S TAKE A BREATHER.
WHAT A RUSH. PHEW.

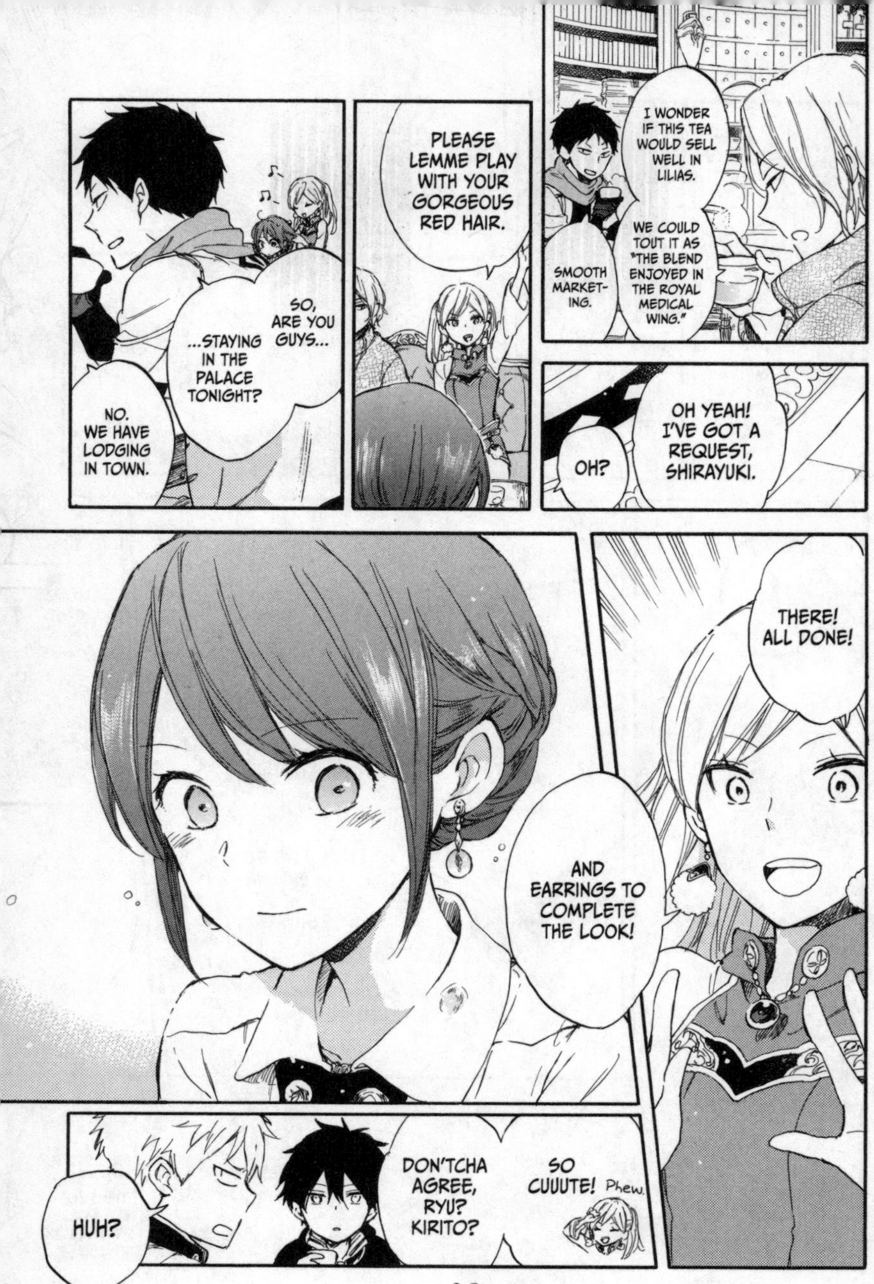
I WONDER IF THIS TEA WOULD SELL WELL IN LILIAS.
WE COULD TOUT IT AS "THE BLEND ENJOYED IN THE ROYAL MEDICAL WING."
SMOOTH MARKET-ING.
OH YEAH! I'VE GOT A REQUEST, SHIRAYUKI.
OH?
PLEASE LEMME PLAY WITH YOUR GORGEOUS RED HAIR.
SO, ARE YOU GUYS...
...STAYING IN THE PALACE TONIGHT?
NO. WE HAVE LODGING IN TOWN.
THERE! ALL DONE!
AND EARRINGS TO COMPLETE THE LOOK!
SO CUUUTE!
Phew.
DON'TCHA AGREE, RYU? KIRITO?
HUH?

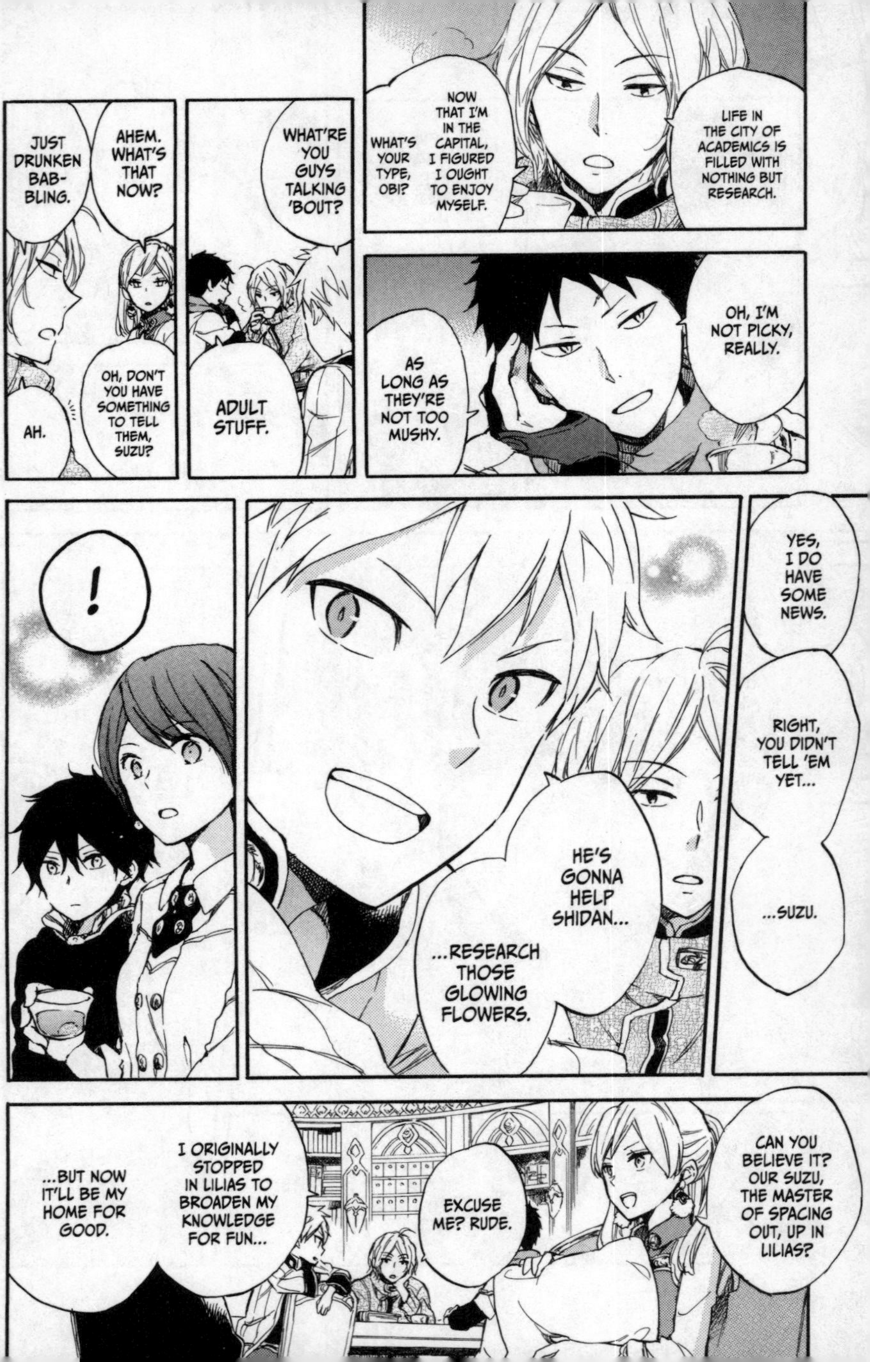
LIFE IN THE CITY OF ACADEMICS IS FILLED WITH NOTHING BUT RESEARCH.
NOW THAT I'M IN THE CAPITAL, I FIGURED I OUGHT TO ENJOY MYSELF.
WHAT'S YOUR TYPE, OBI?
OH, I'M NOT PICKY, REALLY.
AS LONG AS THEY'RE NOT TOO MUSHY.
WHAT'RE YOU GUYS TALKING 'BOUT?
ADULT STUFF.
AHEM. WHAT'S THAT NOW?
JUST DRUNKEN BAB-BLING.
OH, DON'T YOU HAVE SOMETHING TO TELL THEM, SUZU?
AH.
YES, I DO HAVE SOME NEWS.
RIGHT, YOU DIDN'T TELL 'EM YET...
...SUZU.
HE'S GONNA HELP SHIDAN...
...RESEARCH THOSE GLOWING FLOWERS.
!
CAN YOU BELIEVE IT? OUR SUZU, THE MASTER OF SPACING OUT, UP IN LILIAS?
EXCUSE ME? RUDE.
I ORIGINALLY STOPPED IN LILIAS TO BROADEN MY KNOWLEDGE FOR FUN...
...BUT NOW IT'LL BE MY HOME FOR GOOD.

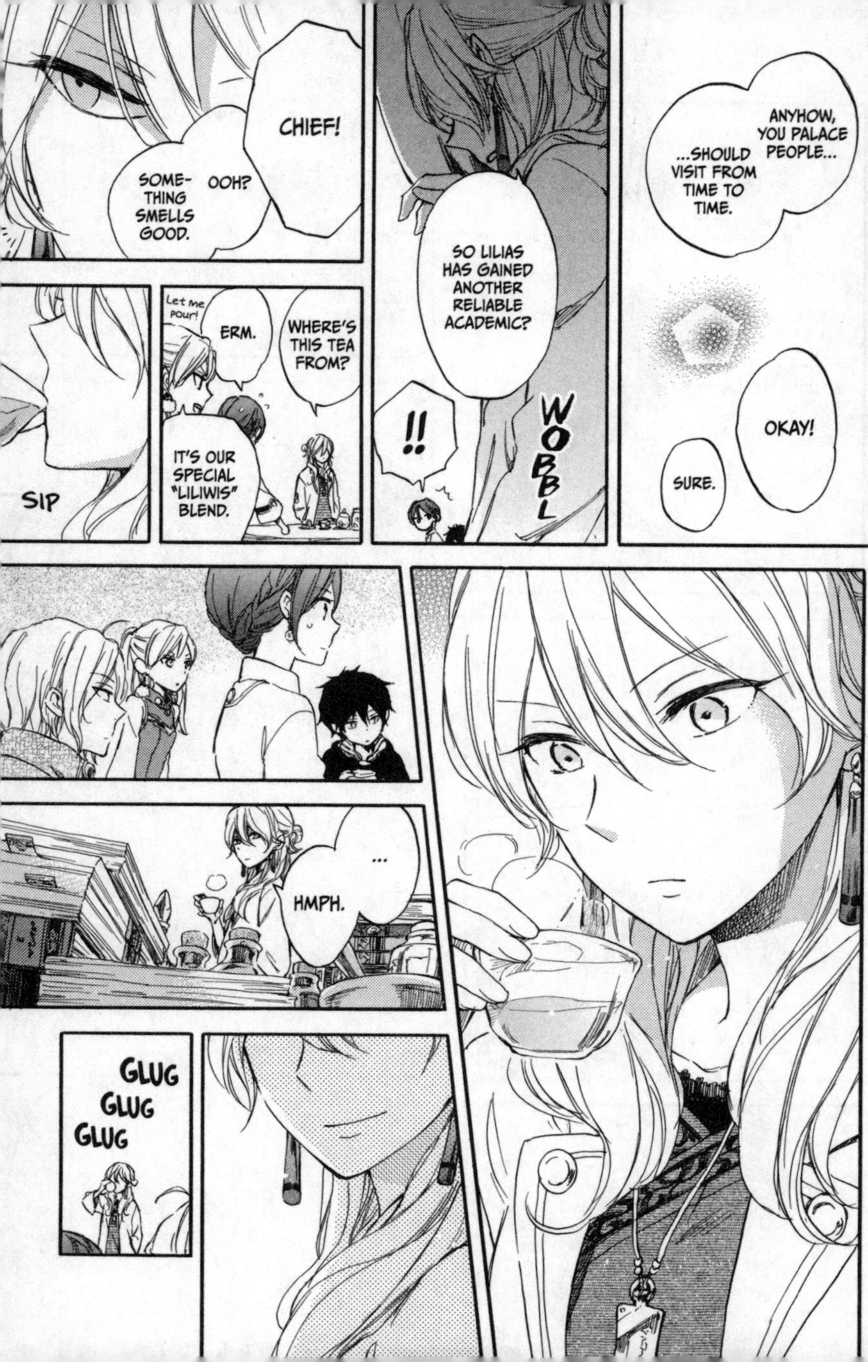

ANYHOW, YOU PALACE PEOPLE...
...SHOULD VISIT FROM TIME TO TIME.
OKAY!
SURE.
SO LILIAS HAS GAINED ANOTHER RELIABLE ACADEMIC?
!!
WOBBL
CHIEF!
OOH?
SOMETHING SMELLS GOOD.
WHERE'S THIS TEA FROM?
ERM.
Let me pour!
IT'S OUR SPECIAL "LILIWIS" BLEND.
SIP
...
HMPH.
GLUG
GLUG
GLUG

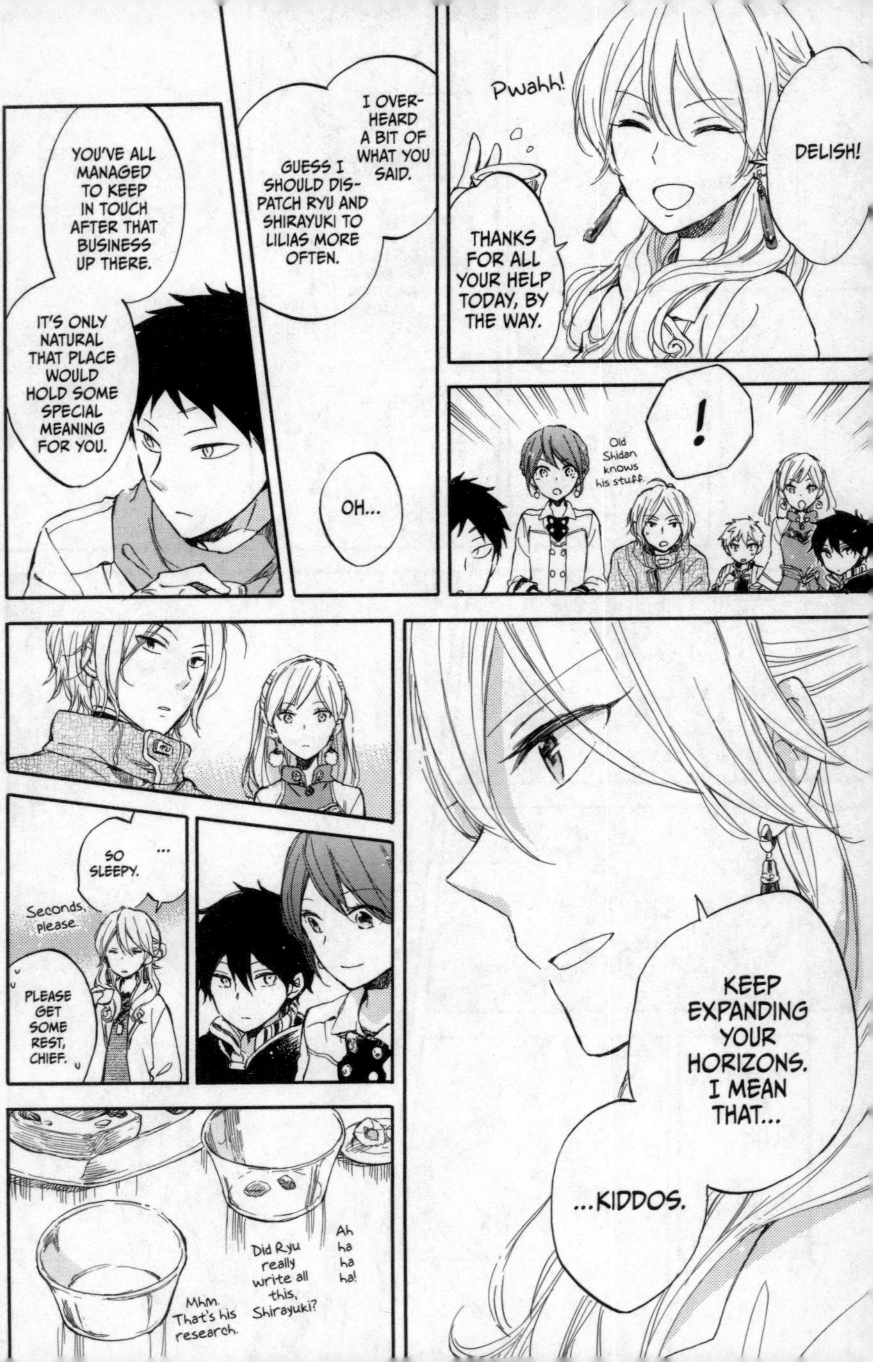
Pwahh!
DELISH!
THANKS FOR ALL YOUR HELP TODAY, BY THE WAY.
!
Old Shidan knows his stuff.
I OVER-HEARD A BIT OF WHAT YOU SAID.
GUESS I SHOULD DIS-PATCH RYU AND SHIRAYUKI TO LILIAS MORE OFTEN.
OH...
YOU'VE ALL MANAGED TO KEEP IN TOUCH AFTER THAT BUSINESS UP THERE.
IT'S ONLY NATURAL THAT PLACE WOULD HOLD SOME SPECIAL MEANING FOR YOU.
KEEP EXPANDING YOUR HORIZONS. I MEAN THAT...
...KIDDOS.
SO SLEEPY. ...
Seconds, please.
PLEASE GET SOME REST, CHIEF.
Ah ha ha ha!
Did Ryu really write all this, Shirayuki?
Mhm. That's his research.

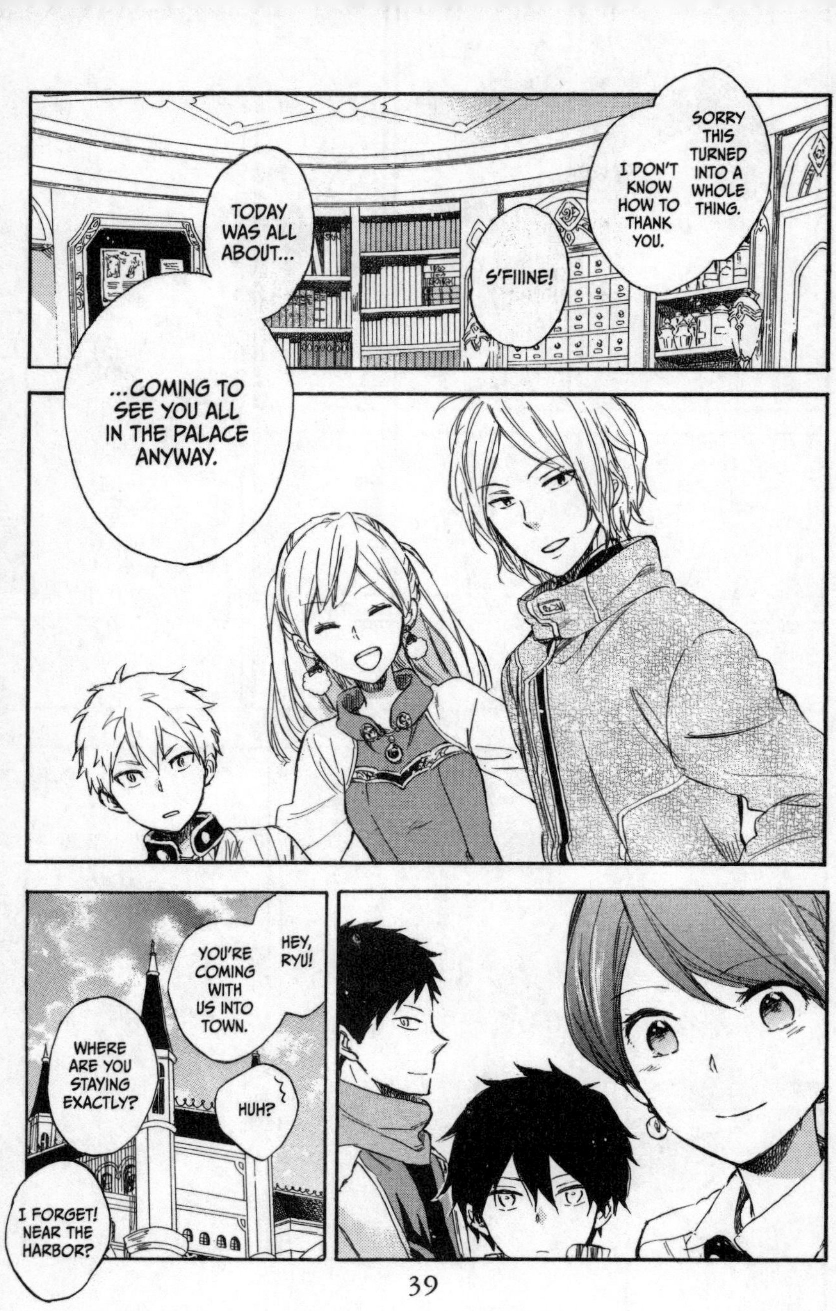
SORRY THIS TURNED INTO A WHOLE THING.
I DON'T KNOW HOW TO THANK YOU.
S'FIIINE!
TODAY WAS ALL ABOUT...
...COMING TO SEE YOU ALL IN THE PALACE ANYWAY.
HEY, RYU!
YOU'RE COMING WITH US INTO TOWN.
HUH?
WHERE ARE YOU STAYING EXACTLY?
I FORGET! NEAR THE HARBOR?

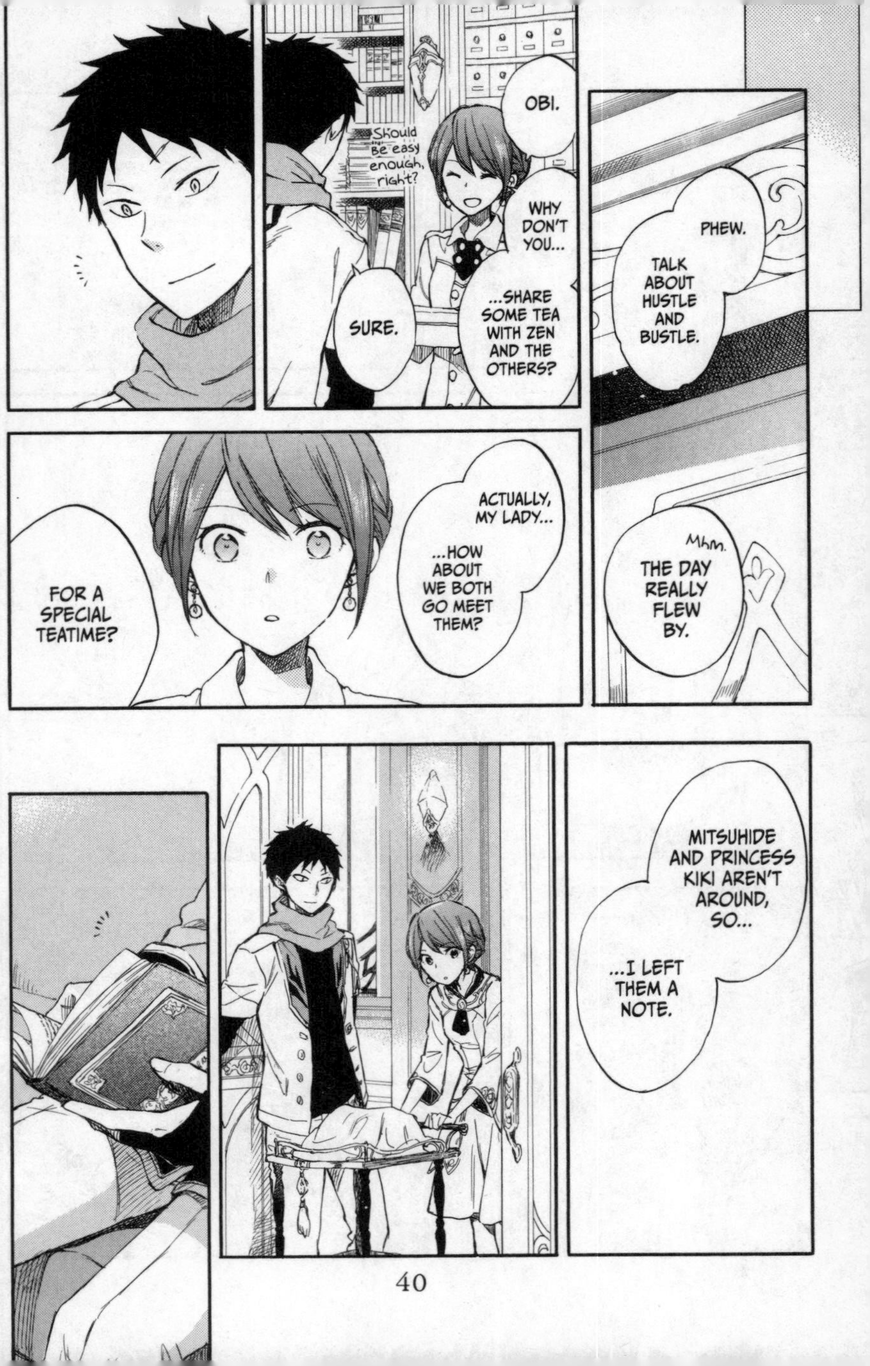
PHEW.
TALK ABOUT HUSTLE AND BUSTLE.
Mhm.
THE DAY REALLY FLEW BY.
OBI.
WHY DON'T YOU...
...SHARE SOME TEA WITH ZEN AND THE OTHERS?
Should be easy enough, right?
SURE.
ACTUALLY, MY LADY...
...HOW ABOUT WE BOTH GO MEET THEM?
FOR A SPECIAL TEATIME?
MITSUHIDE AND PRINCESS KIKI AREN'T AROUND, SO...
...I LEFT THEM A NOTE.

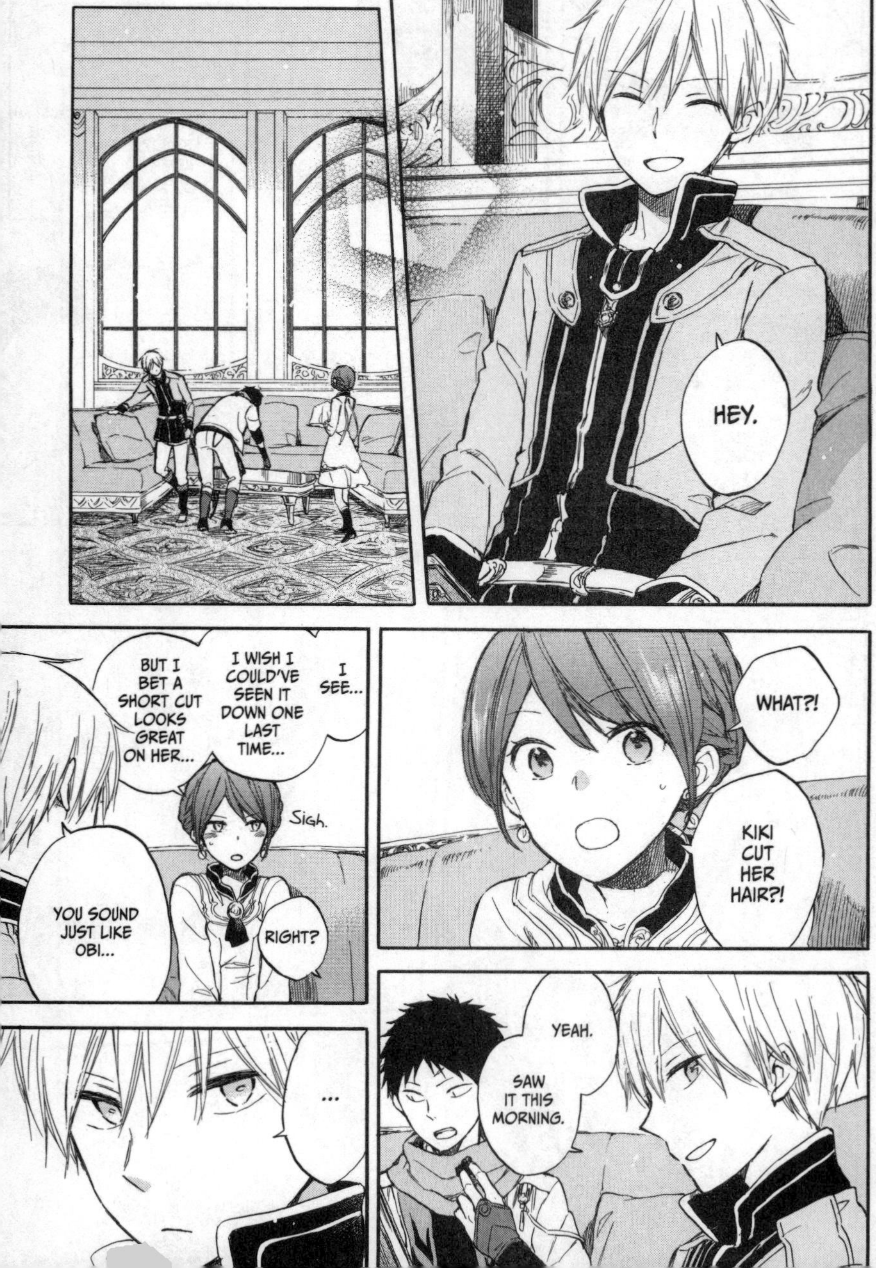
HEY.
WHAT?!
KIKI CUT HER HAIR?!
I SEE...
I WISH I COULD'VE SEEN IT DOWN ONE LAST TIME...
BUT I BET A SHORT CUT LOOKS GREAT ON HER...
Sigh.
RIGHT?
YOU SOUND JUST LIKE OBI...
YEAH.
SAW IT THIS MORNING.
...

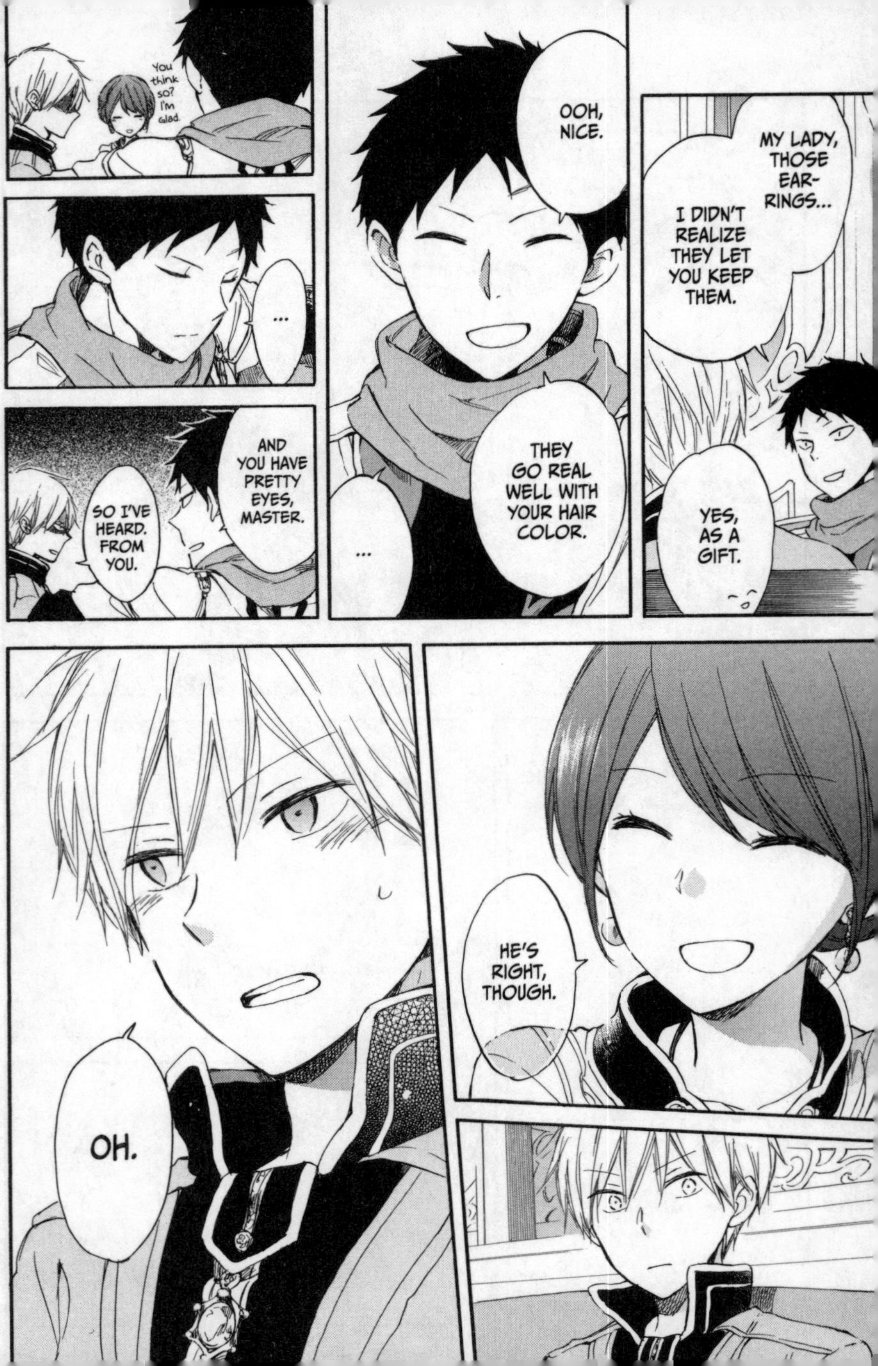
MY LADY, THOSE EAR-RINGS...
I DIDN'T REALIZE THEY LET YOU KEEP THEM.
YES, AS A GIFT.
OOH, NICE.
THEY GO REAL WELL WITH YOUR HAIR COLOR.
...
You think so? I'm Glad.
...
AND YOU HAVE PRETTY EYES, MASTER.
SO I'VE HEARD. FROM YOU.
HE'S RIGHT, THOUGH.
OH.

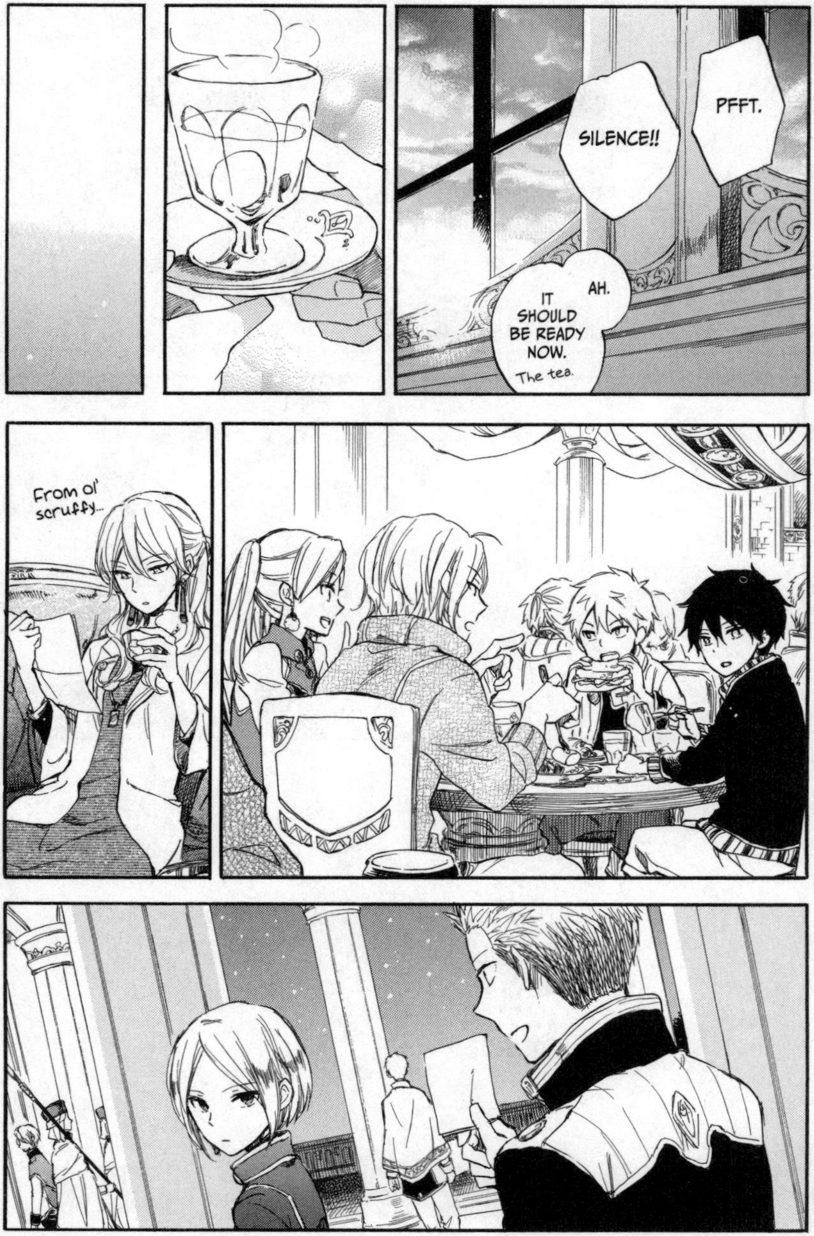
PFFT.
SILENCE!!
AH.
IT SHOULD BE READY NOW.
The tea.
From ol' scruffy...

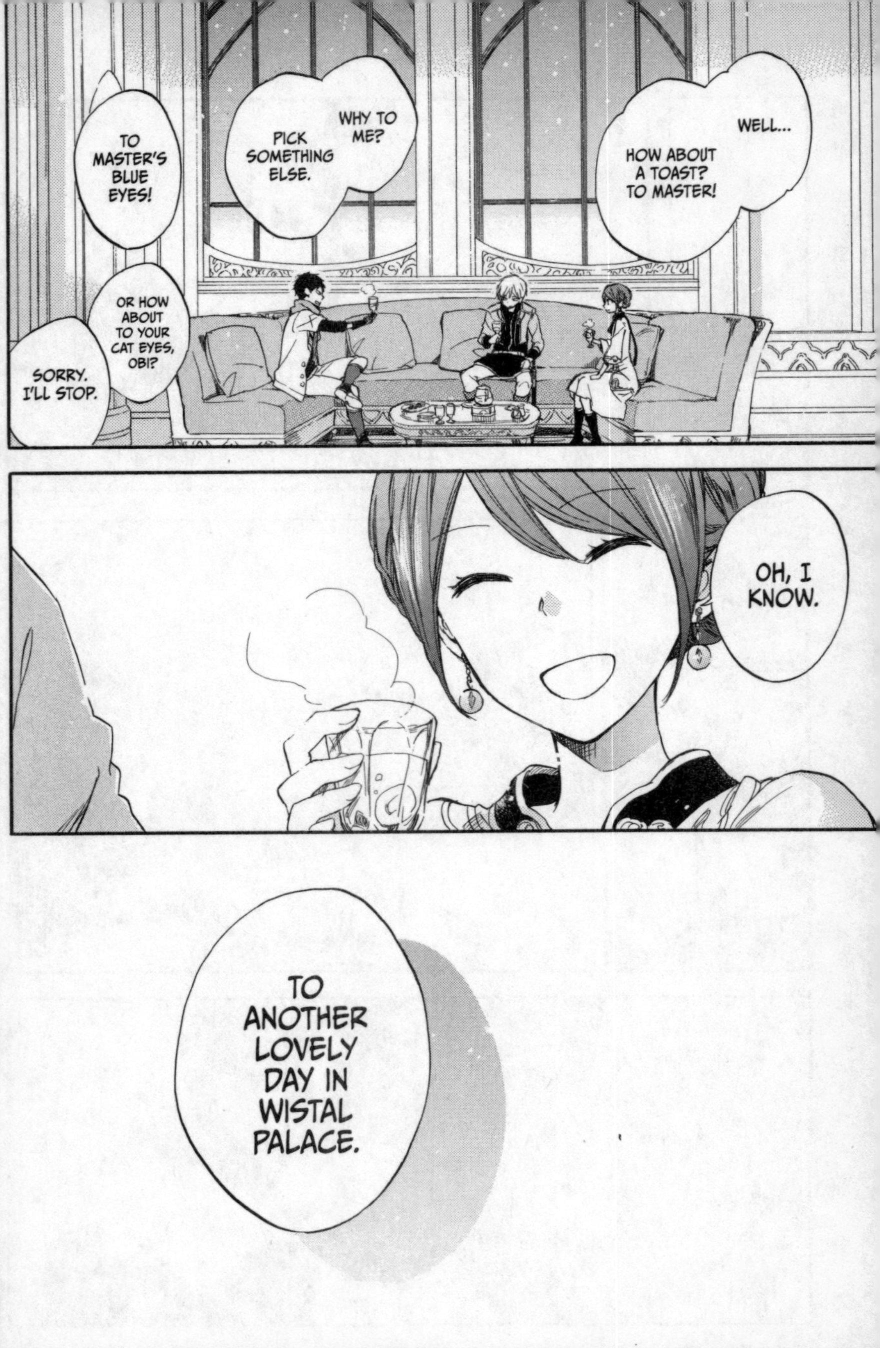
WELL... HOW ABOUT A TOAST? TO MASTER!
WHY TO ME? PICK SOMETHING ELSE.
TO MASTER'S BLUE EYES!
OR HOW ABOUT TO YOUR CAT EYES, OBI?
SORRY. I'LL STOP.
OH, I KNOW.
TO ANOTHER LOVELY DAY IN WISTAL PALACE.

Snow White with the Red Hair

Chapter 45 Preview Image

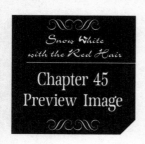

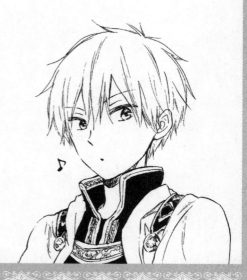

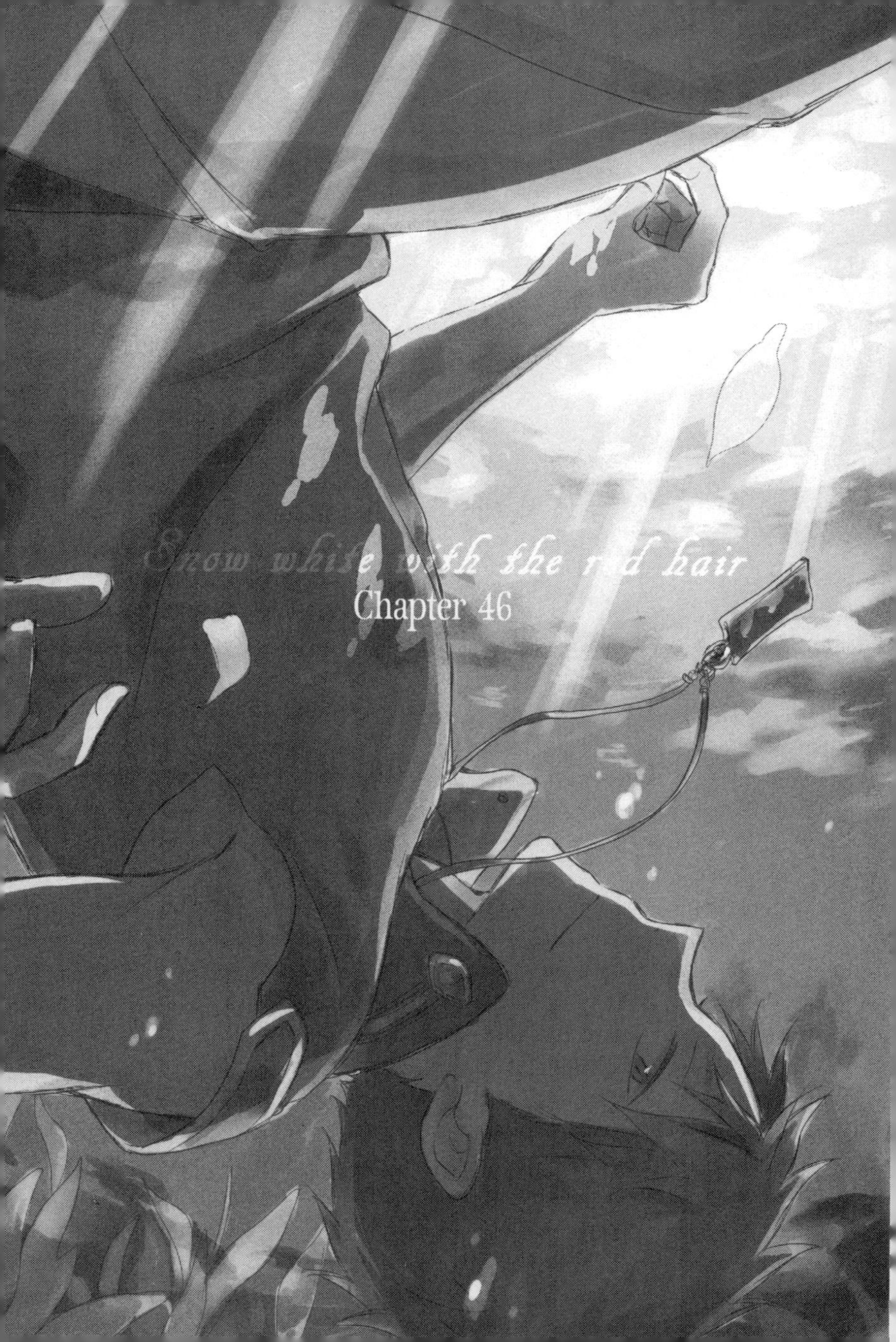
Snow white with the red hair
Chapter 46

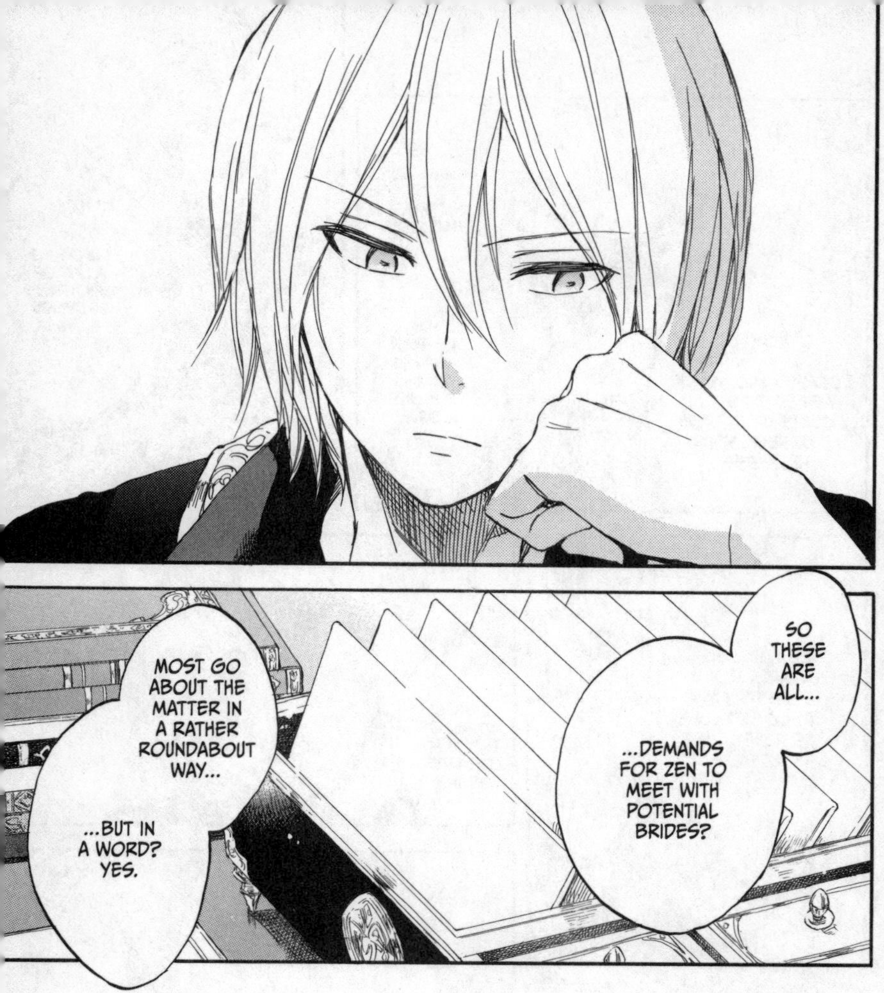
SO THESE ARE ALL...
...DEMANDS FOR ZEN TO MEET WITH POTENTIAL BRIDES?
MOST GO ABOUT THE MATTER IN A RATHER ROUNDABOUT WAY...
...BUT IN A WORD? YES.

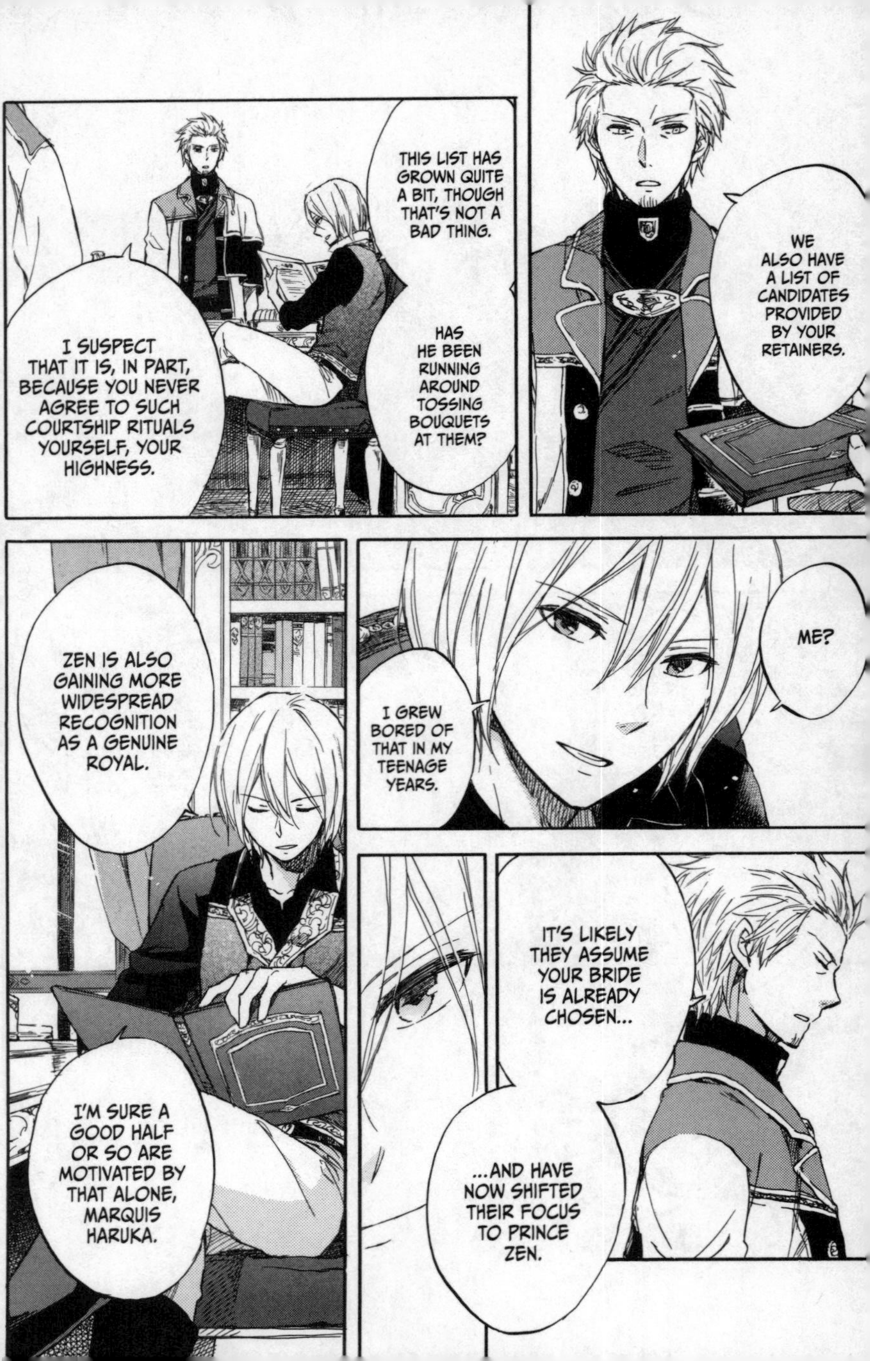
WE ALSO HAVE A LIST OF CANDIDATES PROVIDED BY YOUR RETAINERS.
THIS LIST HAS GROWN QUITE A BIT, THOUGH THAT'S NOT A BAD THING.
HAS HE BEEN RUNNING AROUND TOSSING BOUQUETS AT THEM?
I SUSPECT THAT IT IS, IN PART, BECAUSE YOU NEVER AGREE TO SUCH COURTSHIP RITUALS YOURSELF, YOUR HIGHNESS.
ME?
I GREW BORED OF THAT IN MY TEENAGE YEARS.
IT'S LIKELY THEY ASSUME YOUR BRIDE IS ALREADY CHOSEN...
...AND HAVE NOW SHIFTED THEIR FOCUS TO PRINCE ZEN.
ZEN IS ALSO GAINING MORE WIDESPREAD RECOGNITION AS A GENUINE ROYAL.
I'M SURE A GOOD HALF OR SO ARE MOTIVATED BY THAT ALONE, MARQUIS HARUKA.

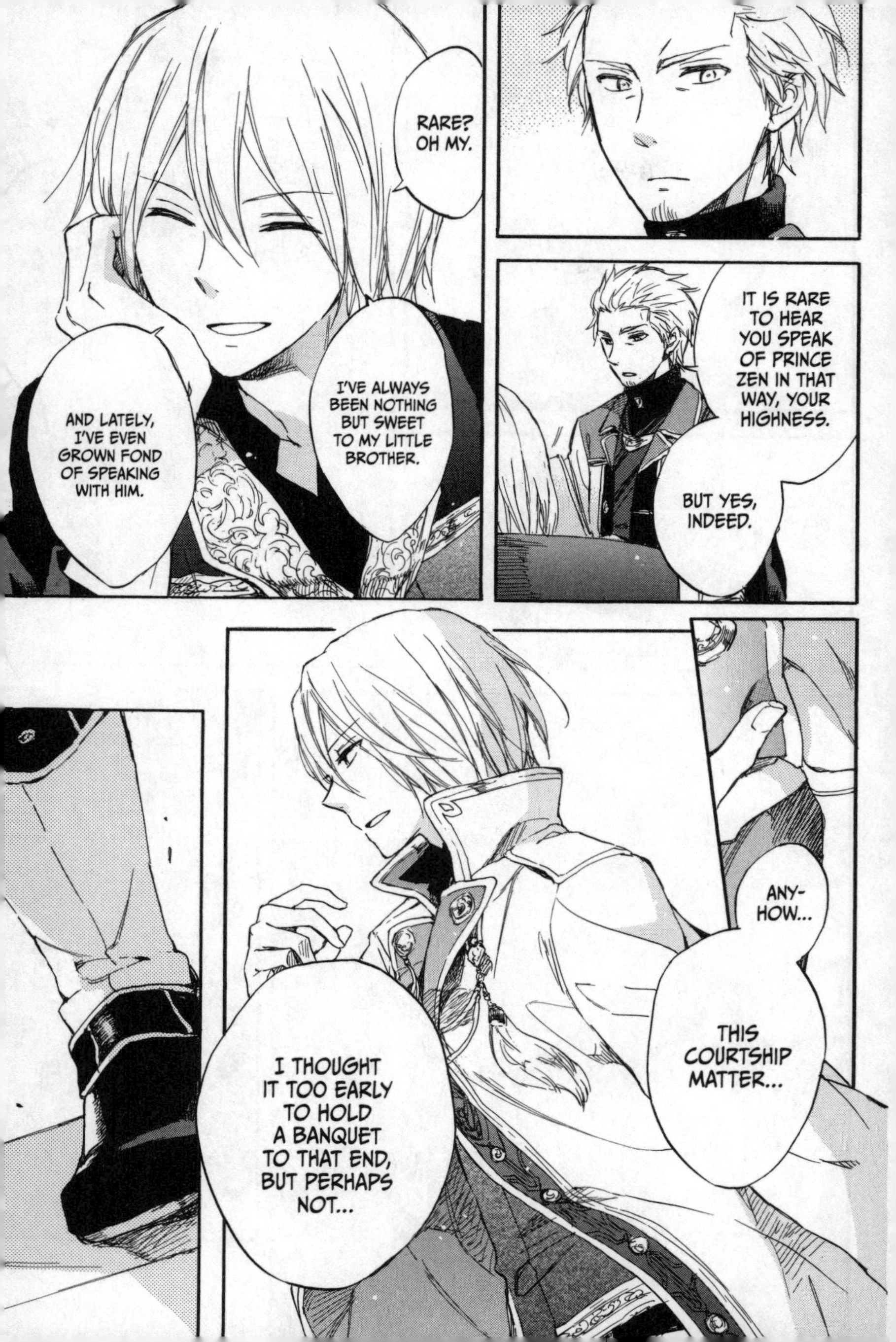
IT IS RARE TO HEAR YOU SPEAK OF PRINCE ZEN IN THAT WAY, YOUR HIGHNESS.
BUT YES, INDEED.
RARE? OH MY.
I'VE ALWAYS BEEN NOTHING BUT SWEET TO MY LITTLE BROTHER.
AND LATELY, I'VE EVEN GROWN FOND OF SPEAKING WITH HIM.
ANY-HOW...
THIS COURTSHIP MATTER...
I THOUGHT IT TOO EARLY TO HOLD A BANQUET TO THAT END, BUT PERHAPS NOT...

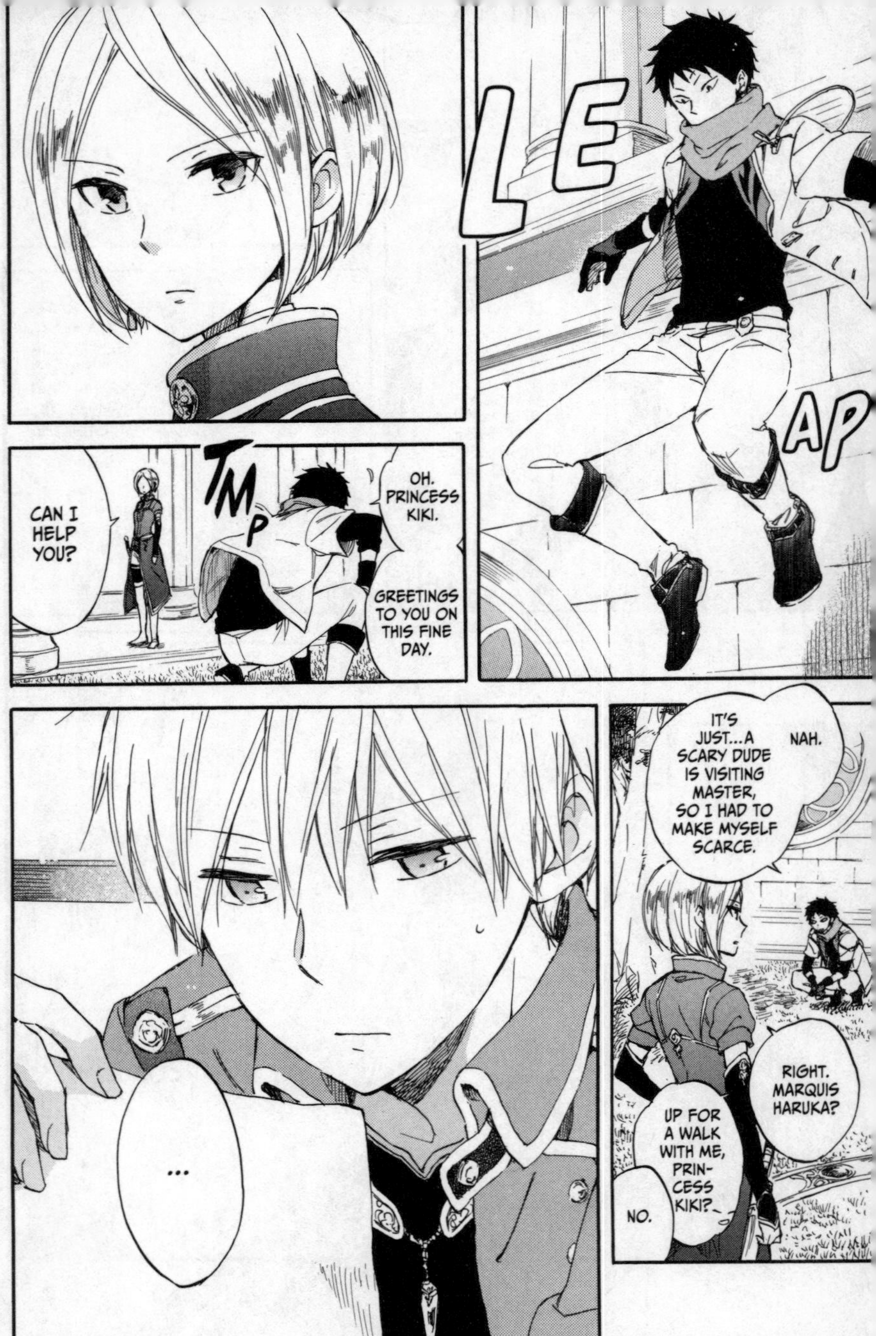
LE
AP
TMP
OH. PRINCESS KIKI.
GREETINGS TO YOU ON THIS FINE DAY.
CAN I HELP YOU?
NAH.
IT'S JUST...A SCARY DUDE IS VISITING MASTER, SO I HAD TO MAKE MYSELF SCARCE.
RIGHT. MARQUIS HARUKA?
UP FOR A WALK WITH ME, PRIN-CESS KIKI?
NO.
...

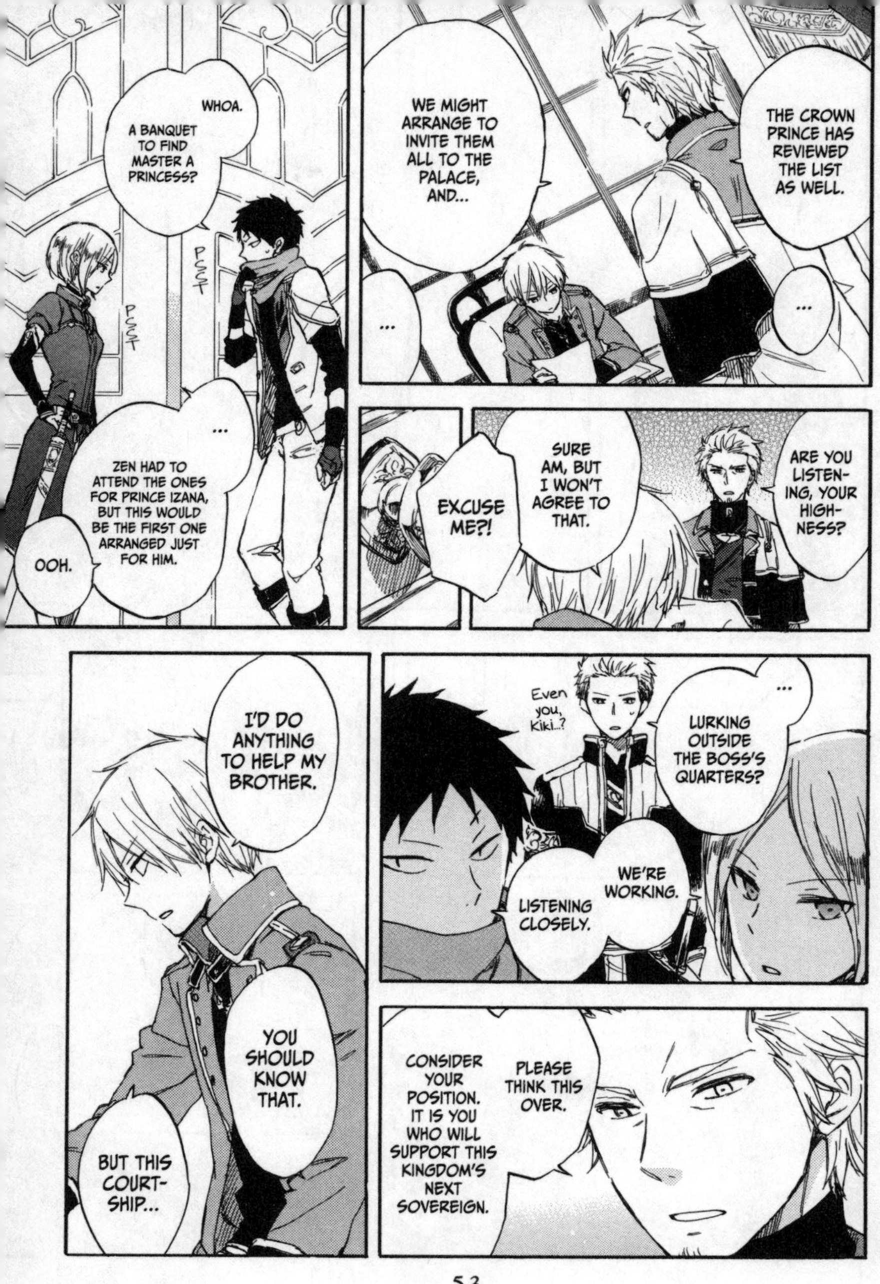
THE CROWN PRINCE HAS REVIEWED THE LIST AS WELL.
...
WE MIGHT ARRANGE TO INVITE THEM ALL TO THE PALACE, AND...
...
ARE YOU LISTENING, YOUR HIGHNESS?
SURE AM, BUT I WON'T AGREE TO THAT.
EXCUSE ME?!
WHOA.
A BANQUET TO FIND MASTER A PRINCESS?
PSST
PSST
...
ZEN HAD TO ATTEND THE ONES FOR PRINCE IZANA, BUT THIS WOULD BE THE FIRST ONE ARRANGED JUST FOR HIM.
OOH.
...
LURKING OUTSIDE THE BOSS'S QUARTERS?
Even you, Kiki...?
WE'RE WORKING.
LISTENING CLOSELY.
PLEASE THINK THIS OVER.
CONSIDER YOUR POSITION. IT IS YOU WHO WILL SUPPORT THIS KINGDOM'S NEXT SOVEREIGN.
I'D DO ANYTHING TO HELP MY BROTHER.
YOU SHOULD KNOW THAT.
BUT THIS COURTSHIP...

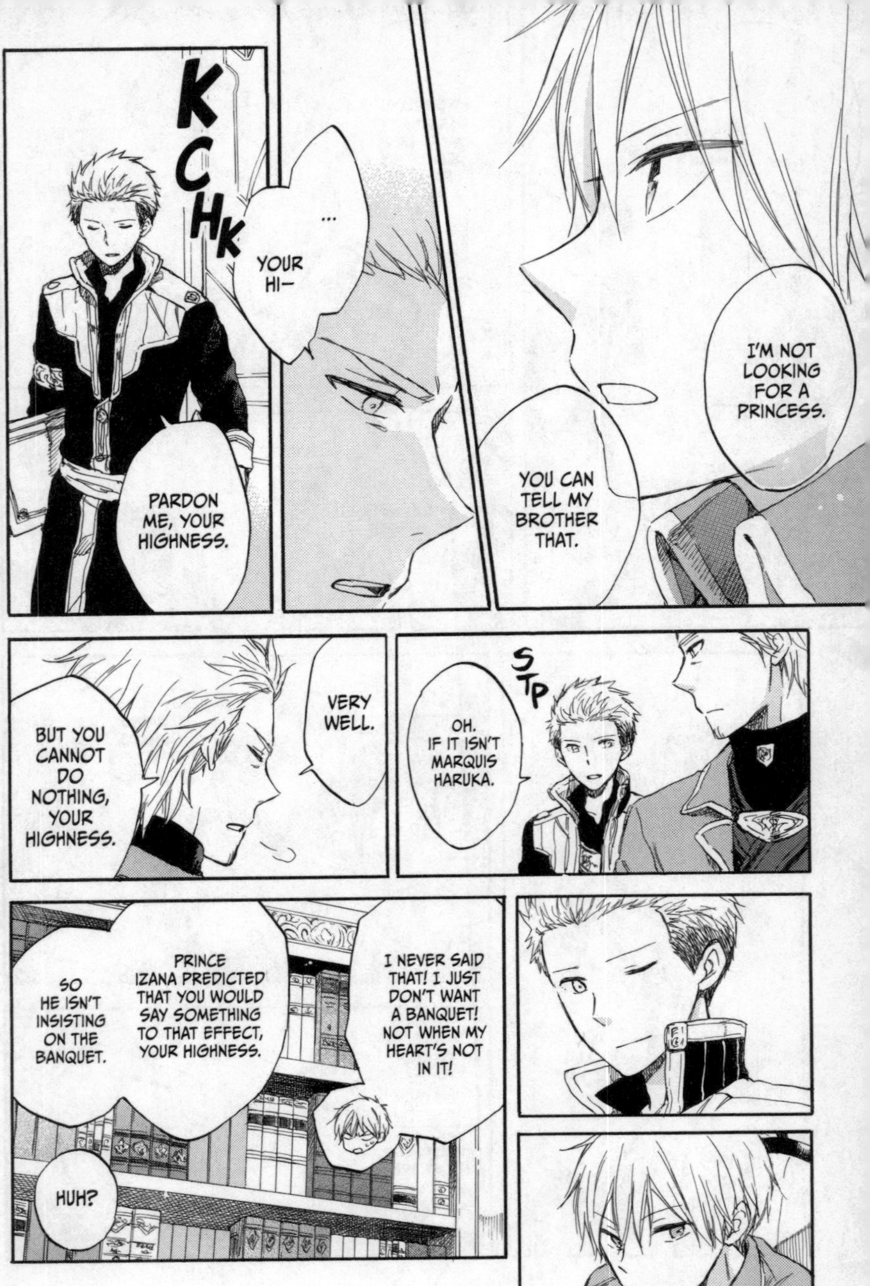
I'M NOT LOOKING FOR A PRINCESS.
YOU CAN TELL MY BROTHER THAT.
...
YOUR HI—
KCHK
PARDON ME, YOUR HIGHNESS.
STP
OH. IF IT ISN'T MARQUIS HARUKA.
VERY WELL.
BUT YOU CANNOT DO NOTHING, YOUR HIGHNESS.
I NEVER SAID THAT! I JUST DON'T WANT A BANQUET! NOT WHEN MY HEART'S NOT IN IT!
PRINCE IZANA PREDICTED THAT YOU WOULD SAY SOMETHING TO THAT EFFECT, YOUR HIGHNESS.
SO HE ISN'T INSISTING ON THE BANQUET.
HUH?

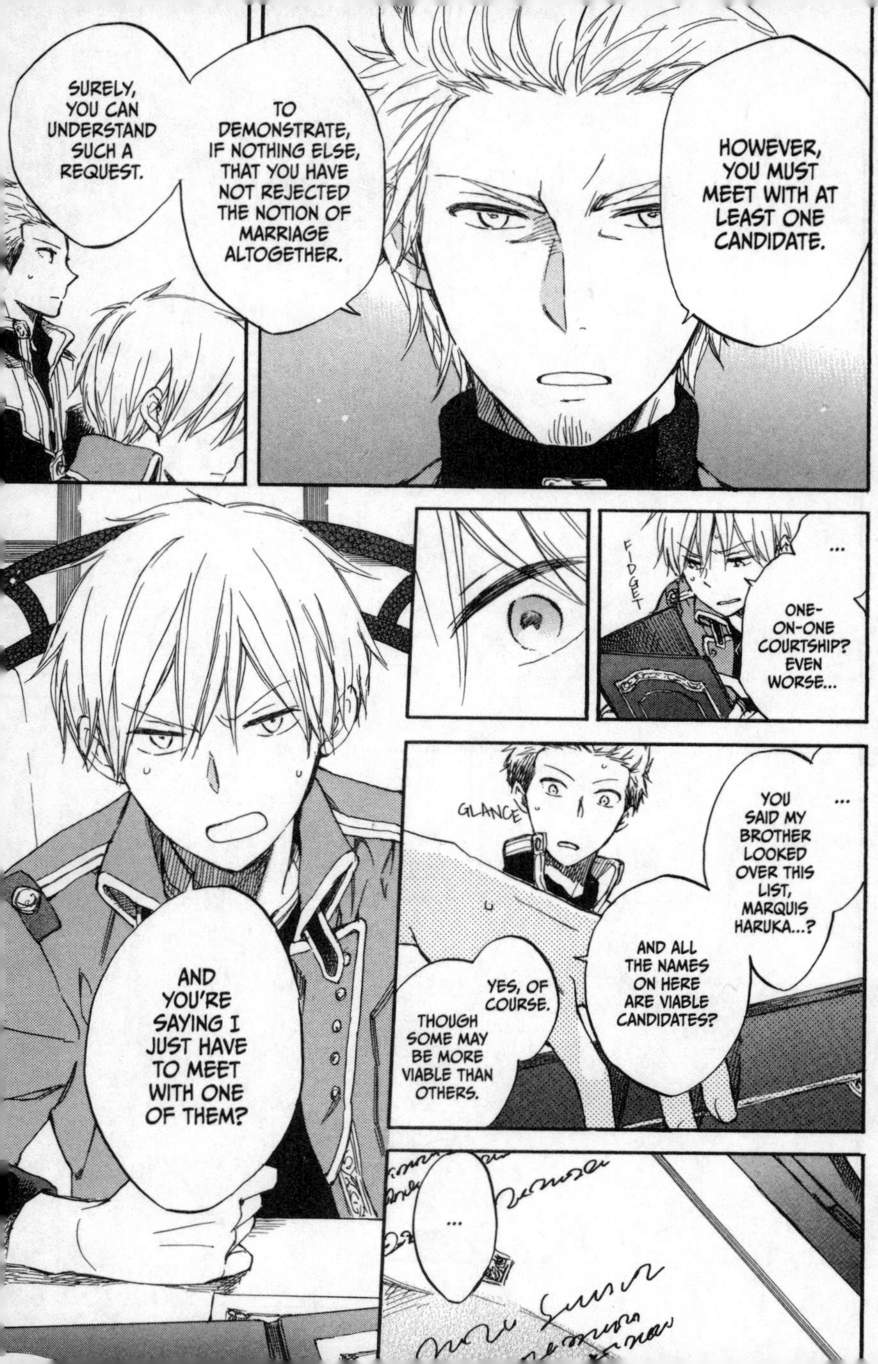
HOWEVER, YOU MUST MEET WITH AT LEAST ONE CANDIDATE.
TO DEMONSTRATE, IF NOTHING ELSE, THAT YOU HAVE NOT REJECTED THE NOTION OF MARRIAGE ALTOGETHER.
SURELY, YOU CAN UNDERSTAND SUCH A REQUEST.
...
FIDGET
ONE-ON-ONE COURTSHIP? EVEN WORSE...
...
YOU SAID MY BROTHER LOOKED OVER THIS LIST, MARQUIS HARUKA...?
GLANCE
AND ALL THE NAMES ON HERE ARE VIABLE CANDIDATES?
YES, OF COURSE.
THOUGH SOME MAY BE MORE VIABLE THAN OTHERS.
...
AND YOU'RE SAYING I JUST HAVE TO MEET WITH ONE OF THEM?

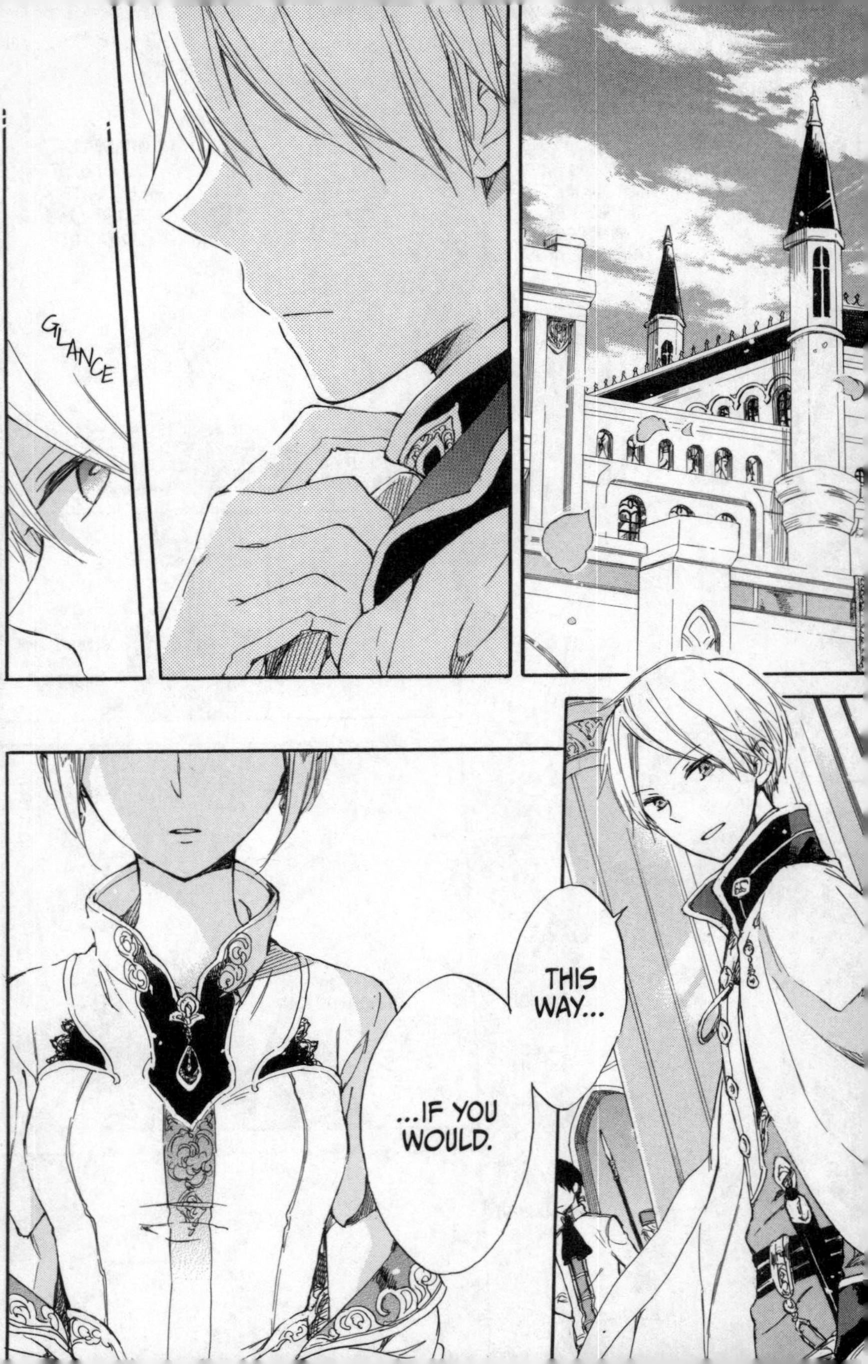
GLANCE
THIS WAY...
...IF YOU WOULD.

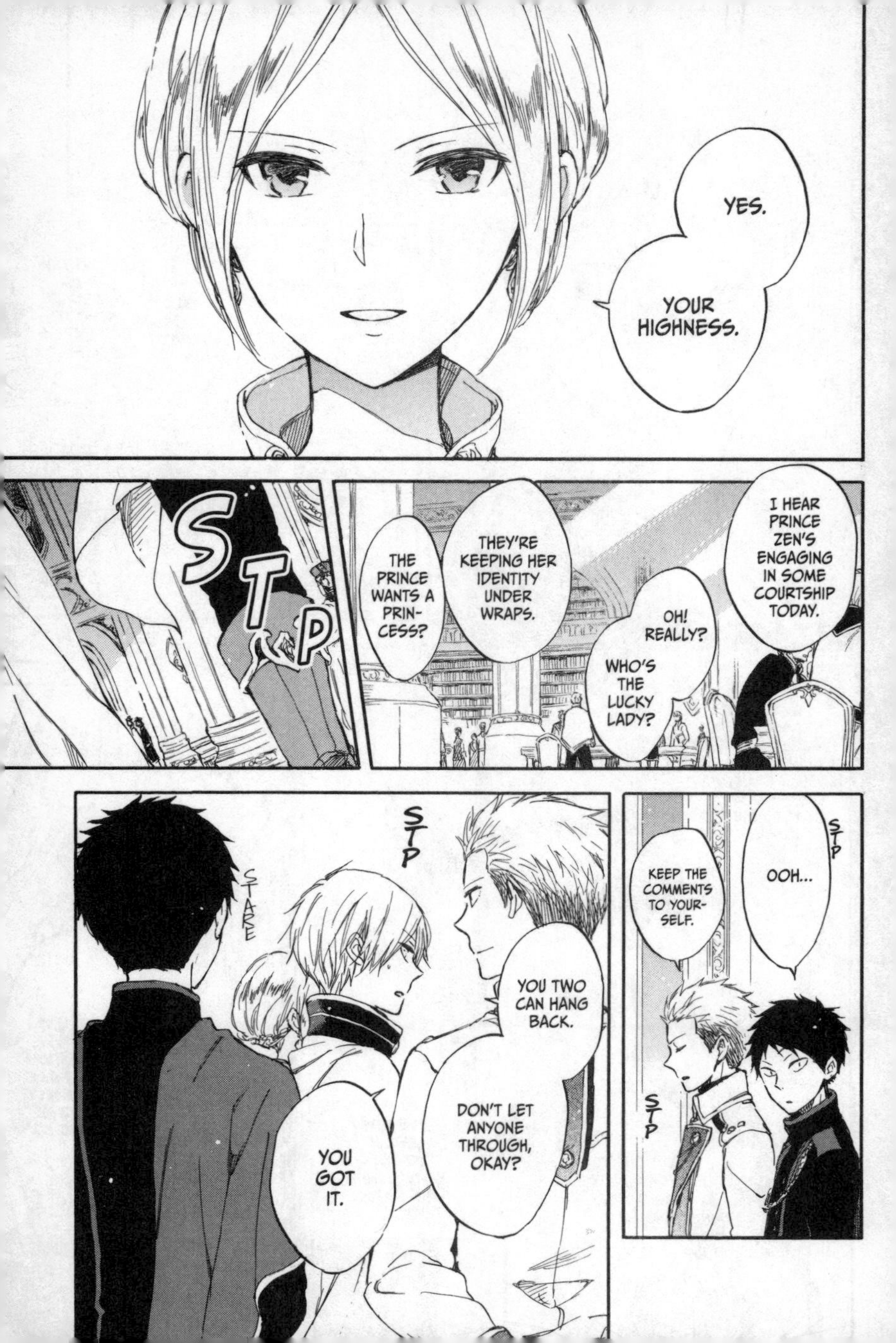
YES.
YOUR HIGHNESS.
I HEAR PRINCE ZEN'S ENGAGING IN SOME COURTSHIP TODAY.
OH! REALLY?
WHO'S THE LUCKY LADY?
THEY'RE KEEPING HER IDENTITY UNDER WRAPS.
THE PRINCE WANTS A PRIN-CESS?
STP
STP
OOH...
KEEP THE COMMENTS TO YOUR-SELF.
STP
STP
YOU TWO CAN HANG BACK.
DON'T LET ANYONE THROUGH, OKAY?
STARE
YOU GOT IT.

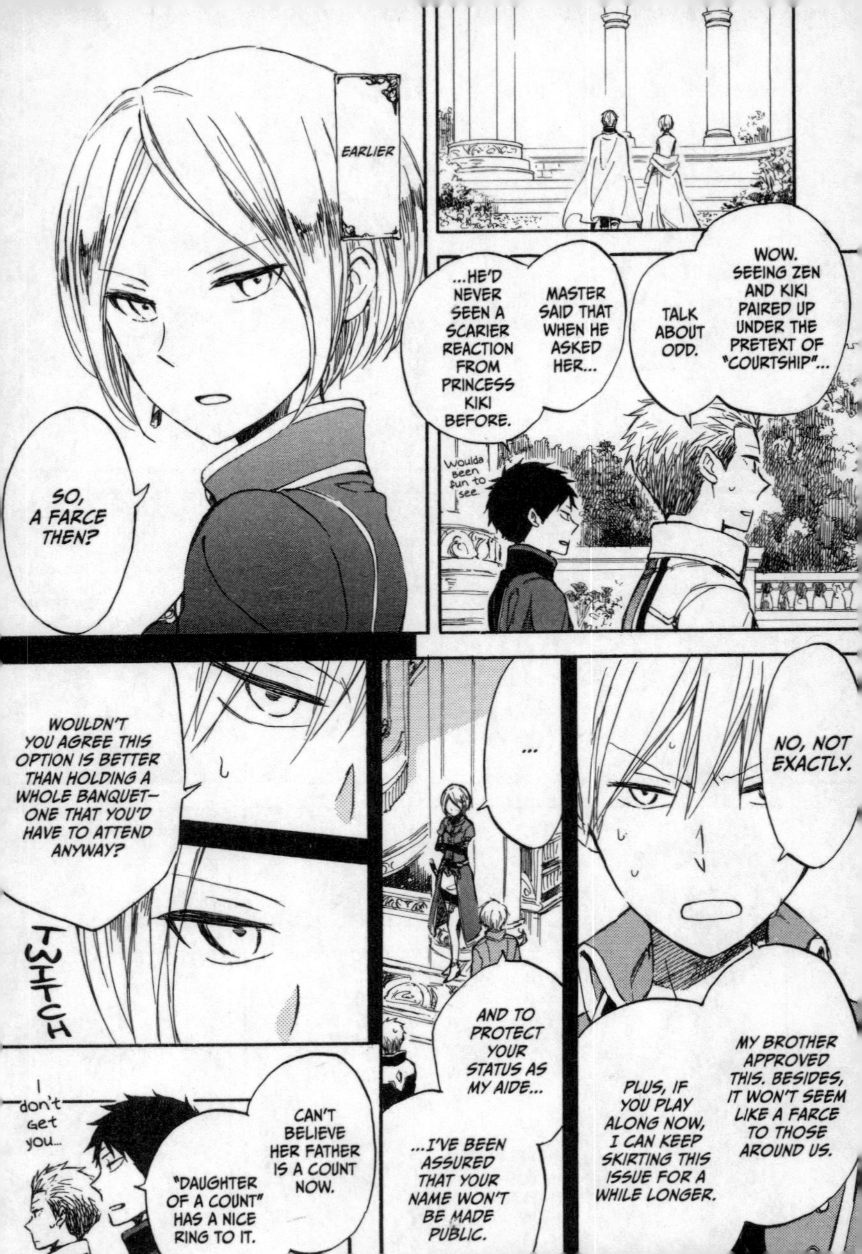
WOW. SEEING ZEN AND KIKI PAIRED UP UNDER THE PRETEXT OF "COURTSHIP"...
TALK ABOUT ODD.
MASTER SAID THAT WHEN HE ASKED HER...
...HE'D NEVER SEEN A SCARIER REACTION FROM PRINCESS KIKI BEFORE.
Woulda been fun to see.
EARLIER
SO, A FARCE THEN?
NO, NOT EXACTLY.
...
WOULDN'T YOU AGREE THIS OPTION IS BETTER THAN HOLDING A WHOLE BANQUET—ONE THAT YOU'D HAVE TO ATTEND ANYWAY?
TWITCH
MY BROTHER APPROVED THIS. BESIDES, IT WON'T SEEM LIKE A FARCE TO THOSE AROUND US.
PLUS, IF YOU PLAY ALONG NOW, I CAN KEEP SKIRTING THIS ISSUE FOR A WHILE LONGER.
AND TO PROTECT YOUR STATUS AS MY AIDE...
...I'VE BEEN ASSURED THAT YOUR NAME WON'T BE MADE PUBLIC.
CAN'T BELIEVE HER FATHER IS A COUNT NOW.
"DAUGHTER OF A COUNT" HAS A NICE RING TO IT.
I don't get you...

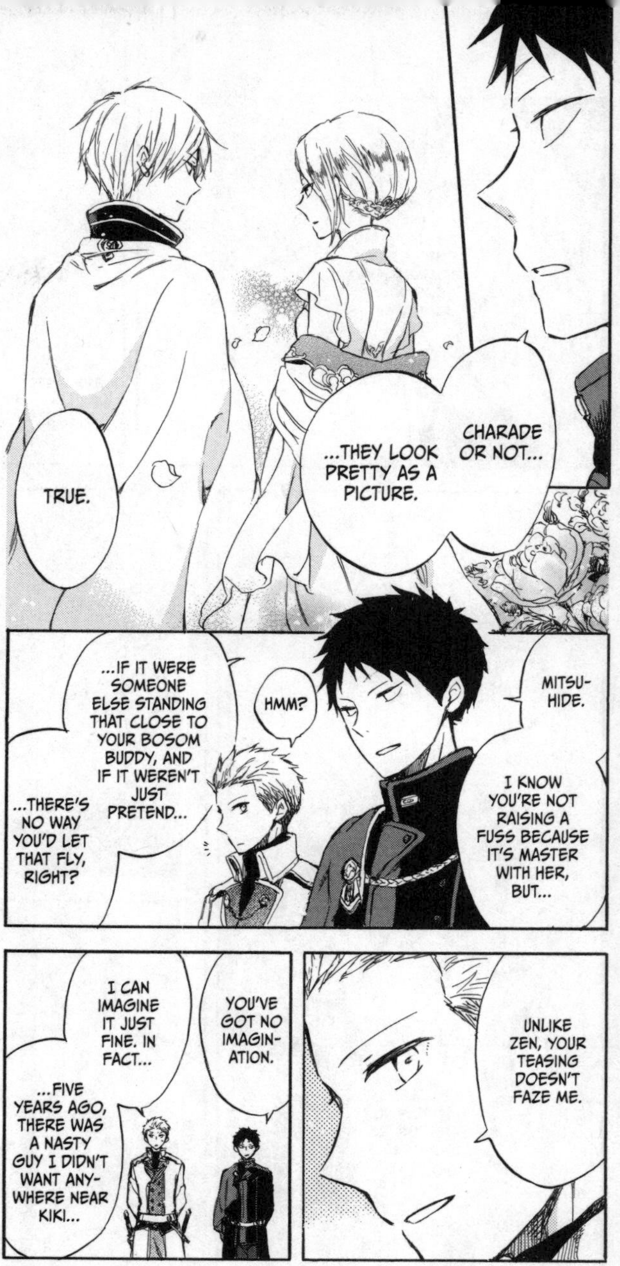
CHARADE OR NOT...
...THEY LOOK PRETTY AS A PICTURE.
TRUE.
MITSU-HIDE.
I KNOW YOU'RE NOT RAISING A FUSS BECAUSE IT'S MASTER WITH HER, BUT...
HMM?
...IF IT WERE SOMEONE ELSE STANDING THAT CLOSE TO YOUR BOSOM BUDDY, AND IF IT WEREN'T JUST PRETEND...
...THERE'S NO WAY YOU'D LET THAT FLY, RIGHT?
UNLIKE ZEN, YOUR TEASING DOESN'T FAZE ME.
YOU'VE GOT NO IMAGIN-ATION.
I CAN IMAGINE IT JUST FINE. IN FACT...
...FIVE YEARS AGO, THERE WAS A NASTY GUY I DIDN'T WANT ANY-WHERE NEAR KIKI...

2

TRIP, PART 1

In May 2013, I traveled to Central Europe with Toki Yajima and Wataru Hibiki.

I was working on volume 10 of this series up until the morning of our departure and ended up missing my bullet train. My heart nearly broke, but Yajima sent me a text saying, "Come on! You can still make it!" So I packed my suitcase and caught a flight to Narita Airport just in the nick of time.

Cooperation!

Family!

I forgot to pack quite a few things, so what do you think I bought first once I arrived in Hungary?

A toothbrush, toothpaste and pocket tissues, of course.

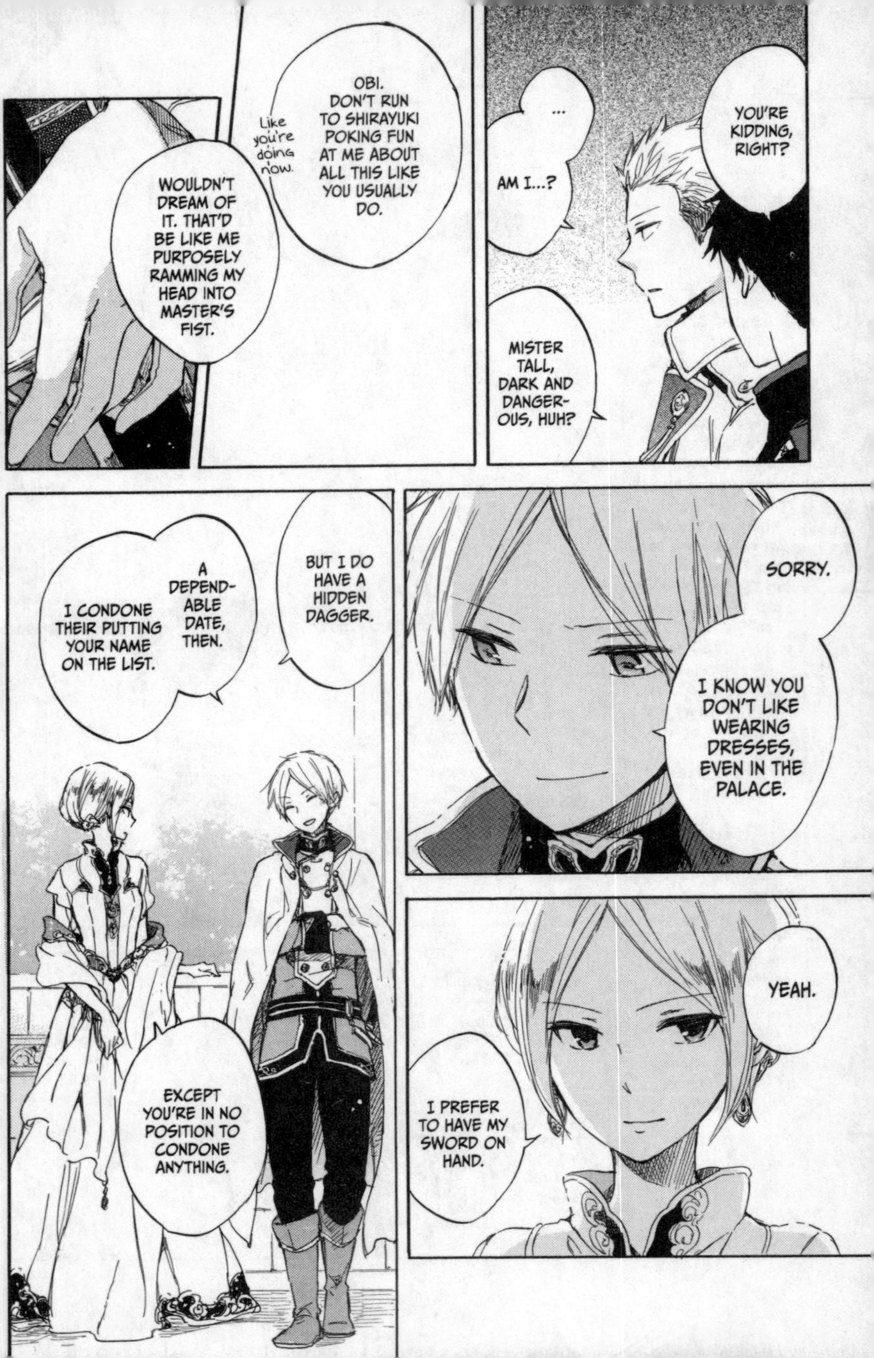
YOU'RE KIDDING, RIGHT?
...
AM I...?
MISTER TALL, DARK AND DANGER-OUS, HUH?
OBI. DON'T RUN TO SHIRAYUKI POKING FUN AT ME ABOUT ALL THIS LIKE YOU USUALLY DO.
Like you're doing now.
WOULDN'T DREAM OF IT. THAT'D BE LIKE ME PURPOSELY RAMMING MY HEAD INTO MASTER'S FIST.
SORRY.
I KNOW YOU DON'T LIKE WEARING DRESSES, EVEN IN THE PALACE.
YEAH.
I PREFER TO HAVE MY SWORD ON HAND.
BUT I DO HAVE A HIDDEN DAGGER.
A DEPEND-ABLE DATE, THEN.
I CONDONE THEIR PUTTING YOUR NAME ON THE LIST.
EXCEPT YOU'RE IN NO POSITION TO CONDONE ANYTHING.

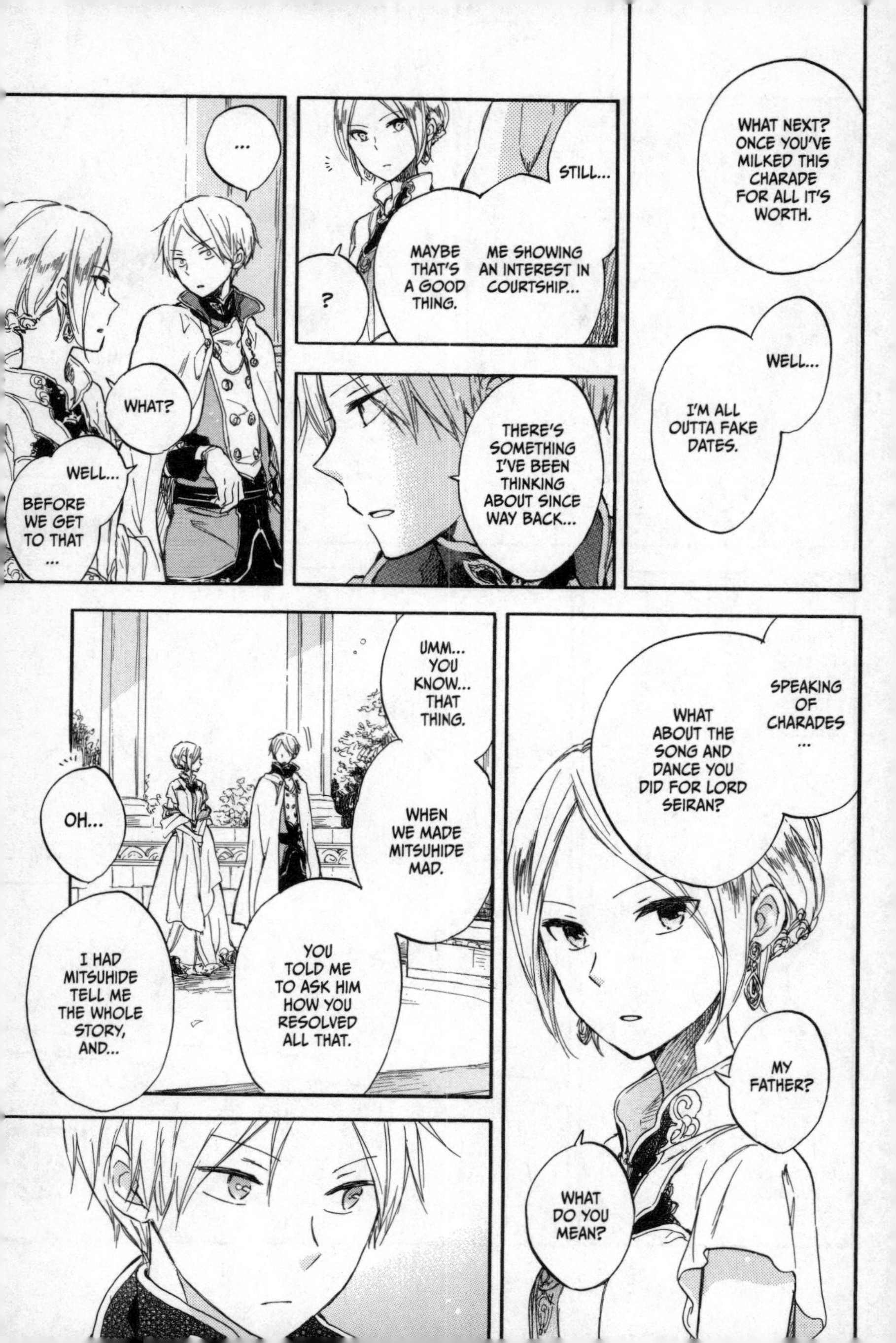
WHAT NEXT? ONCE YOU'VE MILKED THIS CHARADE FOR ALL IT'S WORTH.
WELL...
I'M ALL OUTTA FAKE DATES.
STILL...
ME SHOWING AN INTEREST IN COURTSHIP...
MAYBE THAT'S A GOOD THING.
?
THERE'S SOMETHING I'VE BEEN THINKING ABOUT SINCE WAY BACK...
...
WHAT?
WELL...
BEFORE WE GET TO THAT ...
SPEAKING OF CHARADES ...
WHAT ABOUT THE SONG AND DANCE YOU DID FOR LORD SEIRAN?
MY FATHER?
WHAT DO YOU MEAN?
UMM... YOU KNOW... THAT THING.
WHEN WE MADE MITSUHIDE MAD.
YOU TOLD ME TO ASK HIM HOW YOU RESOLVED ALL THAT.
OH...
I HAD MITSUHIDE TELL ME THE WHOLE STORY, AND...

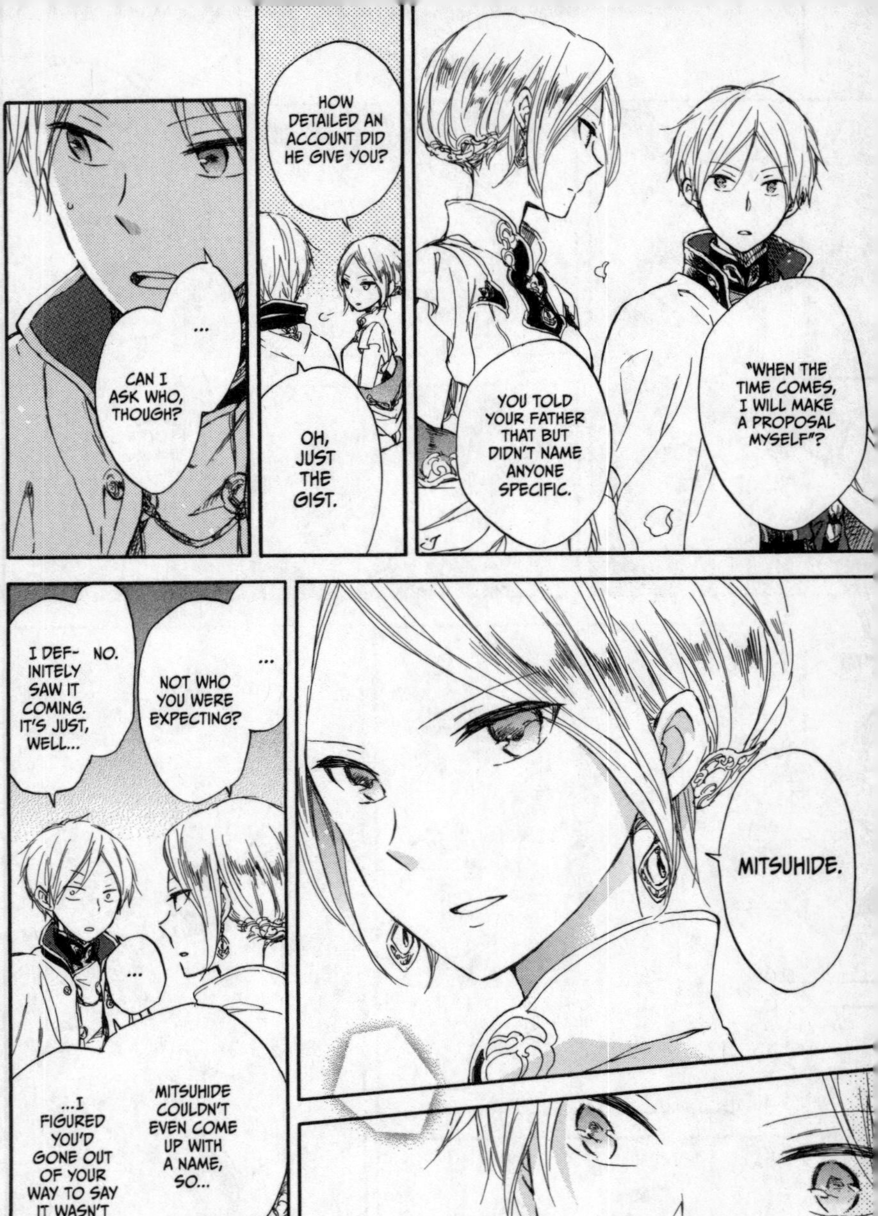
"WHEN THE TIME COMES, I WILL MAKE A PROPOSAL MYSELF"?
YOU TOLD YOUR FATHER THAT BUT DIDN'T NAME ANYONE SPECIFIC.
HOW DETAILED AN ACCOUNT DID HE GIVE YOU?
OH, JUST THE GIST.
...
CAN I ASK WHO, THOUGH?
MITSUHIDE.
...
NOT WHO YOU WERE EXPECTING?
NO.
I DEF-INITELY SAW IT COMING. IT'S JUST, WELL...
...
MITSUHIDE COULDN'T EVEN COME UP WITH A NAME, SO...
...I FIGURED YOU'D GONE OUT OF YOUR WAY TO SAY IT WASN'T HIM.

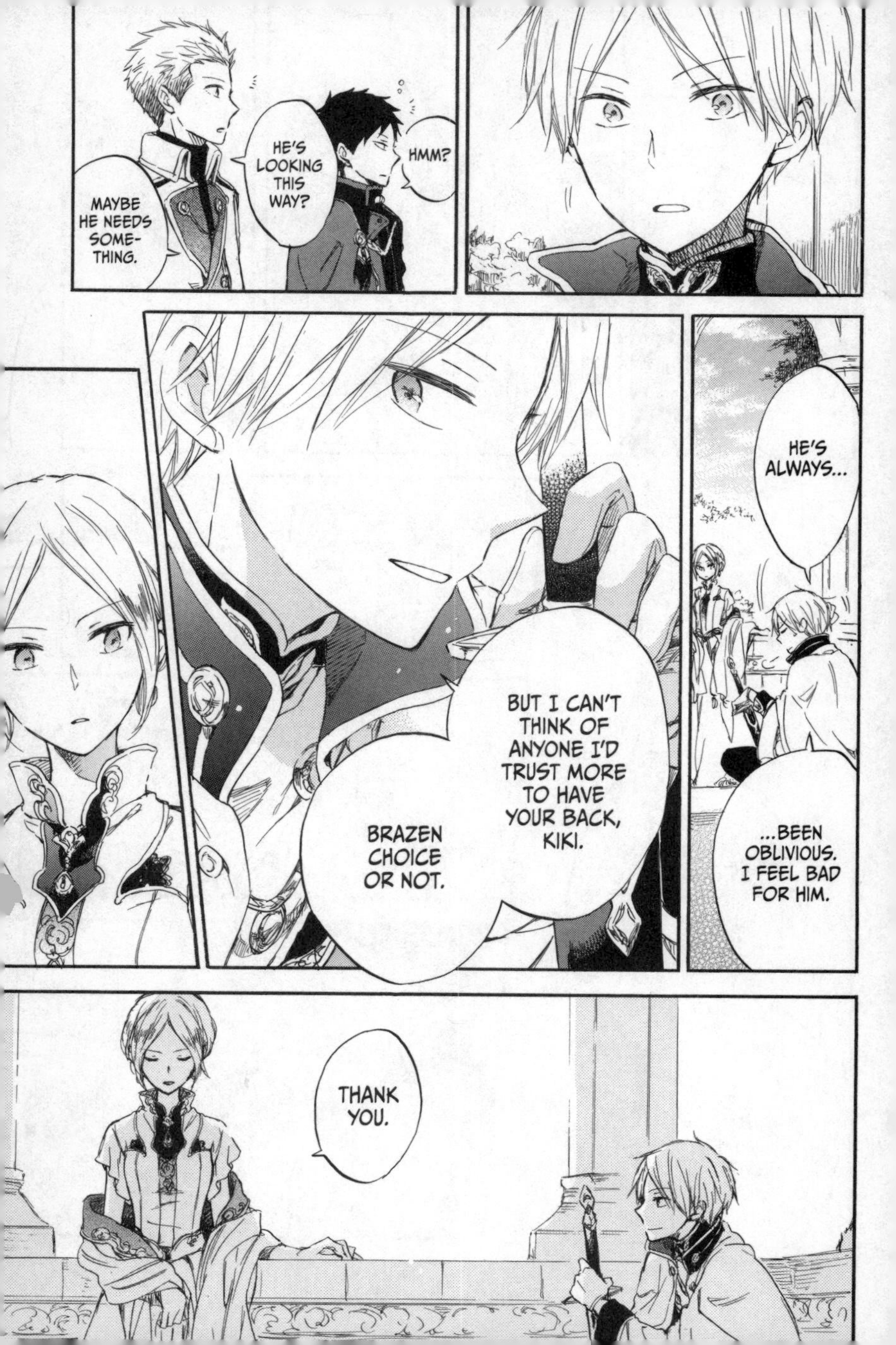
HMM?
HE'S LOOKING THIS WAY?
MAYBE HE NEEDS SOME-THING.
HE'S ALWAYS...
...BEEN OBLIVIOUS. I FEEL BAD FOR HIM.
BUT I CAN'T THINK OF ANYONE I'D TRUST MORE TO HAVE YOUR BACK, KIKI.
BRAZEN CHOICE OR NOT.
THANK YOU.

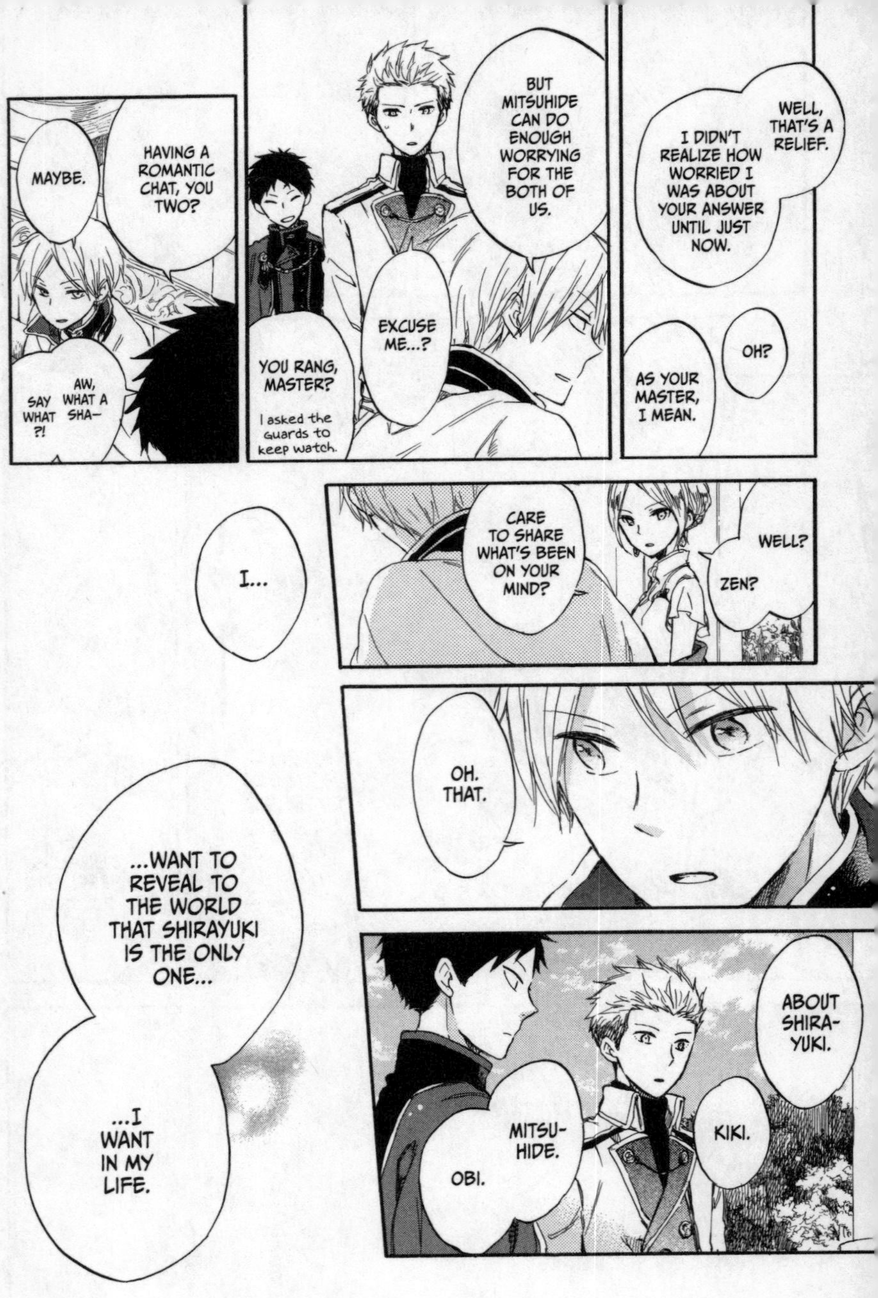
WELL, THAT'S A RELIEF.
I DIDN'T REALIZE HOW WORRIED I WAS ABOUT YOUR ANSWER UNTIL JUST NOW.
OH?
AS YOUR MASTER, I MEAN.
BUT MITSUHIDE CAN DO ENOUGH WORRYING FOR THE BOTH OF US.
EXCUSE ME...?
YOU RANG, MASTER?
I asked the guards to keep watch.
HAVING A ROMANTIC CHAT, YOU TWO?
MAYBE.
AW, WHAT A SHA—
SAY WHAT ?!
WELL?
ZEN?
CARE TO SHARE WHAT'S BEEN ON YOUR MIND?
I...
OH. THAT.
ABOUT SHIRAYUKI.
KIKI.
MITSUHIDE.
OBI.
...WANT TO REVEAL TO THE WORLD THAT SHIRAYUKI IS THE ONLY ONE...
...I WANT IN MY LIFE.

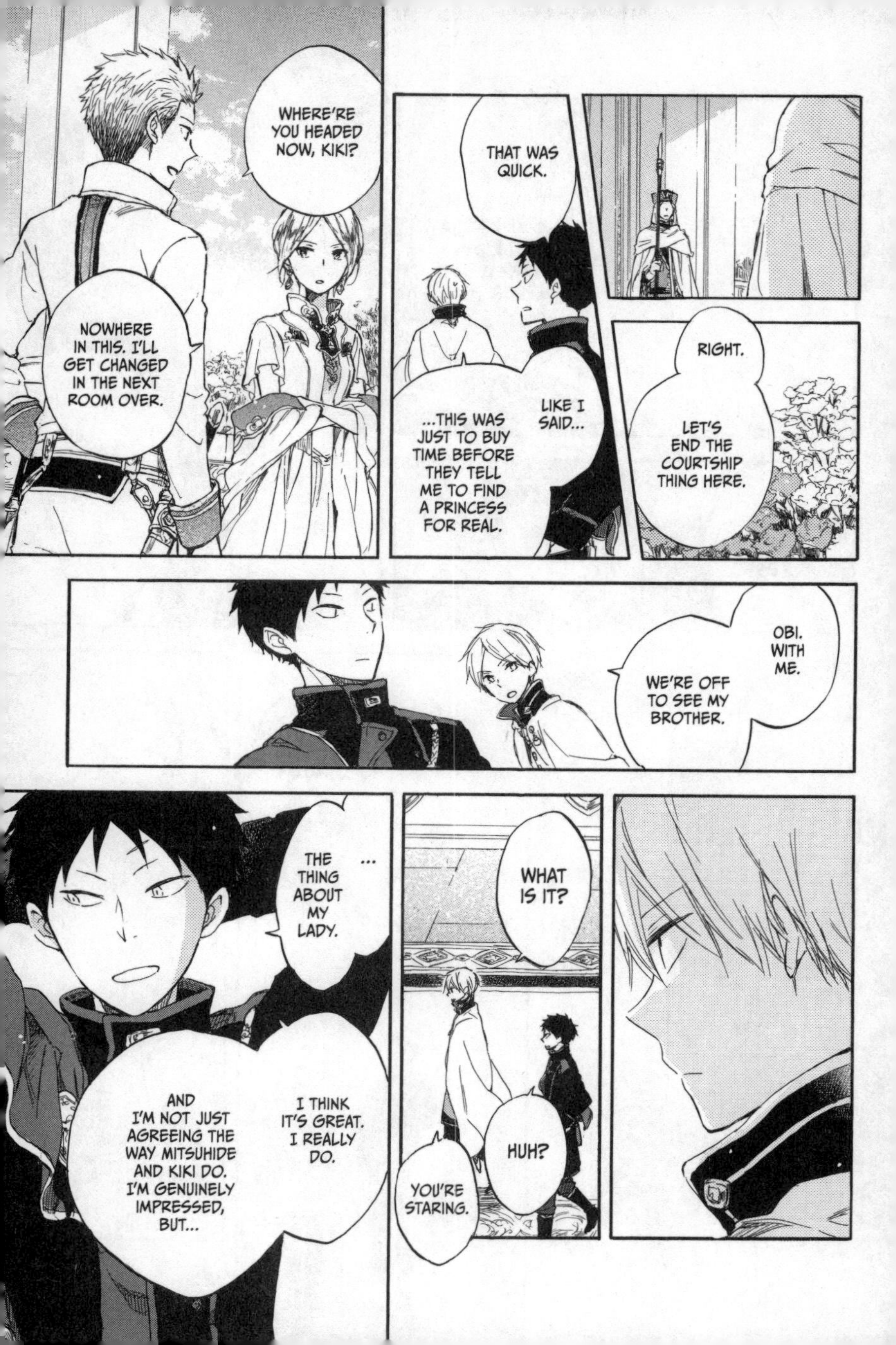
RIGHT.
LET'S END THE COURTSHIP THING HERE.
THAT WAS QUICK.
LIKE I SAID...
...THIS WAS JUST TO BUY TIME BEFORE THEY TELL ME TO FIND A PRINCESS FOR REAL.
WHERE'RE YOU HEADED NOW, KIKI?
NOWHERE IN THIS. I'LL GET CHANGED IN THE NEXT ROOM OVER.
OBI. WITH ME.
WE'RE OFF TO SEE MY BROTHER.
WHAT IS IT?
HUH?
YOU'RE STARING.
...
THE THING ABOUT MY LADY.
I THINK IT'S GREAT. I REALLY DO.
AND I'M NOT JUST AGREEING THE WAY MITSUHIDE AND KIKI DO. I'M GENUINELY IMPRESSED, BUT...

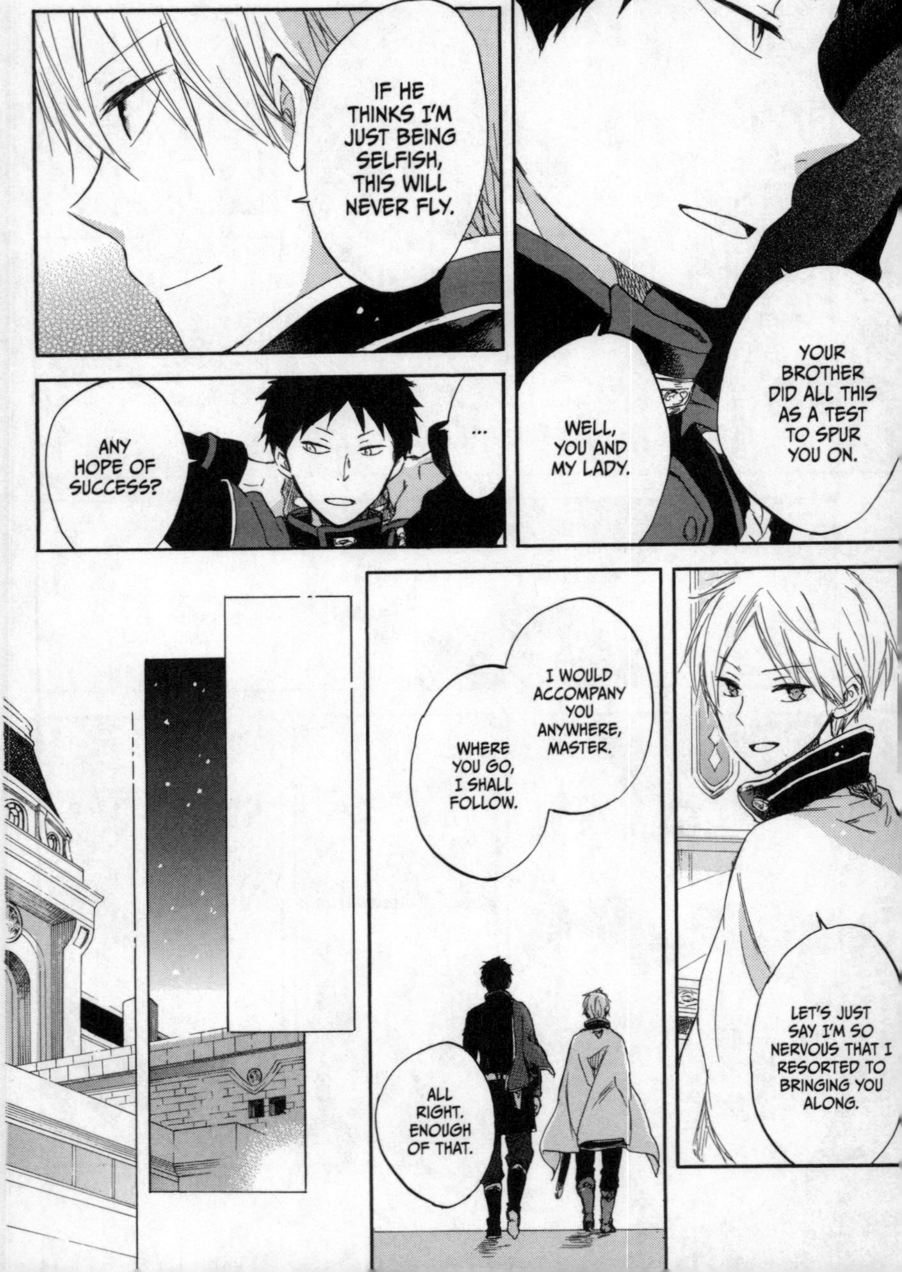
YOUR BROTHER DID ALL THIS AS A TEST TO SPUR YOU ON.
WELL, YOU AND MY LADY.
IF HE THINKS I'M JUST BEING SELFISH, THIS WILL NEVER FLY.
...
ANY HOPE OF SUCCESS?
LET'S JUST SAY I'M SO NERVOUS THAT I RESORTED TO BRINGING YOU ALONG.
I WOULD ACCOMPANY YOU ANYWHERE, MASTER.
WHERE YOU GO, I SHALL FOLLOW.
ALL RIGHT. ENOUGH OF THAT.

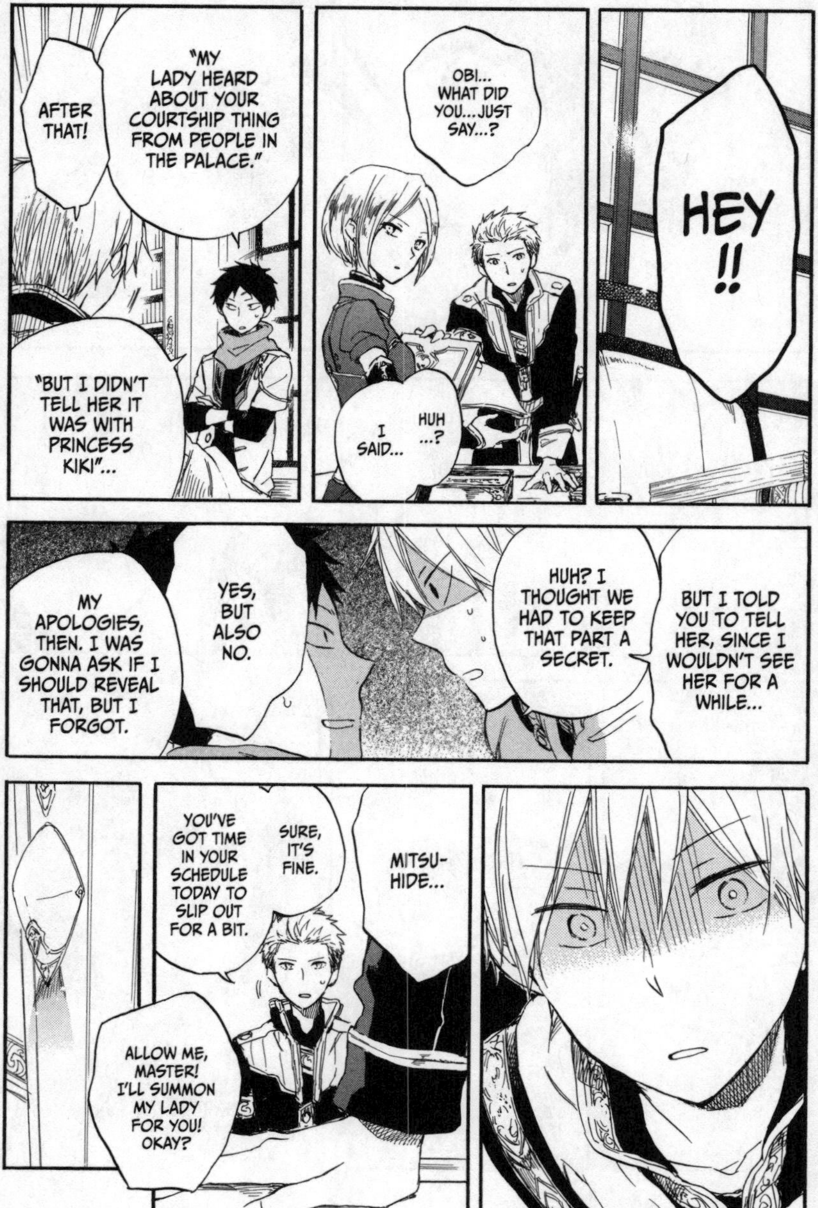
HEY !!
OBI... WHAT DID YOU... JUST SAY...?
HUH ...?
I SAID...
"MY LADY HEARD ABOUT YOUR COURTSHIP THING FROM PEOPLE IN THE PALACE."
AFTER THAT!
"BUT I DIDN'T TELL HER IT WAS WITH PRINCESS KIKI"...
BUT I TOLD YOU TO TELL HER, SINCE I WOULDN'T SEE HER FOR A WHILE...
HUH? I THOUGHT WE HAD TO KEEP THAT PART A SECRET.
YES, BUT ALSO NO.
MY APOLOGIES, THEN. I WAS GONNA ASK IF I SHOULD REVEAL THAT, BUT I FORGOT.
MITSU-HIDE...
SURE, IT'S FINE.
YOU'VE GOT TIME IN YOUR SCHEDULE TODAY TO SLIP OUT FOR A BIT.
ALLOW ME, MASTER! I'LL SUMMON MY LADY FOR YOU! OKAY?

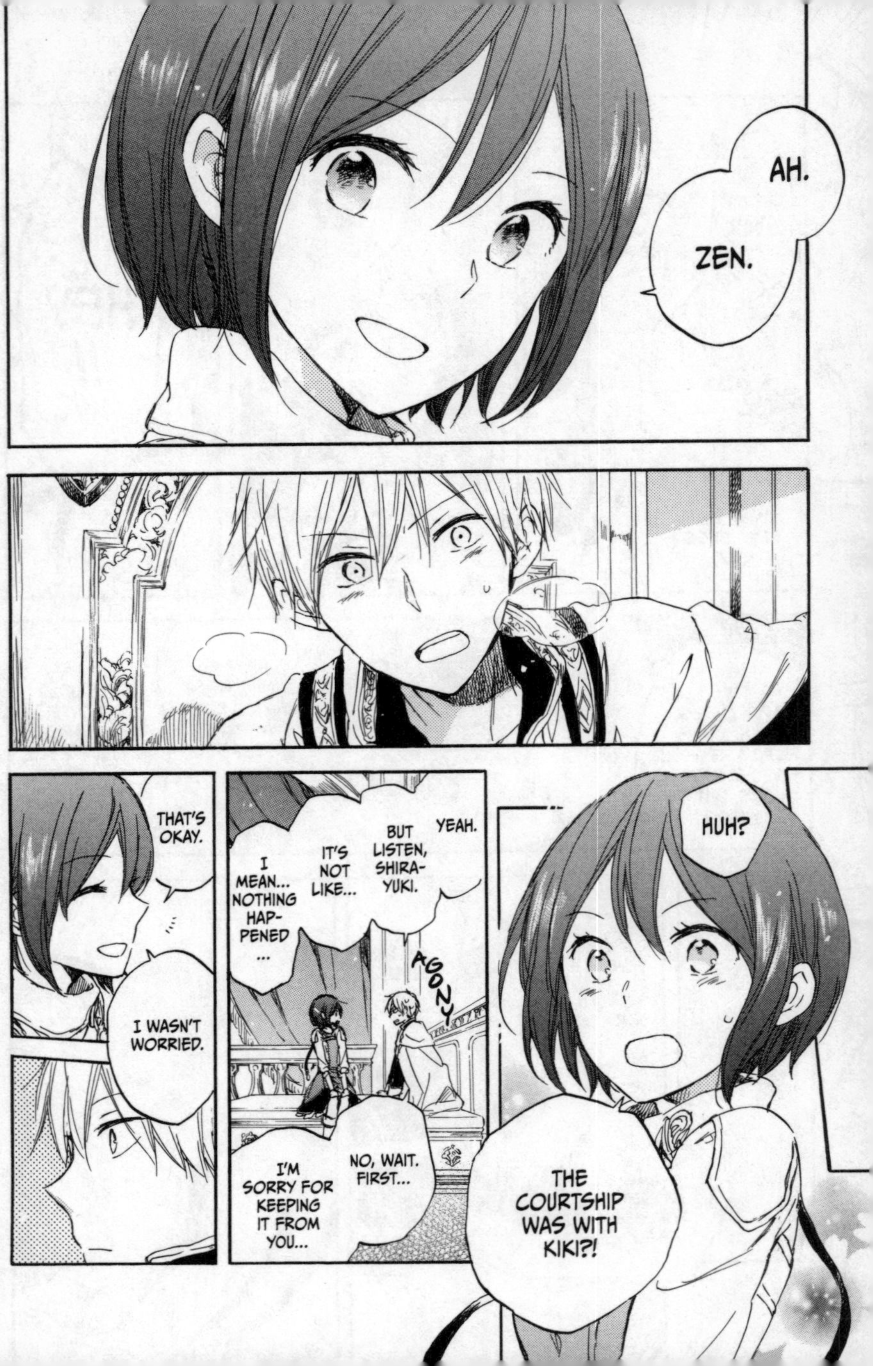
AH.
ZEN.
HUH?
THE COURTSHIP WAS WITH KIKI?!
YEAH.
BUT LISTEN, SHIRA-YUKI.
IT'S NOT LIKE...
I MEAN... NOTHING HAP-PENED ...
AGONY
NO, WAIT. FIRST...
I'M SORRY FOR KEEPING IT FROM YOU...
THAT'S OKAY.
...
I WASN'T WORRIED.

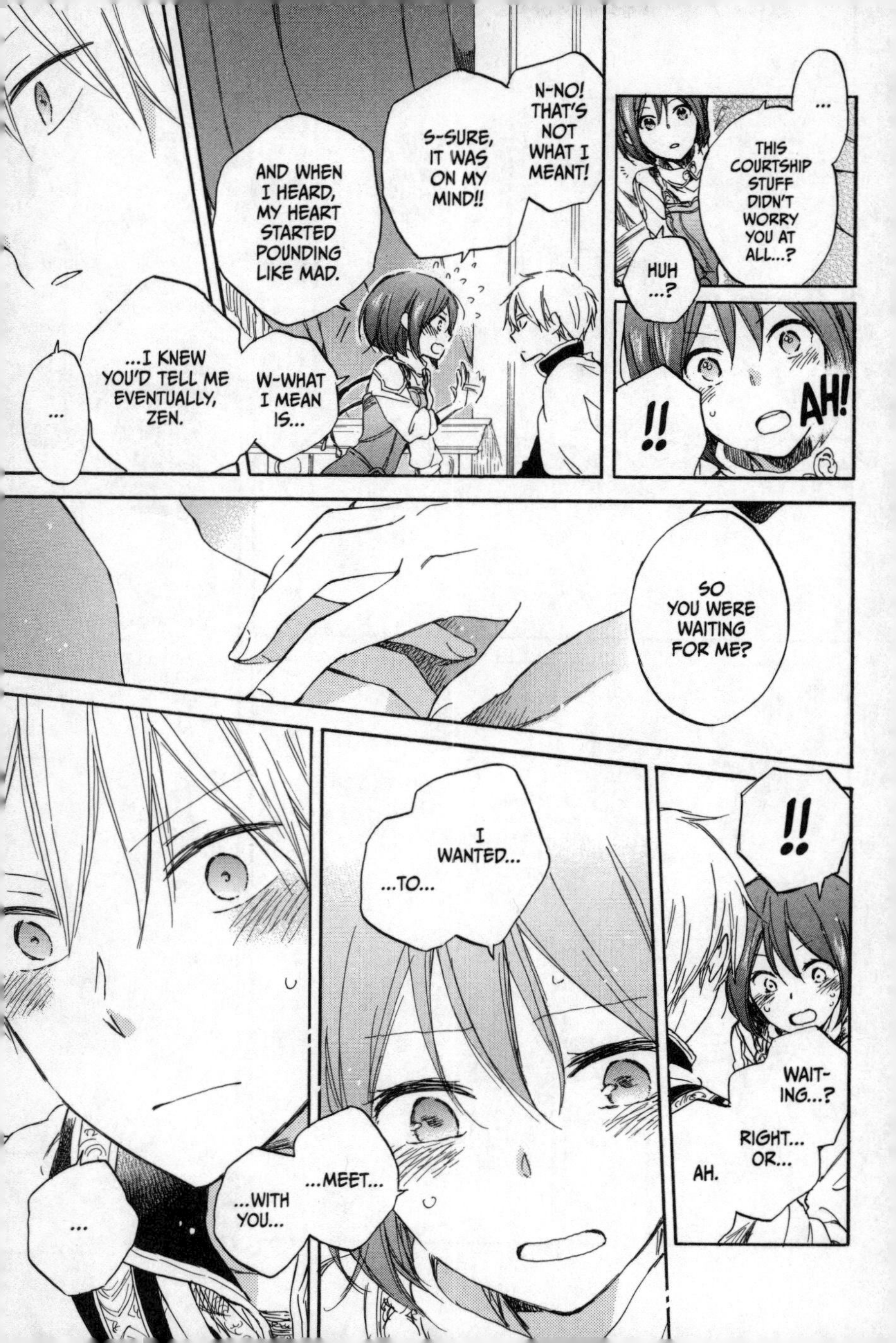
...
THIS COURTSHIP STUFF DIDN'T WORRY YOU AT ALL...?
HUH ...?
AH!
!!
N-NO! THAT'S NOT WHAT I MEANT!
S-SURE, IT WAS ON MY MIND!!
AND WHEN I HEARD, MY HEART STARTED POUNDING LIKE MAD.
W-WHAT I MEAN IS...
...I KNEW YOU'D TELL ME EVENTUALLY, ZEN.
...
SO YOU WERE WAITING FOR ME?
!!
WAIT-ING...?
RIGHT... OR...
AH.
I WANTED...
...TO...
...MEET...
...WITH YOU...
...

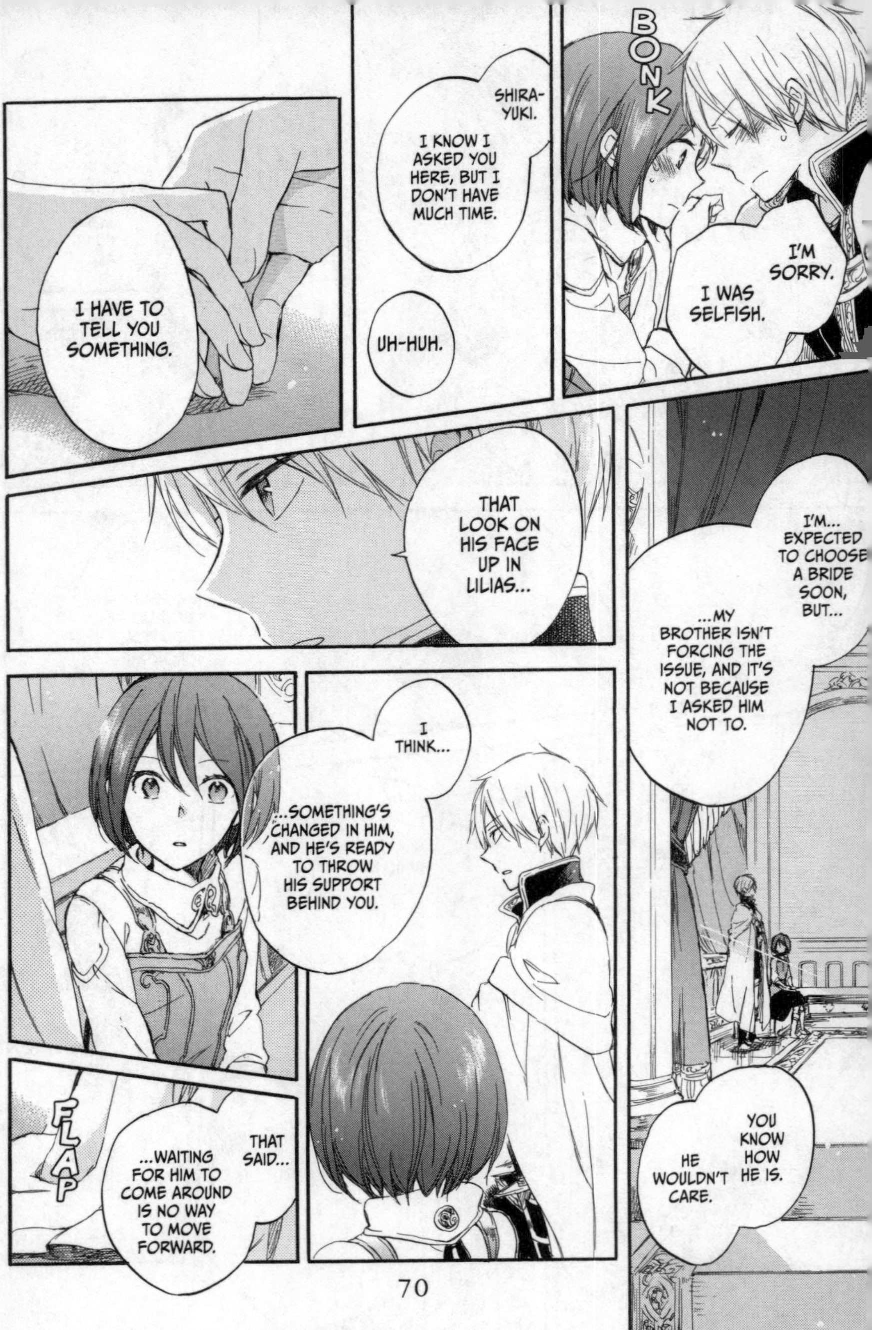
BONK
I'M SORRY.
I WAS SELFISH.
SHIRA-YUKI.
I KNOW I ASKED YOU HERE, BUT I DON'T HAVE MUCH TIME.
UH-HUH.
I HAVE TO TELL YOU SOMETHING.
I'M... EXPECTED TO CHOOSE A BRIDE SOON, BUT...
...MY BROTHER ISN'T FORCING THE ISSUE, AND IT'S NOT BECAUSE I ASKED HIM NOT TO.
YOU KNOW HOW HE IS.
HE WOULDN'T CARE.
THAT LOOK ON HIS FACE UP IN LILIAS...
I THINK...
...SOMETHING'S CHANGED IN HIM, AND HE'S READY TO THROW HIS SUPPORT BEHIND YOU.
FLAP
THAT SAID...
...WAITING FOR HIM TO COME AROUND IS NO WAY TO MOVE FORWARD.

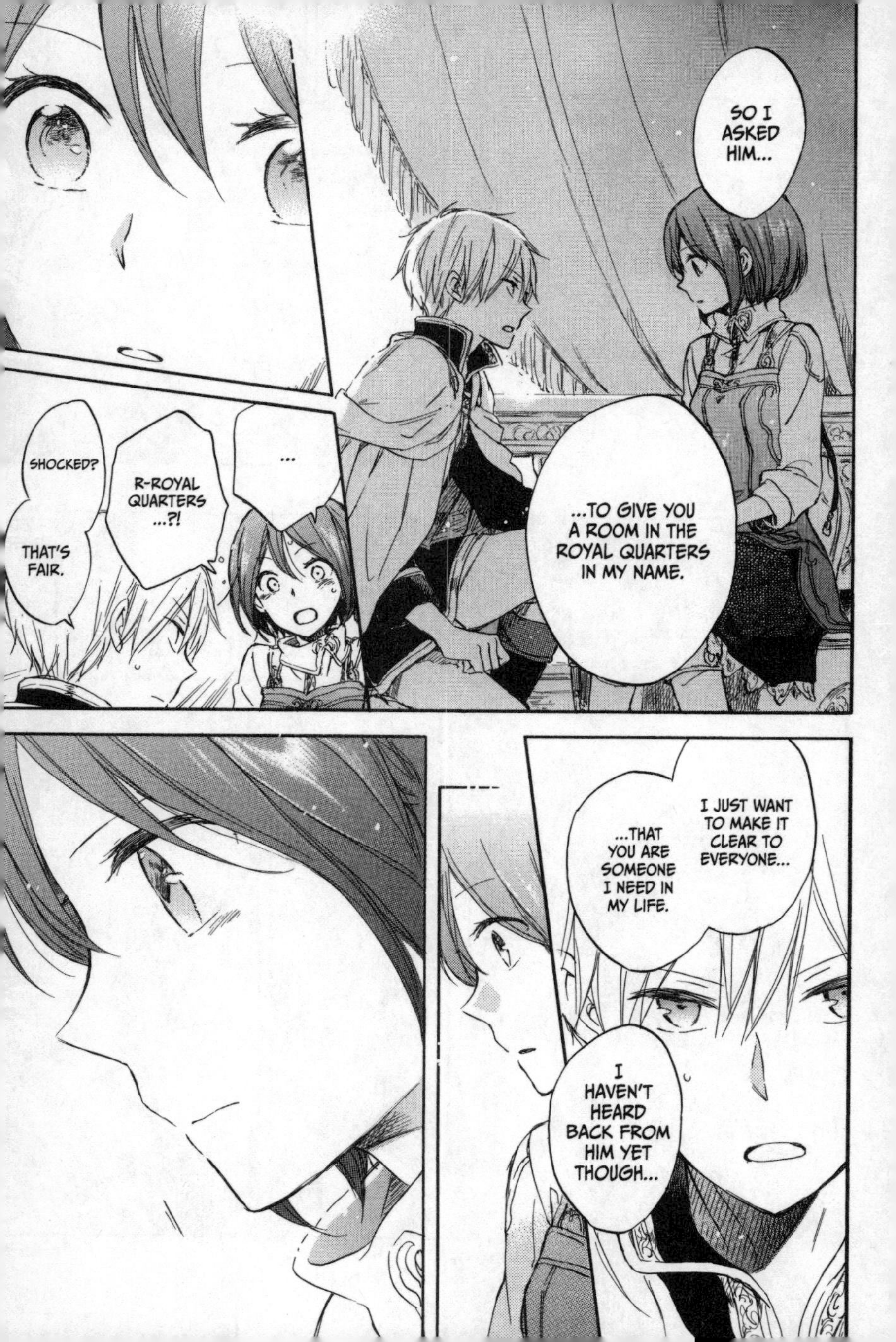
SO I ASKED HIM...
...TO GIVE YOU A ROOM IN THE ROYAL QUARTERS IN MY NAME.
...
R-ROYAL QUARTERS ...?!
SHOCKED?
THAT'S FAIR.
I JUST WANT TO MAKE IT CLEAR TO EVERYONE...
...THAT YOU ARE SOMEONE I NEED IN MY LIFE.
I HAVEN'T HEARD BACK FROM HIM YET THOUGH...

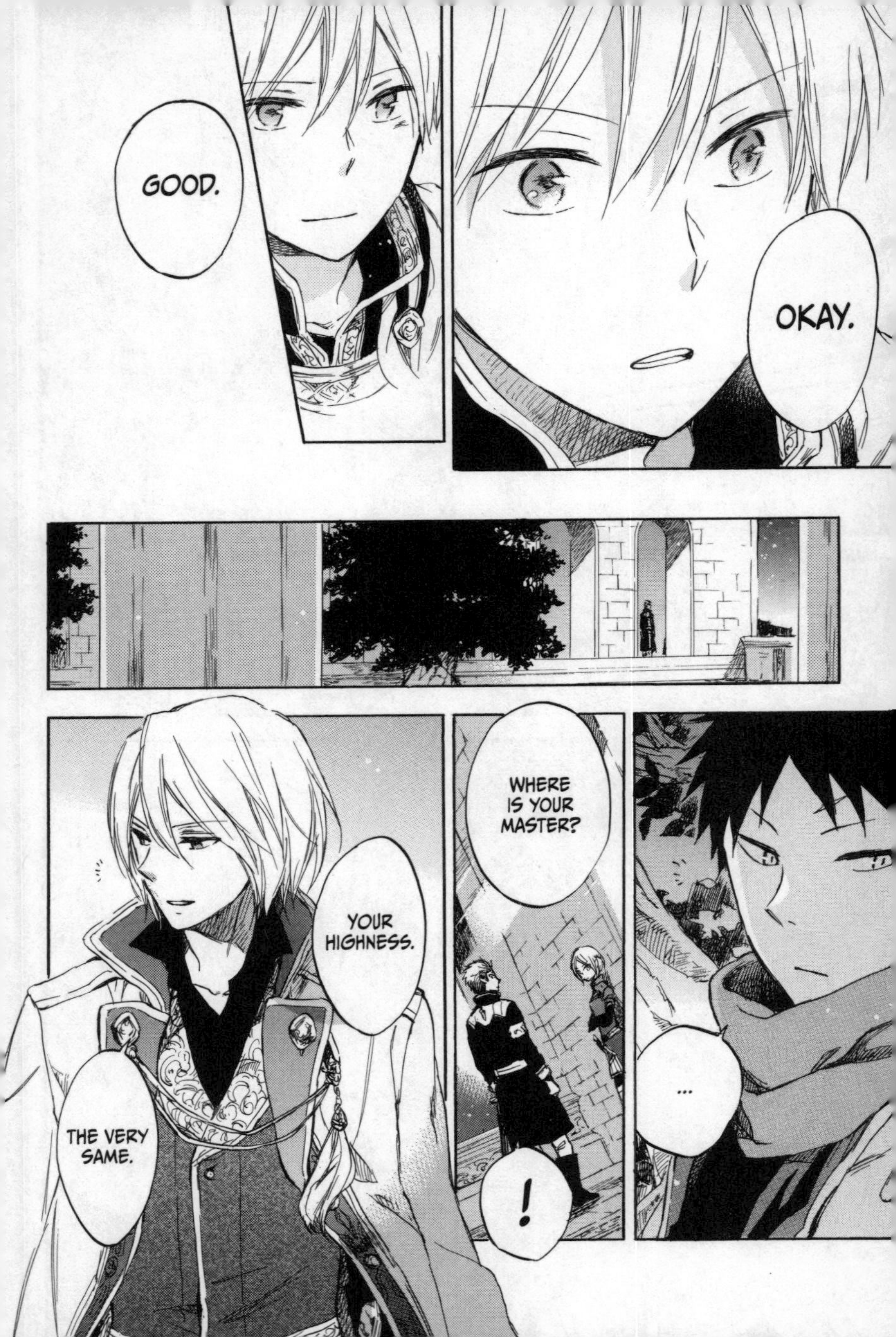
OKAY.
GOOD.
...
WHERE IS YOUR MASTER?
!
YOUR HIGHNESS.
THE VERY SAME.

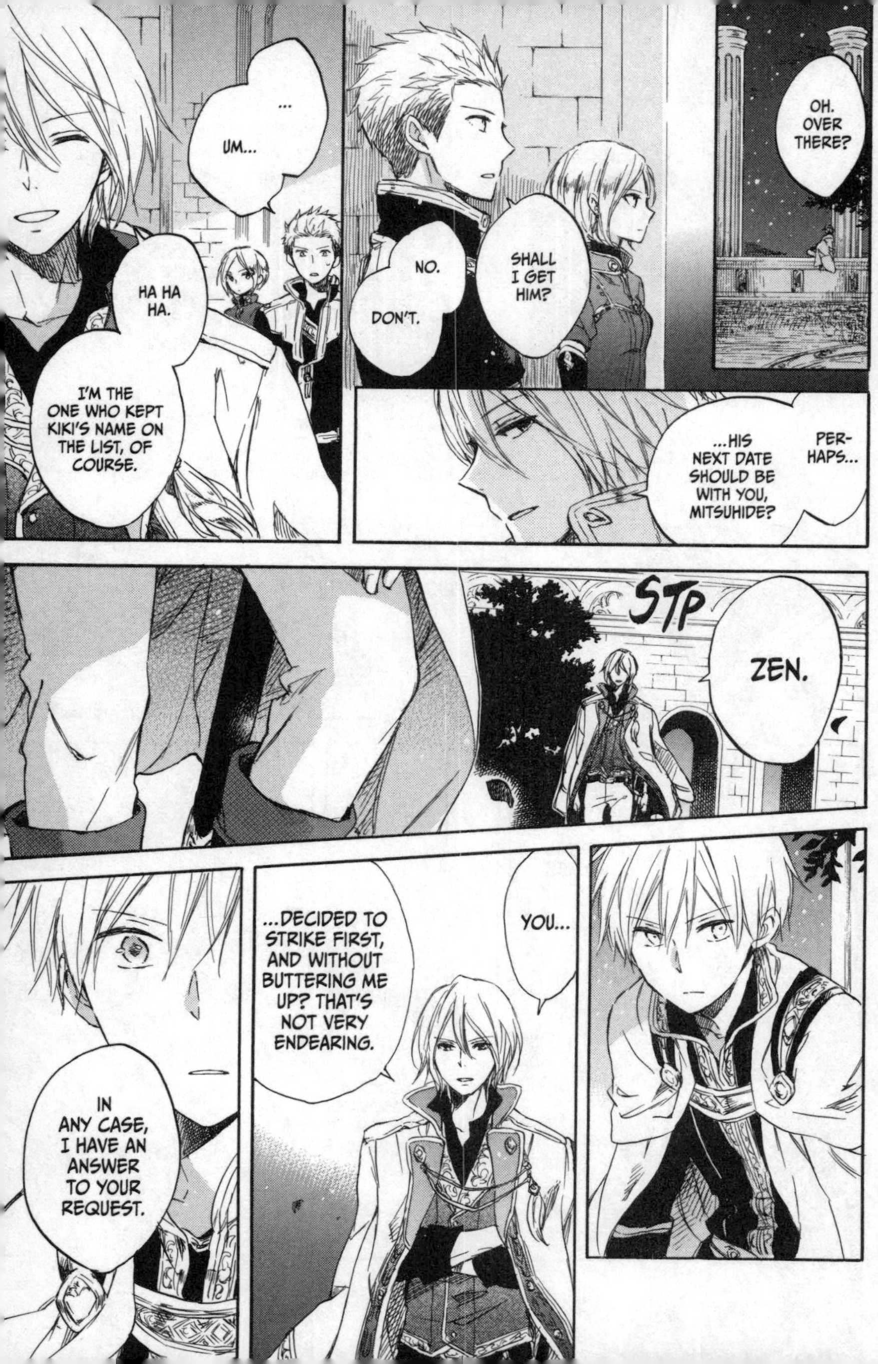
OH. OVER THERE?
SHALL I GET HIM?
NO.
DON'T.
PER-HAPS...
...HIS NEXT DATE SHOULD BE WITH YOU, MITSUHIDE?
...
UM...
HA HA HA.
I'M THE ONE WHO KEPT KIKI'S NAME ON THE LIST, OF COURSE.
STP
ZEN.
YOU...
...DECIDED TO STRIKE FIRST, AND WITHOUT BUTTERING ME UP? THAT'S NOT VERY ENDEARING.
IN ANY CASE, I HAVE AN ANSWER TO YOUR REQUEST.

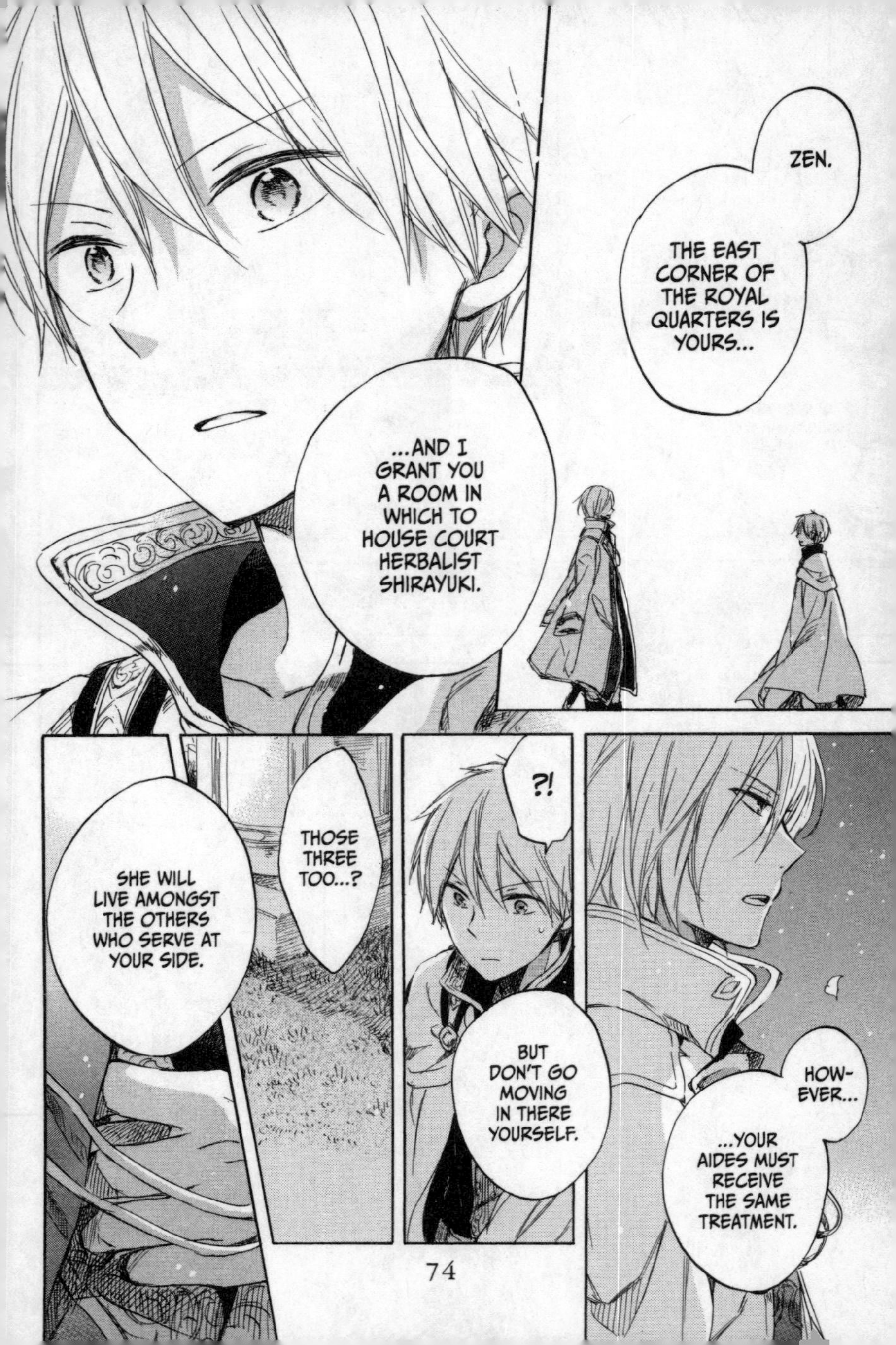
ZEN.
THE EAST CORNER OF THE ROYAL QUARTERS IS YOURS...
...AND I GRANT YOU A ROOM IN WHICH TO HOUSE COURT HERBALIST SHIRAYUKI.
HOW-EVER...
...YOUR AIDES MUST RECEIVE THE SAME TREATMENT.
?!
BUT DON'T GO MOVING IN THERE YOURSELF.
THOSE THREE TOO...?
SHE WILL LIVE AMONGST THE OTHERS WHO SERVE AT YOUR SIDE.

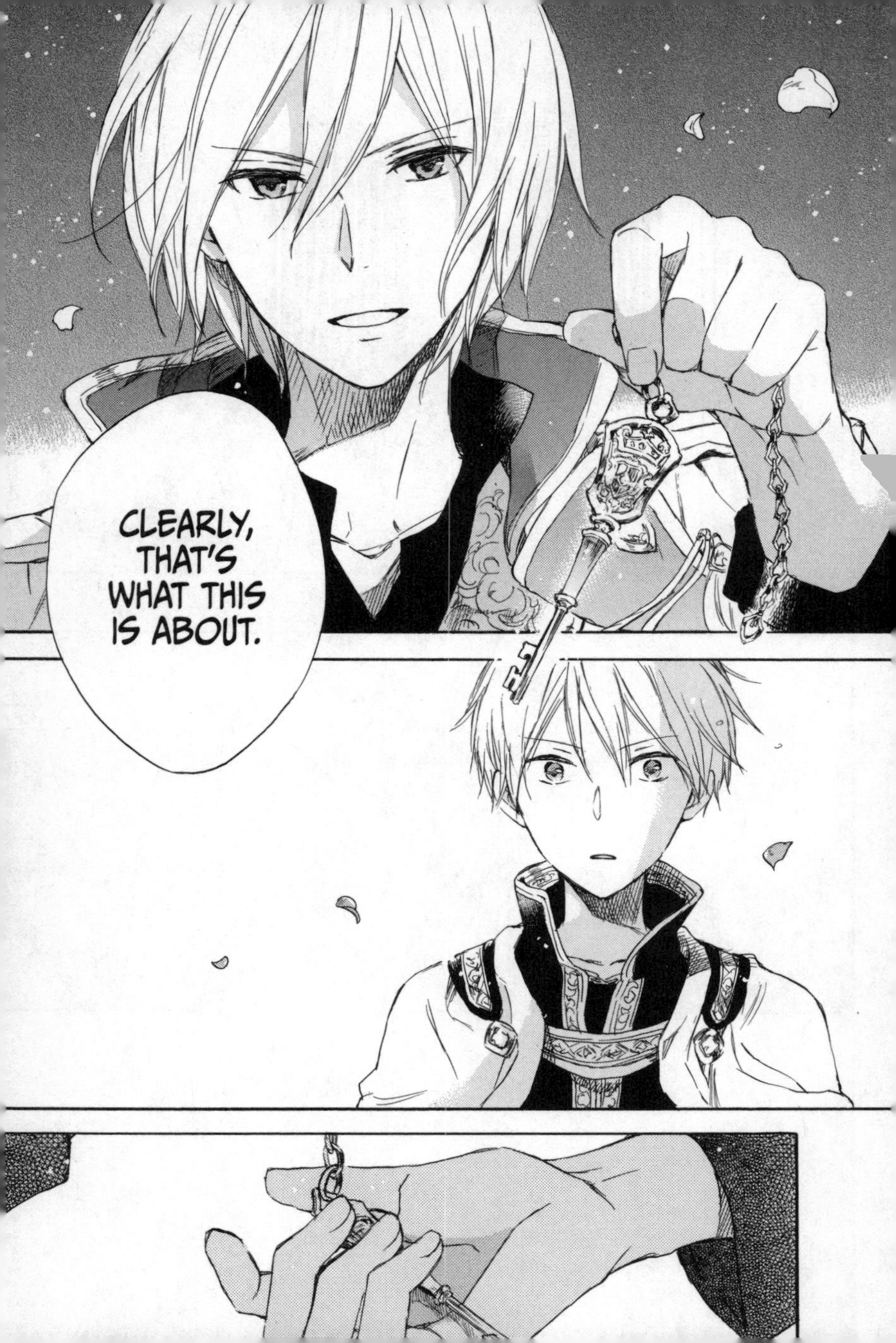
CLEARLY, THAT'S WHAT THIS IS ABOUT.

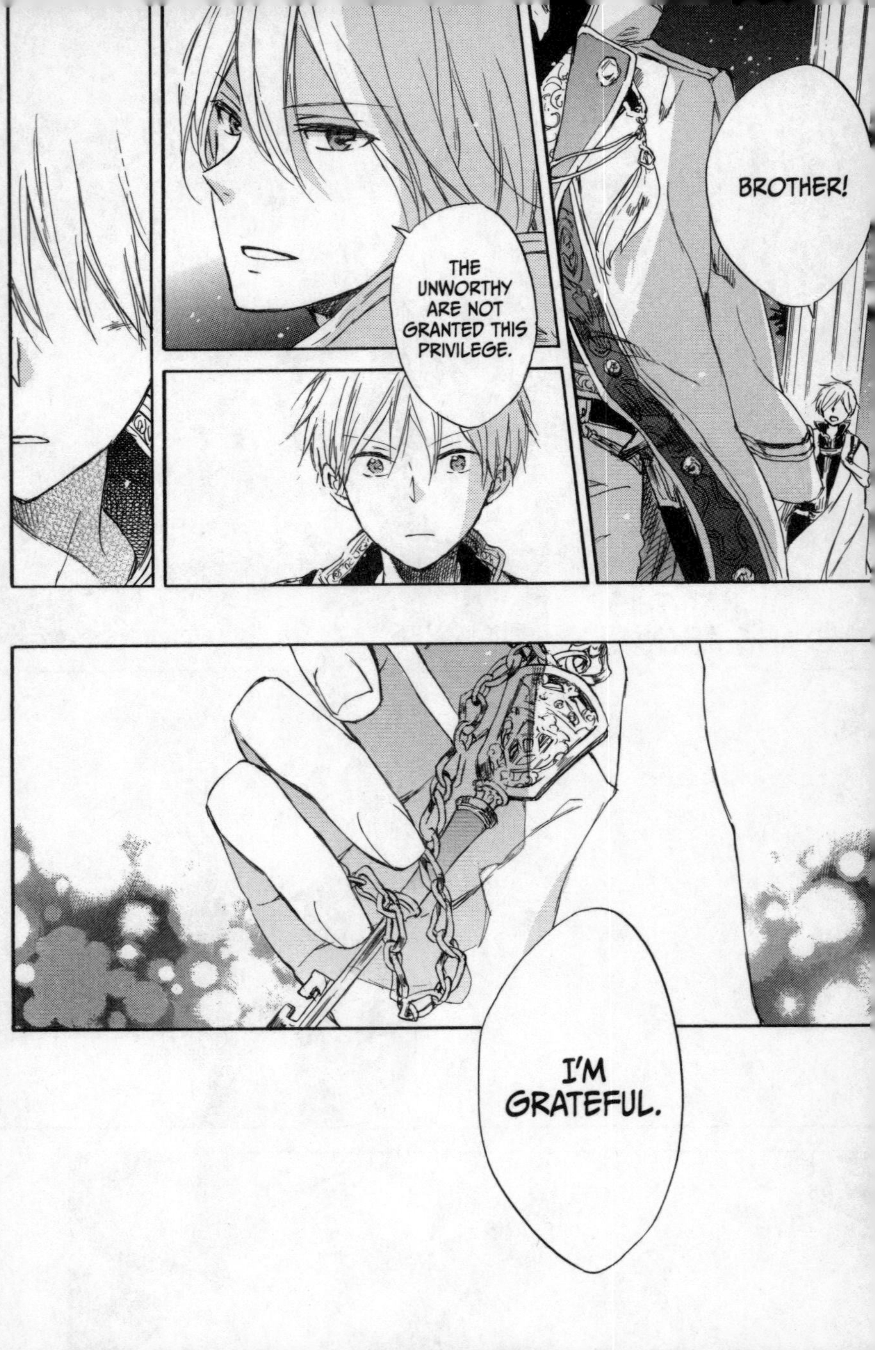
BROTHER!
THE UNWORTHY ARE NOT GRANTED THIS PRIVILEGE.
I'M GRATEFUL.

Snow White with the Red Hair

Chapter 46 Preview Image

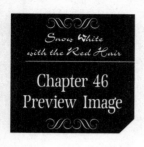

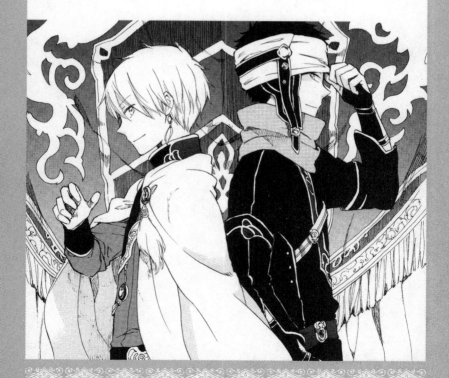

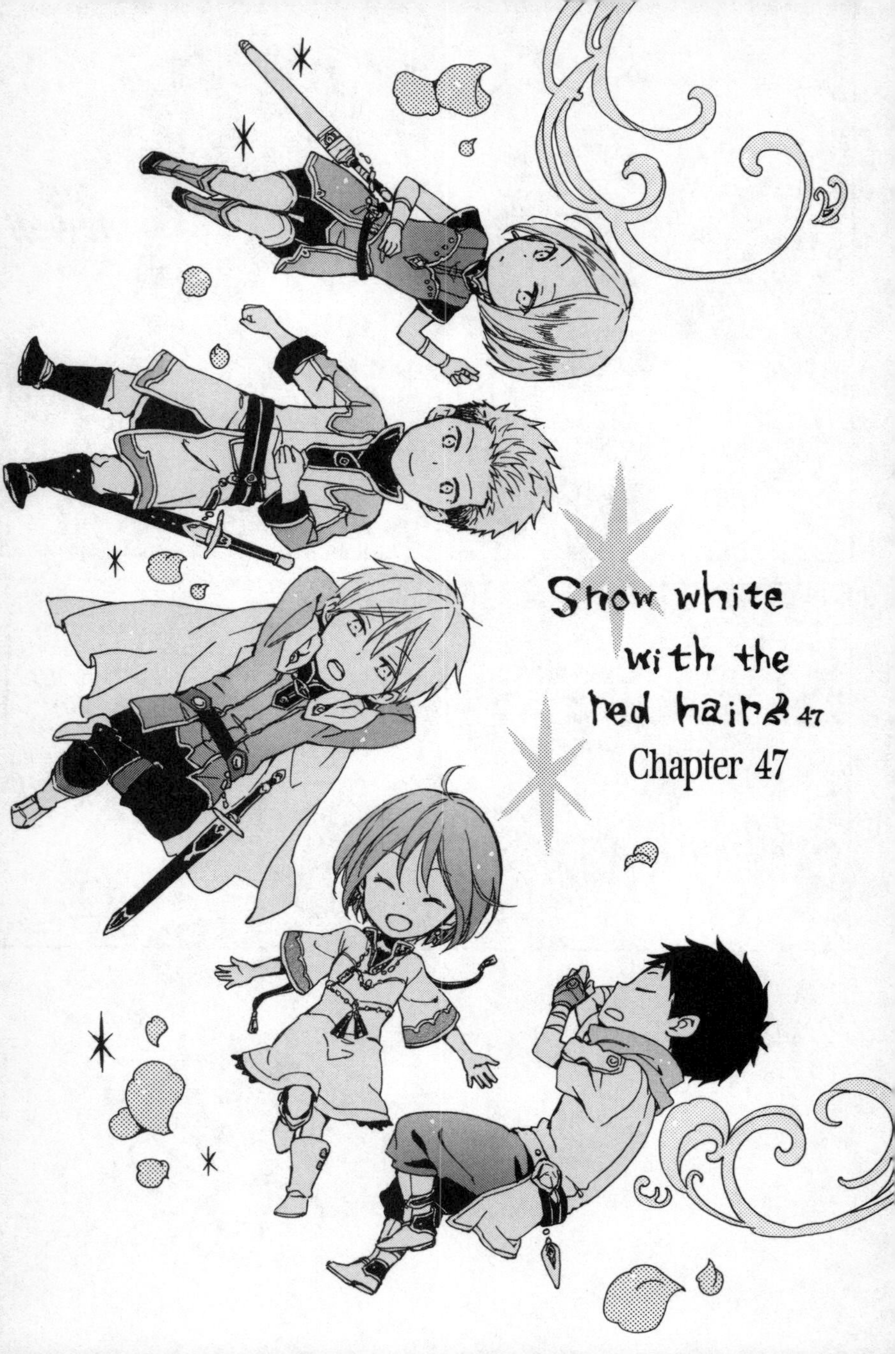
Snow White with the Red Hair 47
Chapter 47

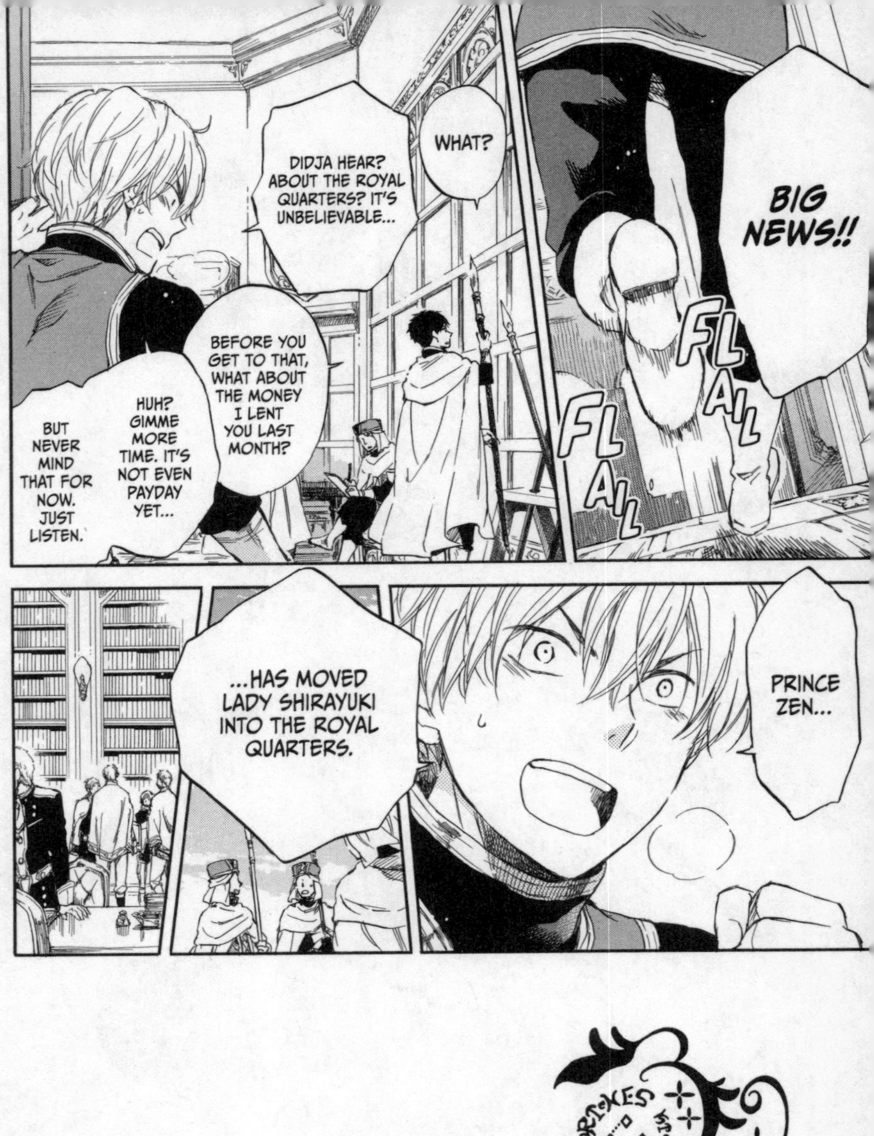
BIG NEWS!!
FLAIL
FLAIL
WHAT?
DIDJA HEAR? ABOUT THE ROYAL QUARTERS? IT'S UNBELIEVABLE...
BEFORE YOU GET TO THAT, WHAT ABOUT THE MONEY I LENT YOU LAST MONTH?
HUH? GIMME MORE TIME. IT'S NOT EVEN PAYDAY YET...
BUT NEVER MIND THAT FOR NOW. JUST LISTEN.
PRINCE ZEN...
...HAS MOVED LADY SHIRAYUKI INTO THE ROYAL QUARTERS.

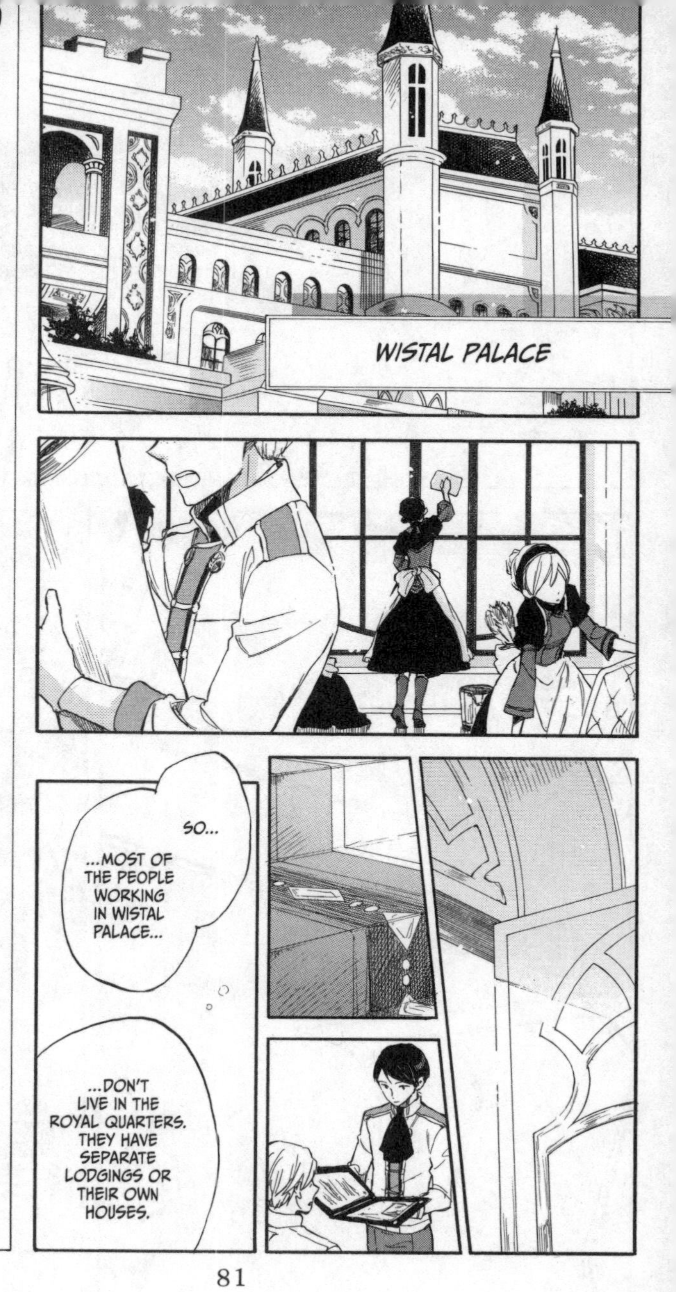
WISTAL PALACE
SO...
...MOST OF THE PEOPLE WORKING IN WISTAL PALACE...
...DON'T LIVE IN THE ROYAL QUARTERS. THEY HAVE SEPARATE LODGINGS OR THEIR OWN HOUSES.

3

TRIP, PART 2

Since this was a tour of Central Europe, we visited multiple countries, but at nearly every place we stopped, we were offered soup with every meal.

What kind of soup, you ask...?

Salty soup.

Wherever we went, even if the dish went by a different name, it was still...

...salty soup.

Unwaveringly salty soup. By the end of our trip, we even created a little song and dance about it. It goes... "Here we go... It's soup time."

The veggies were extra delicious.

Tomatooo!

Bell pepperrrs!

Also, I drank cranberry juice for the first time. Yummy!

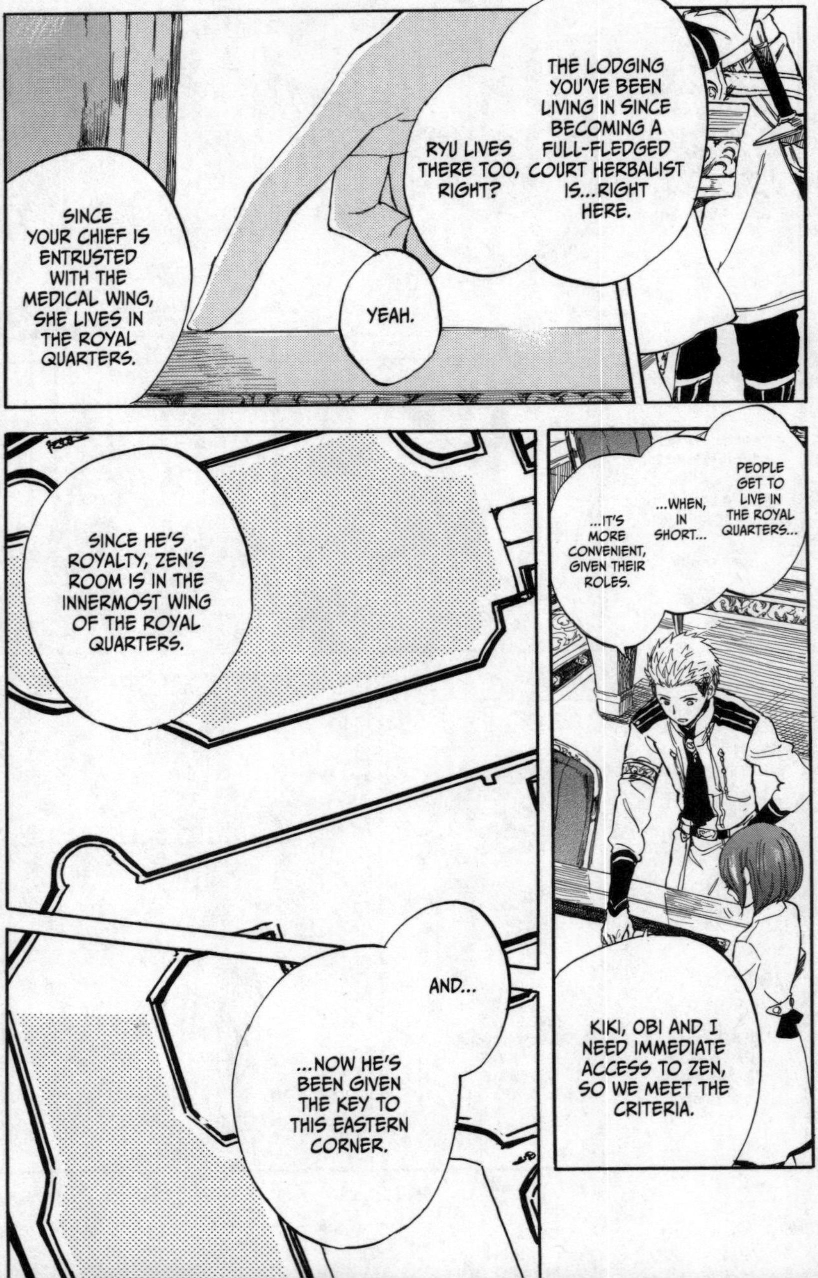
THE LODGING YOU'VE BEEN LIVING IN SINCE BECOMING A FULL-FLEDGED COURT HERBALIST IS...RIGHT HERE.
RYU LIVES THERE TOO, RIGHT?
YEAH.
SINCE YOUR CHIEF IS ENTRUSTED WITH THE MEDICAL WING, SHE LIVES IN THE ROYAL QUARTERS.
PEOPLE GET TO LIVE IN THE ROYAL QUARTERS...
...WHEN, IN SHORT...
...IT'S MORE CONVENIENT, GIVEN THEIR ROLES.
KIKI, OBI AND I NEED IMMEDIATE ACCESS TO ZEN, SO WE MEET THE CRITERIA.
SINCE HE'S ROYALTY, ZEN'S ROOM IS IN THE INNERMOST WING OF THE ROYAL QUARTERS.
AND...
...NOW HE'S BEEN GIVEN THE KEY TO THIS EASTERN CORNER.

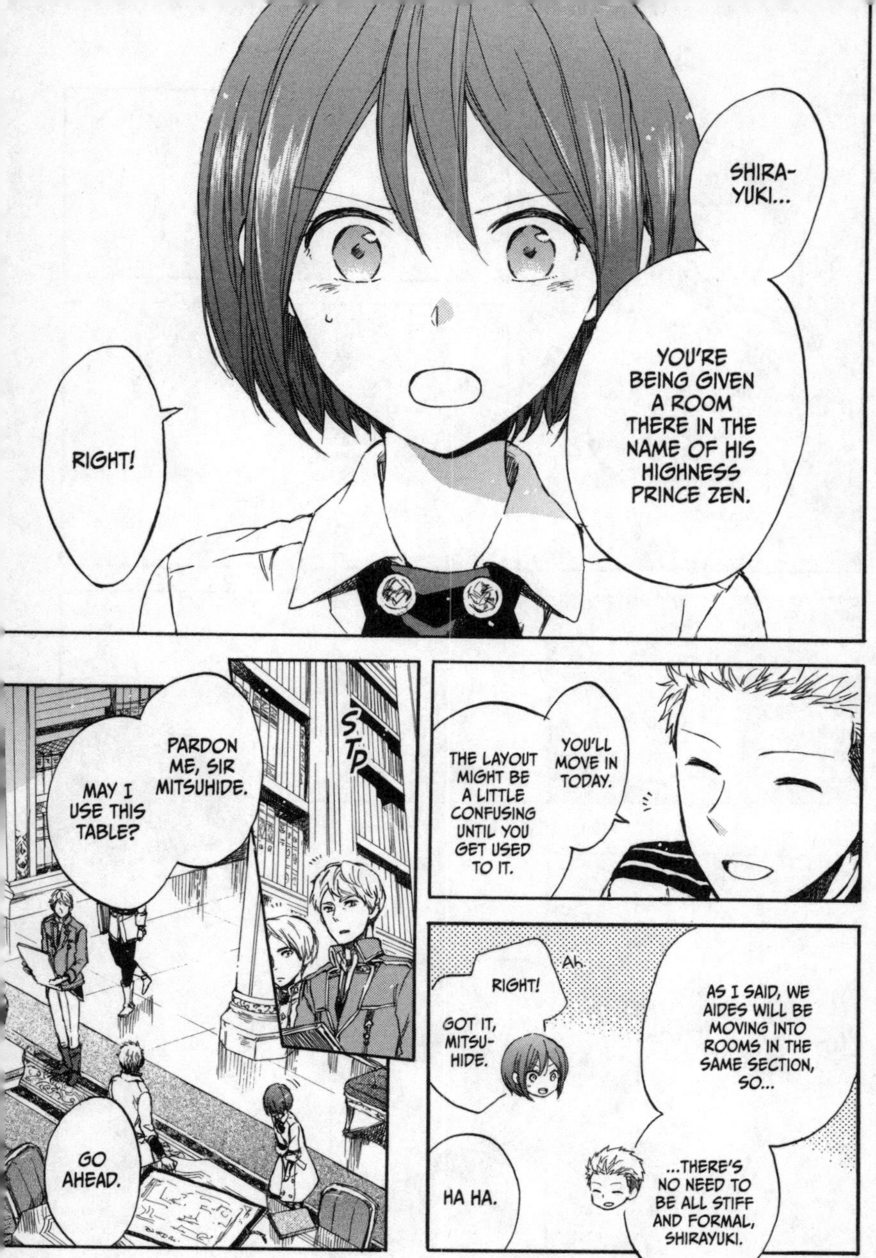

SHIRA-YUKI...
YOU'RE BEING GIVEN A ROOM THERE IN THE NAME OF HIS HIGHNESS PRINCE ZEN.
RIGHT!
YOU'LL MOVE IN TODAY.
THE LAYOUT MIGHT BE A LITTLE CONFUSING UNTIL YOU GET USED TO IT.
AS I SAID, WE AIDES WILL BE MOVING INTO ROOMS IN THE SAME SECTION, SO...
...THERE'S NO NEED TO BE ALL STIFF AND FORMAL, SHIRAYUKI.
Ah
RIGHT!
GOT IT, MITSU-HIDE.
HA HA.
STP
PARDON ME, SIR MITSUHIDE.
MAY I USE THIS TABLE?
GO AHEAD.

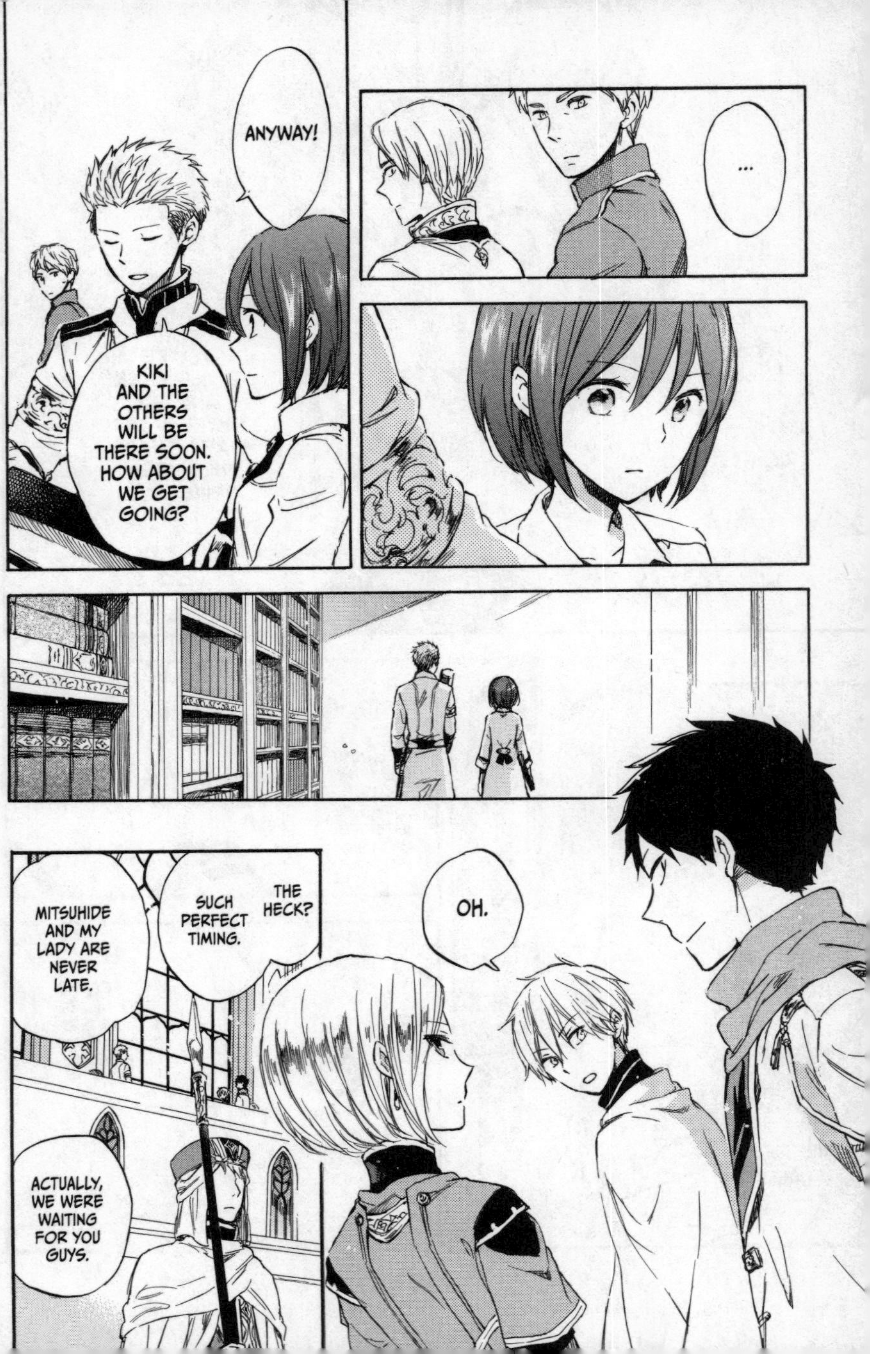
...
ANYWAY!
KIKI AND THE OTHERS WILL BE THERE SOON. HOW ABOUT WE GET GOING?
OH.
THE HECK?
SUCH PERFECT TIMING.
MITSUHIDE AND MY LADY ARE NEVER LATE.
ACTUALLY, WE WERE WAITING FOR YOU GUYS.

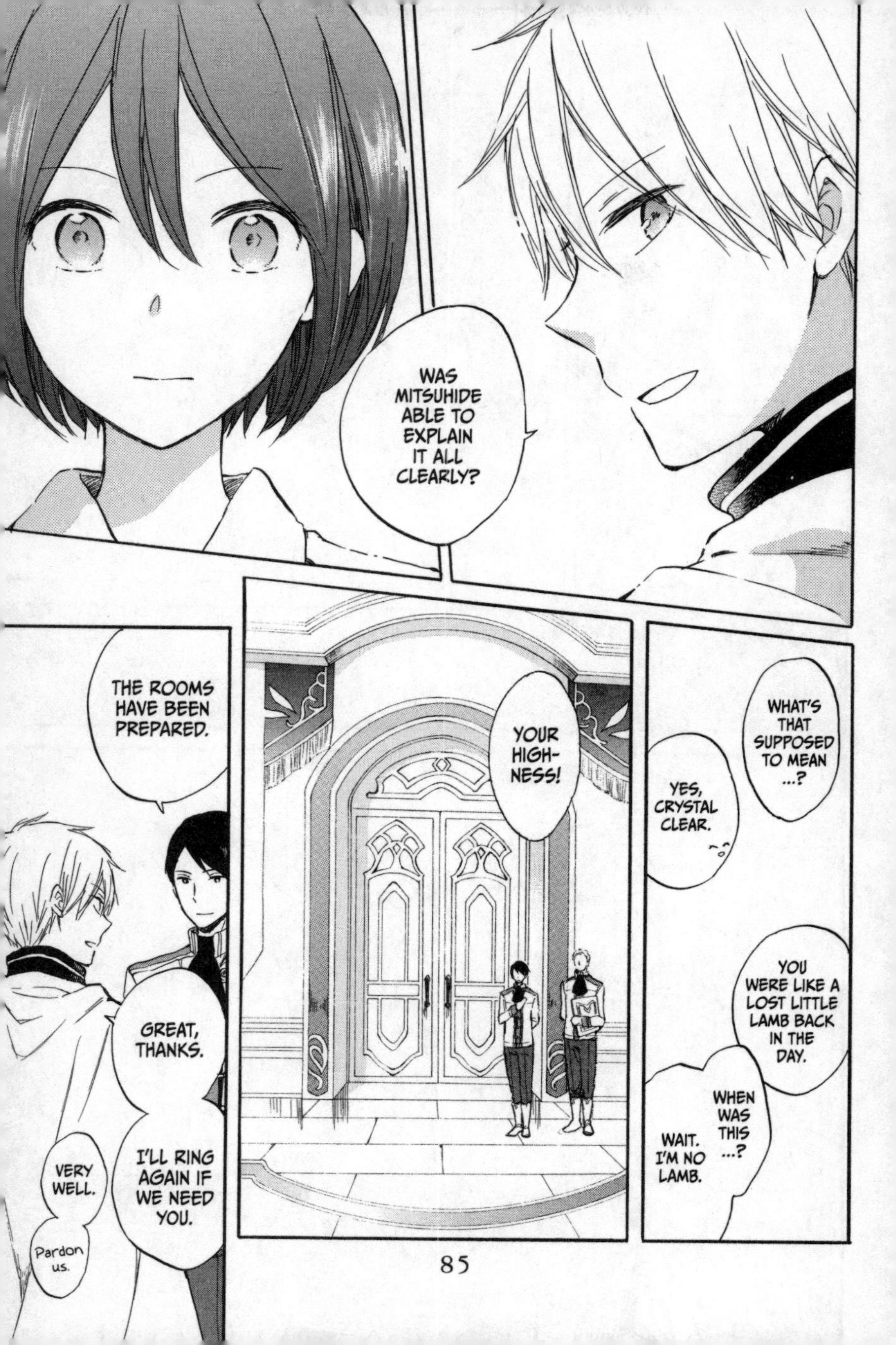
WAS MITSUHIDE ABLE TO EXPLAIN IT ALL CLEARLY?
YES, CRYSTAL CLEAR.
WHAT'S THAT SUPPOSED TO MEAN ...?
YOU WERE LIKE A LOST LITTLE LAMB BACK IN THE DAY.
WHEN WAS THIS ...?
WAIT. I'M NO LAMB.
YOUR HIGH-NESS!
THE ROOMS HAVE BEEN PREPARED.
GREAT, THANKS.
I'LL RING AGAIN IF WE NEED YOU.
VERY WELL.
Pardon us.

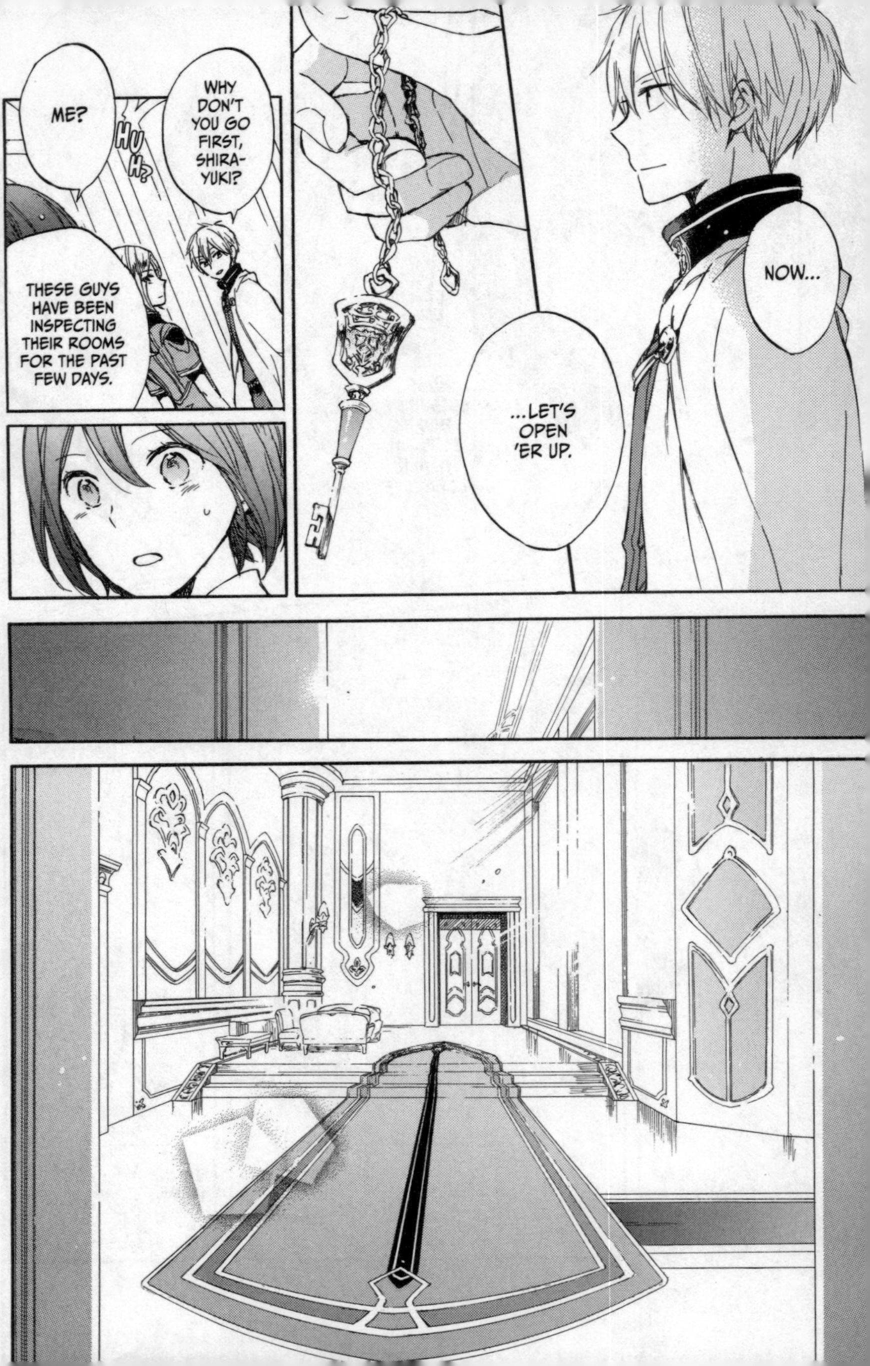
NOW...
...LET'S OPEN 'ER UP.
WHY DON'T YOU GO FIRST, SHIRA-YUKI?
HUH?
ME?
THESE GUYS HAVE BEEN INSPECTING THEIR ROOMS FOR THE PAST FEW DAYS.

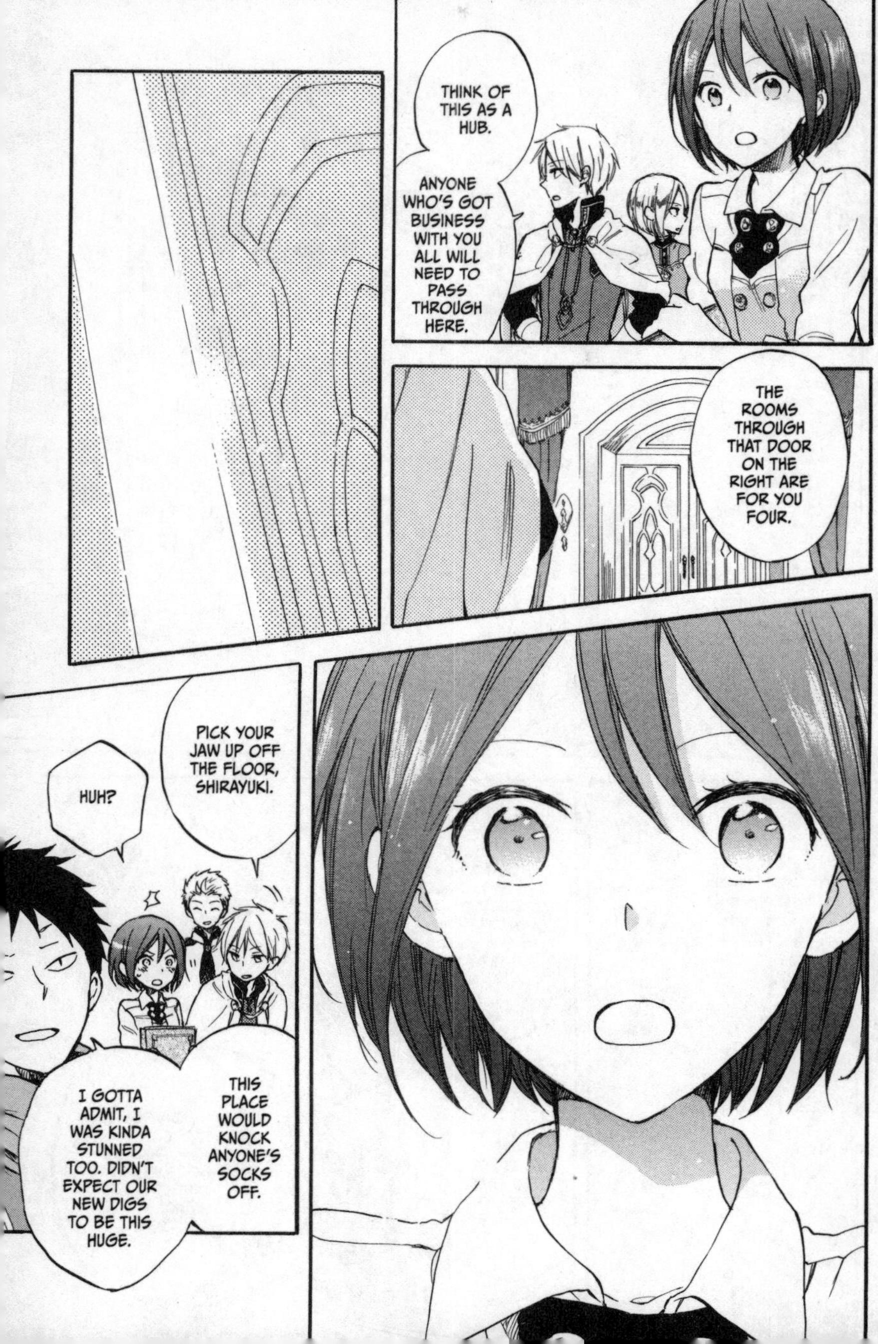
THINK OF THIS AS A HUB.
ANYONE WHO'S GOT BUSINESS WITH YOU ALL WILL NEED TO PASS THROUGH HERE.
THE ROOMS THROUGH THAT DOOR ON THE RIGHT ARE FOR YOU FOUR.
PICK YOUR JAW UP OFF THE FLOOR, SHIRAYUKI.
HUH?
THIS PLACE WOULD KNOCK ANYONE'S SOCKS OFF.
I GOTTA ADMIT, I WAS KINDA STUNNED TOO. DIDN'T EXPECT OUR NEW DIGS TO BE THIS HUGE.

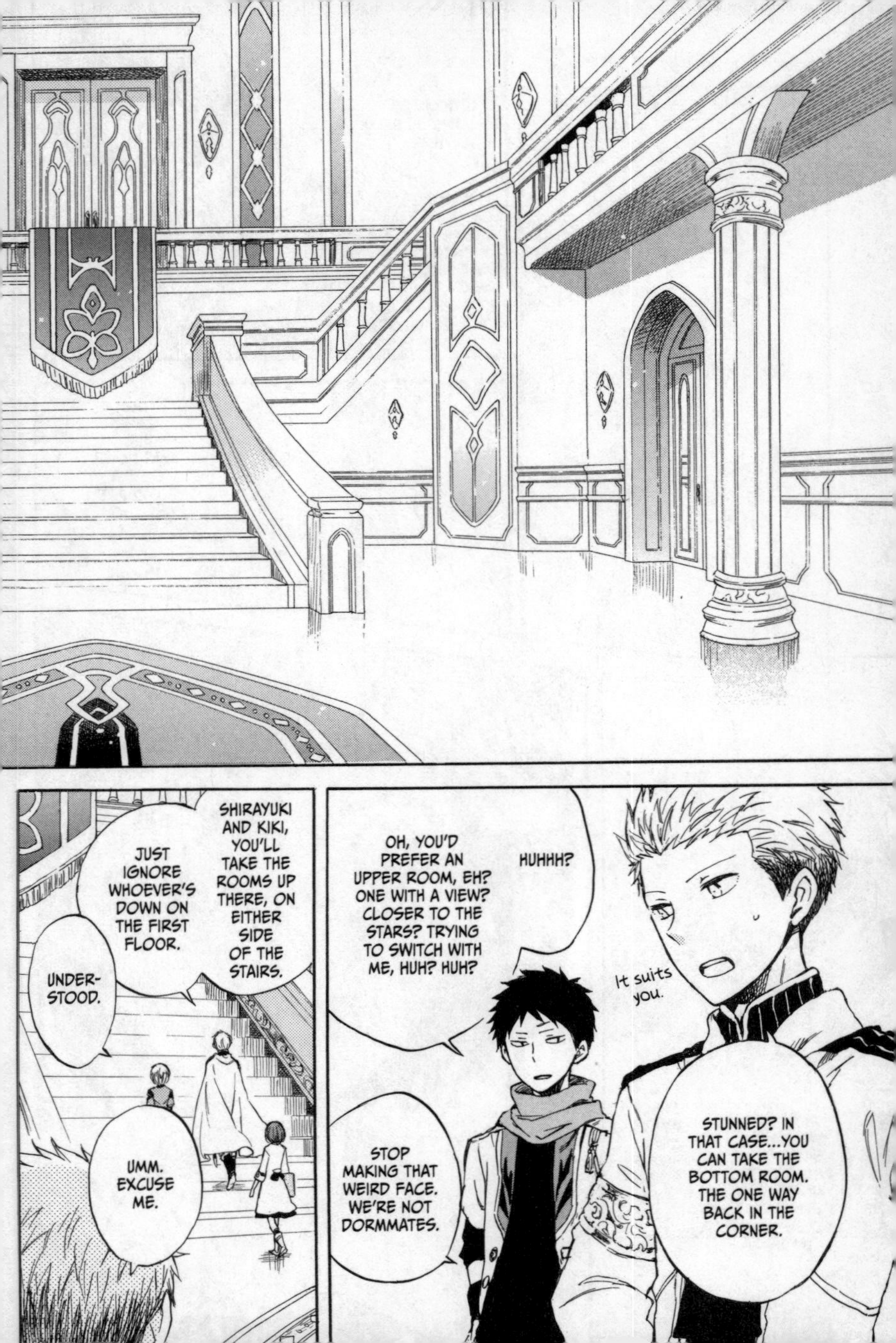
HUHHH?
OH, YOU'D PREFER AN UPPER ROOM, EH? ONE WITH A VIEW? CLOSER TO THE STARS? TRYING TO SWITCH WITH ME, HUH? HUH?
It suits you.
STUNNED? IN THAT CASE...YOU CAN TAKE THE BOTTOM ROOM. THE ONE WAY BACK IN THE CORNER.
STOP MAKING THAT WEIRD FACE. WE'RE NOT DORMMATES.
SHIRAYUKI AND KIKI, YOU'LL TAKE THE ROOMS UP THERE, ON EITHER SIDE OF THE STAIRS.
JUST IGNORE WHOEVER'S DOWN ON THE FIRST FLOOR.
UNDER-STOOD.
UMM. EXCUSE ME.

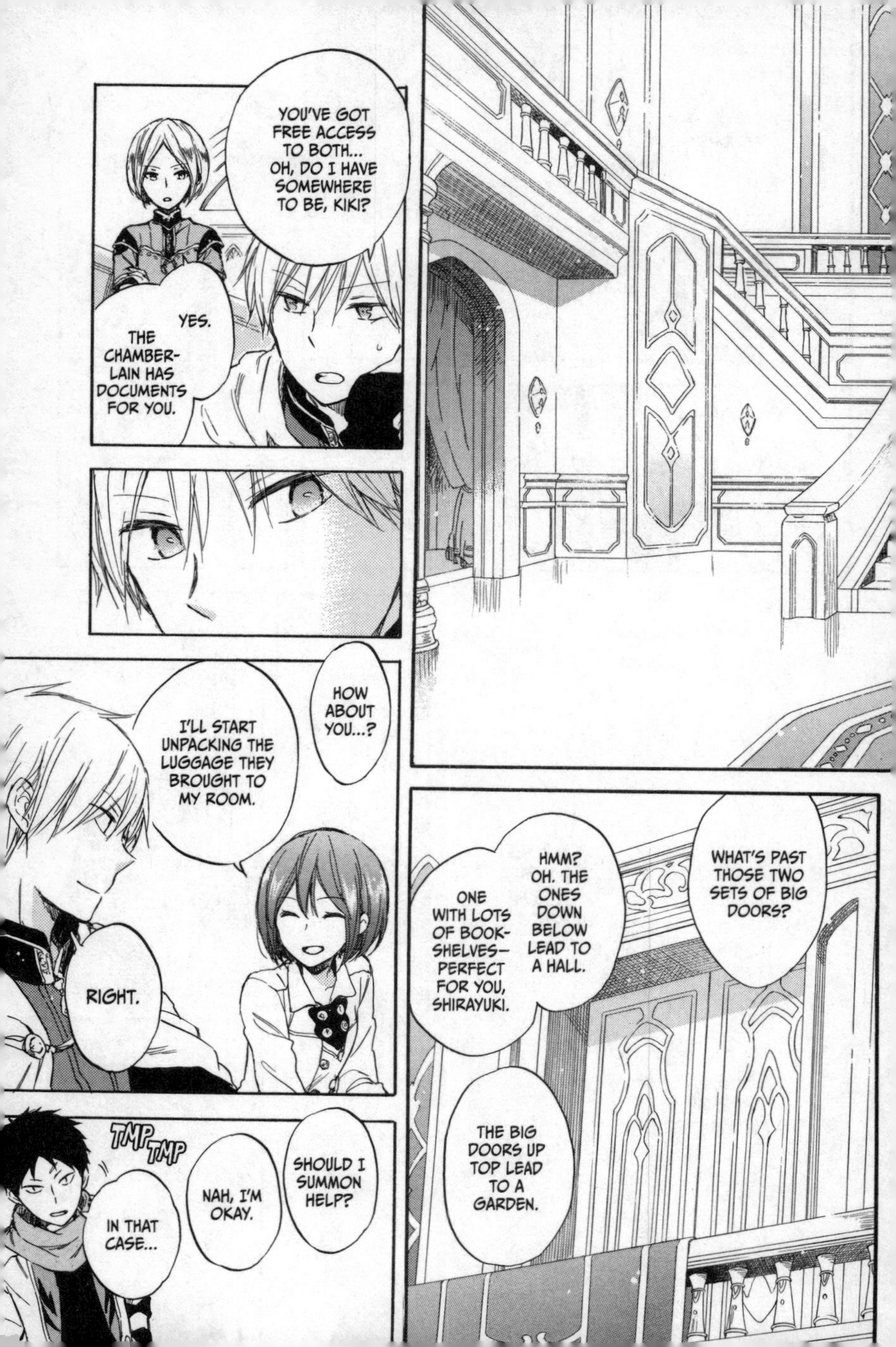
YOU'VE GOT FREE ACCESS TO BOTH... OH, DO I HAVE SOMEWHERE TO BE, KIKI?
YES. THE CHAMBER-LAIN HAS DOCUMENTS FOR YOU.
WHAT'S PAST THOSE TWO SETS OF BIG DOORS?
HMM? OH. THE ONES DOWN BELOW LEAD TO A HALL.
ONE WITH LOTS OF BOOK-SHELVES—PERFECT FOR YOU, SHIRAYUKI.
THE BIG DOORS UP TOP LEAD TO A GARDEN.
HOW ABOUT YOU...?
I'LL START UNPACKING THE LUGGAGE THEY BROUGHT TO MY ROOM.
RIGHT.
TMP TMP
SHOULD I SUMMON HELP?
NAH, I'M OKAY.
IN THAT CASE...

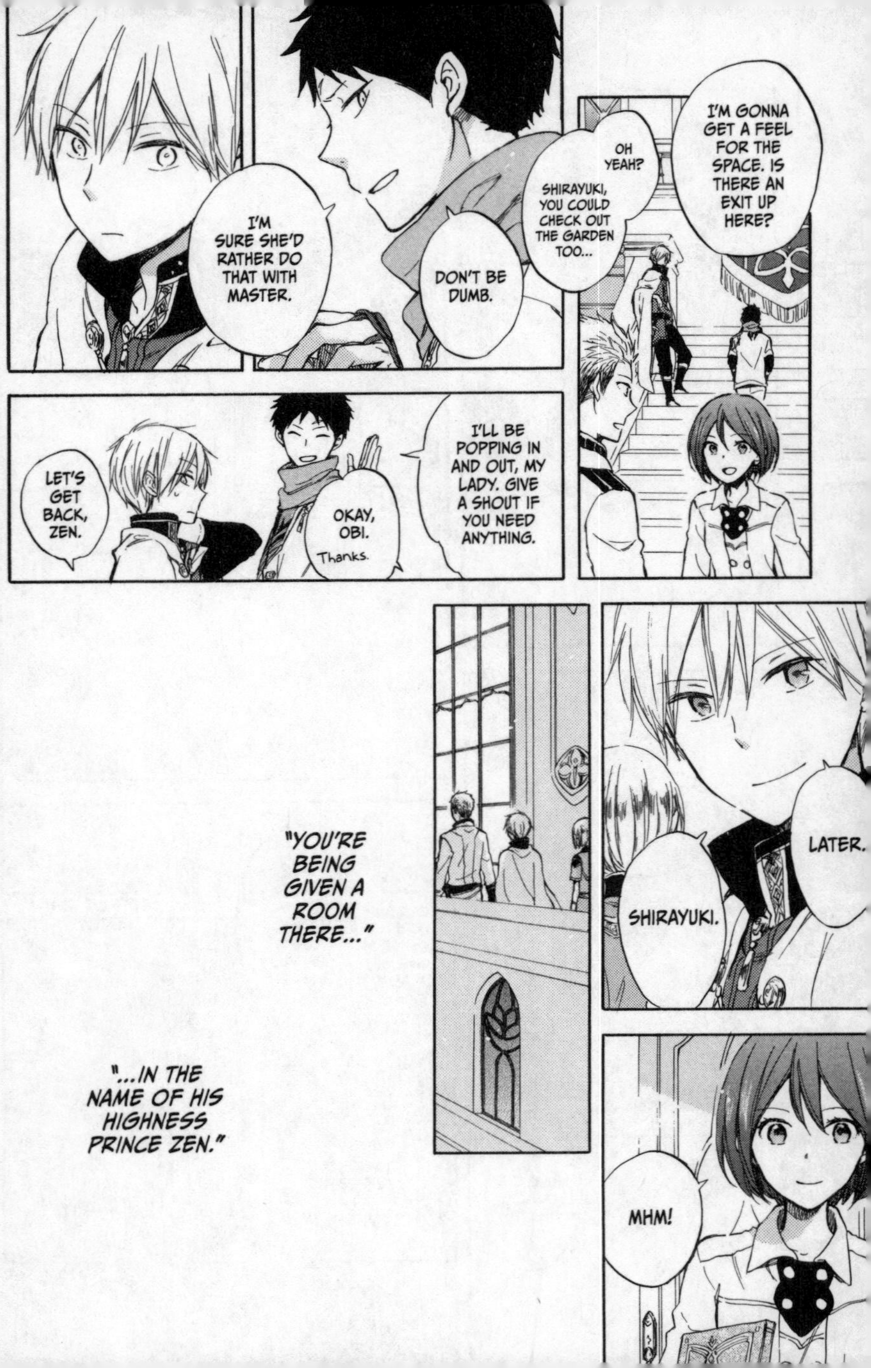
I'M GONNA GET A FEEL FOR THE SPACE. IS THERE AN EXIT UP HERE?
OH YEAH?
SHIRAYUKI, YOU COULD CHECK OUT THE GARDEN TOO...
DON'T BE DUMB.
I'M SURE SHE'D RATHER DO THAT WITH MASTER.
I'LL BE POPPING IN AND OUT, MY LADY. GIVE A SHOUT IF YOU NEED ANYTHING.
OKAY, OBI.
Thanks.
LET'S GET BACK, ZEN.
LATER.
SHIRAYUKI.
MHM!
"YOU'RE BEING GIVEN A ROOM THERE..."
"...IN THE NAME OF HIS HIGHNESS PRINCE ZEN."

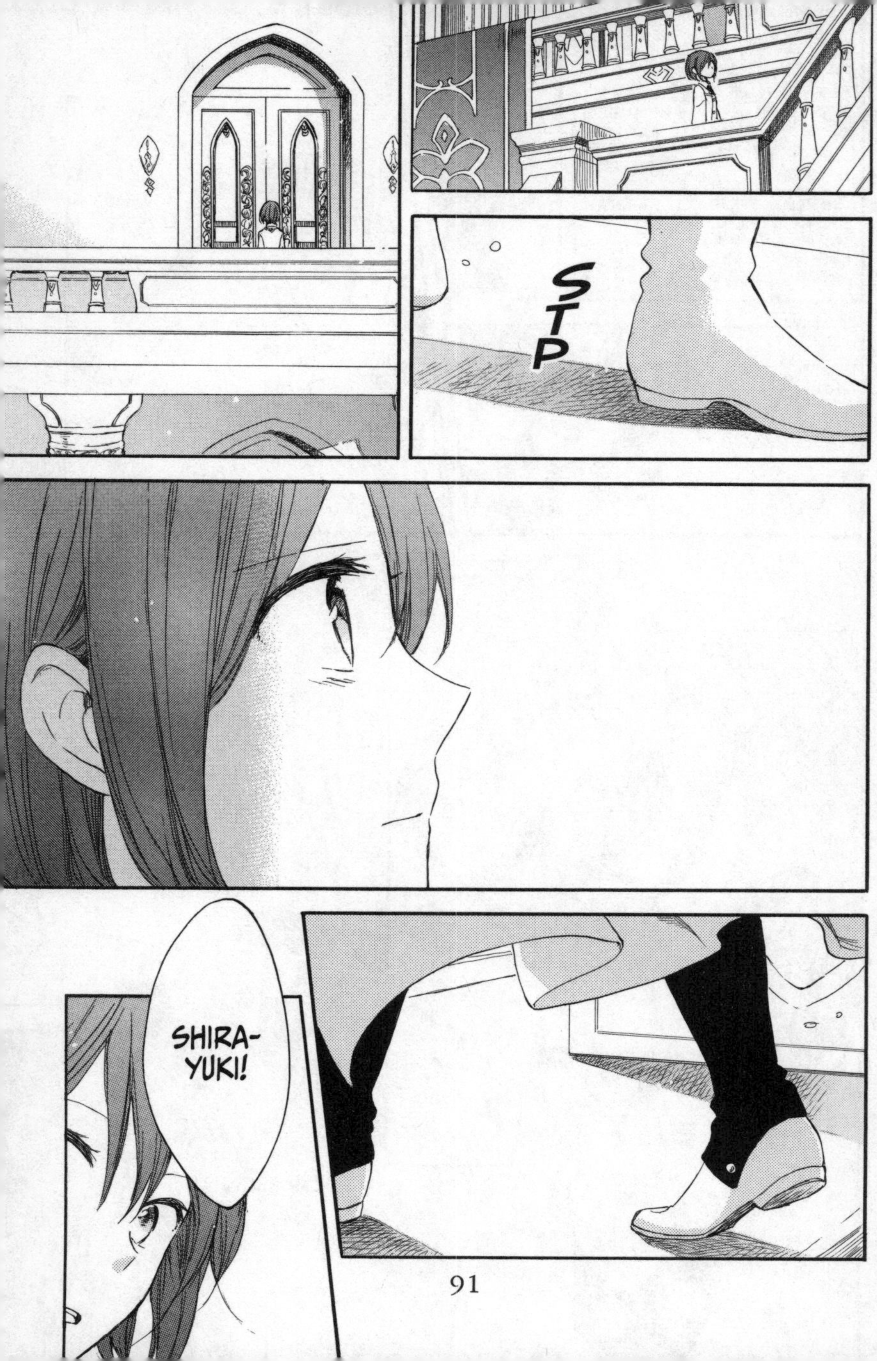
STP
SHIRA-YUKI!

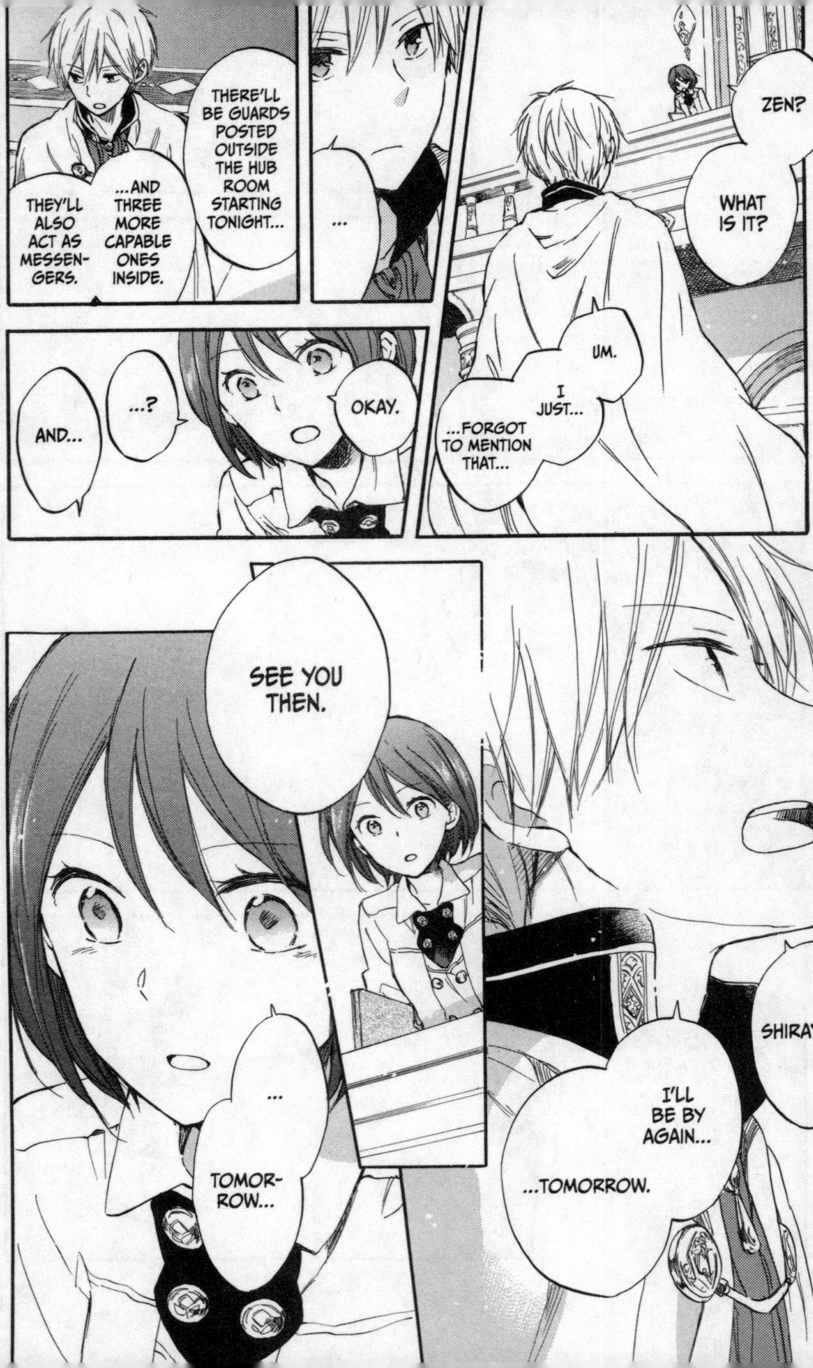
ZEN?
WHAT IS IT?
UM.
I JUST...
...FORGOT TO MENTION THAT...
...
THERE'LL BE GUARDS POSTED OUTSIDE THE HUB ROOM STARTING TONIGHT...
...AND THREE MORE CAPABLE ONES INSIDE.
THEY'LL ALSO ACT AS MESSEN-GERS.
OKAY.
...?
AND...
SHIRAYUKI.
I'LL BE BY AGAIN...
...TOMORROW.
...
TOMOR-ROW...
SEE YOU THEN.

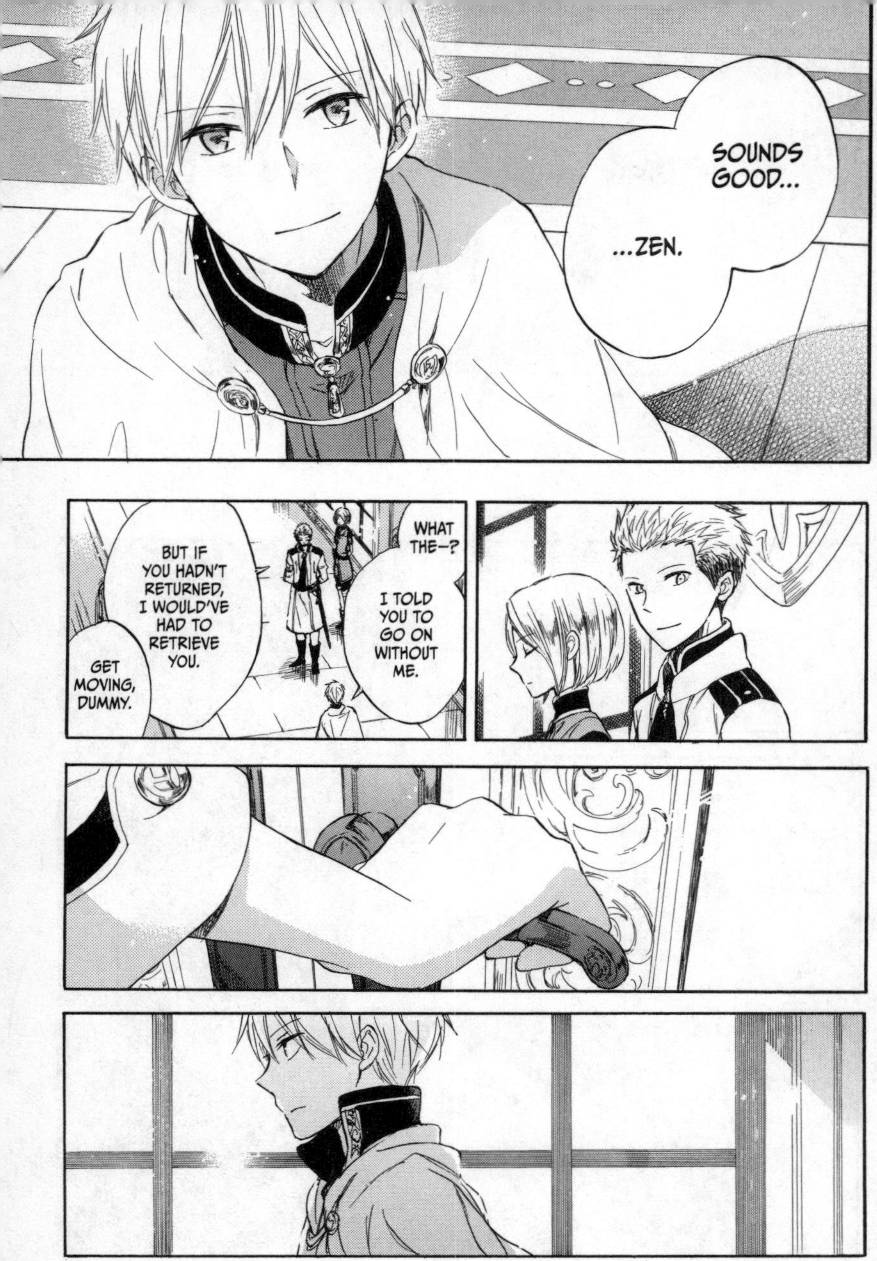
SOUNDS GOOD...
...ZEN.
WHAT THE–?
I TOLD YOU TO GO ON WITHOUT ME.
BUT IF YOU HADN'T RETURNED, I WOULD'VE HAD TO RETRIEVE YOU.
GET MOVING, DUMMY.

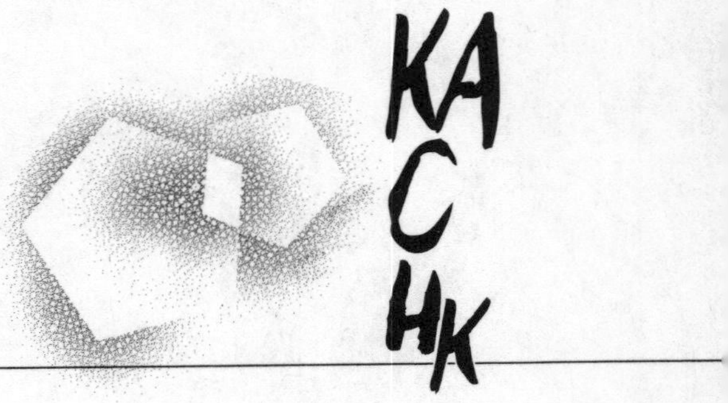
KACHK

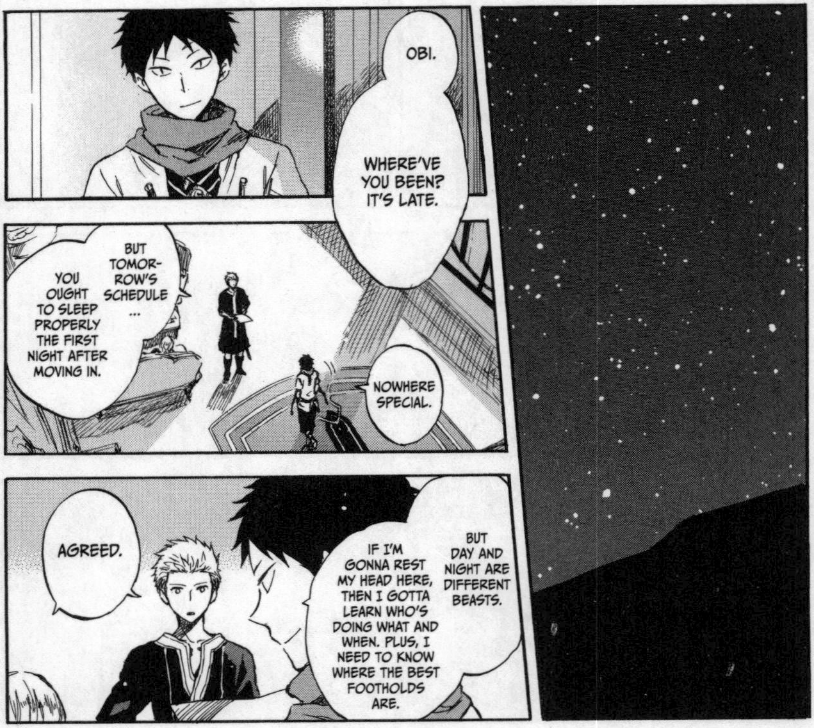
OBI.
WHERE'VE YOU BEEN? IT'S LATE.
NOWHERE SPECIAL.
BUT TOMOR-ROW'S SCHEDULE ...
YOU OUGHT TO SLEEP PROPERLY THE FIRST NIGHT AFTER MOVING IN.
BUT DAY AND NIGHT ARE DIFFERENT BEASTS.
IF I'M GONNA REST MY HEAD HERE, THEN I GOTTA LEARN WHO'S DOING WHAT AND WHEN. PLUS, I NEED TO KNOW WHERE THE BEST FOOTHOLDS ARE.
AGREED.

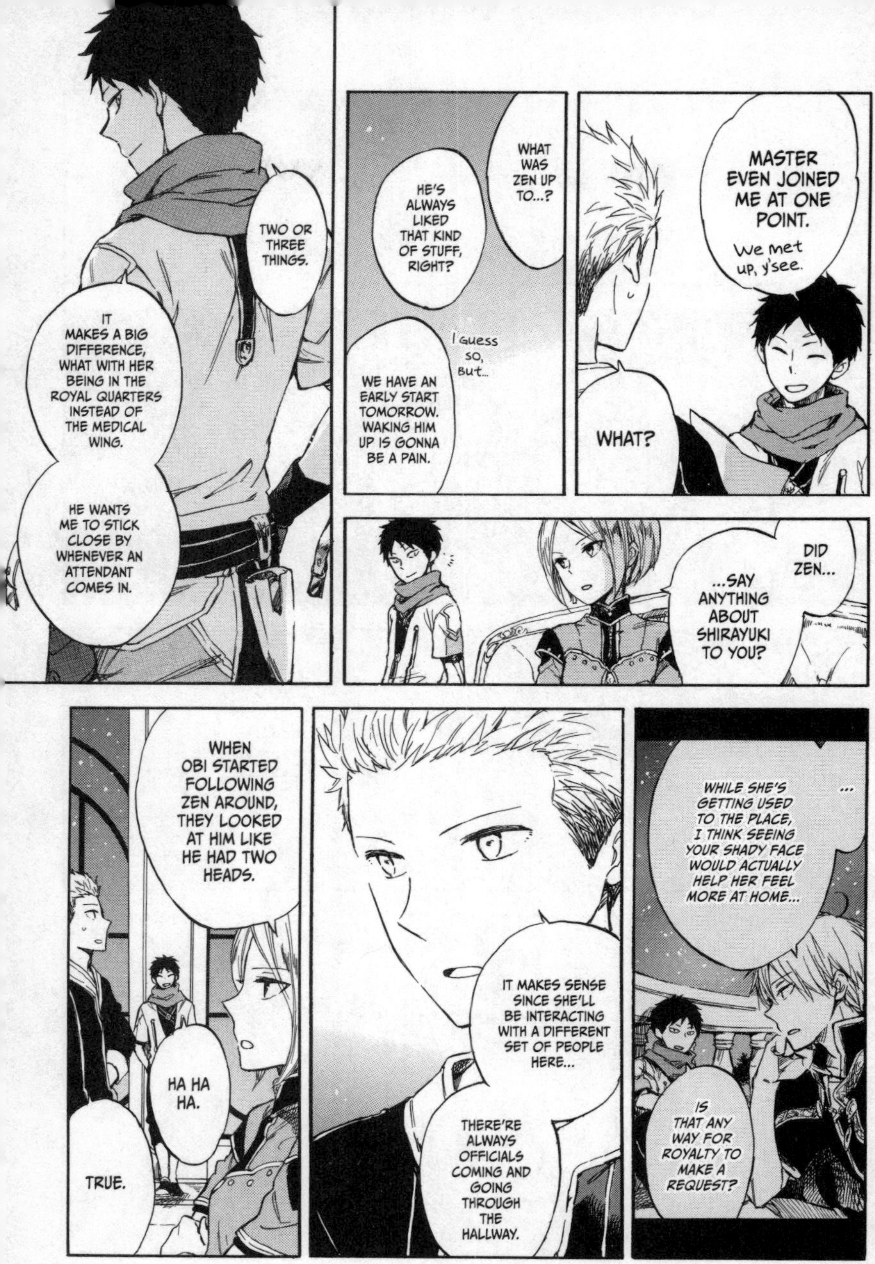
MASTER EVEN JOINED ME AT ONE POINT.
We met up, y'see.
WHAT?
WHAT WAS ZEN UP TO...?
HE'S ALWAYS LIKED THAT KIND OF STUFF, RIGHT?
I guess so, but...
WE HAVE AN EARLY START TOMORROW. WAKING HIM UP IS GONNA BE A PAIN.
DID ZEN...
...SAY ANYTHING ABOUT SHIRAYUKI TO YOU?
TWO OR THREE THINGS.
IT MAKES A BIG DIFFERENCE, WHAT WITH HER BEING IN THE ROYAL QUARTERS INSTEAD OF THE MEDICAL WING.
HE WANTS ME TO STICK CLOSE BY WHENEVER AN ATTENDANT COMES IN.
...
WHILE SHE'S GETTING USED TO THE PLACE, I THINK SEEING YOUR SHADY FACE WOULD ACTUALLY HELP HER FEEL MORE AT HOME...
IS THAT ANY WAY FOR ROYALTY TO MAKE A REQUEST?
IT MAKES SENSE SINCE SHE'LL BE INTERACTING WITH A DIFFERENT SET OF PEOPLE HERE...
THERE'RE ALWAYS OFFICIALS COMING AND GOING THROUGH THE HALLWAY.
WHEN OBI STARTED FOLLOWING ZEN AROUND, THEY LOOKED AT HIM LIKE HE HAD TWO HEADS.
HA HA HA.
TRUE.

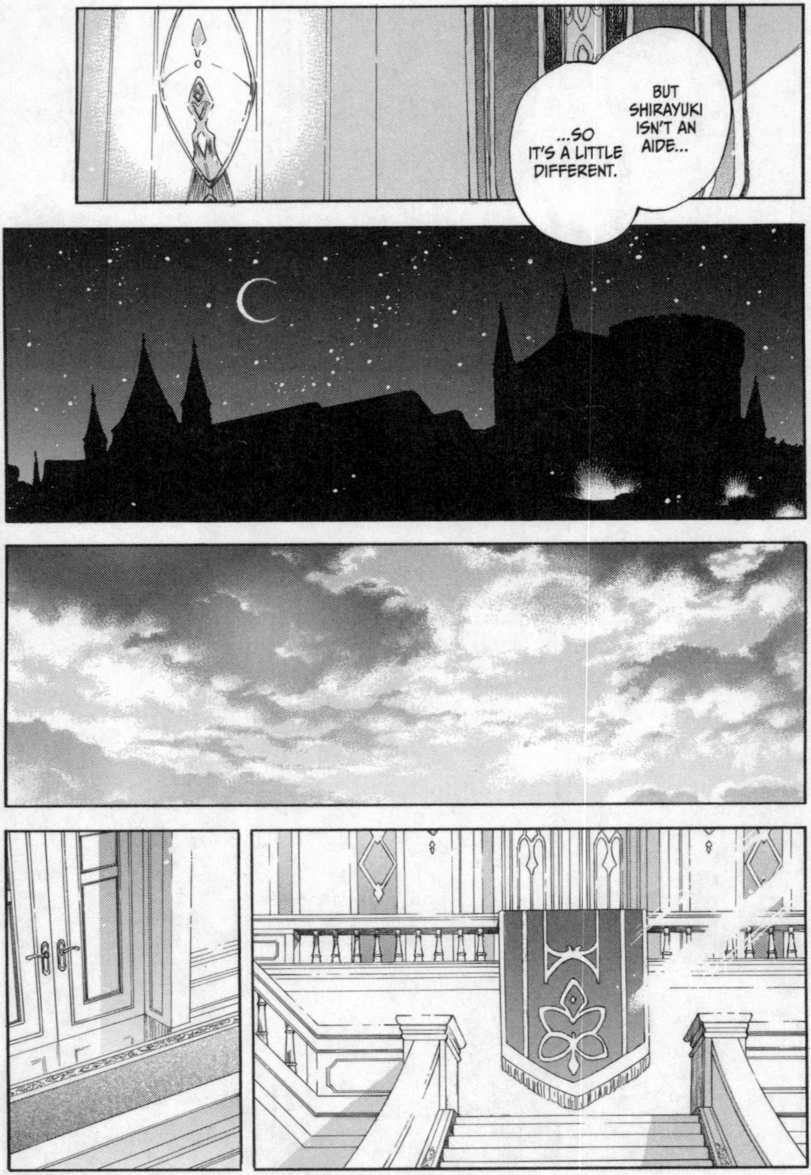
BUT SHIRAYUKI ISN'T AN AIDE...
...SO IT'S A LITTLE DIFFERENT.

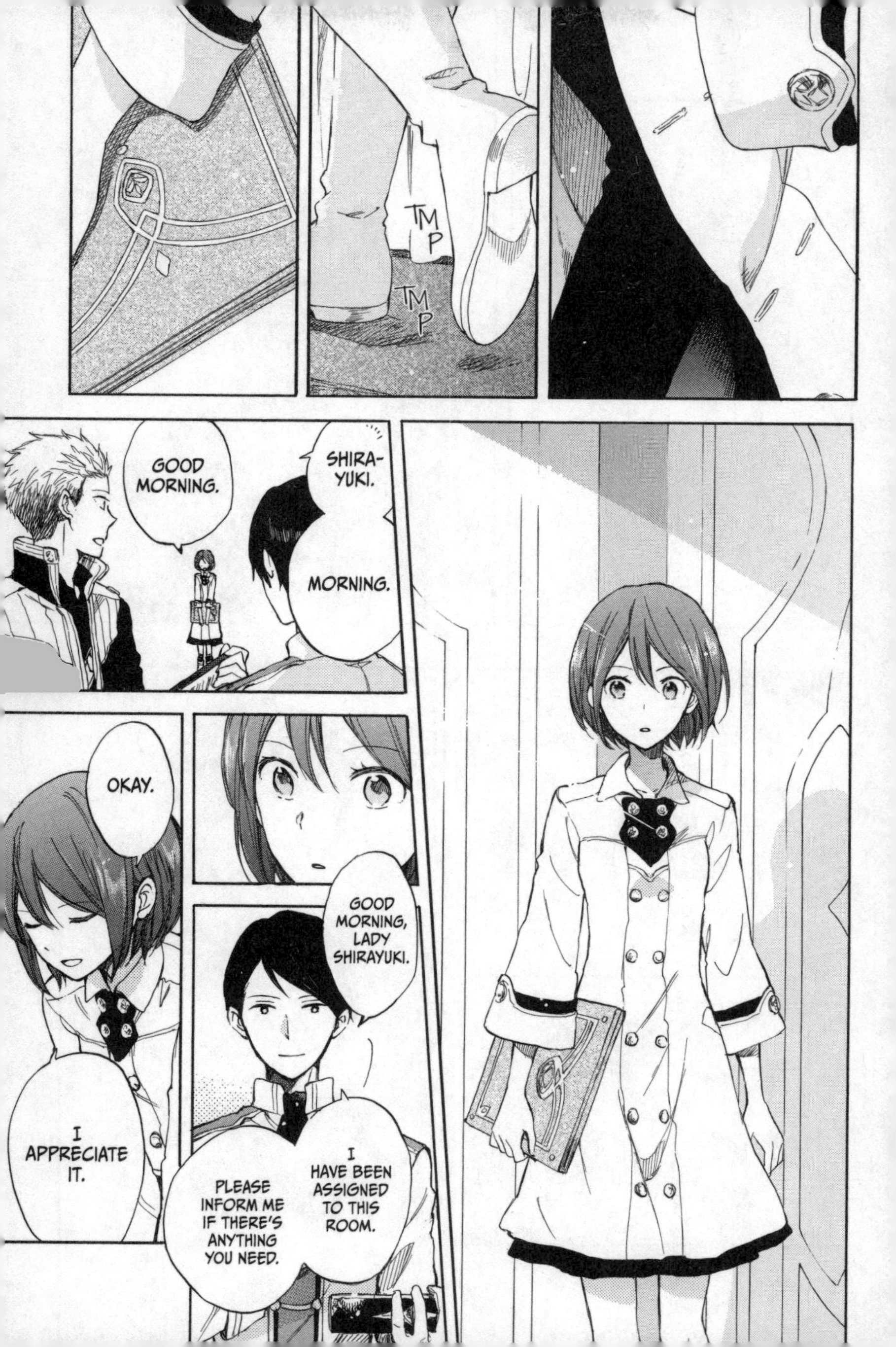
TMP
TMP
SHIRA-YUKI.
GOOD MORNING.
MORNING.
GOOD MORNING, LADY SHIRAYUKI.
I HAVE BEEN ASSIGNED TO THIS ROOM.
PLEASE INFORM ME IF THERE'S ANYTHING YOU NEED.
OKAY.
I APPRECIATE IT.

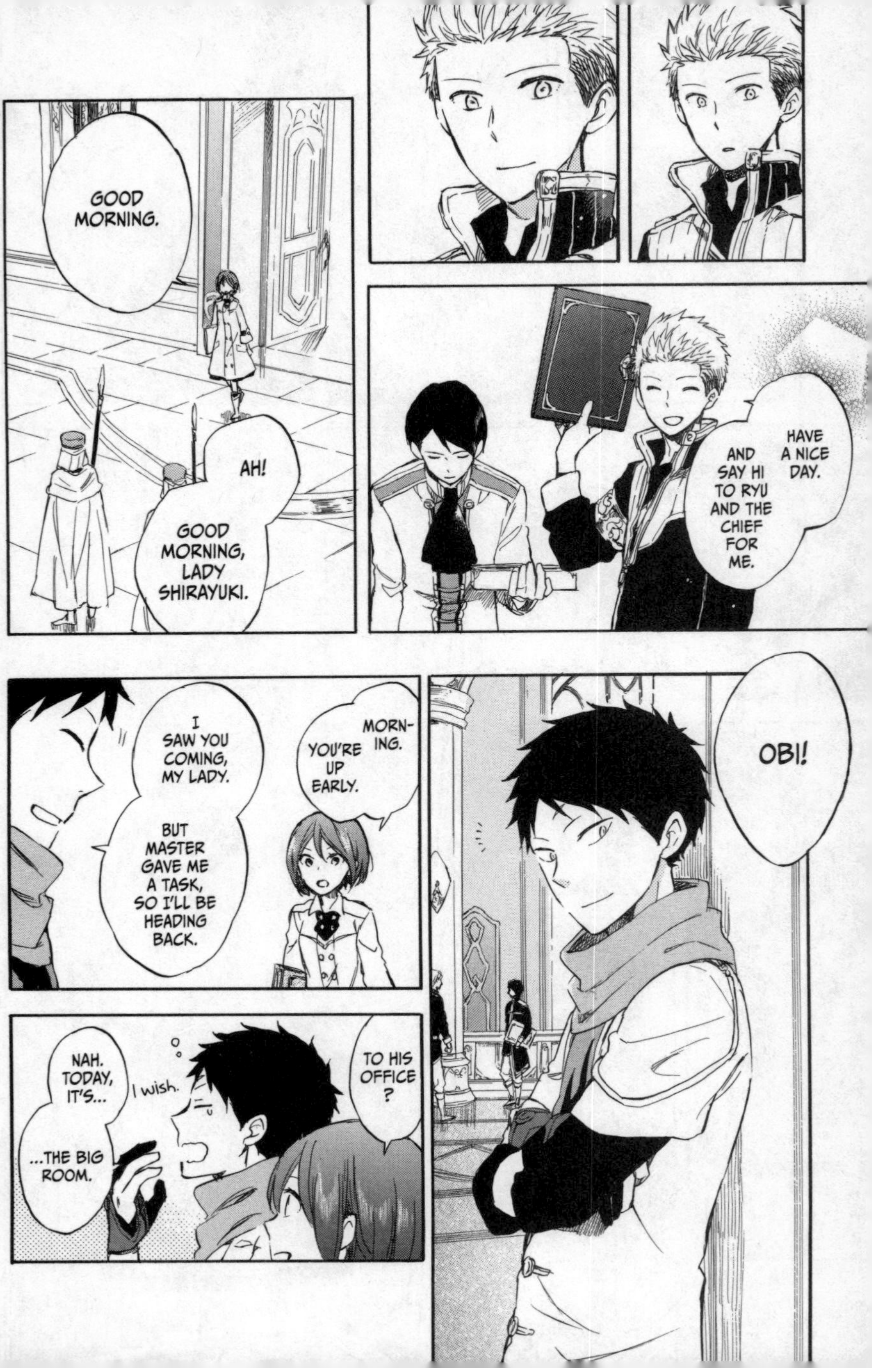
HAVE A NICE DAY.
AND SAY HI TO RYU AND THE CHIEF FOR ME.
GOOD MORNING.
AH!
GOOD MORNING, LADY SHIRAYUKI.
OBI!
MORNING.
YOU'RE UP EARLY.
I SAW YOU COMING, MY LADY.
BUT MASTER GAVE ME A TASK, SO I'LL BE HEADING BACK.
TO HIS OFFICE?
NAH. TODAY, IT'S...
I wish.
...THE BIG ROOM.

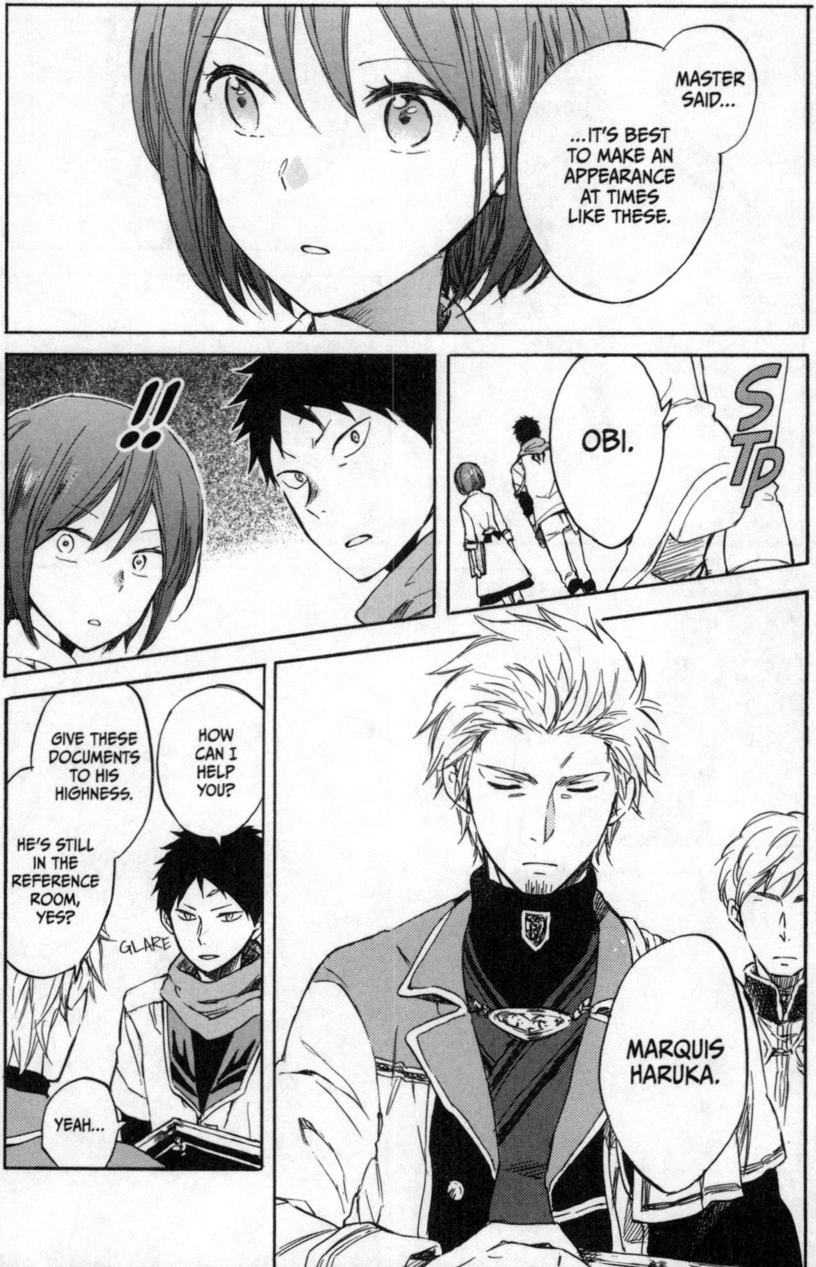
MASTER SAID...
...IT'S BEST TO MAKE AN APPEARANCE AT TIMES LIKE THESE.
OBI.
STP
!!
MARQUIS HARUKA.
HOW CAN I HELP YOU?
GIVE THESE DOCUMENTS TO HIS HIGHNESS.
HE'S STILL IN THE REFERENCE ROOM, YES?
GLARE
YEAH...

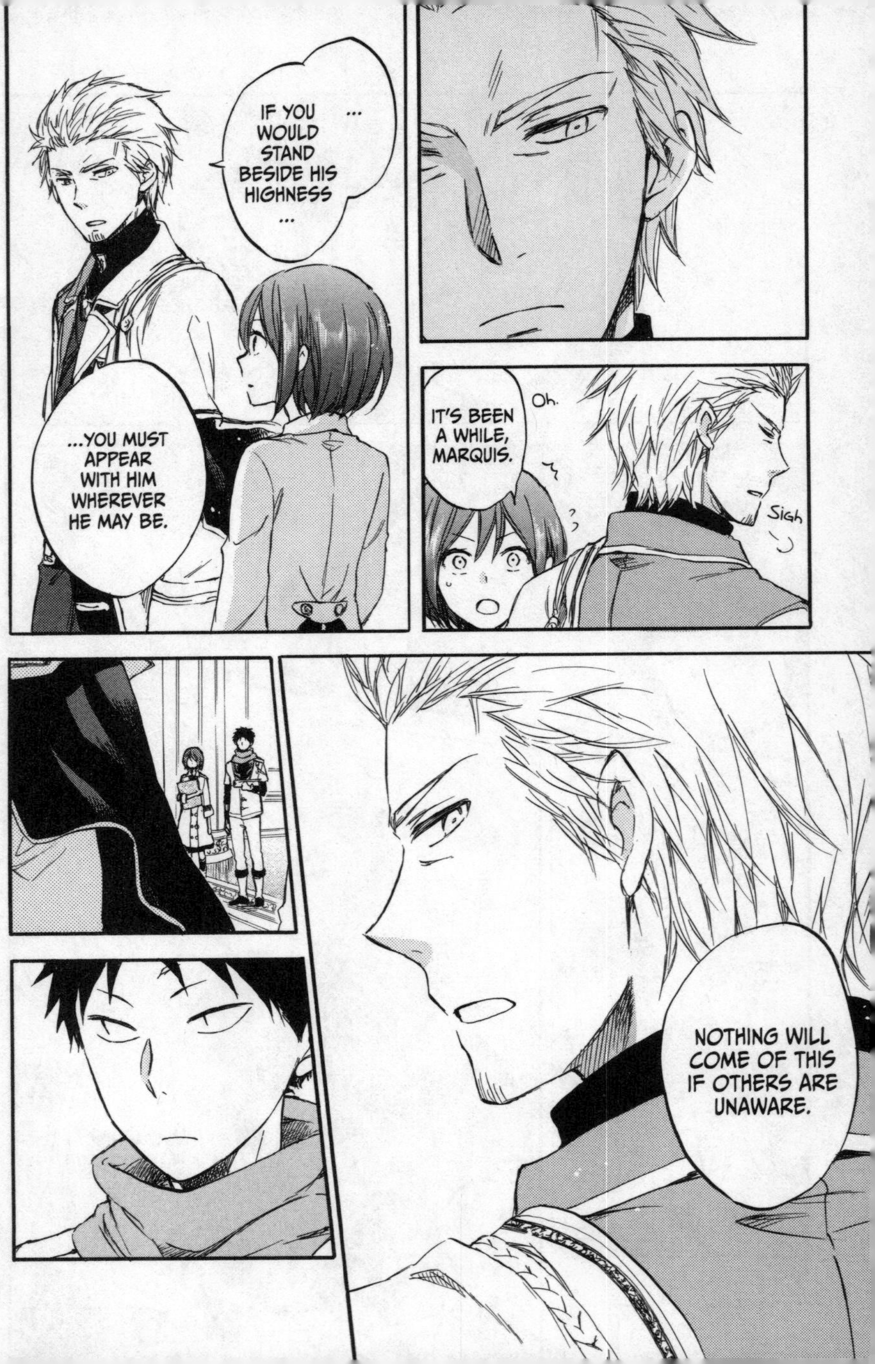
Oh.
IT'S BEEN A WHILE, MARQUIS.
Sigh
... IF YOU WOULD STAND BESIDE HIS HIGHNESS ...
...YOU MUST APPEAR WITH HIM WHEREVER HE MAY BE.
NOTHING WILL COME OF THIS IF OTHERS ARE UNAWARE.

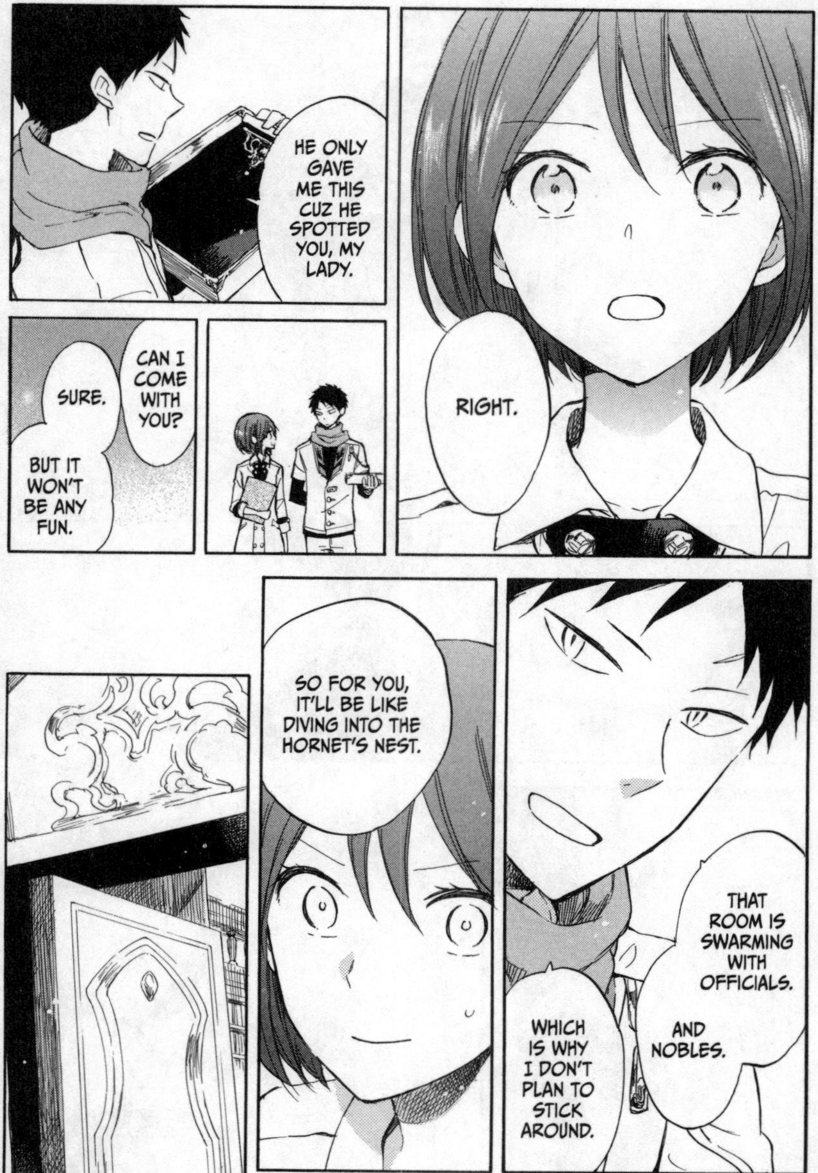
RIGHT.
HE ONLY GAVE ME THIS CUZ HE SPOTTED YOU, MY LADY.
CAN I COME WITH YOU?
SURE.
BUT IT WON'T BE ANY FUN.
THAT ROOM IS SWARMING WITH OFFICIALS.
AND NOBLES.
WHICH IS WHY I DON'T PLAN TO STICK AROUND.
SO FOR YOU, IT'LL BE LIKE DIVING INTO THE HORNET'S NEST.

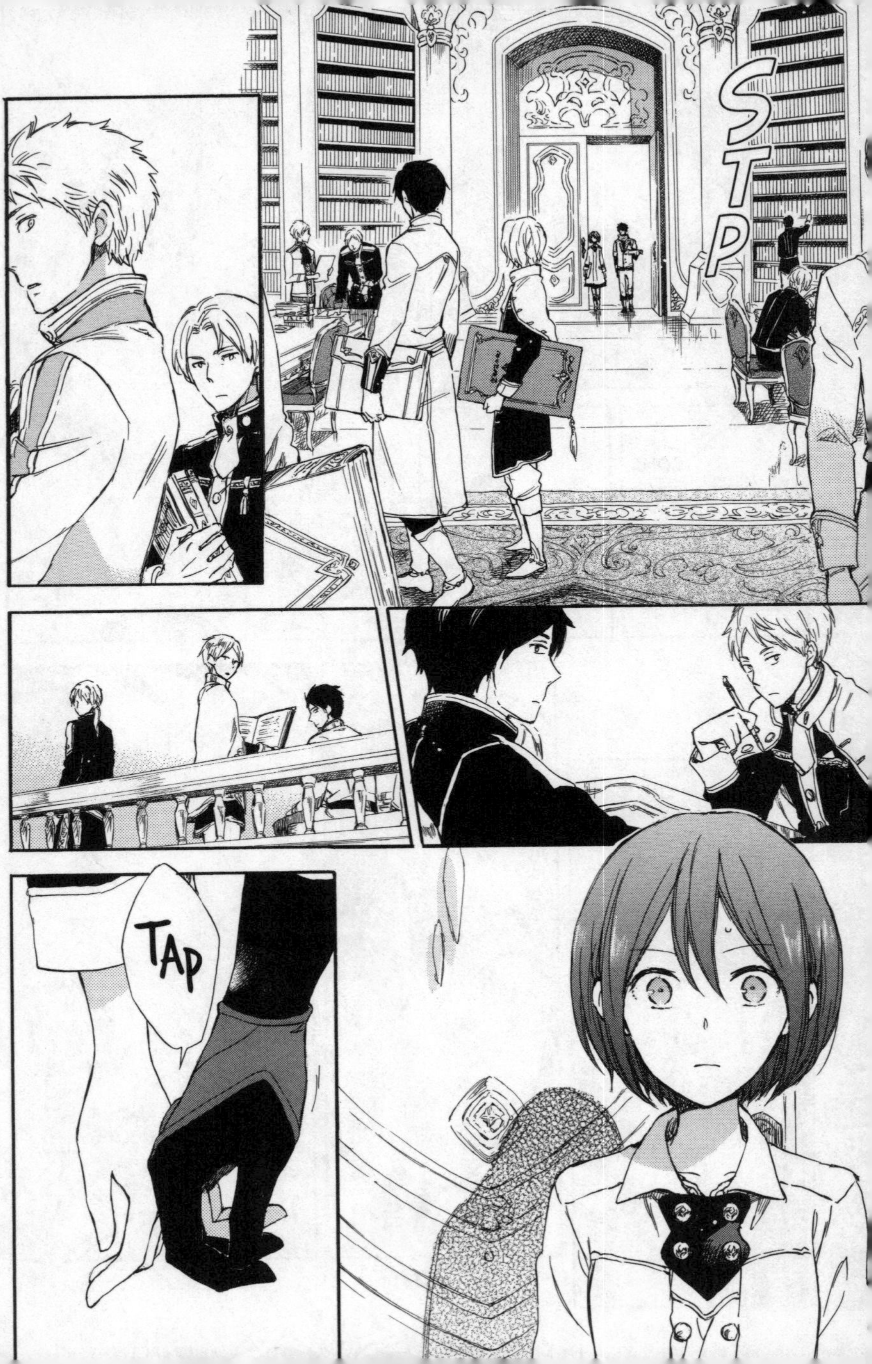
STP
TAP

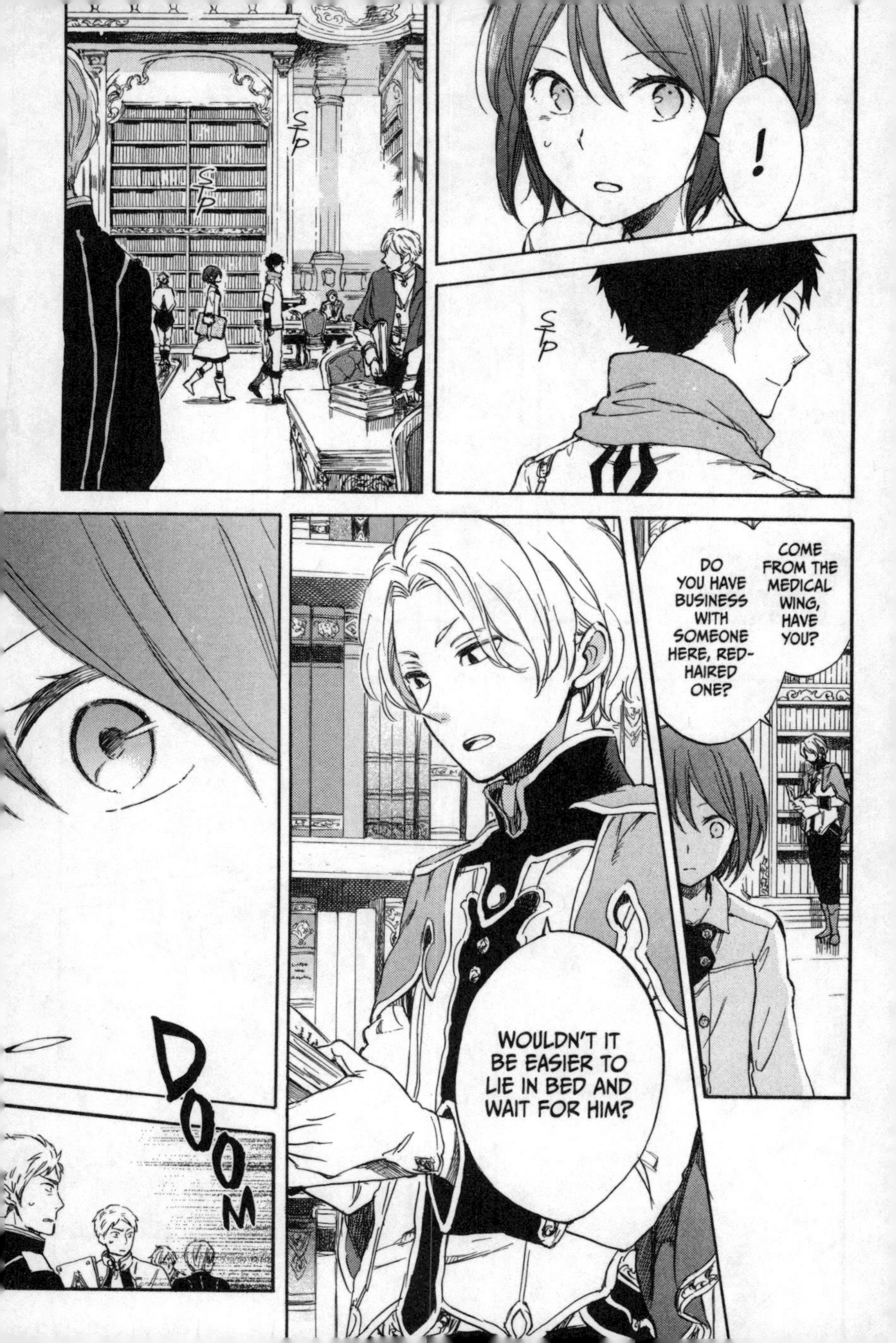
!
STP
STP
STP
COME FROM THE MEDICAL WING, HAVE YOU?
DO YOU HAVE BUSINESS WITH SOMEONE HERE, RED-HAIRED ONE?
WOULDN'T IT BE EASIER TO LIE IN BED AND WAIT FOR HIM?
DOOM

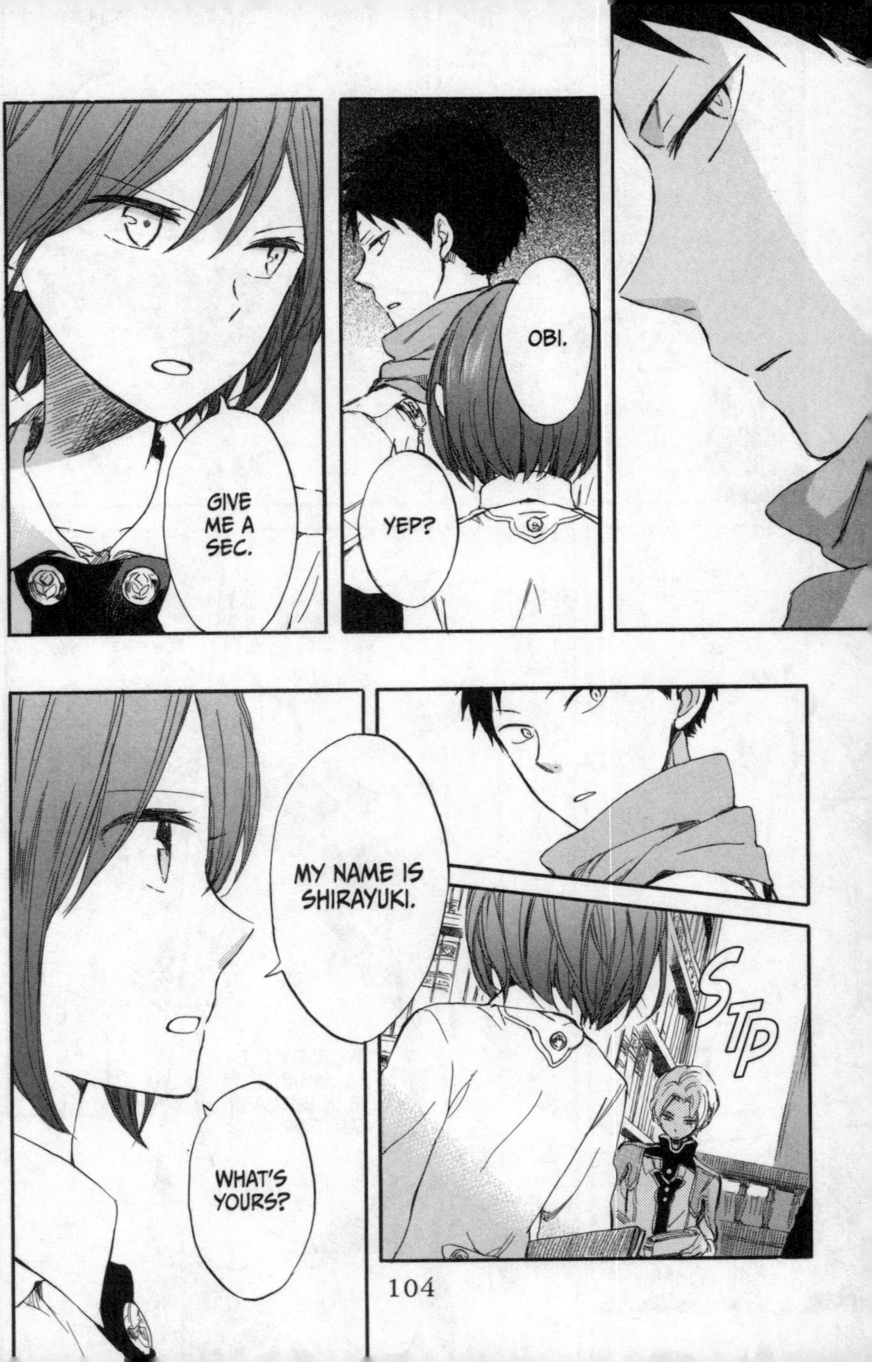
OBI.
YEP?
GIVE ME A SEC.
STP
MY NAME IS SHIRAYUKI.
WHAT'S YOURS?

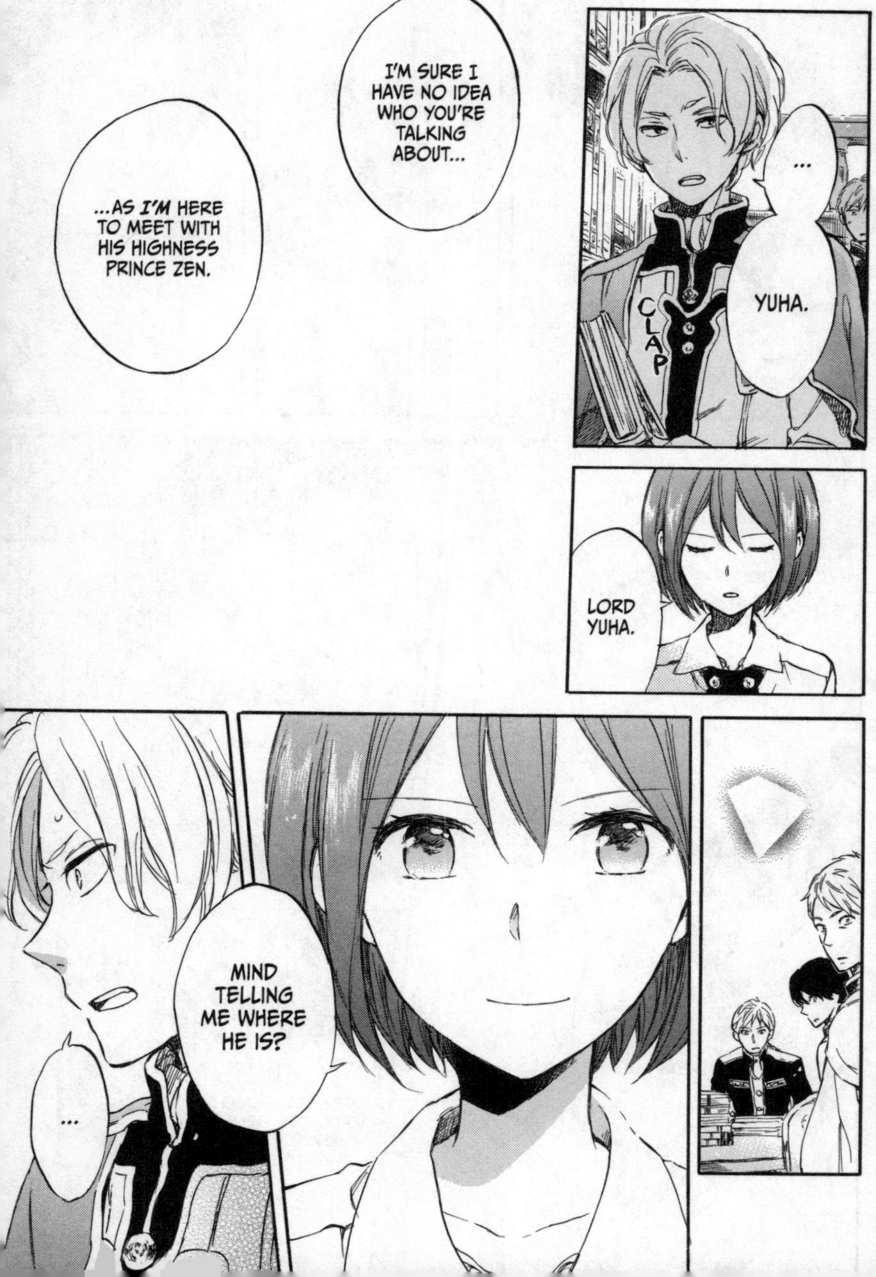
...
YUHA.
CLAP
LORD YUHA.
I'M SURE I HAVE NO IDEA WHO YOU'RE TALKING ABOUT...
...AS *I'M* HERE TO MEET WITH HIS HIGHNESS PRINCE ZEN.
MIND TELLING ME WHERE HE IS?
...

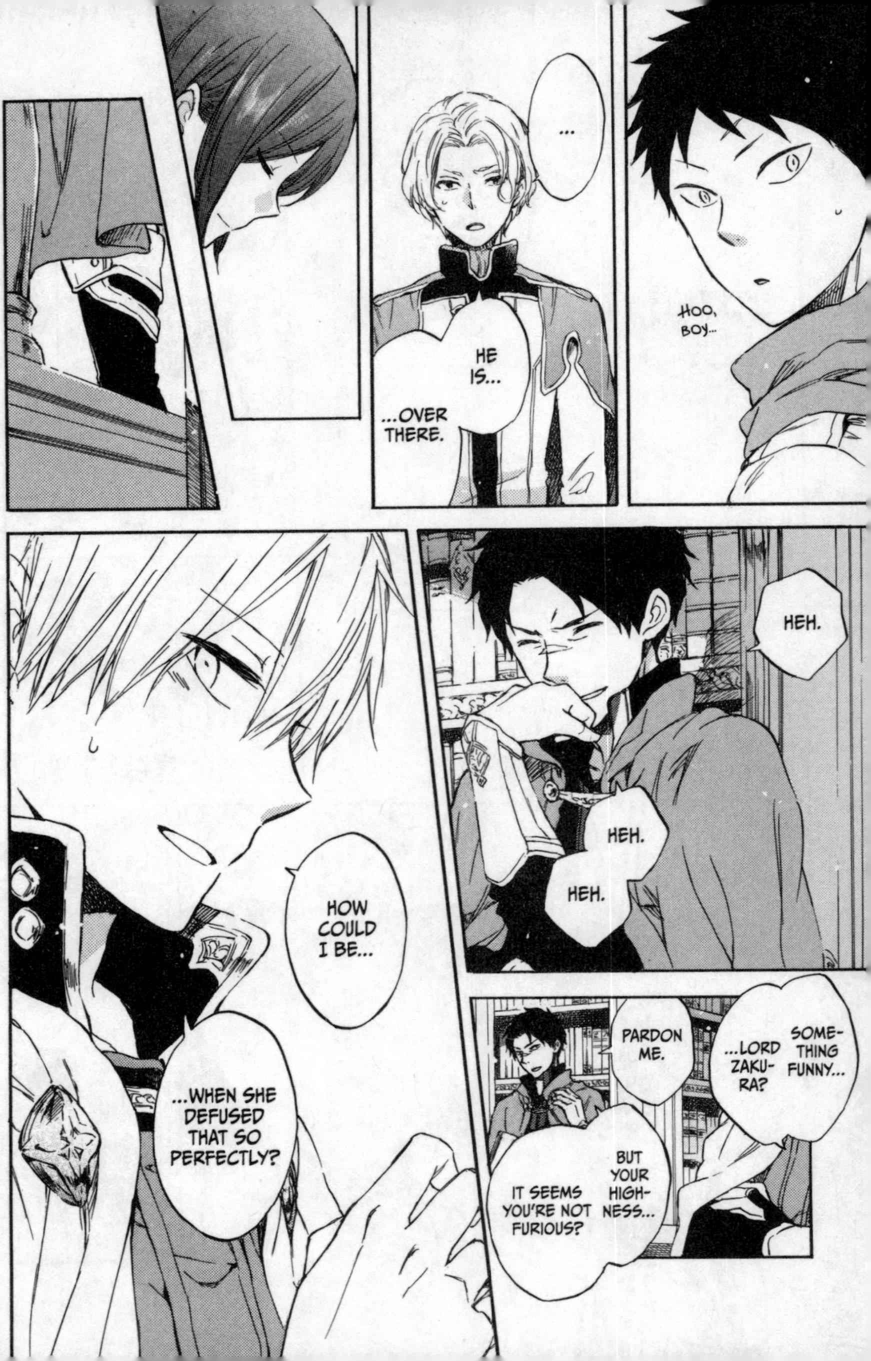
HOO, BOY...
...
HE IS...
...OVER THERE.
HEH.
HEH.
HEH.
SOMETHING FUNNY...
...LORD ZAKURA?
PARDON ME.
BUT YOUR HIGHNESS...
IT SEEMS YOU'RE NOT FURIOUS?
HOW COULD I BE...
...WHEN SHE DEFUSED THAT SO PERFECTLY?

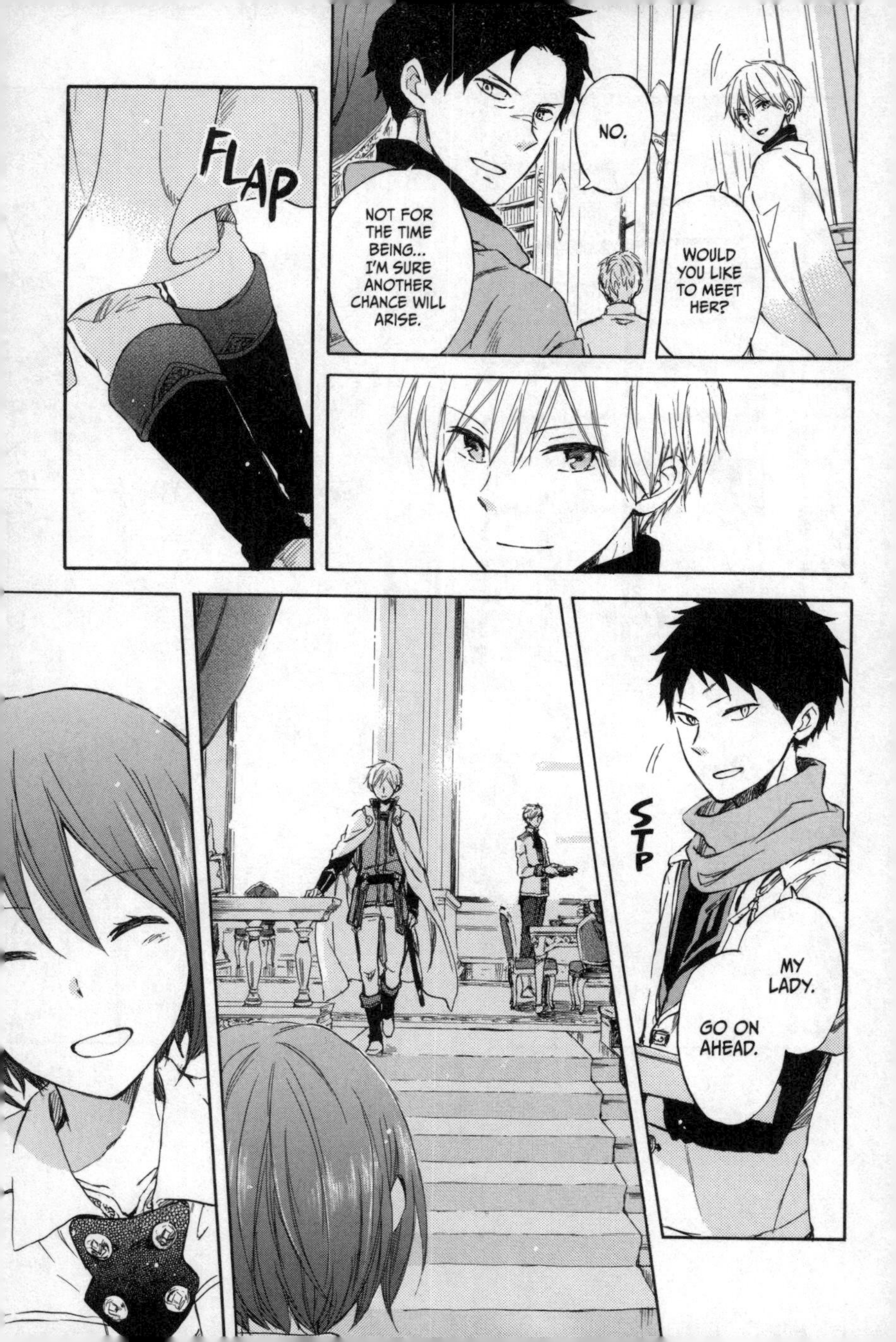
WOULD YOU LIKE TO MEET HER?
NO.
NOT FOR THE TIME BEING... I'M SURE ANOTHER CHANCE WILL ARISE.
FLAP
STP
MY LADY.
GO ON AHEAD.

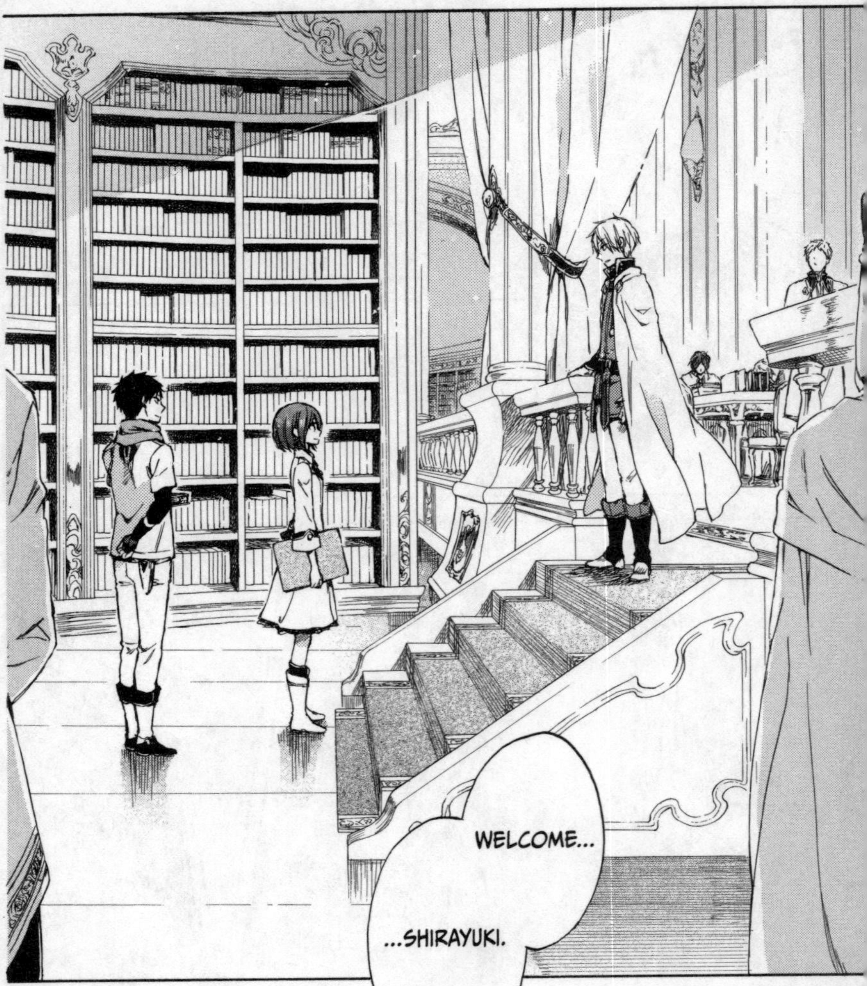
WELCOME...
...SHIRAYUKI.

Snow White with the Red Hair

Chapter 48 Preview Image

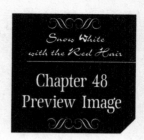

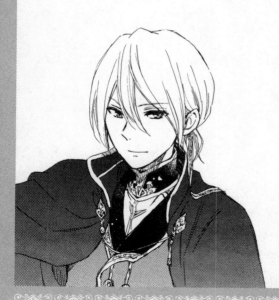

Chapter 48

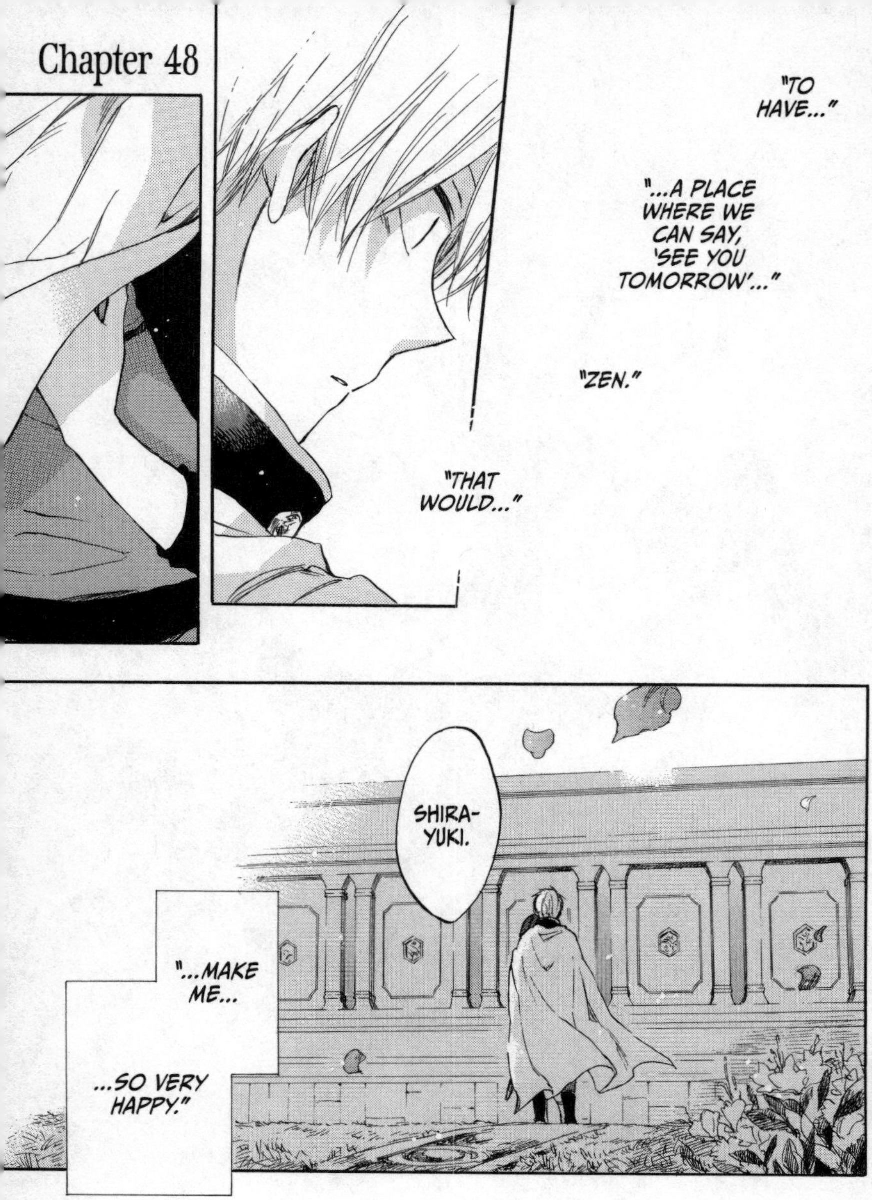
"TO HAVE..."
"...A PLACE WHERE WE CAN SAY, 'SEE YOU TOMORROW'..."
"ZEN."
"THAT WOULD..."
SHIRA-YUKI.
"...MAKE ME...
...SO VERY HAPPY."

Chapter 48

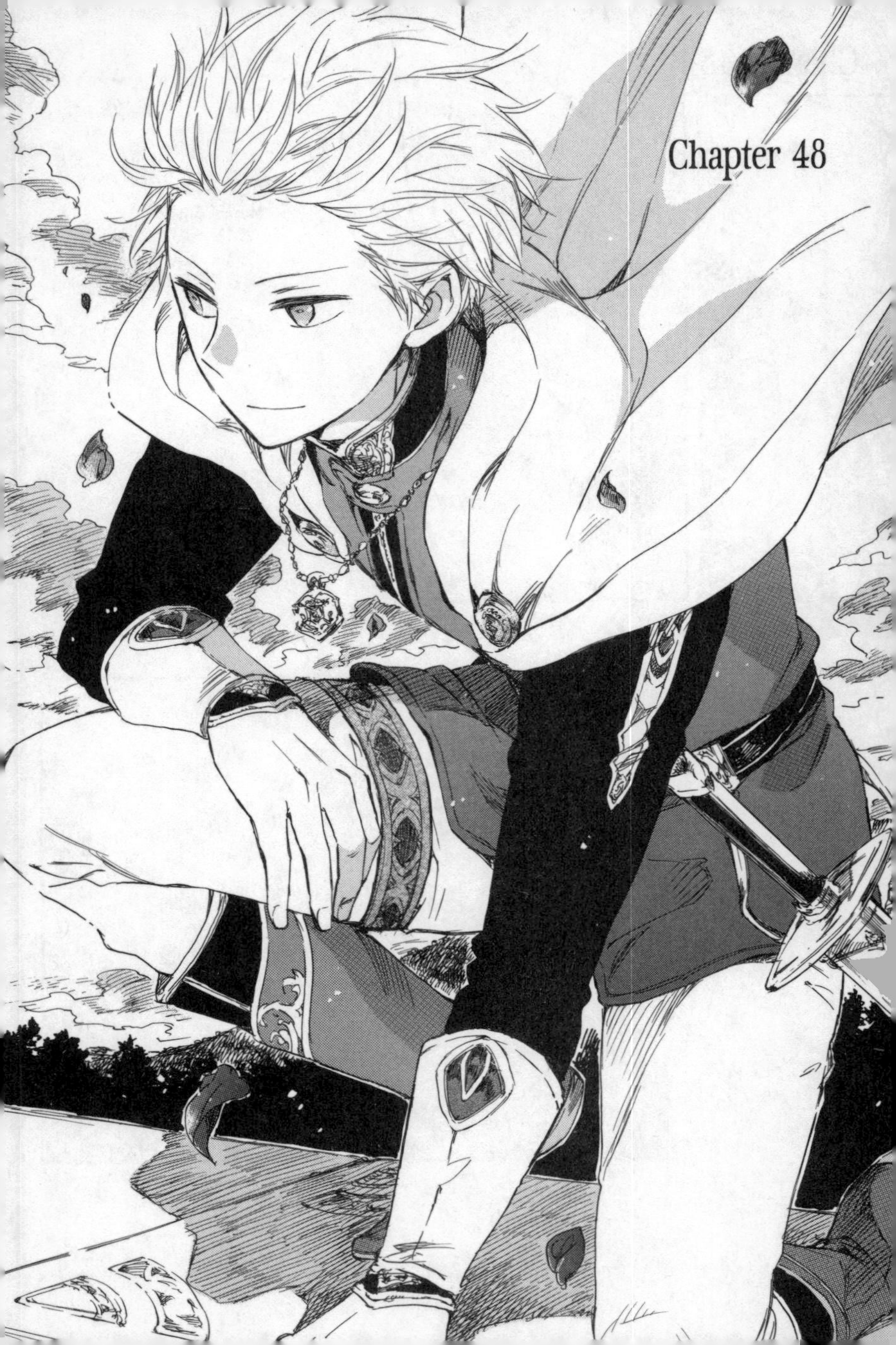

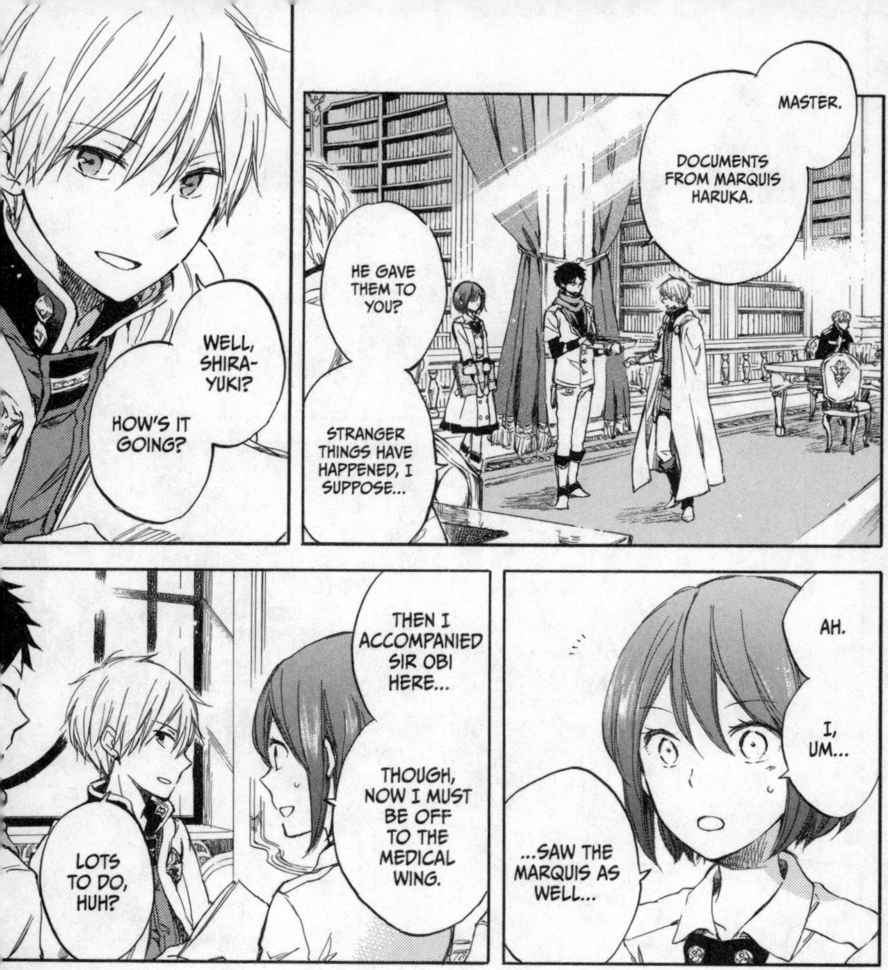
MASTER.
DOCUMENTS FROM MARQUIS HARUKA.
HE GAVE THEM TO YOU?
STRANGER THINGS HAVE HAPPENED, I SUPPOSE...
WELL, SHIRA-YUKI?
HOW'S IT GOING?
AH.
I, UM...
...SAW THE MARQUIS AS WELL...
THEN I ACCOMPANIED SIR OBI HERE...
THOUGH, NOW I MUST BE OFF TO THE MEDICAL WING.
LOTS TO DO, HUH?

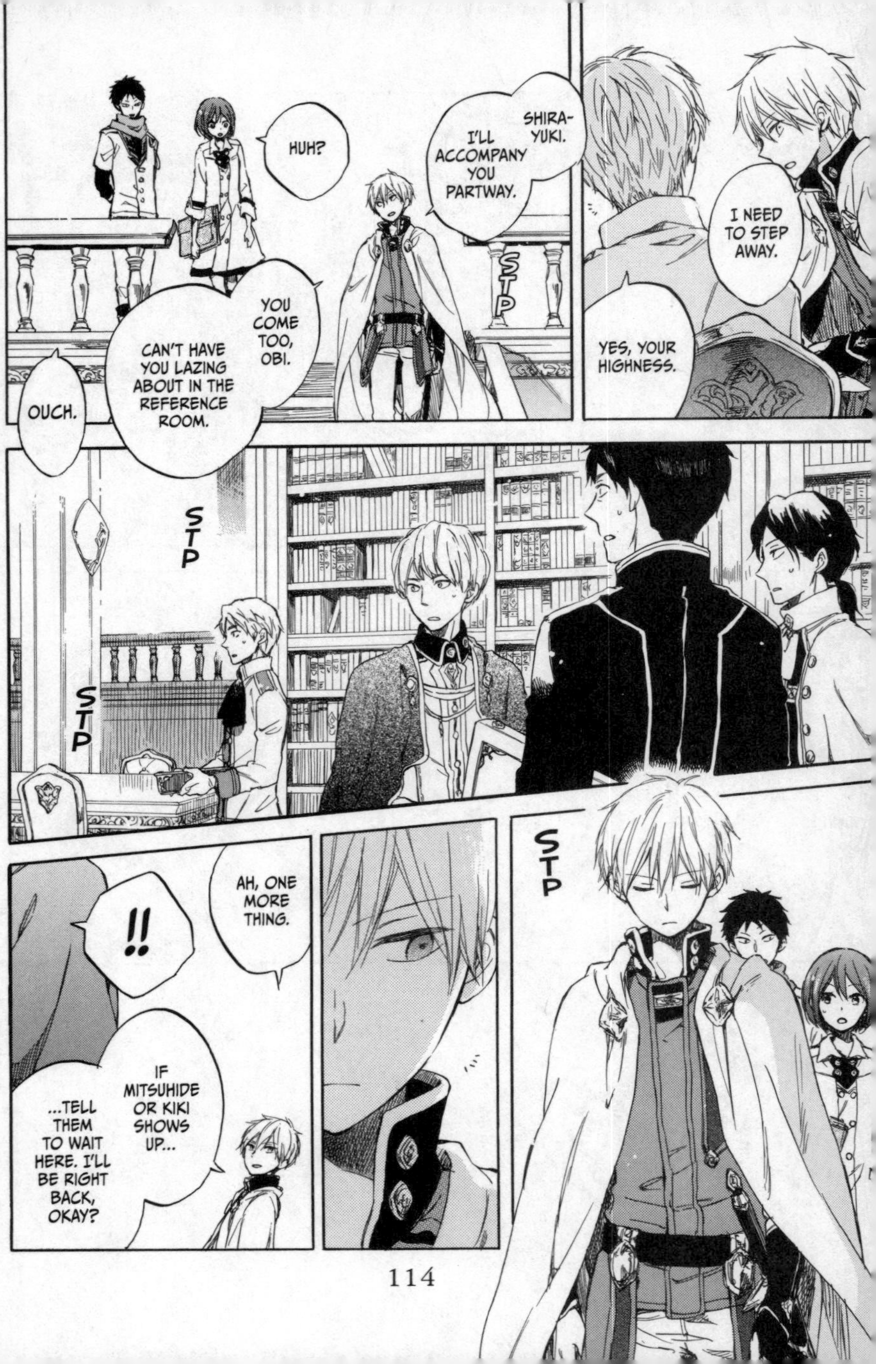
I NEED TO STEP AWAY.
YES, YOUR HIGHNESS.
SHIRA-YUKI.
I'LL ACCOMPANY YOU PARTWAY.
HUH?
STP
YOU COME TOO, OBI.
CAN'T HAVE YOU LAZING ABOUT IN THE REFERENCE ROOM.
OUCH.
STP
STP
STP
AH, ONE MORE THING.
!!
IF MITSUHIDE OR KIKI SHOWS UP...
...TELL THEM TO WAIT HERE. I'LL BE RIGHT BACK, OKAY?

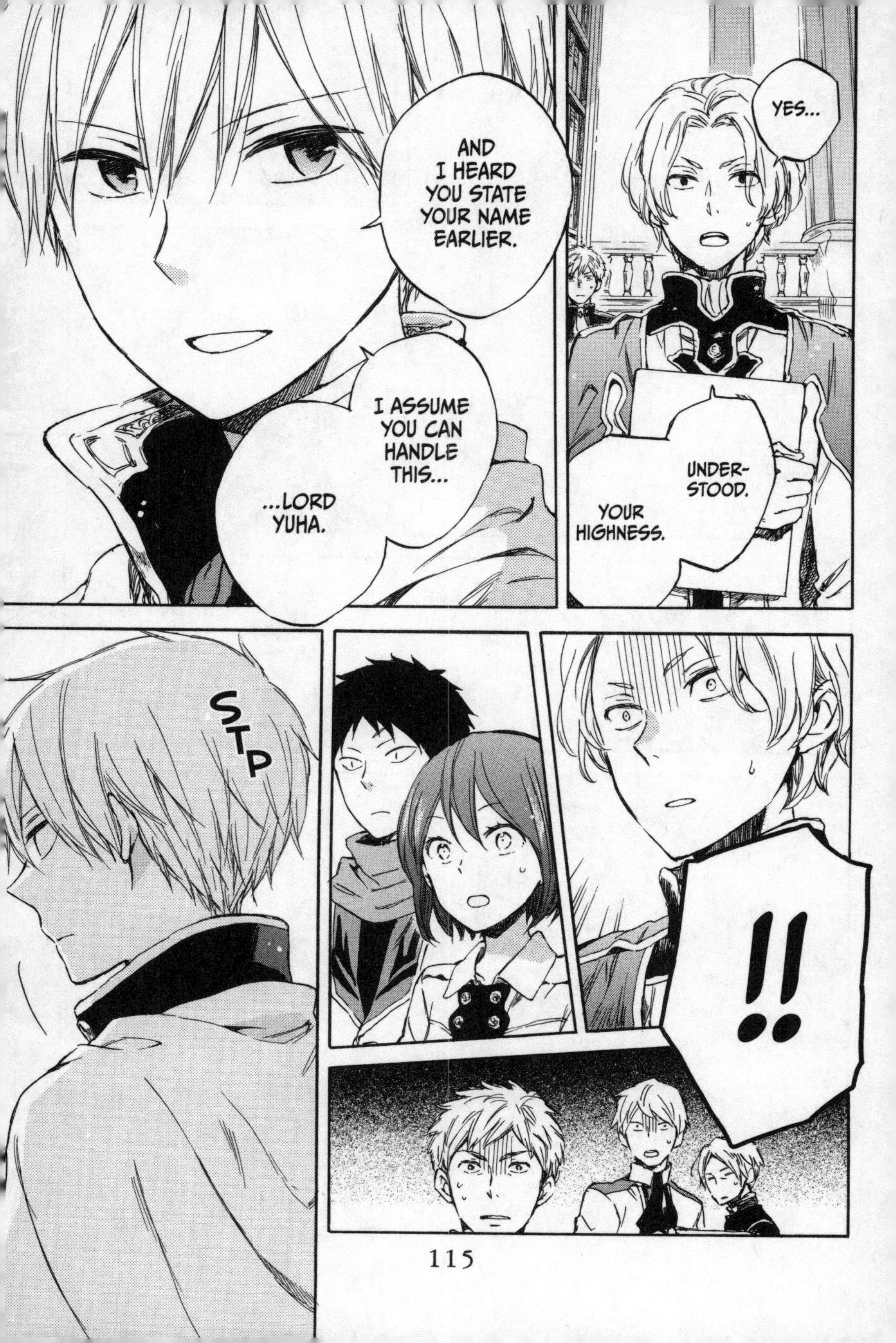
YES...
UNDERSTOOD. YOUR HIGHNESS.
AND I HEARD YOU STATE YOUR NAME EARLIER.
I ASSUME YOU CAN HANDLE THIS...
...LORD YUHA.
!!
STP

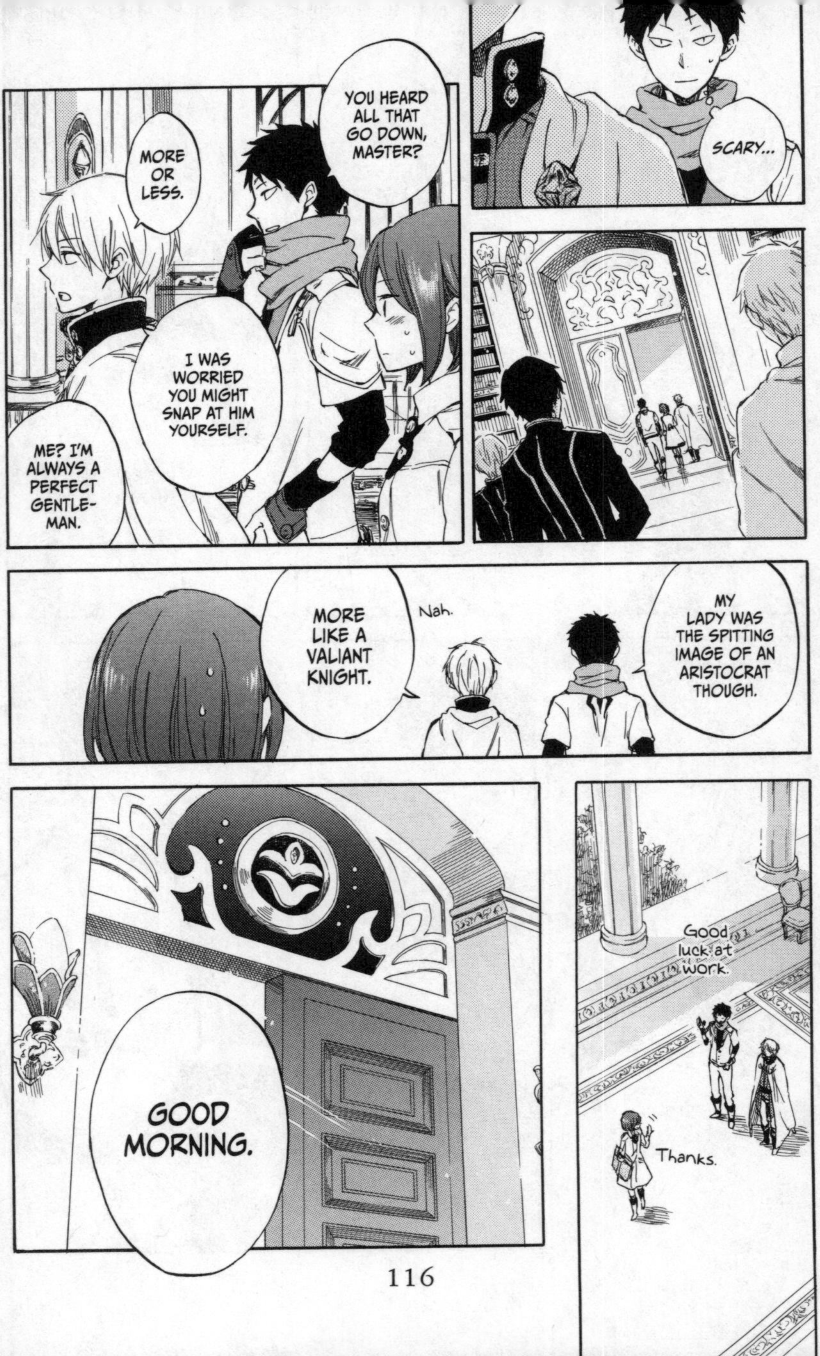
SCARY...
YOU HEARD ALL THAT GO DOWN, MASTER?
MORE OR LESS.
I WAS WORRIED YOU MIGHT SNAP AT HIM YOURSELF.
ME? I'M ALWAYS A PERFECT GENTLEMAN.
MY LADY WAS THE SPITTING IMAGE OF AN ARISTOCRAT THOUGH.
Nah.
MORE LIKE A VALIANT KNIGHT.
Good luck at work.
Thanks.
GOOD MORNING.

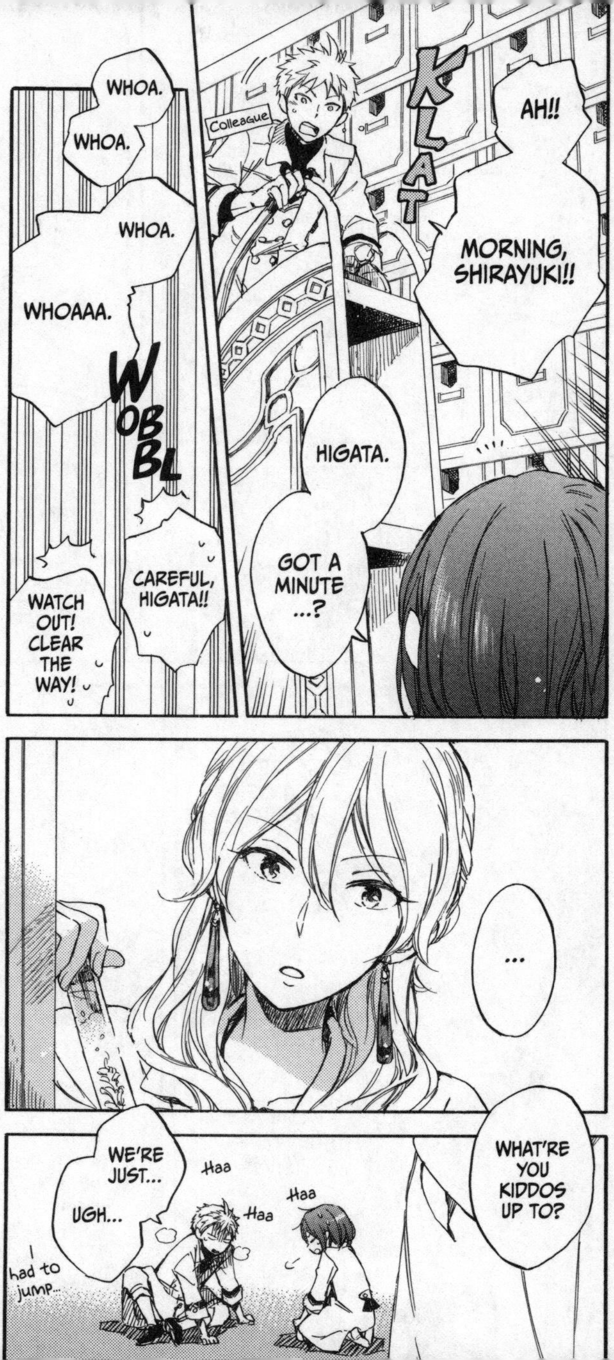
AH!!
MORNING, SHIRAYUKI!!
KLAT
Colleague
HIGATA.
GOT A MINUTE ...?
WHOA.
WHOA.
WHOA.
WHOAAA.
WOBBL
CAREFUL, HIGATA!!
WATCH OUT! CLEAR THE WAY!
...
WHAT'RE YOU KIDDOS UP TO?
WE'RE JUST...
Haa
Haa
Haa
UGH...
I had to jump...

4

TRIP, PART 3

-A digital camera that ran out of juice

-A night cruise featuring the beautiful sights of Hungary

-A sublime library in Vienna

-A group of foreigners who, surprisingly, started singing behind us while visiting the royal palace

-Salty things

-Apple-flavored chocolate chips

-Our set greeting to each other each morning: "How's that rough draft coming along?"

-The potato chips Hachi simply had to buy on this trip

-The muscle soreness Hibiki experienced after playing a game on the airplane

-Truly blue skies

-The guide who only wanted to talk to us about Japanese TV shows

-The Fanta soda I received after ordering orange juice

-A mountain of meat we couldn't possibly finish

-A cheery live performance by some old men

-Oh wait—that was actually a really well-made Czech cuckoo clock

wheeze *wheeze*

My trip to Central Europe was a lot of fun!

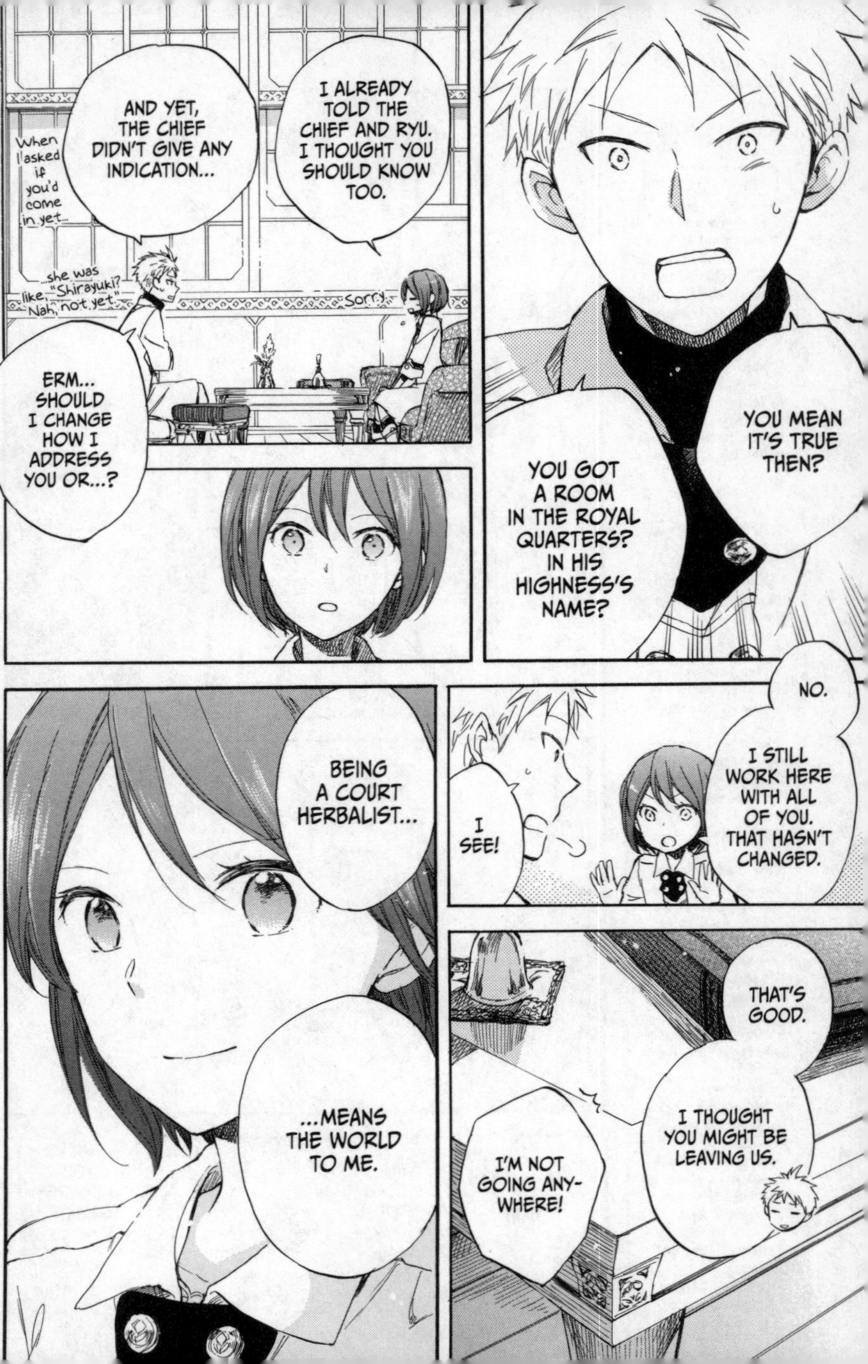
YOU MEAN IT'S TRUE THEN?
YOU GOT A ROOM IN THE ROYAL QUARTERS? IN HIS HIGHNESS'S NAME?
I ALREADY TOLD THE CHIEF AND RYU. I THOUGHT YOU SHOULD KNOW TOO.
AND YET, THE CHIEF DIDN'T GIVE ANY INDICATION...
When I asked if you'd come in yet...
...she was like, "Shirayuki? Nah, not yet."
Sorry.
ERM... SHOULD I CHANGE HOW I ADDRESS YOU OR...?
NO.
I STILL WORK HERE WITH ALL OF YOU. THAT HASN'T CHANGED.
I SEE!
THAT'S GOOD.
I THOUGHT YOU MIGHT BE LEAVING US.
I'M NOT GOING ANY-WHERE!
BEING A COURT HERBALIST...
...MEANS THE WORLD TO ME.

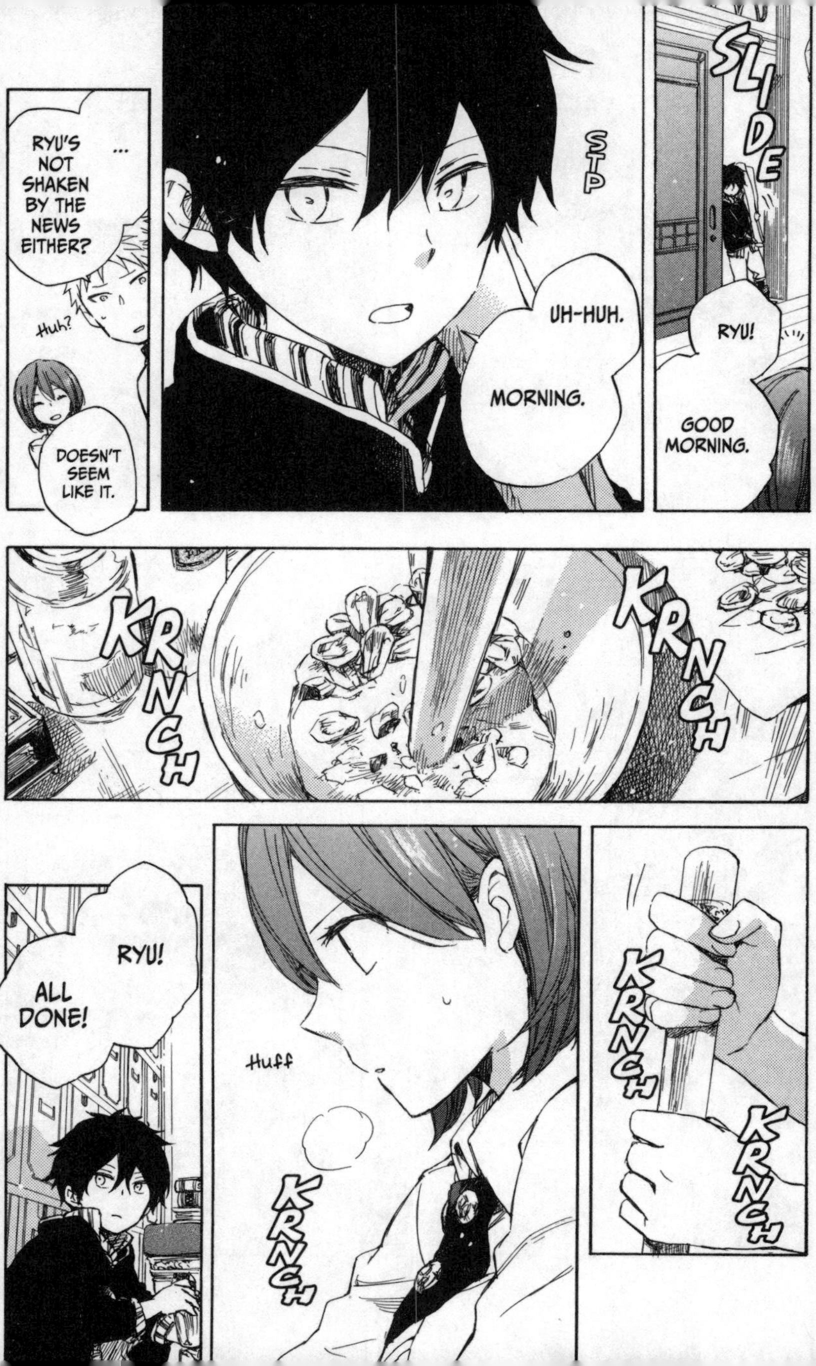
SLIDE
RYU!
GOOD MORNING.
STP
UH-HUH.
MORNING.
...
RYU'S NOT SHAKEN BY THE NEWS EITHER?
Huh?
DOESN'T SEEM LIKE IT.
KRNCH
KRNCH
KRNCH
KRNCH
Huff
KRNCH
RYU!
ALL DONE!

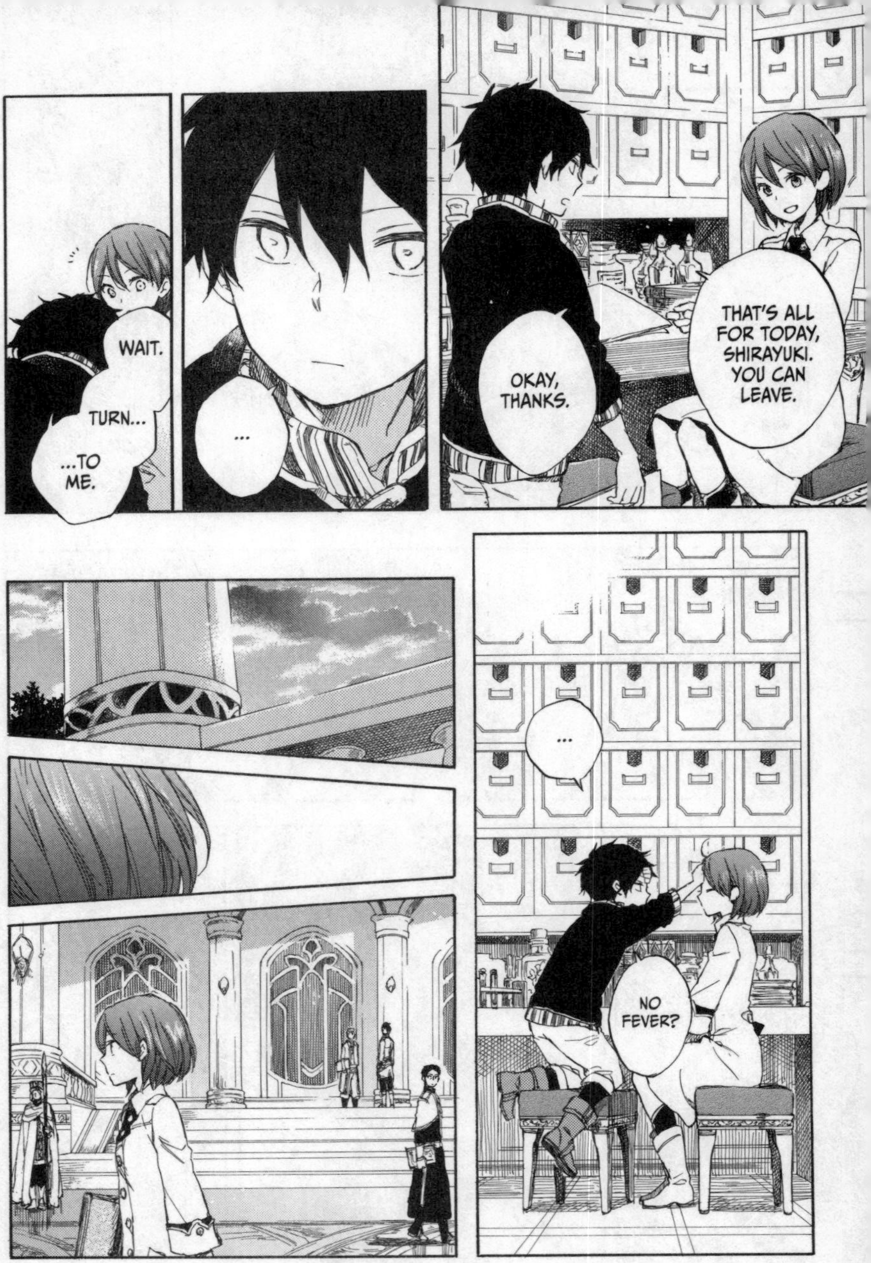
THAT'S ALL FOR TODAY, SHIRAYUKI. YOU CAN LEAVE.
OKAY, THANKS.
...
WAIT.
TURN...
...TO ME.
...
NO FEVER?

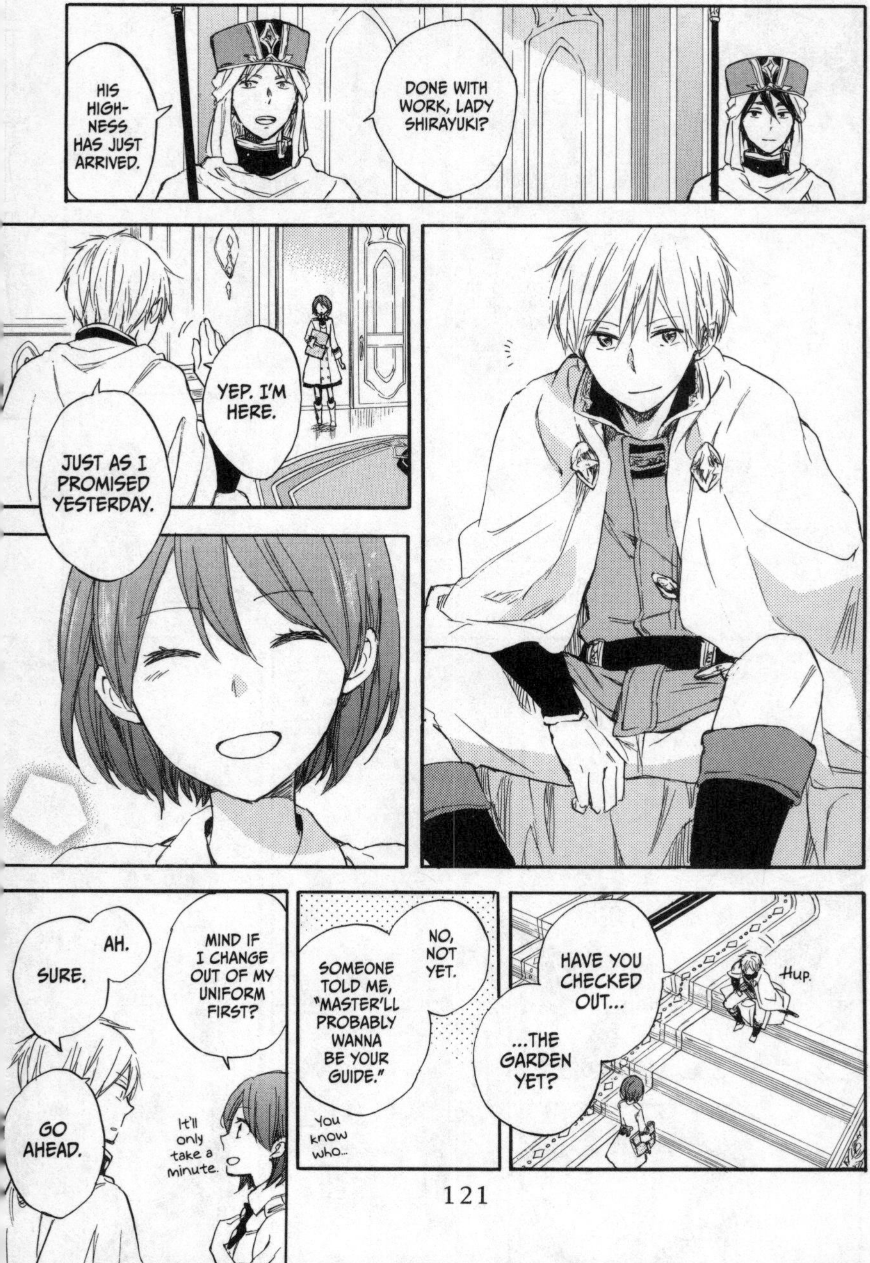
DONE WITH WORK, LADY SHIRAYUKI?
HIS HIGHNESS HAS JUST ARRIVED.
YEP. I'M HERE.
JUST AS I PROMISED YESTERDAY.
HAVE YOU CHECKED OUT...
...THE GARDEN YET?
Hup.
NO, NOT YET.
SOMEONE TOLD ME, "MASTER'LL PROBABLY WANNA BE YOUR GUIDE."
You know who...
MIND IF I CHANGE OUT OF MY UNIFORM FIRST?
It'll only take a minute.
AH.
SURE.
GO AHEAD.

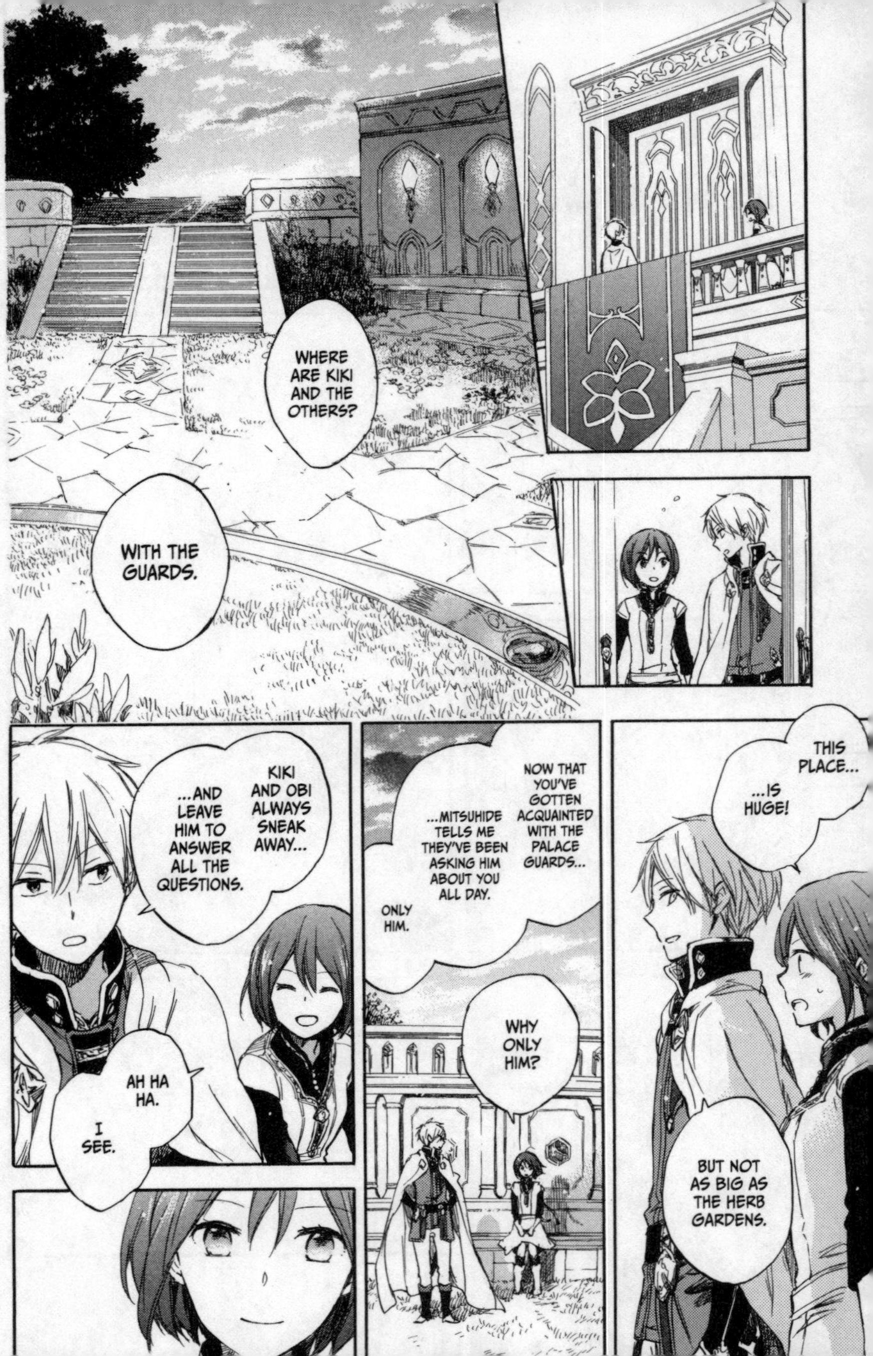
WHERE ARE KIKI AND THE OTHERS?
WITH THE GUARDS.
THIS PLACE...
...IS HUGE!
BUT NOT AS BIG AS THE HERB GARDENS.
NOW THAT YOU'VE GOTTEN ACQUAINTED WITH THE PALACE GUARDS...
...MITSUHIDE TELLS ME THEY'VE BEEN ASKING HIM ABOUT YOU ALL DAY.
ONLY HIM.
WHY ONLY HIM?
KIKI AND OBI ALWAYS SNEAK AWAY...
...AND LEAVE HIM TO ANSWER ALL THE QUESTIONS.
AH HA HA.
I SEE.

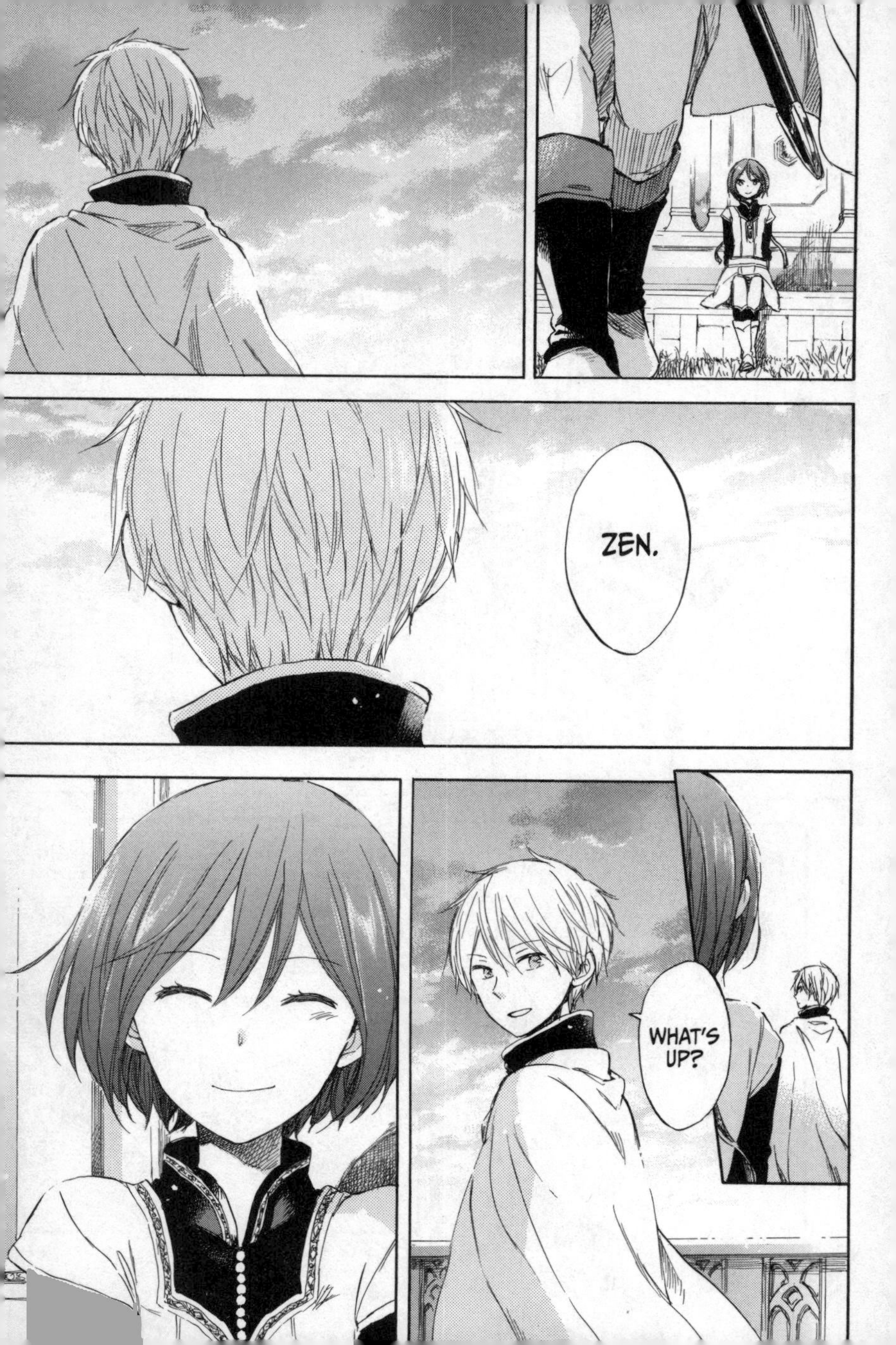
ZEN.
WHAT'S UP?

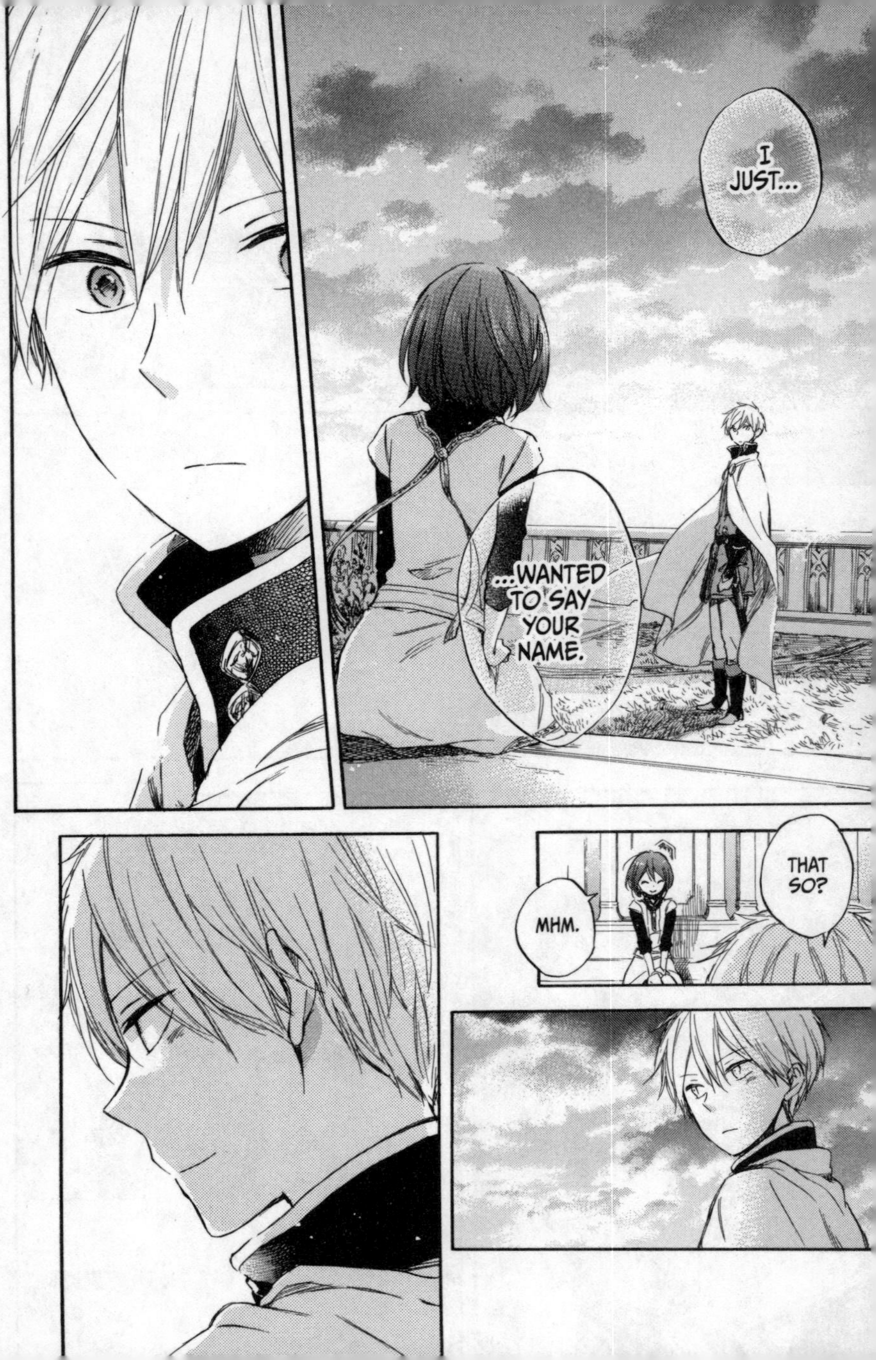
I JUST...
...WANTED TO SAY YOUR NAME.
THAT SO?
MHM.

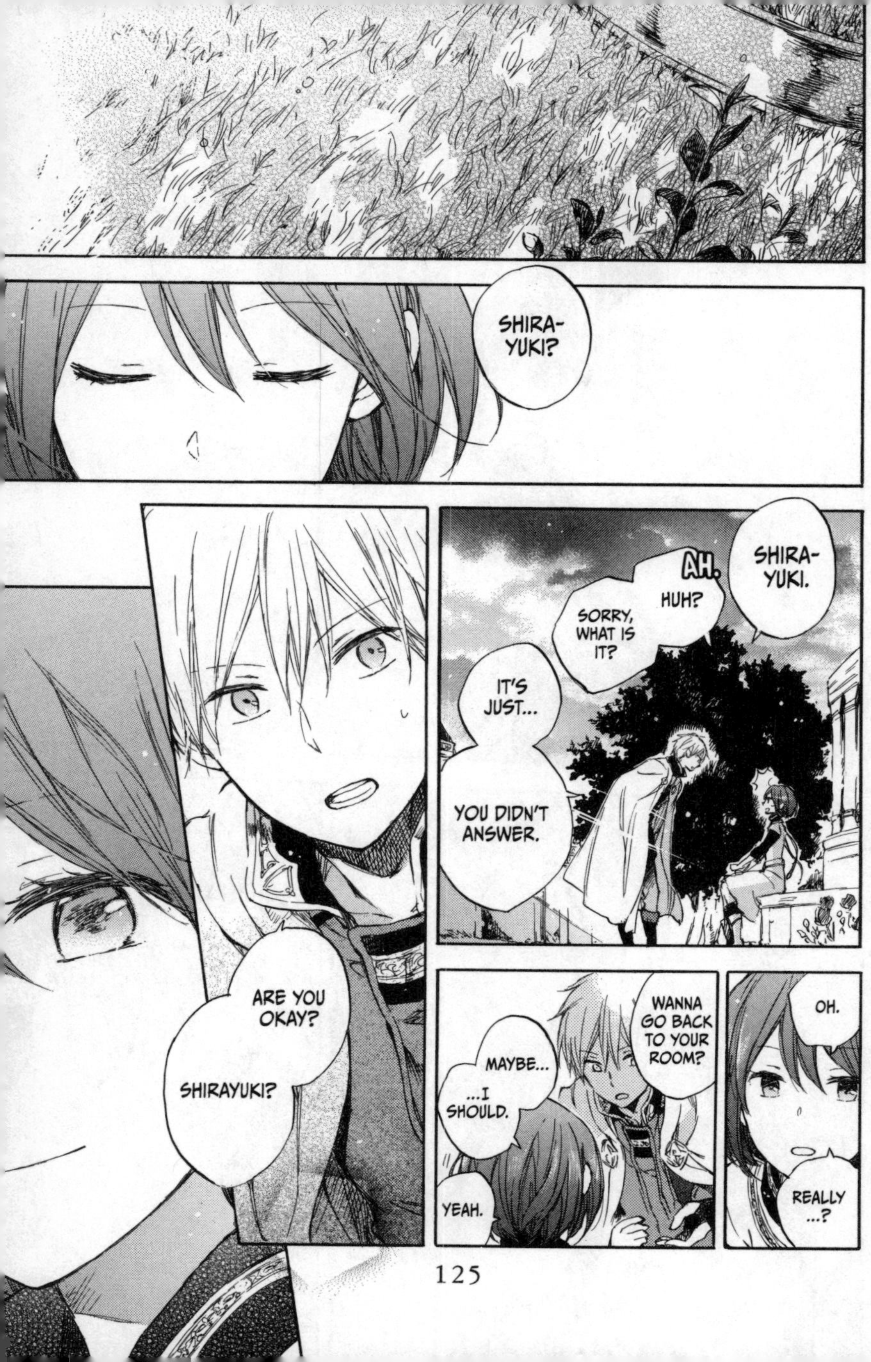
SHIRA-YUKI?
SHIRA-YUKI.
AH.
HUH?
SORRY, WHAT IS IT?
IT'S JUST...
YOU DIDN'T ANSWER.
OH.
REALLY ...?
WANNA GO BACK TO YOUR ROOM?
MAYBE...
...I SHOULD.
YEAH.
ARE YOU OKAY?
SHIRAYUKI?

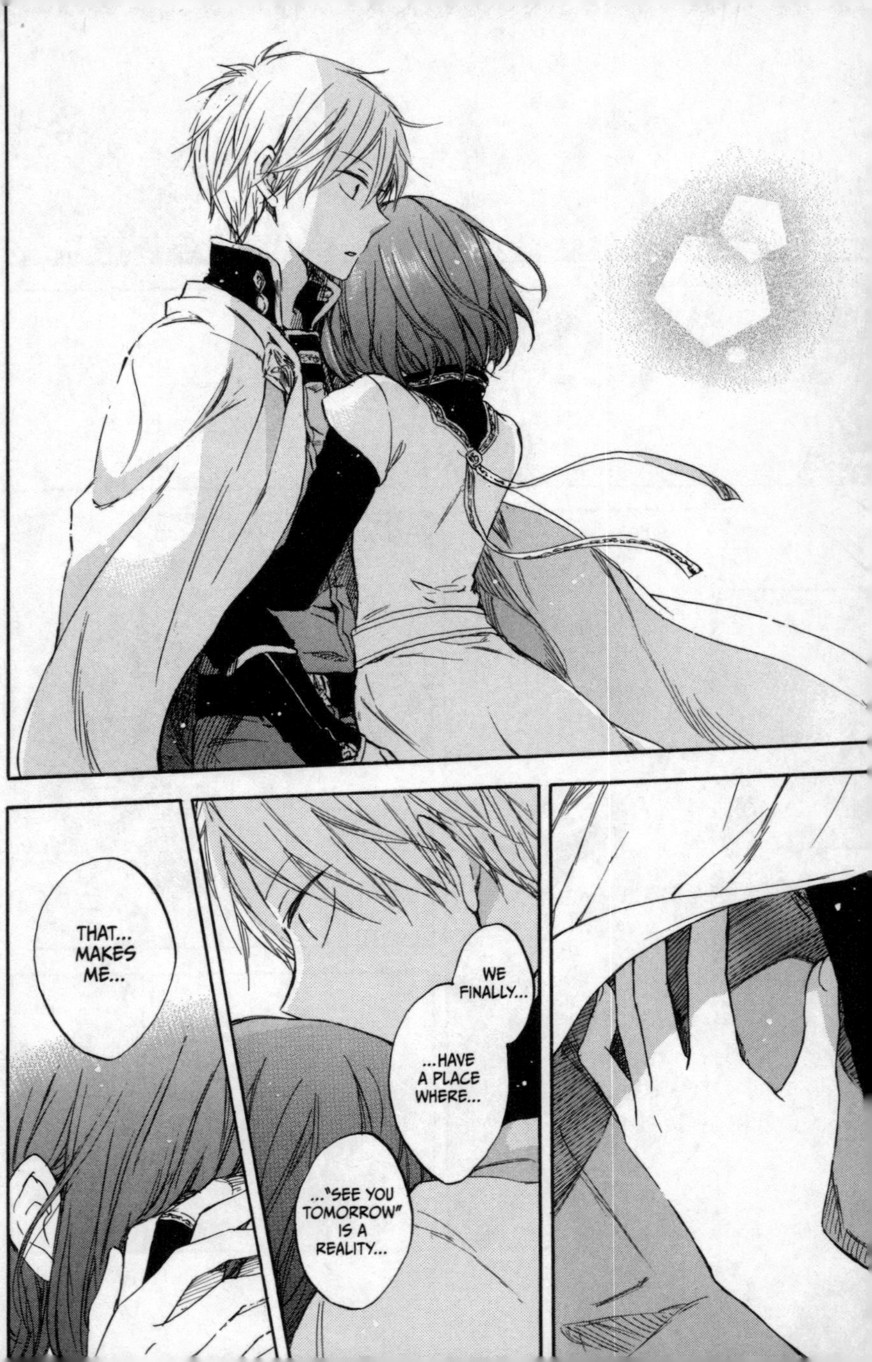
WE FINALLY...
...HAVE A PLACE WHERE...
..."SEE YOU TOMORROW" IS A REALITY...
THAT... MAKES ME...

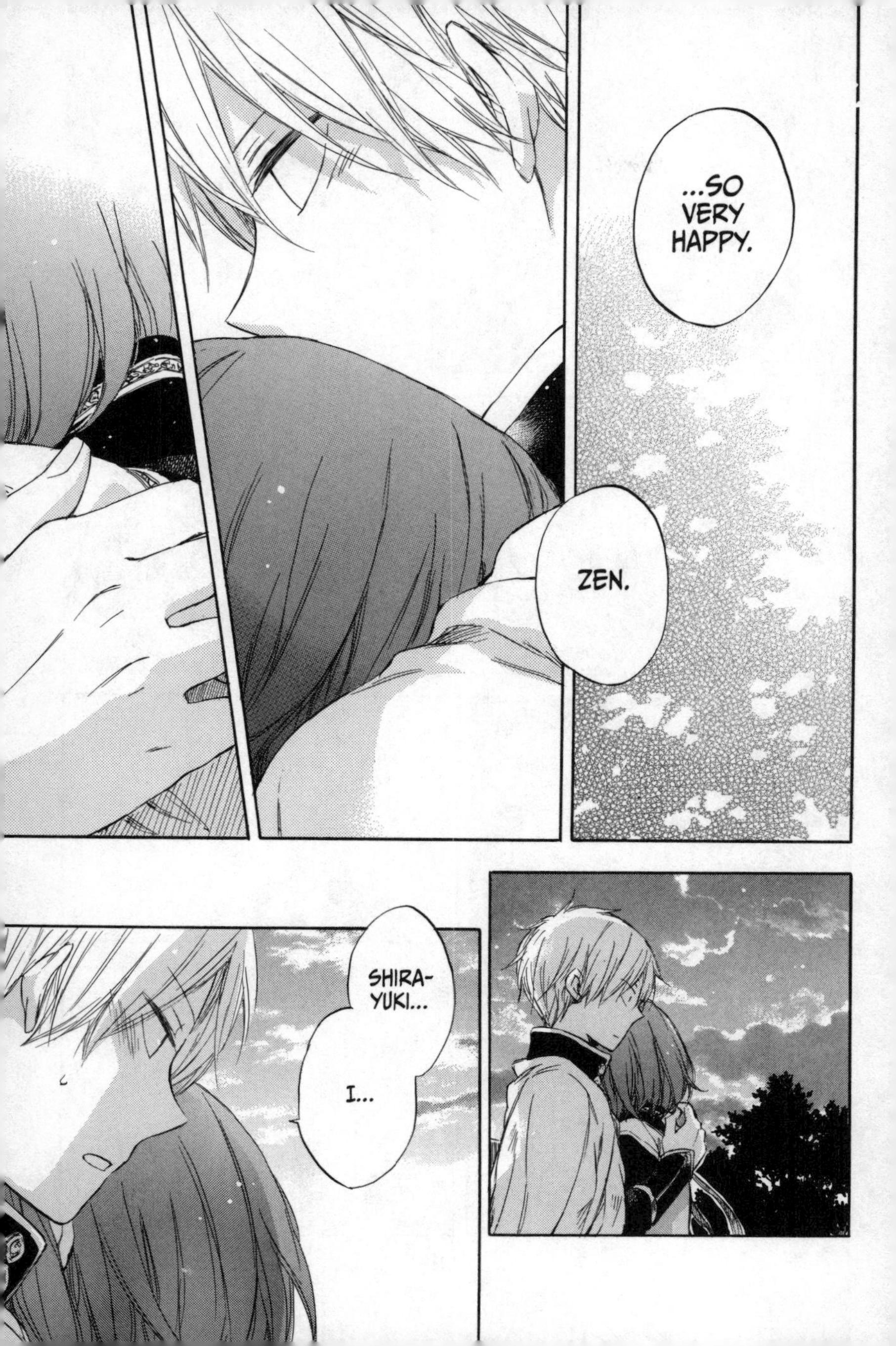
...SO VERY HAPPY.
ZEN.
SHIRA-YUKI...
I...

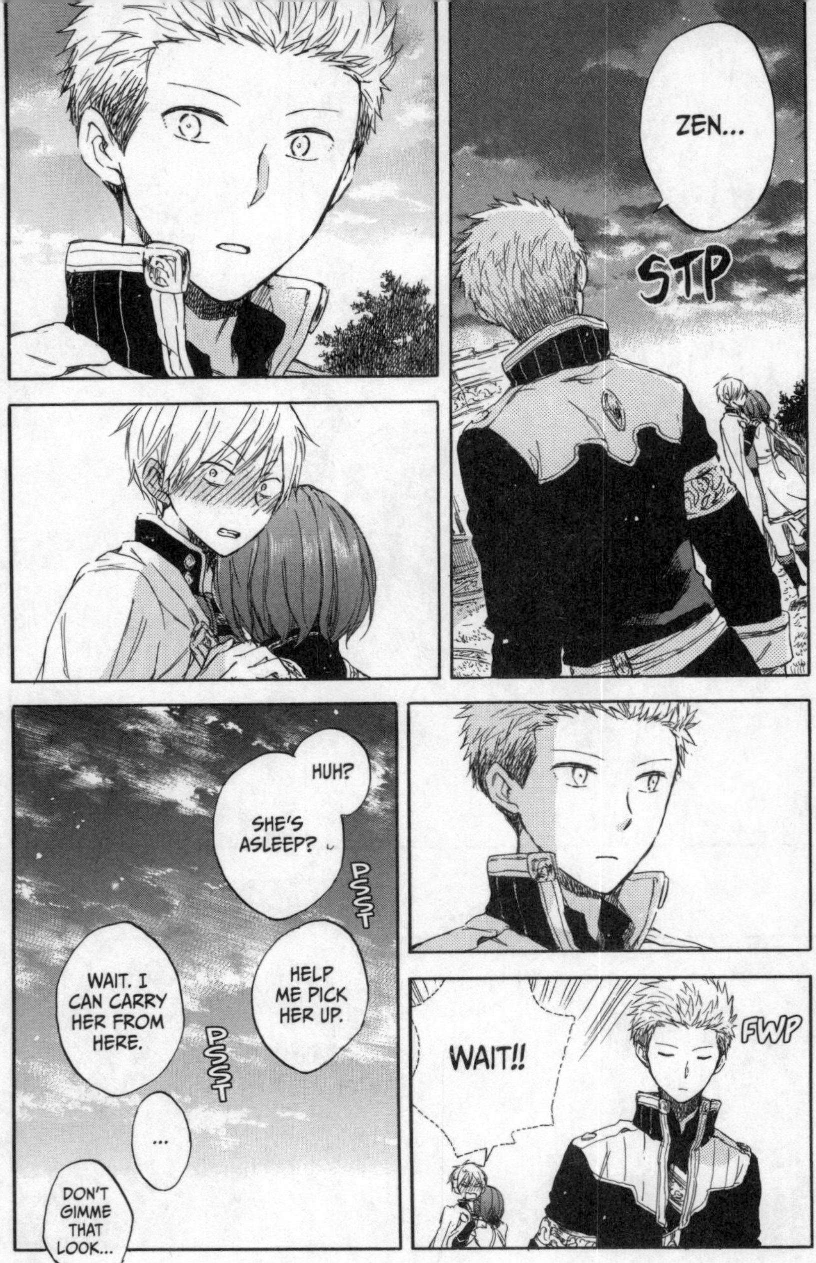
ZEN...
STP
WAIT!!
FWP
HUH?
SHE'S ASLEEP?
PSST
HELP ME PICK HER UP.
WAIT. I CAN CARRY HER FROM HERE.
PSST
...
DON'T GIMME THAT LOOK...

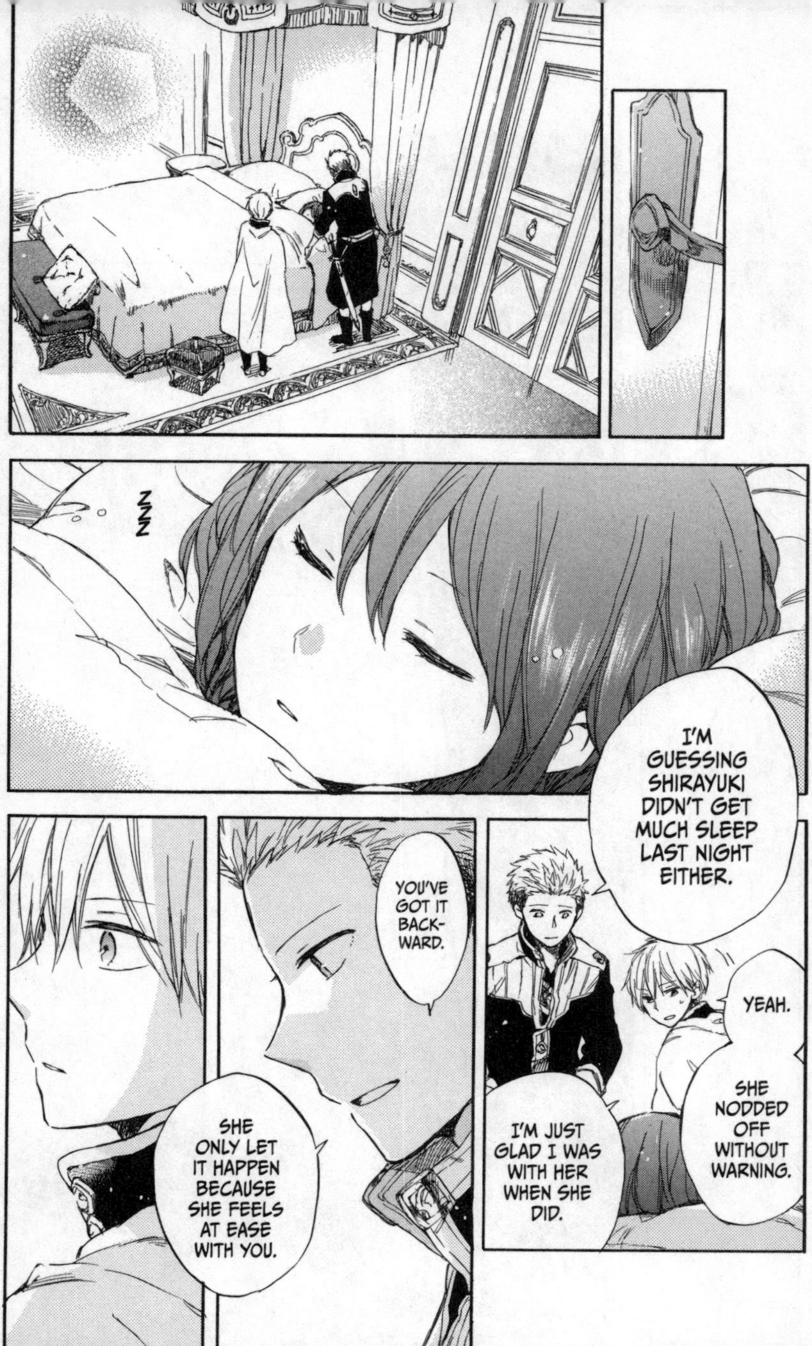
ZZZ
I'M GUESSING SHIRAYUKI DIDN'T GET MUCH SLEEP LAST NIGHT EITHER.
YEAH.
SHE NODDED OFF WITHOUT WARNING.
I'M JUST GLAD I WAS WITH HER WHEN SHE DID.
YOU'VE GOT IT BACK-WARD.
SHE ONLY LET IT HAPPEN BECAUSE SHE FEELS AT EASE WITH YOU.

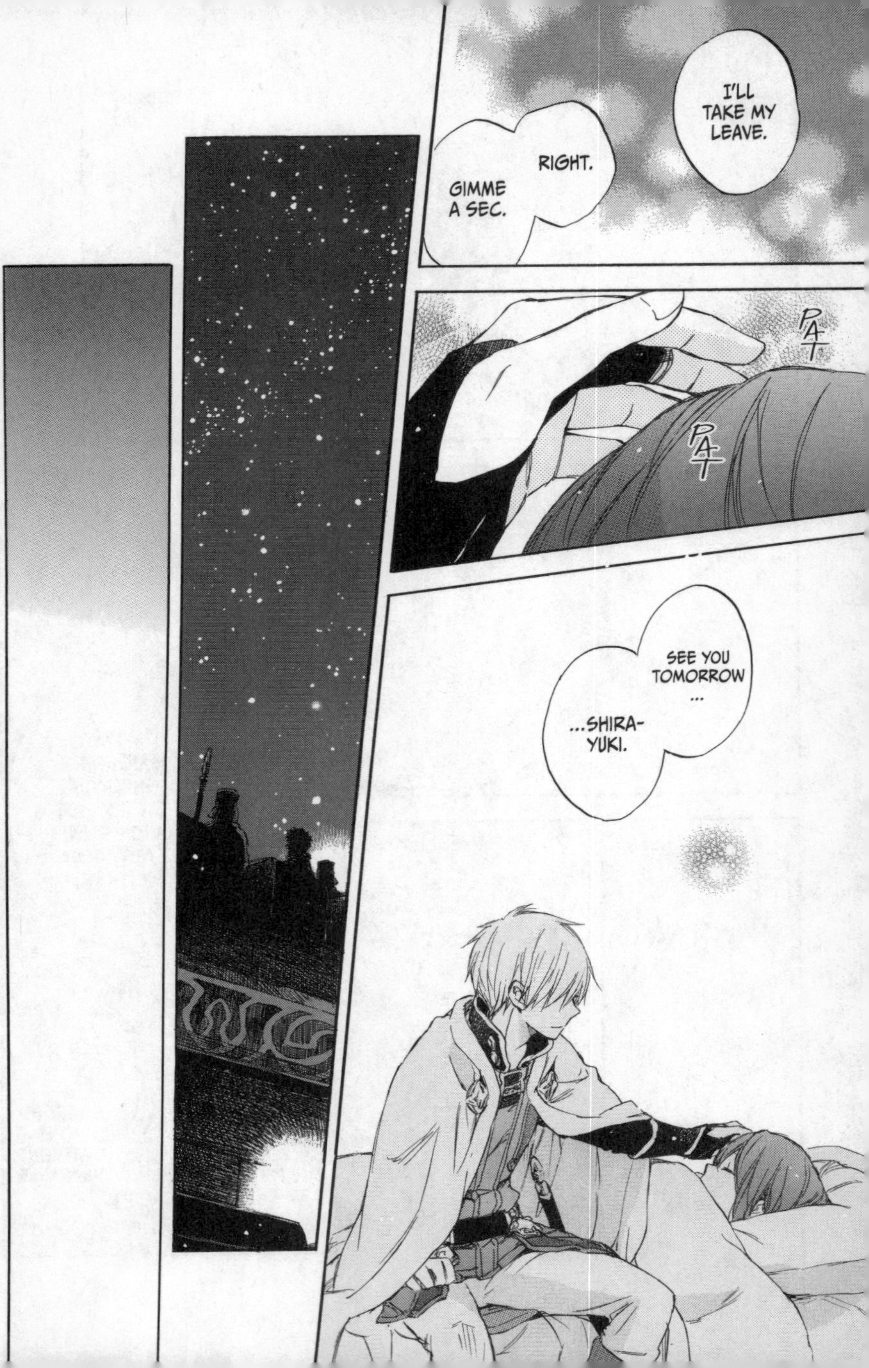
I'LL TAKE MY LEAVE.
RIGHT. GIMME A SEC.
PAT
PAT
SEE YOU TOMORROW ... ...SHIRA-YUKI.

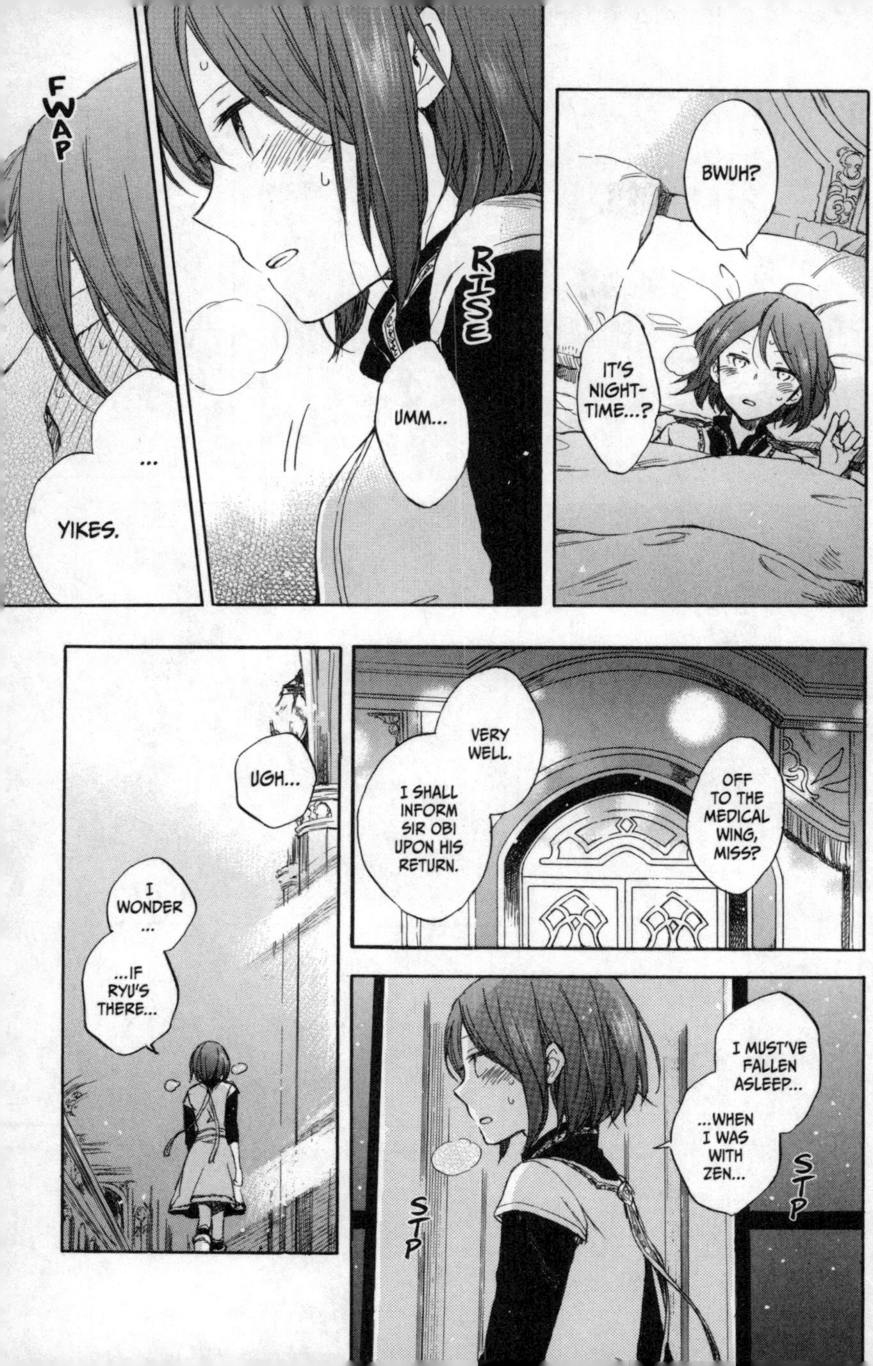
BWUH?
IT'S NIGHT-TIME...?
RISE
UMM...
FWAP
...
YIKES.
OFF TO THE MEDICAL WING, MISS?
VERY WELL.
I SHALL INFORM SIR OBI UPON HIS RETURN.
I MUST'VE FALLEN ASLEEP...
...WHEN I WAS WITH ZEN...
STP
STP
UGH...
I WONDER...
...IF RYU'S THERE...

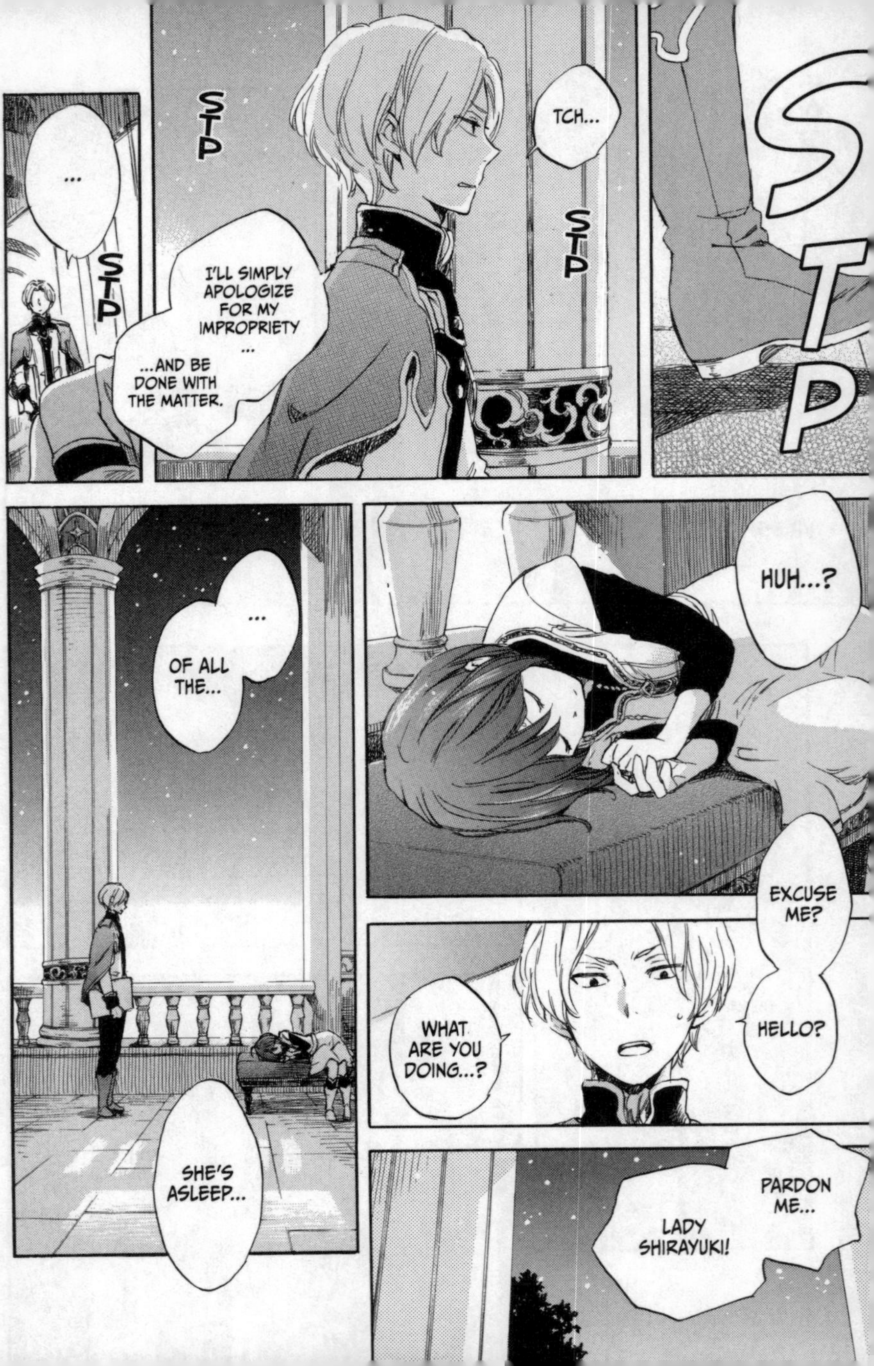
STP
TCH...
STP
STP
I'LL SIMPLY APOLOGIZE FOR MY IMPROPRIETY...
...AND BE DONE WITH THE MATTER.
...
STP
HUH...?
EXCUSE ME?
HELLO?
WHAT ARE YOU DOING...?
PARDON ME...
LADY SHIRAYUKI!
...
OF ALL THE...
SHE'S ASLEEP...

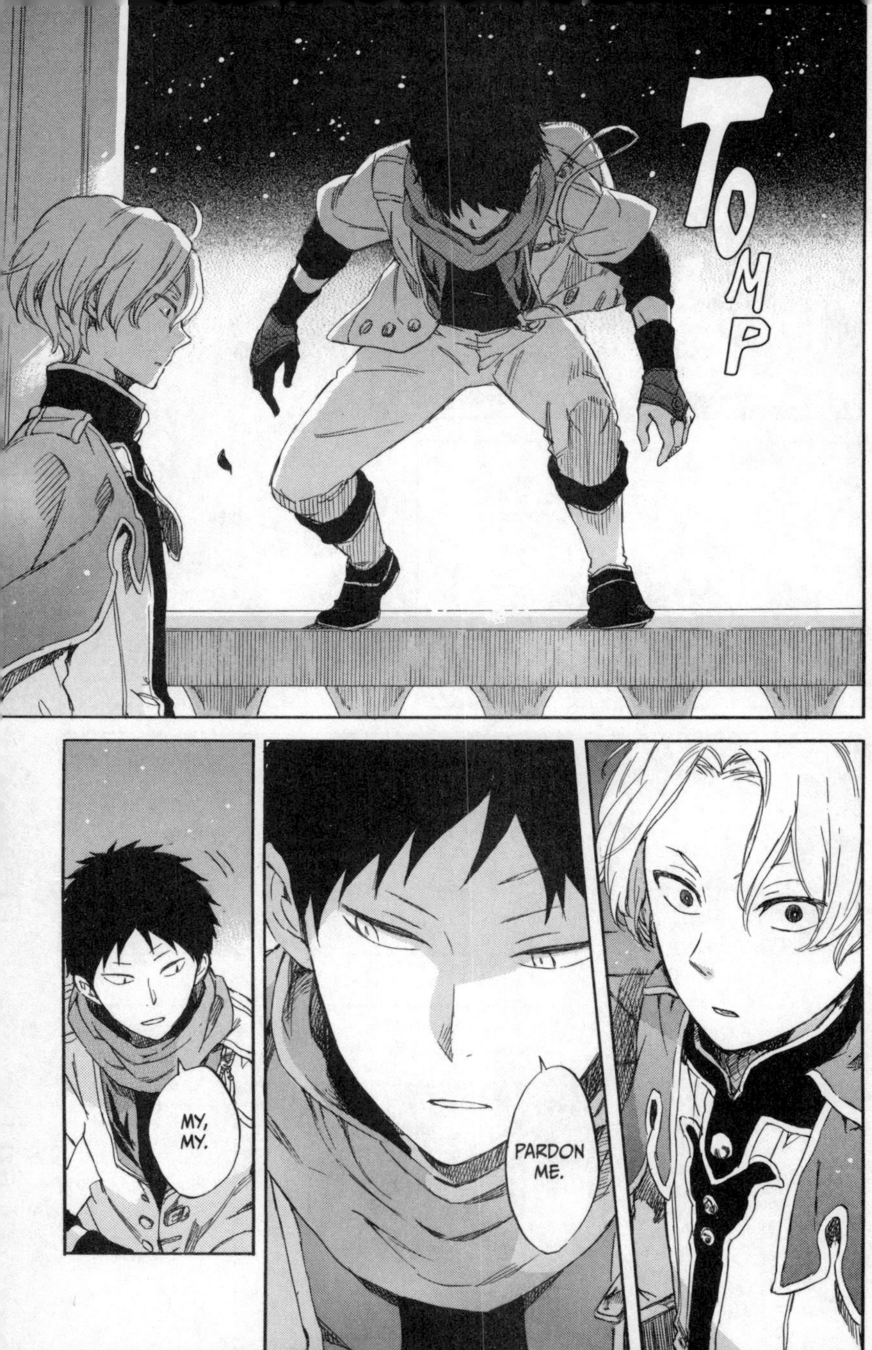
TOMP
PARDON ME.
MY, MY.

A FEVER? HUH?

THOUGHT I'D MAKE IT...

...TO MEDICAL...

COULDN'T MANAGE, HUH?

I gotcha.

MY LADY!

!

UGH...

OBI...

G-GOOD. IT'S YOU.

ME? NO.

DID YOU HAVE BUSINESS WITH MY LADY?

AND YOU...

I WAS PASSING BY AND DISCOVERED HER IN THAT STATE.

Ugh...

I'd best be off.

OH.

TOMP

TOMP

WHAT'S GOING ON?

SIR OBI?

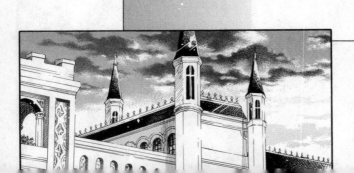

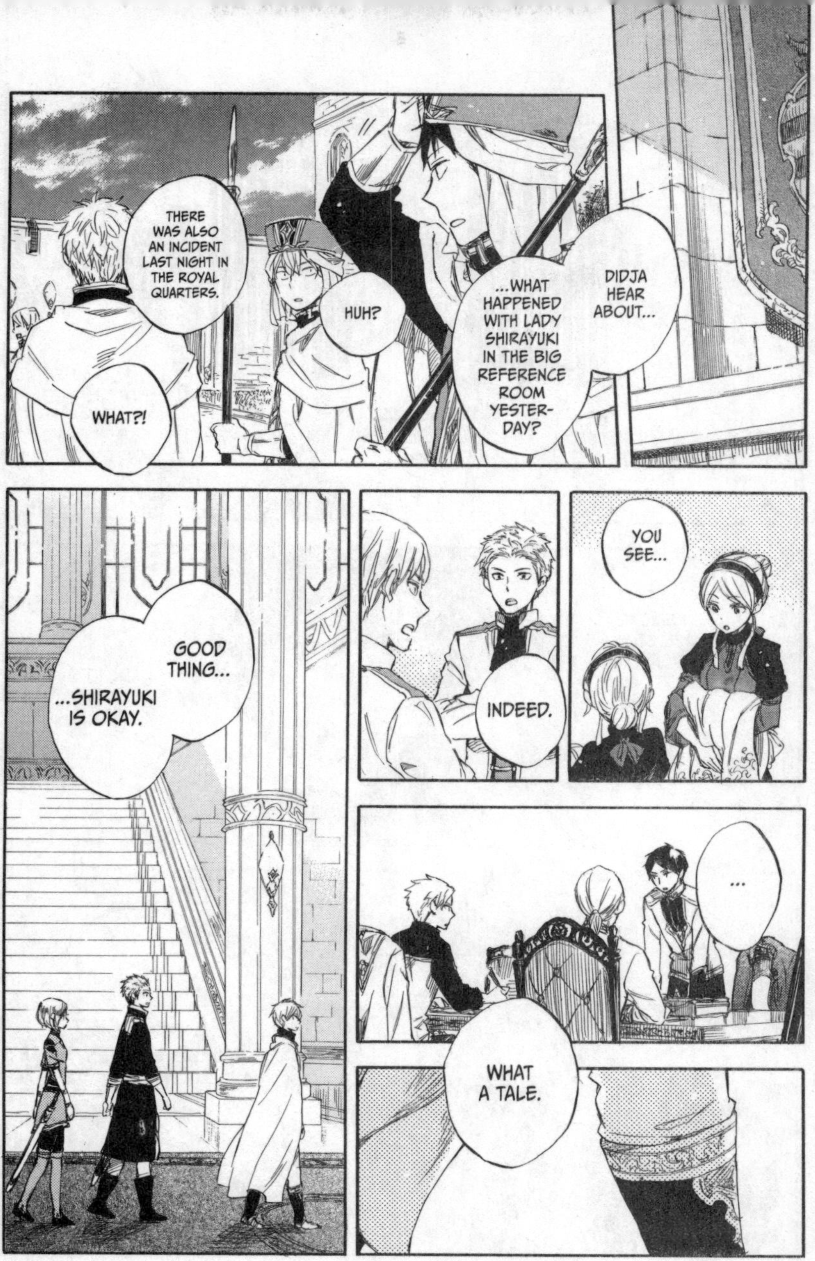

DIDJA HEAR ABOUT...
...WHAT HAPPENED WITH LADY SHIRAYUKI IN THE BIG REFERENCE ROOM YESTER-DAY?
HUH?
THERE WAS ALSO AN INCIDENT LAST NIGHT IN THE ROYAL QUARTERS.
WHAT?!
YOU SEE...
INDEED.
...
WHAT A TALE.
GOOD THING...
...SHIRAYUKI IS OKAY.

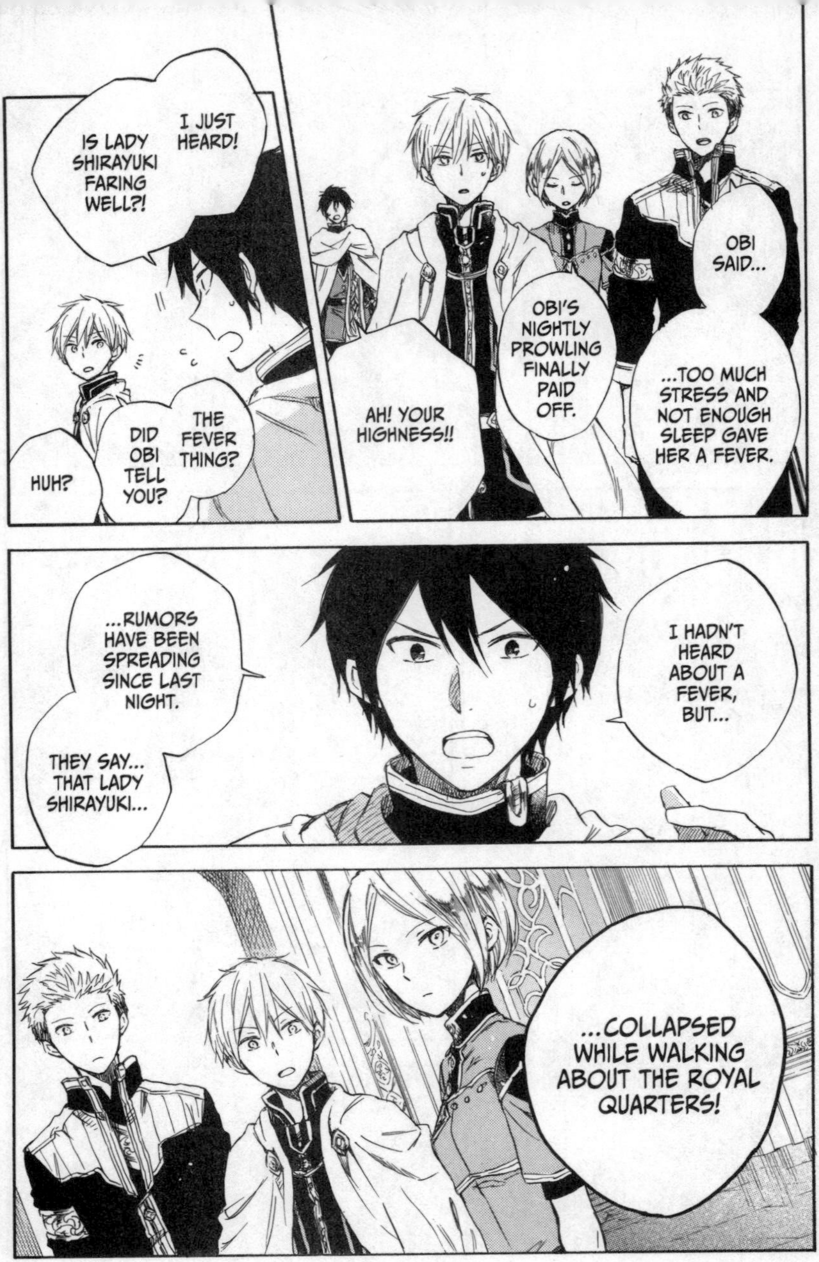
OBI SAID...
...TOO MUCH STRESS AND NOT ENOUGH SLEEP GAVE HER A FEVER.
OBI'S NIGHTLY PROWLING FINALLY PAID OFF.
AH! YOUR HIGHNESS!!
I JUST HEARD!
IS LADY SHIRAYUKI FARING WELL?!
THE FEVER THING?
DID OBI TELL YOU?
HUH?
I HADN'T HEARD ABOUT A FEVER, BUT...
...RUMORS HAVE BEEN SPREADING SINCE LAST NIGHT.
THEY SAY... THAT LADY SHIRAYUKI...
...COLLAPSED WHILE WALKING ABOUT THE ROYAL QUARTERS!

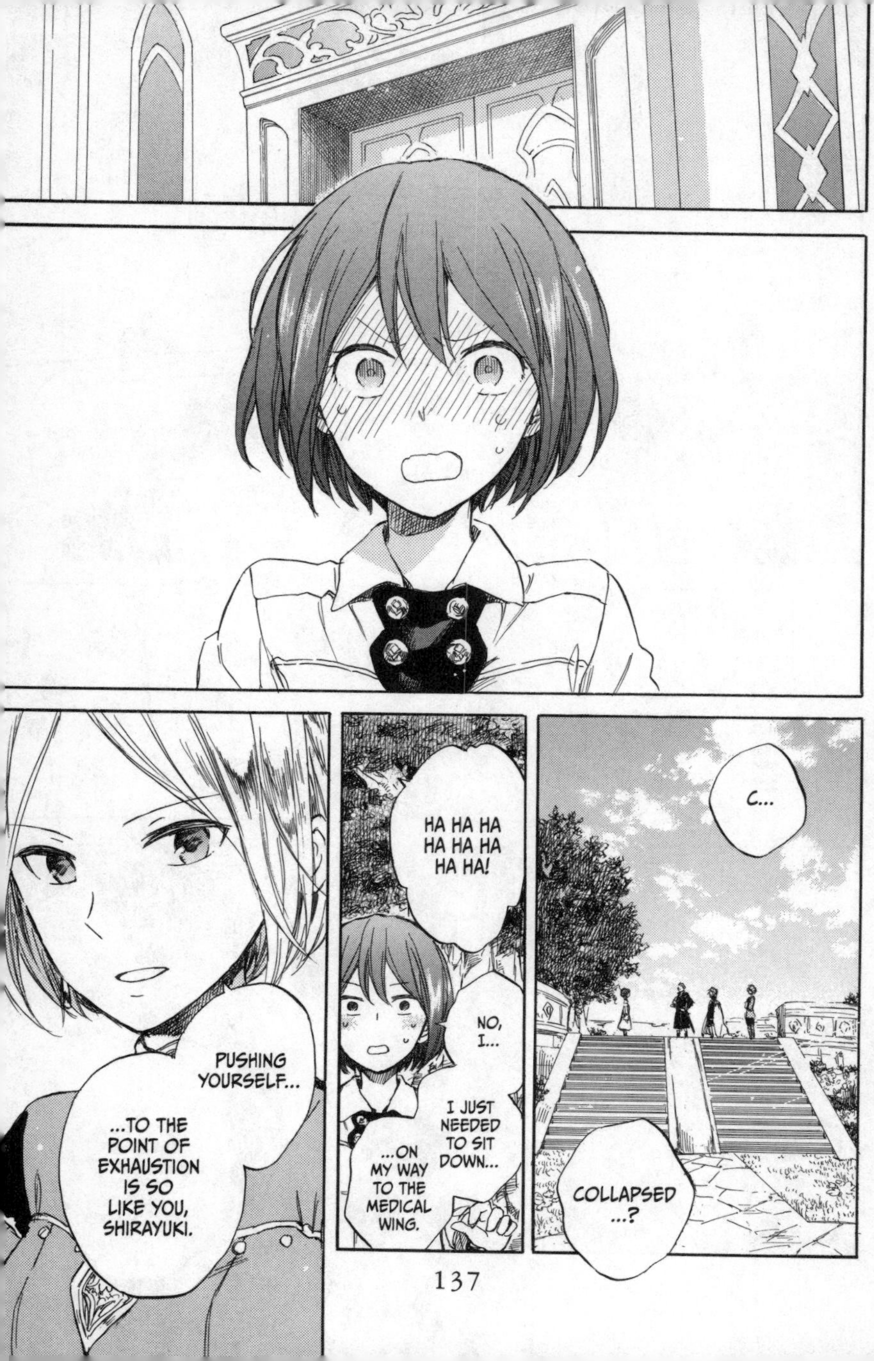
C...
COLLAPSED ...?
HA HA HA HA HA HA HA HA!
NO, I...
I JUST NEEDED TO SIT DOWN...
...ON MY WAY TO THE MEDICAL WING.
PUSHING YOURSELF...
...TO THE POINT OF EXHAUSTION IS SO LIKE YOU, SHIRAYUKI.

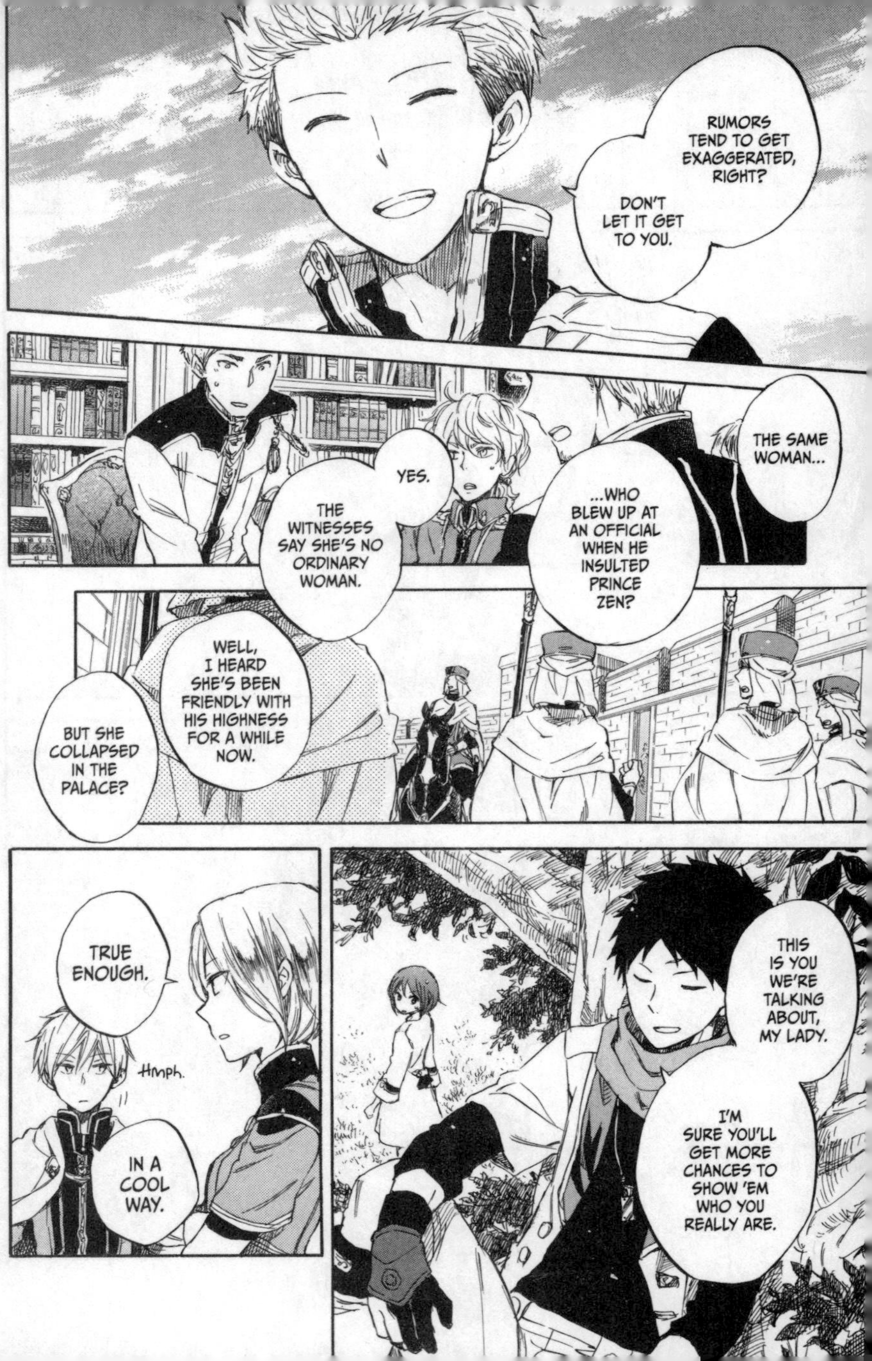
RUMORS TEND TO GET EXAGGERATED, RIGHT?
DON'T LET IT GET TO YOU.
THE SAME WOMAN...
...WHO BLEW UP AT AN OFFICIAL WHEN HE INSULTED PRINCE ZEN?
YES.
THE WITNESSES SAY SHE'S NO ORDINARY WOMAN.
WELL, I HEARD SHE'S BEEN FRIENDLY WITH HIS HIGHNESS FOR A WHILE NOW.
BUT SHE COLLAPSED IN THE PALACE?
THIS IS YOU WE'RE TALKING ABOUT, MY LADY.
I'M SURE YOU'LL GET MORE CHANCES TO SHOW 'EM WHO YOU REALLY ARE.
TRUE ENOUGH.
Hmph.
IN A COOL WAY.

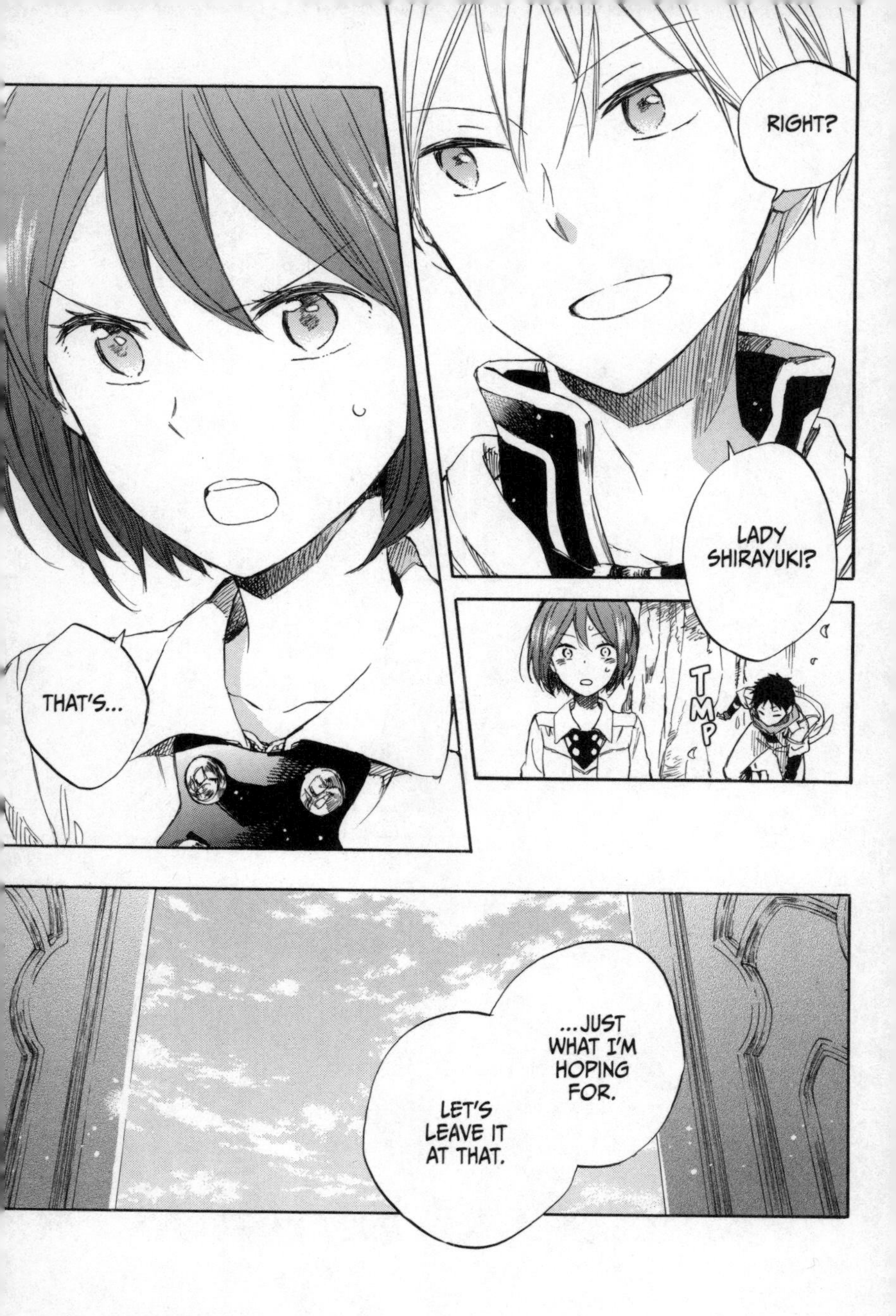
RIGHT?
LADY SHIRAYUKI?
TMP
THAT'S...
...JUST WHAT I'M HOPING FOR.
LET'S LEAVE IT AT THAT.

Chapter 49

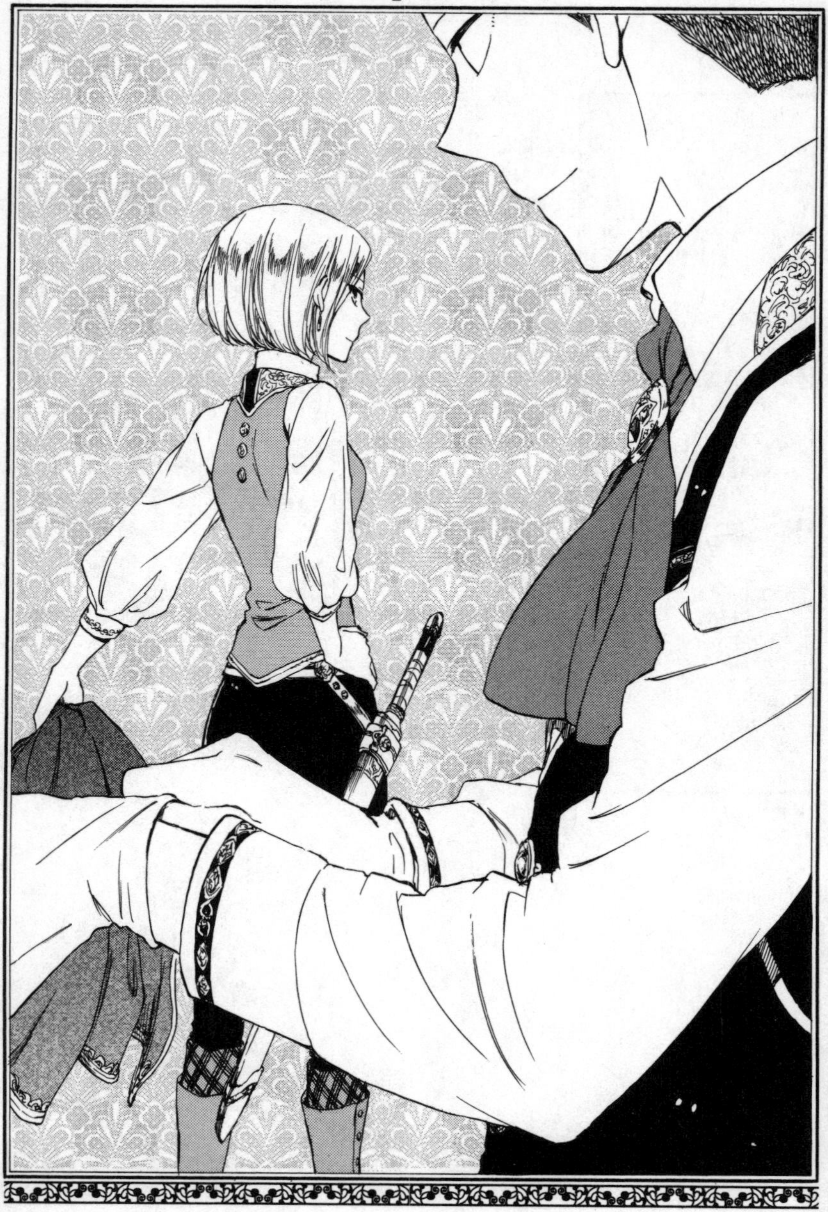

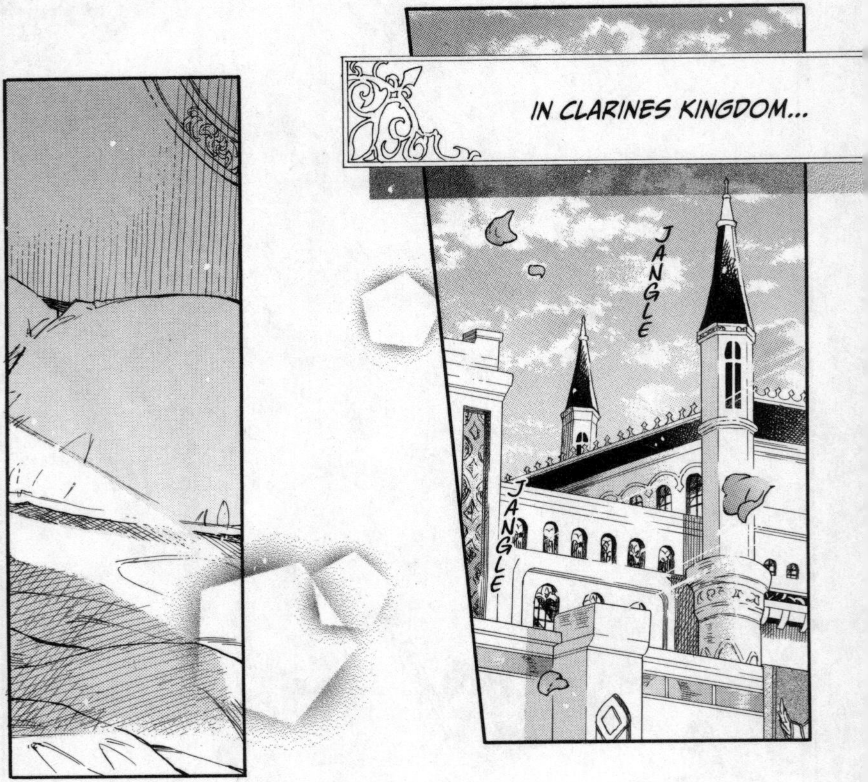
IN CLARINES KINGDOM...
JANGLE
JANGLE

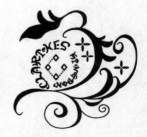

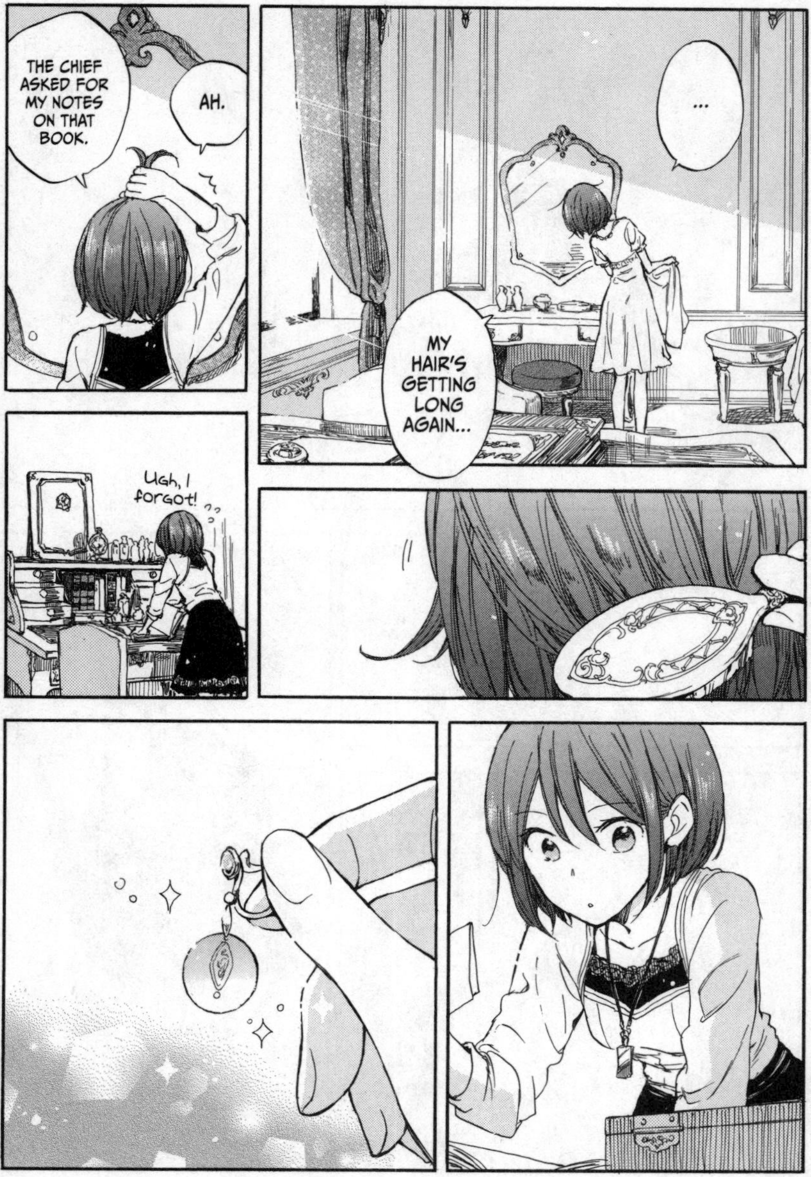
...
MY HAIR'S GETTING LONG AGAIN...
AH.
THE CHIEF ASKED FOR MY NOTES ON THAT BOOK.
Ugh, I forgot!

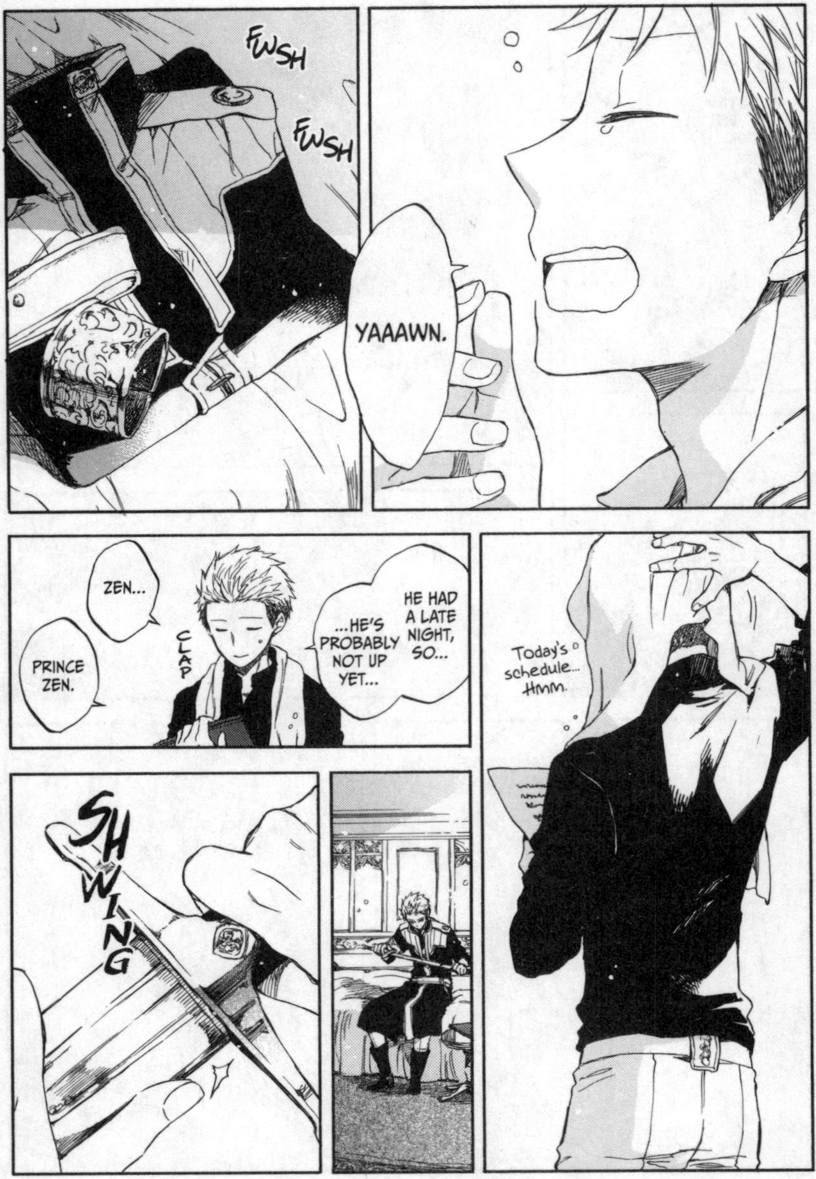
YAAAWN.
FWSH
FWSH
Today's schedule... Hmm.
HE HAD A LATE NIGHT, SO...
...HE'S PROBABLY NOT UP YET...
CLAP
ZEN...
PRINCE ZEN.
SHWING

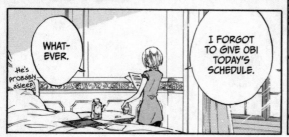

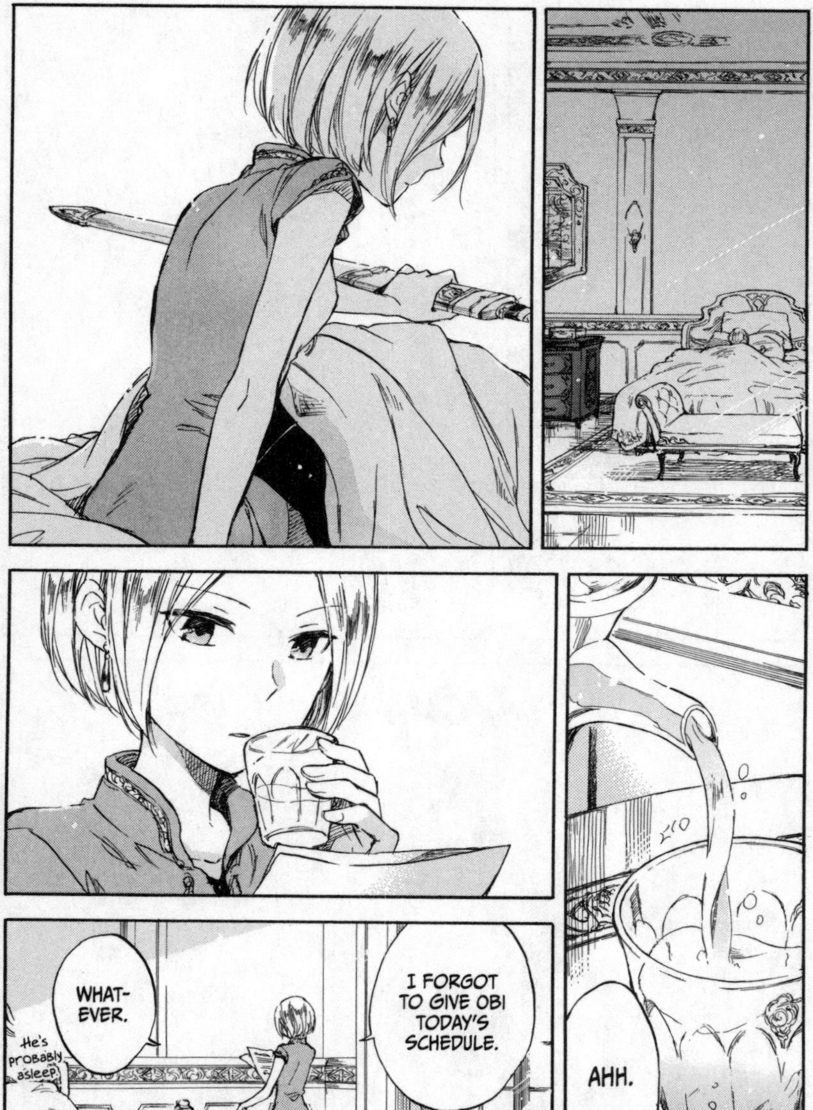
AHH.
I FORGOT TO GIVE OBI TODAY'S SCHEDULE.
WHAT-EVER.
He's probably asleep.

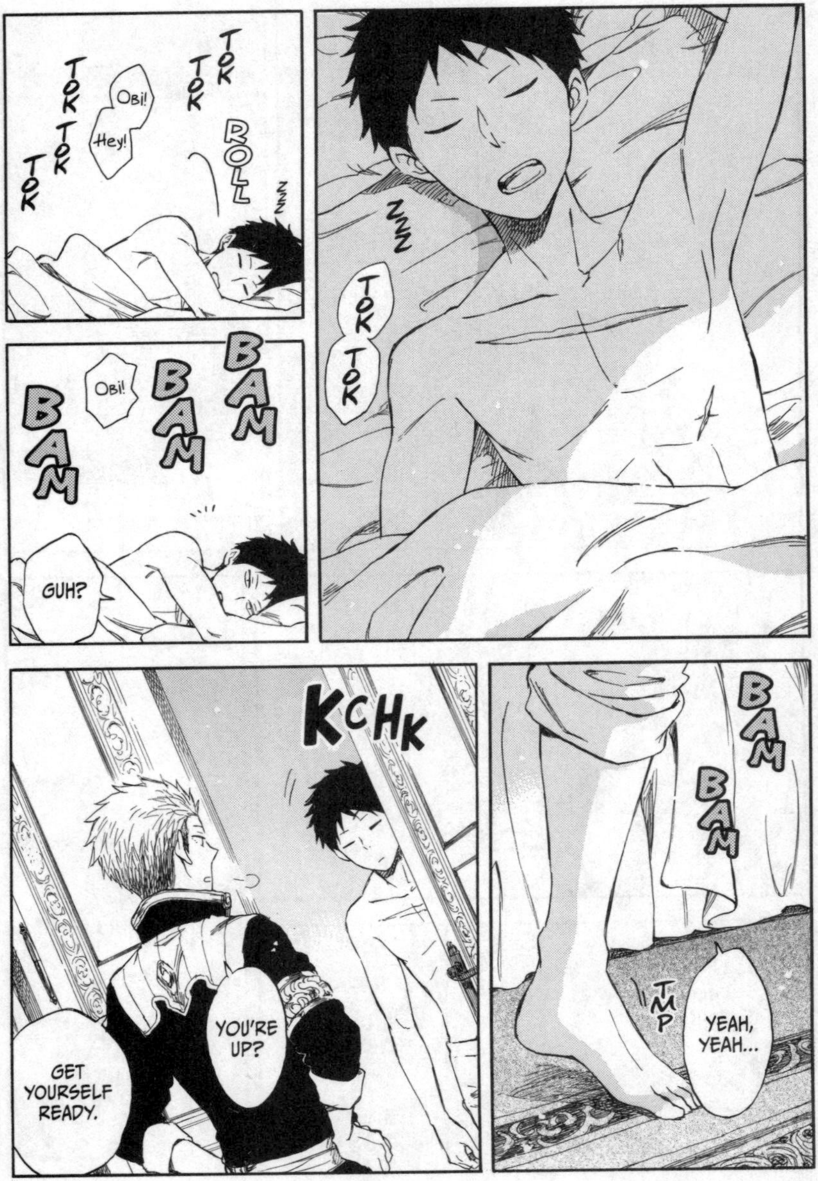
ZZZ
TOK TOK
TOK TOK TOK TOK TOK
Obi!
Hey!
ROLL
ZZZ
BAM BAM BAM
Obi!
GUH?
BAM BAM
TMP
YEAH, YEAH...
KCHK
YOU'RE UP?
GET YOURSELF READY.

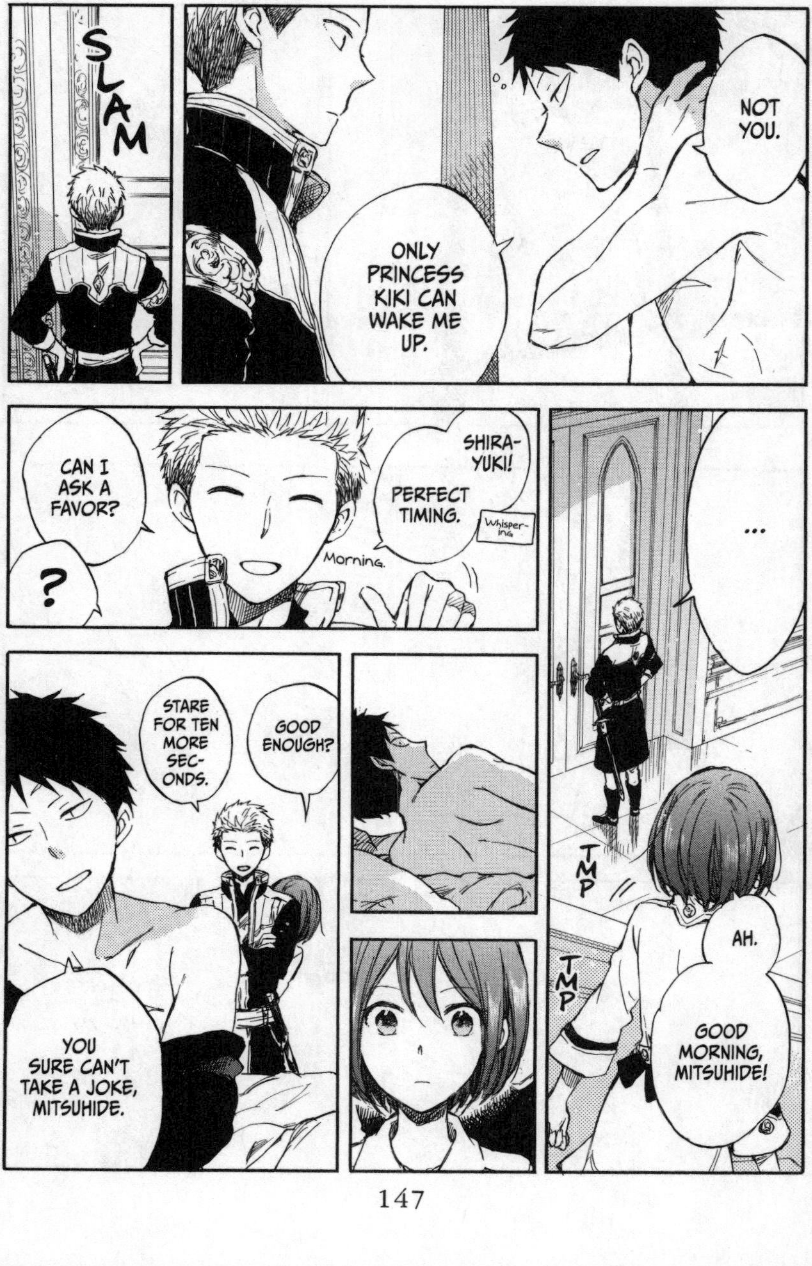
NOT YOU.
ONLY PRINCESS KIKI CAN WAKE ME UP.
SLAM
...
TMP
TMP
AH.
GOOD MORNING, MITSUHIDE!
SHIRA-YUKI!
PERFECT TIMING.
Whisper-ing
Morning.
CAN I ASK A FAVOR?
?
GOOD ENOUGH?
STARE FOR TEN MORE SEC-ONDS.
YOU SURE CAN'T TAKE A JOKE, MITSUHIDE.

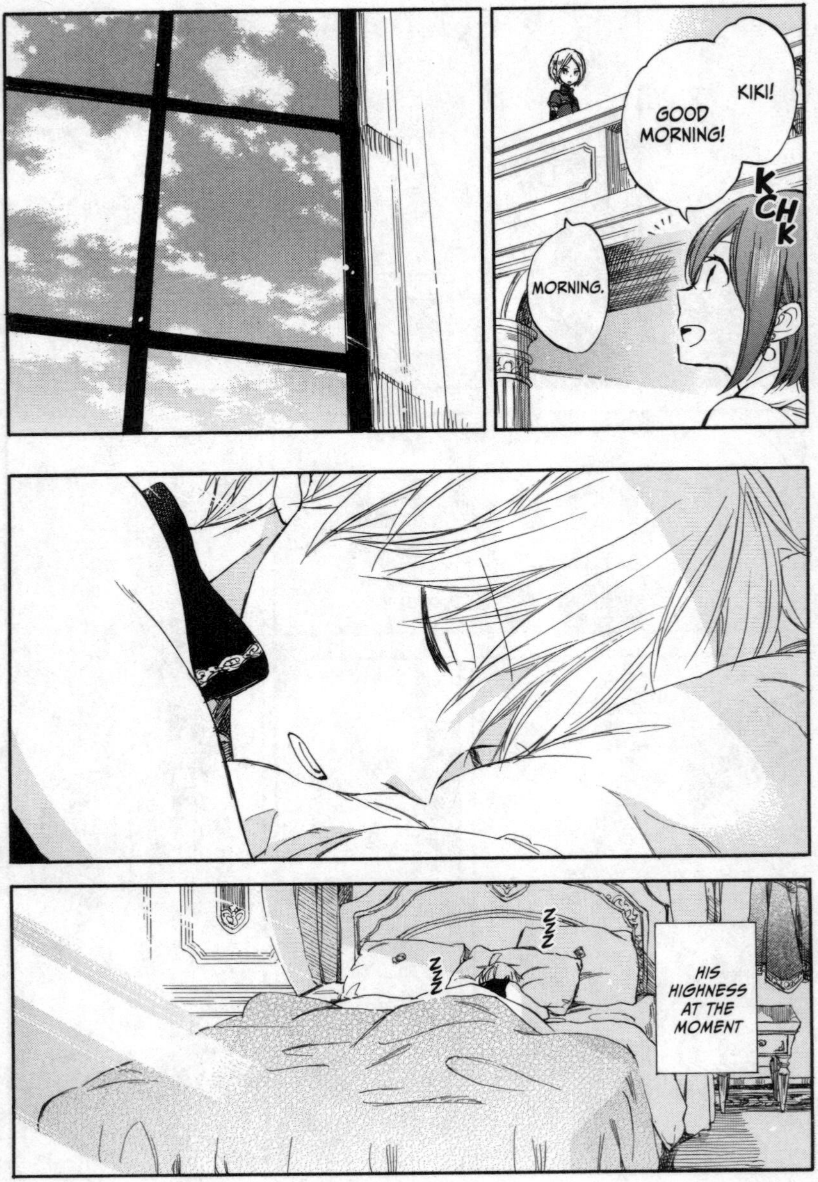
KIKI! GOOD MORNING!
KCHK
MORNING.
ZZZ
ZZZ
HIS HIGHNESS AT THE MOMENT

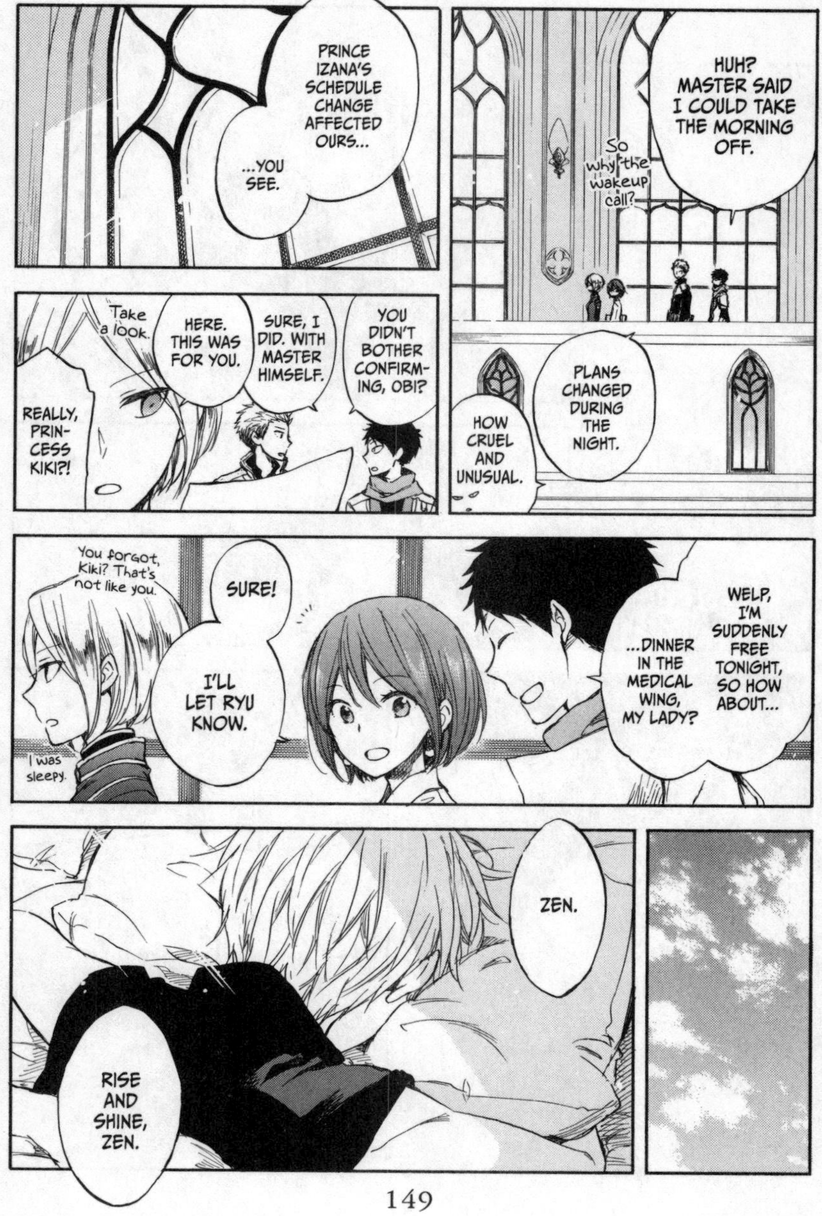
HUH? MASTER SAID I COULD TAKE THE MORNING OFF.
So why the wakeup call?
PLANS CHANGED DURING THE NIGHT.
HOW CRUEL AND UNUSUAL.
PRINCE IZANA'S SCHEDULE CHANGE AFFECTED OURS...
...YOU SEE.
YOU DIDN'T BOTHER CONFIRMING, OBI?
SURE, I DID. WITH MASTER HIMSELF.
HERE. THIS WAS FOR YOU.
Take a look.
REALLY, PRINCESS KIKI?!
WELP, I'M SUDDENLY FREE TONIGHT, SO HOW ABOUT...
...DINNER IN THE MEDICAL WING, MY LADY?
SURE!
I'LL LET RYU KNOW.
You forgot, Kiki? That's not like you.
I was sleepy.
ZEN.
RISE AND SHINE, ZEN.

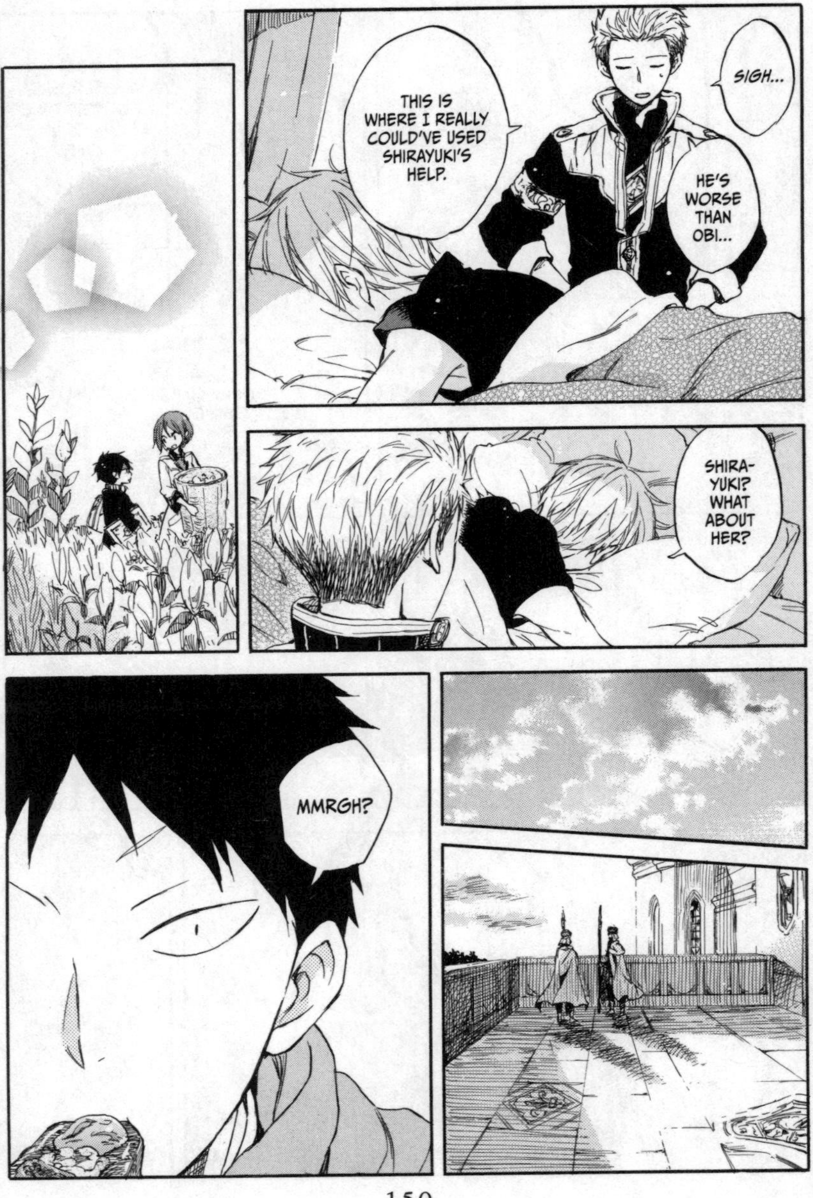

SIGH...
HE'S WORSE THAN OBI...
THIS IS WHERE I REALLY COULD'VE USED SHIRAYUKI'S HELP.
SHIRA-YUKI? WHAT ABOUT HER?
MMRGH?

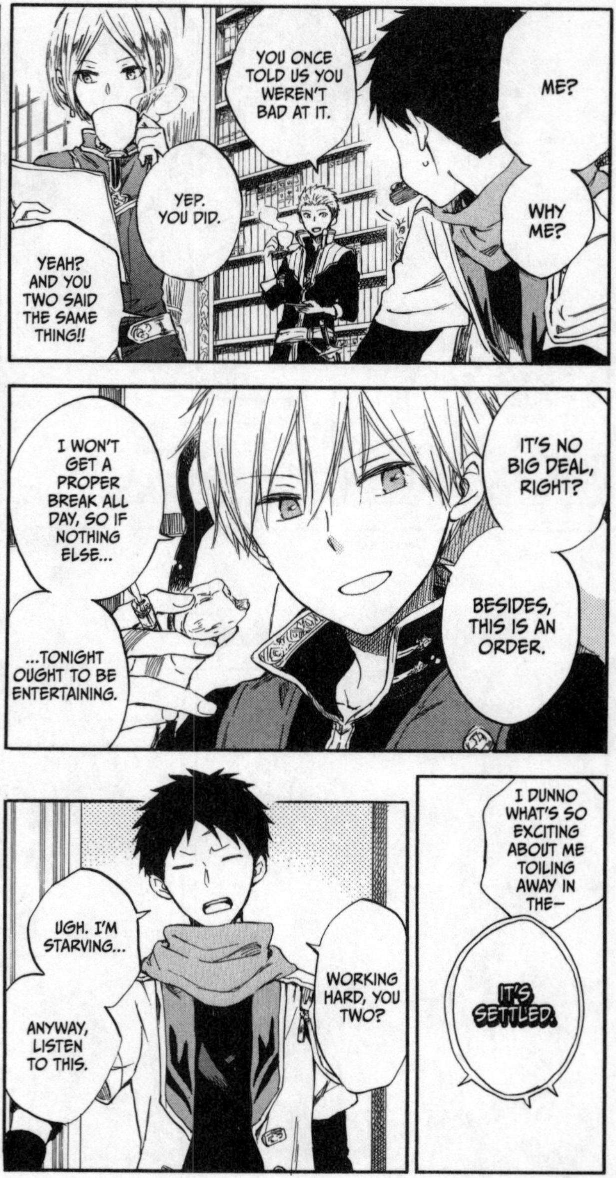
ME?
WHY ME?
YOU ONCE TOLD US YOU WEREN'T BAD AT IT.
YEP. YOU DID.
YEAH? AND YOU TWO SAID THE SAME THING!!
IT'S NO BIG DEAL, RIGHT?
BESIDES, THIS IS AN ORDER.
I WON'T GET A PROPER BREAK ALL DAY, SO IF NOTHING ELSE...
...TONIGHT OUGHT TO BE ENTERTAINING.
I DUNNO WHAT'S SO EXCITING ABOUT ME TOILING AWAY IN THE—
IT'S SETTLED.
WORKING HARD, YOU TWO?
UGH. I'M STARVING...
ANYWAY, LISTEN TO THIS.

5

There was a spin-off edition of the magazine called *LaLa Fantasy*, and my contribution was an eight-page bonus chapter.

I was allowed to make it about any characters I wanted. I wasn't sure who to choose at first, but in the end, I went with my trusty trio—and thrust Mitsuhide into the spotlight.

I personally wanted to include another certain character, but there just wasn't enough demand, so I abandoned that idea.

Too bad.

Too bad, huh?

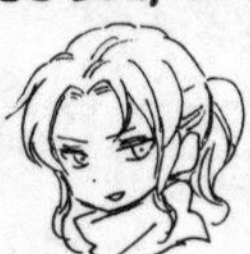

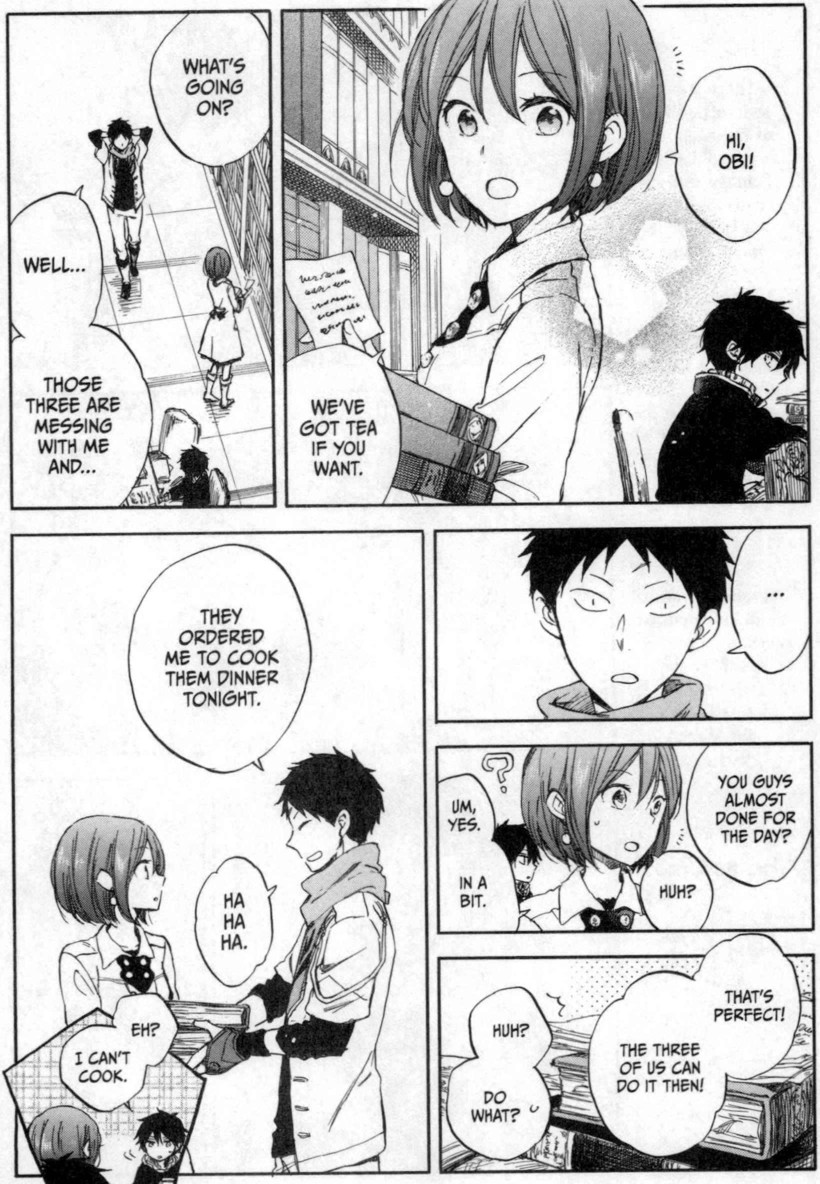
HI, OBI!
WE'VE GOT TEA IF YOU WANT.
WHAT'S GOING ON?
WELL...
THOSE THREE ARE MESSING WITH ME AND...
...
YOU GUYS ALMOST DONE FOR THE DAY?
HUH?
UM, YES.
IN A BIT.
THAT'S PERFECT!
THE THREE OF US CAN DO IT THEN!
HUH?
DO WHAT?
THEY ORDERED ME TO COOK THEM DINNER TONIGHT.
HA HA HA.
EH?
I CAN'T COOK.

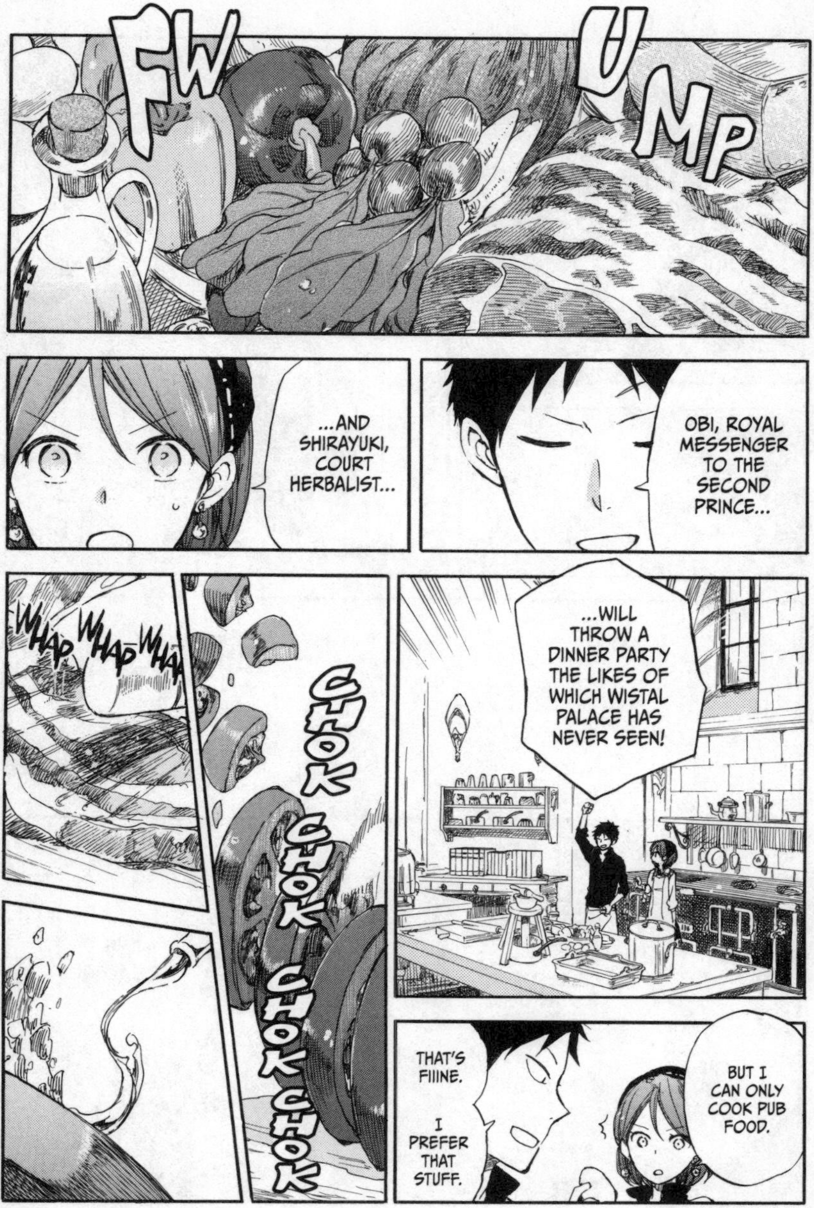
FWUMP
OBI, ROYAL MESSENGER TO THE SECOND PRINCE...
...AND SHIRAYUKI, COURT HERBALIST...
...WILL THROW A DINNER PARTY THE LIKES OF WHICH WISTAL PALACE HAS NEVER SEEN!
CHOK CHOK CHOK CHOK CHOK
WHAP WHAP WHAP
BUT I CAN ONLY COOK PUB FOOD.
THAT'S FIIINE.
I PREFER THAT STUFF.

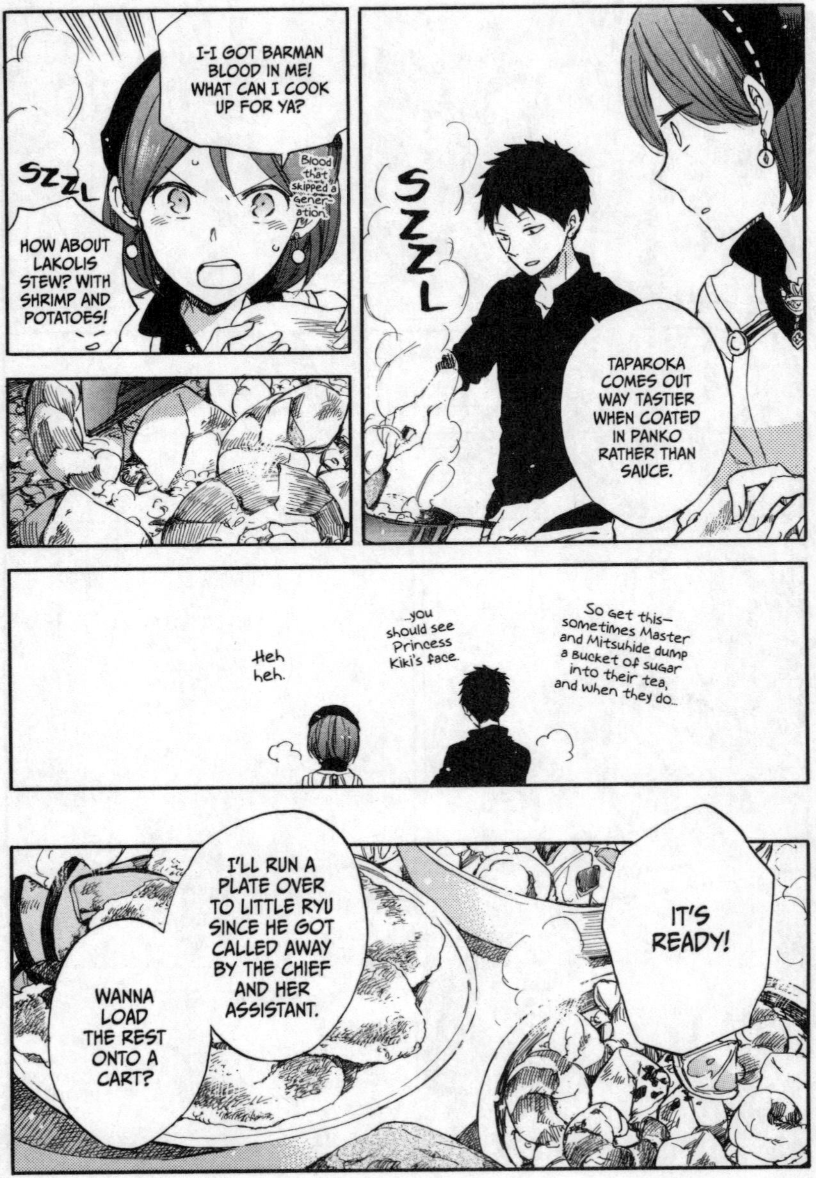
SZZL
TAPAROKA COMES OUT WAY TASTIER WHEN COATED IN PANKO RATHER THAN SAUCE.
I-I GOT BARMAN BLOOD IN ME! WHAT CAN I COOK UP FOR YA?
Blood that skipped a generation.
SZZL
HOW ABOUT LAKOLIS STEW? WITH SHRIMP AND POTATOES!
So get this— sometimes Master and Mitsuhide dump a bucket of sugar into their tea, and when they do...
...you should see Princess Kiki's face.
Heh heh.
IT'S READY!
I'LL RUN A PLATE OVER TO LITTLE RYU SINCE HE GOT CALLED AWAY BY THE CHIEF AND HER ASSISTANT.
WANNA LOAD THE REST ONTO A CART?

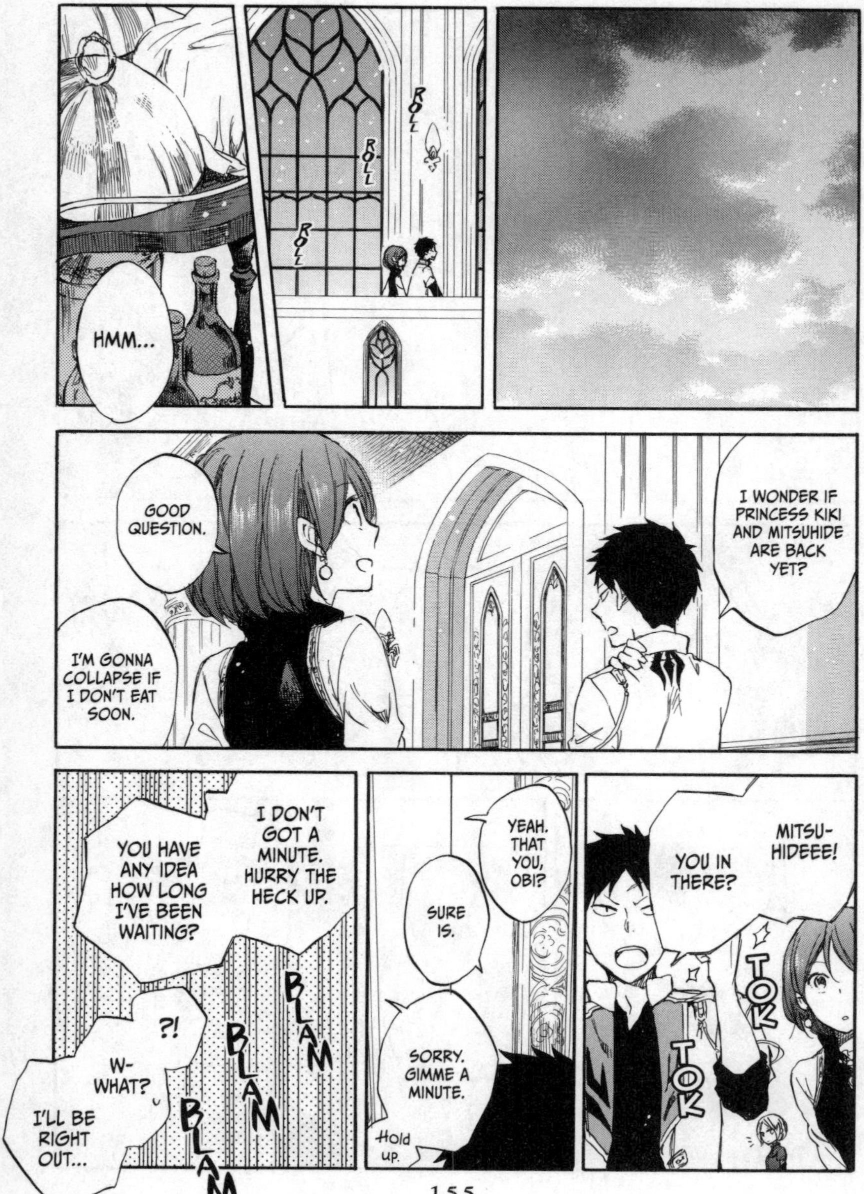

ROLL
ROLL
ROLL
HMM...
I WONDER IF PRINCESS KIKI AND MITSUHIDE ARE BACK YET?
GOOD QUESTION.
I'M GONNA COLLAPSE IF I DON'T EAT SOON.
MITSU-HIDEEE!
YOU IN THERE?
TOK
TOK
YEAH. THAT YOU, OBI?
SURE IS.
SORRY. GIMME A MINUTE.
Hold up.
I DON'T GOT A MINUTE. HURRY THE HECK UP.
YOU HAVE ANY IDEA HOW LONG I'VE BEEN WAITING?
BLAM
BLAM
BLAM
BLAM
?!
W-WHAT?
I'LL BE RIGHT OUT...

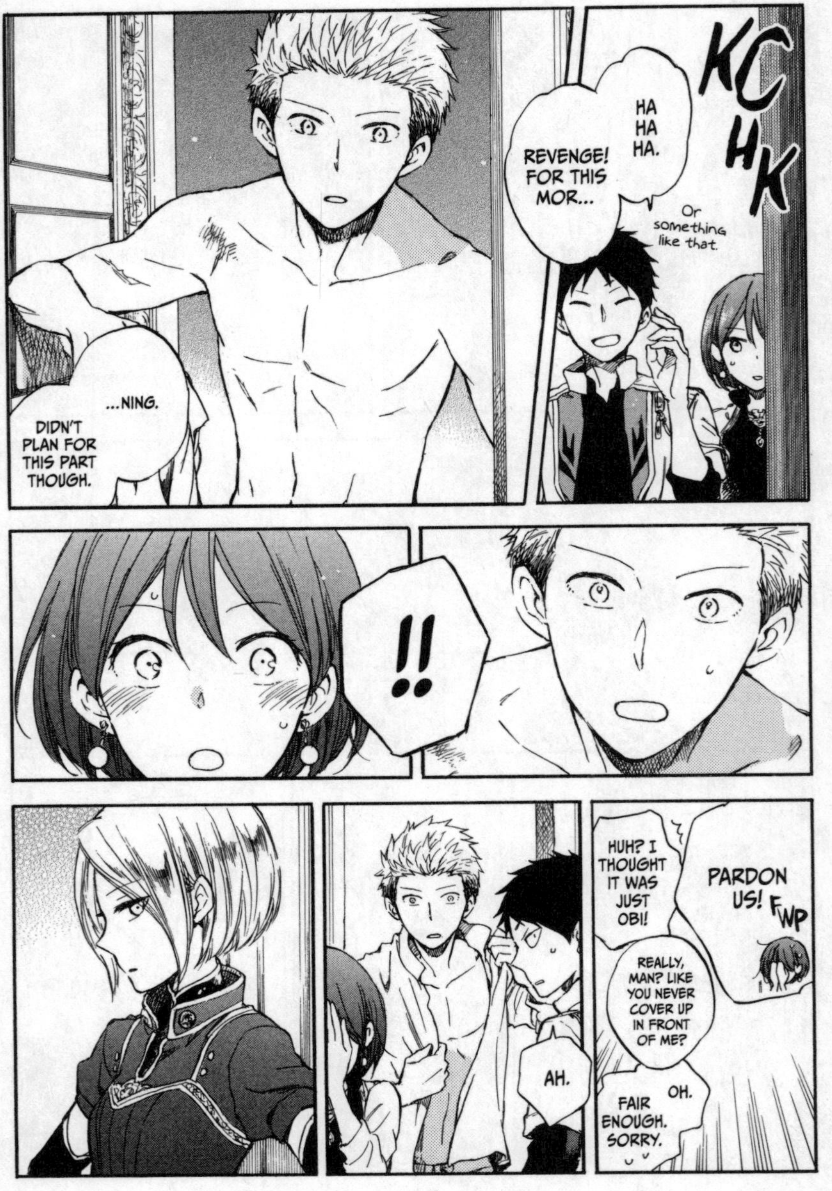
KCHK
HA HA HA.
REVENGE! FOR THIS MOR...
Or something like that.
...NING.
DIDN'T PLAN FOR THIS PART THOUGH.
!!
PARDON US!
FWP
HUH? I THOUGHT IT WAS JUST OBI!
REALLY, MAN? LIKE YOU NEVER COVER UP IN FRONT OF ME?
OH.
FAIR ENOUGH. SORRY.
AH.

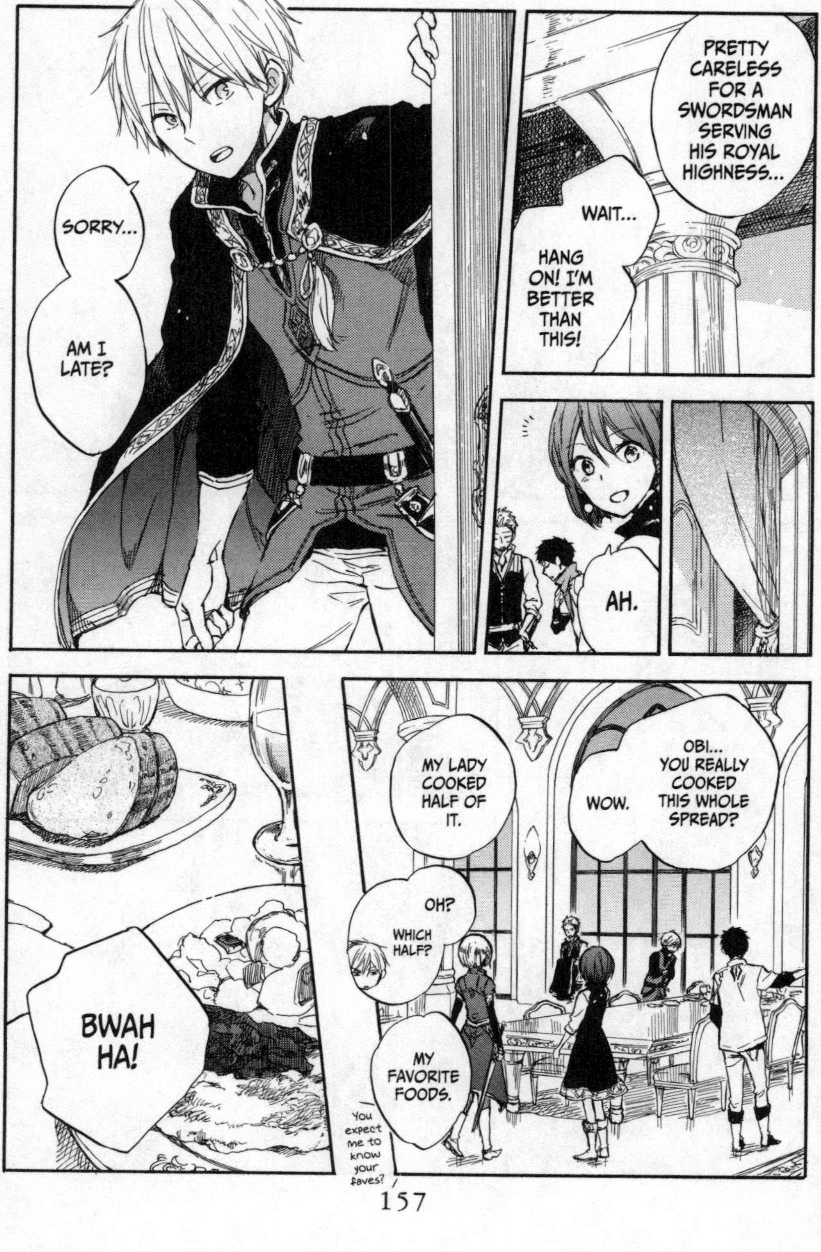
PRETTY CARELESS FOR A SWORDSMAN SERVING HIS ROYAL HIGHNESS...
WAIT...
HANG ON! I'M BETTER THAN THIS!
AH.
SORRY...
AM I LATE?
OBI... YOU REALLY COOKED THIS WHOLE SPREAD?
WOW.
MY LADY COOKED HALF OF IT.
OH?
WHICH HALF?
MY FAVORITE FOODS.
You expect me to know your faves?
BWAH HA!

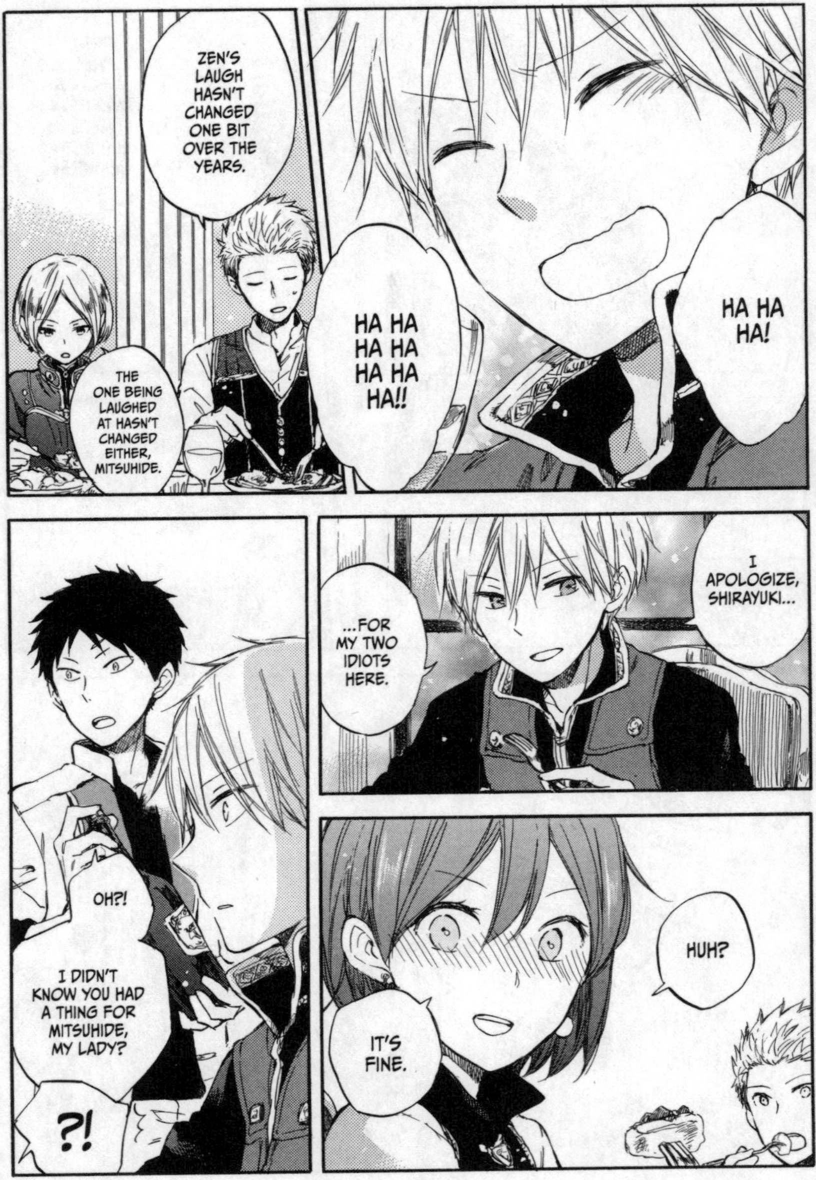
HA HA HA!
HA HA HA HA HA HA HA!!
ZEN'S LAUGH HASN'T CHANGED ONE BIT OVER THE YEARS.
THE ONE BEING LAUGHED AT HASN'T CHANGED EITHER, MITSUHIDE.
I APOLOGIZE, SHIRAYUKI...
...FOR MY TWO IDIOTS HERE.
HUH?
IT'S FINE.
OH?!
I DIDN'T KNOW YOU HAD A THING FOR MITSUHIDE, MY LADY?
?!

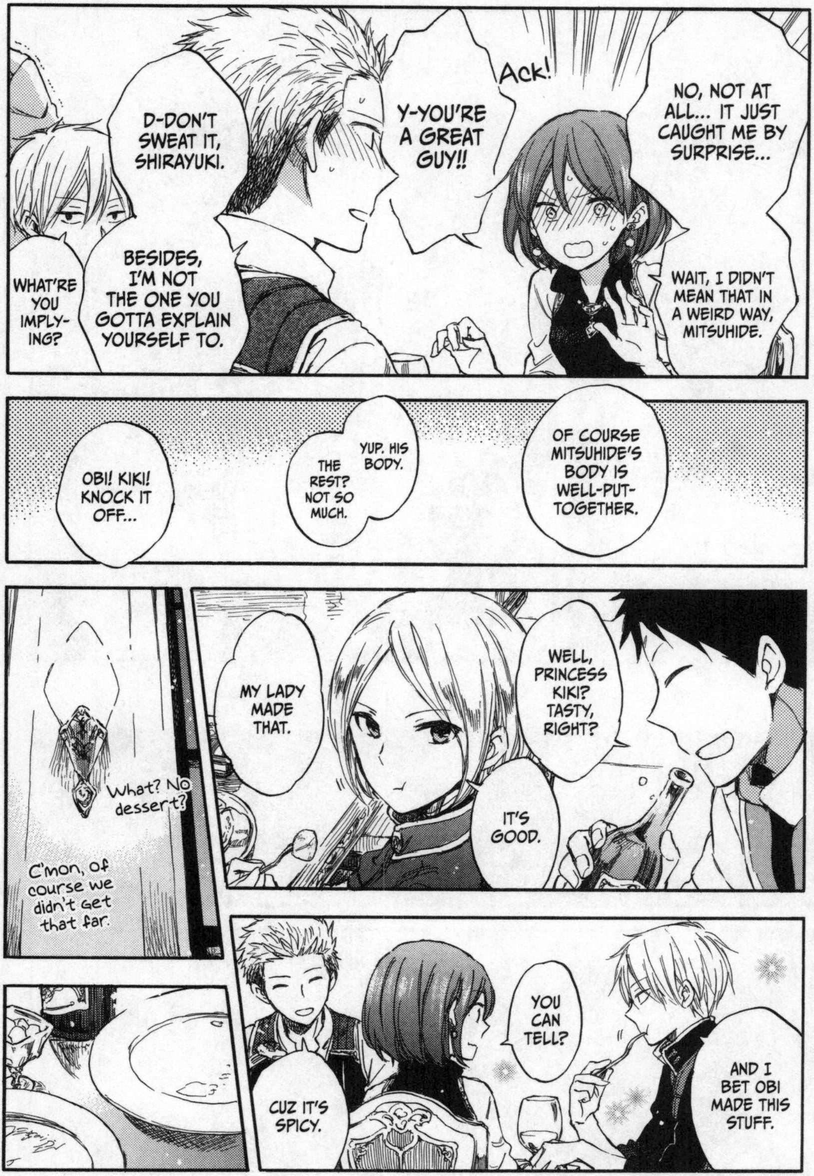
NO, NOT AT ALL... IT JUST CAUGHT ME BY SURPRISE...
WAIT, I DIDN'T MEAN THAT IN A WEIRD WAY, MITSUHIDE.
Ack!
Y-YOU'RE A GREAT GUY!!
D-DON'T SWEAT IT, SHIRAYUKI.
BESIDES, I'M NOT THE ONE YOU GOTTA EXPLAIN YOURSELF TO.
WHAT'RE YOU IMPLYING?
OF COURSE MITSUHIDE'S BODY IS WELL-PUT-TOGETHER.
YUP. HIS BODY.
THE REST? NOT SO MUCH.
OBI! KIKI! KNOCK IT OFF...
WELL, PRINCESS KIKI? TASTY, RIGHT?
IT'S GOOD.
MY LADY MADE THAT.
AND I BET OBI MADE THIS STUFF.
YOU CAN TELL?
CUZ IT'S SPICY.
What? No dessert?
C'mon, of course we didn't get that far.

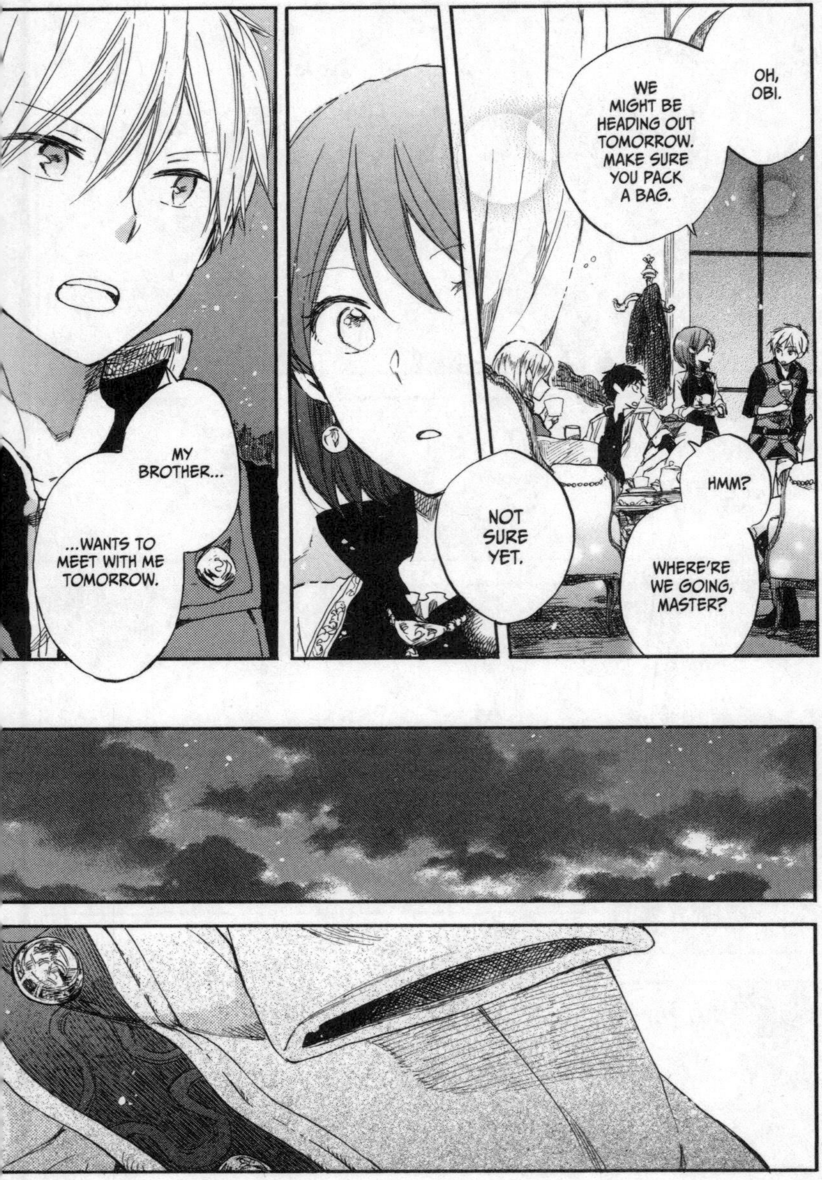
OH, OBI.
WE MIGHT BE HEADING OUT TOMORROW. MAKE SURE YOU PACK A BAG.
HMM?
WHERE'RE WE GOING, MASTER?
NOT SURE YET.
MY BROTHER...
...WANTS TO MEET WITH ME TOMORROW.

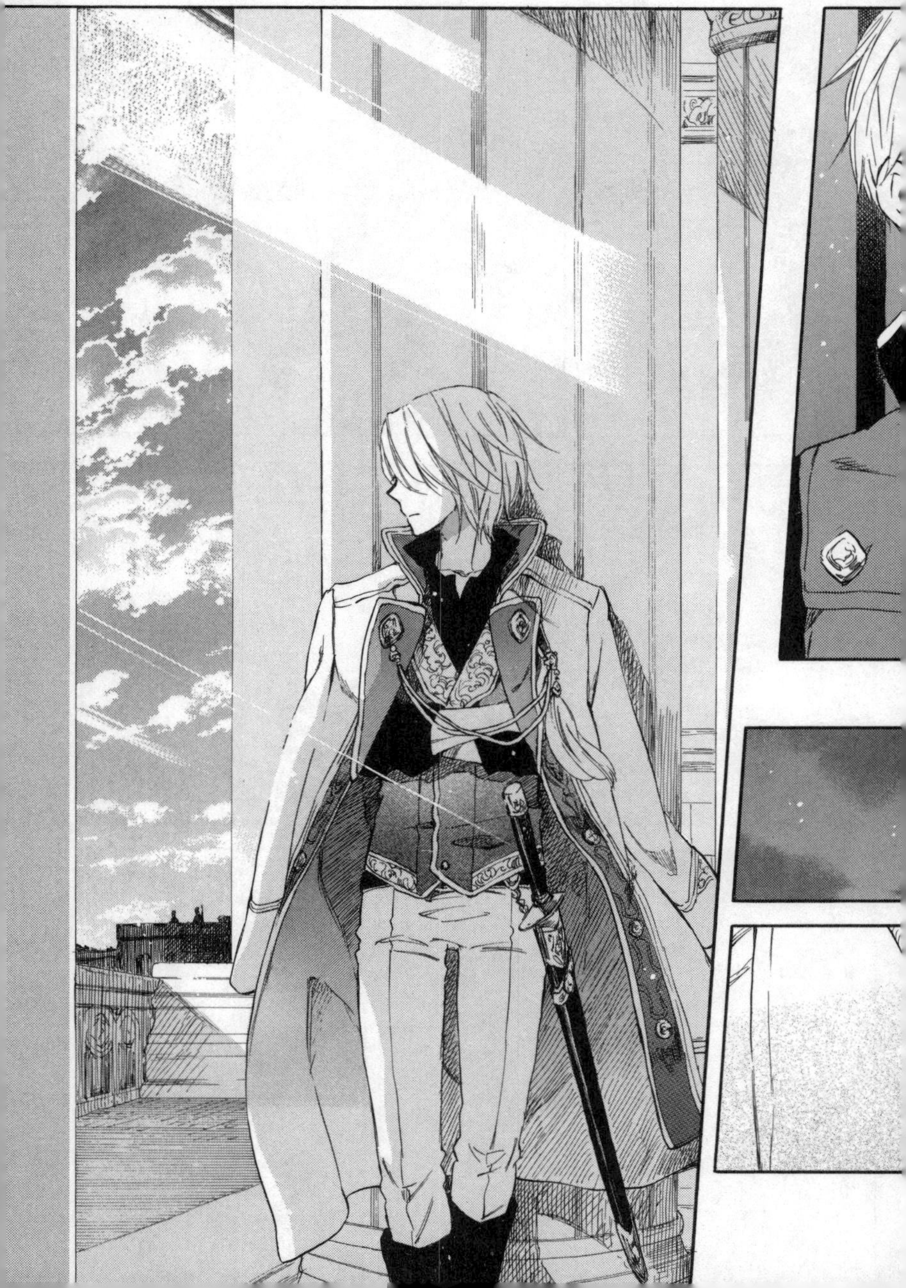

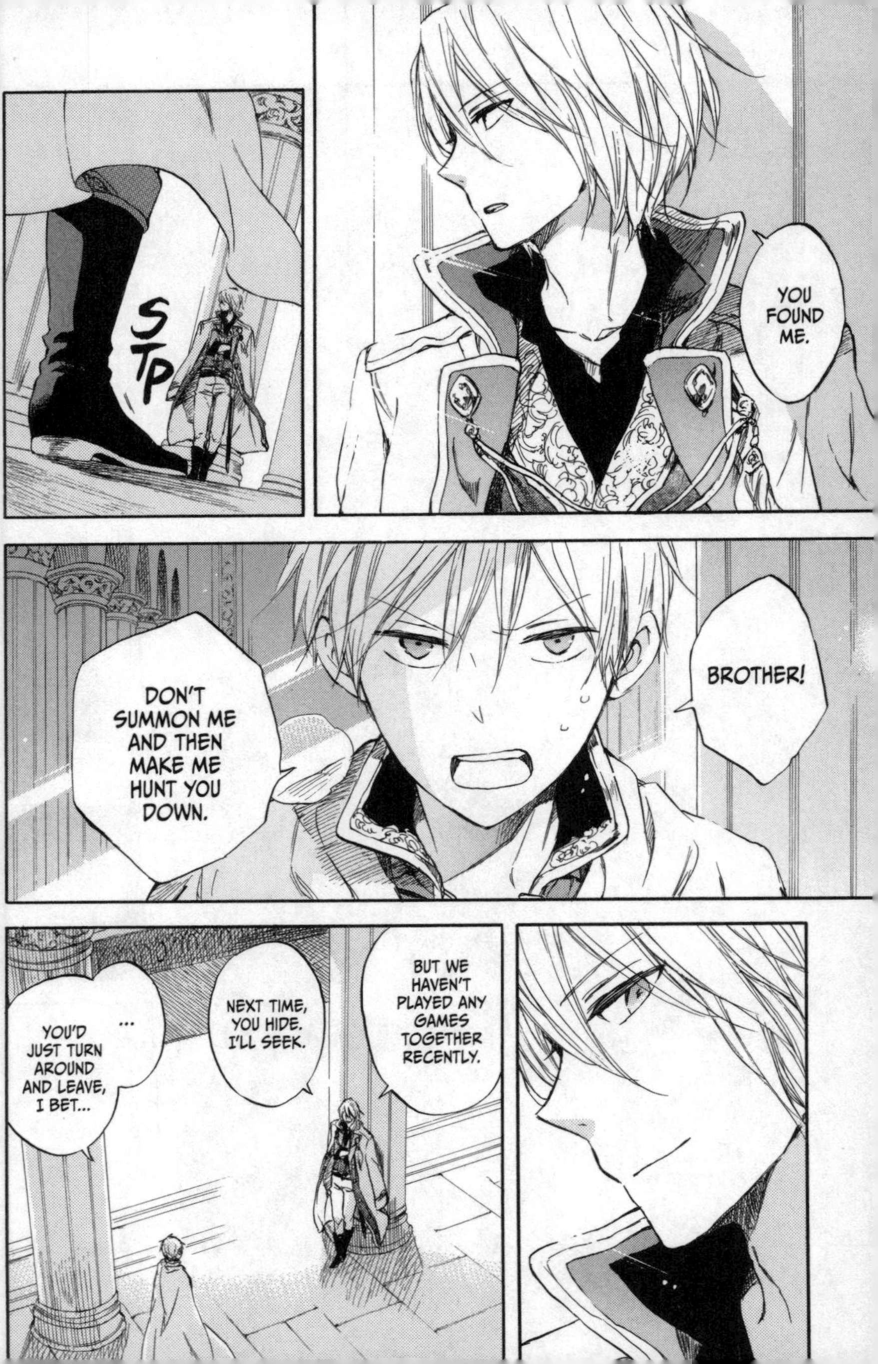
YOU FOUND ME.
STP
BROTHER!
DON'T SUMMON ME AND THEN MAKE ME HUNT YOU DOWN.
BUT WE HAVEN'T PLAYED ANY GAMES TOGETHER RECENTLY.
NEXT TIME, YOU HIDE. I'LL SEEK.
...
YOU'D JUST TURN AROUND AND LEAVE, I BET...

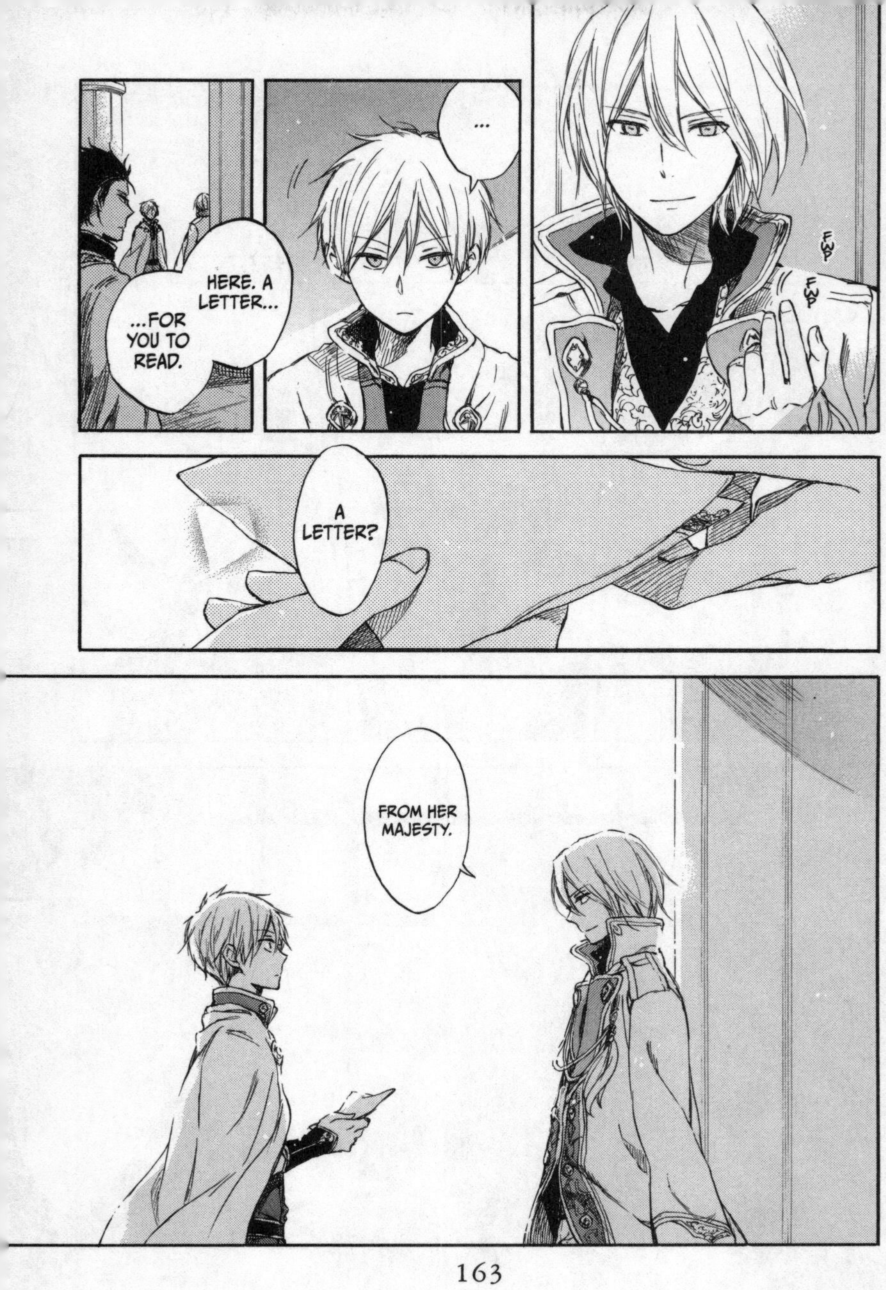
FWP
FWP
...
HERE. A LETTER...
...FOR YOU TO READ.
A LETTER?
FROM HER MAJESTY.

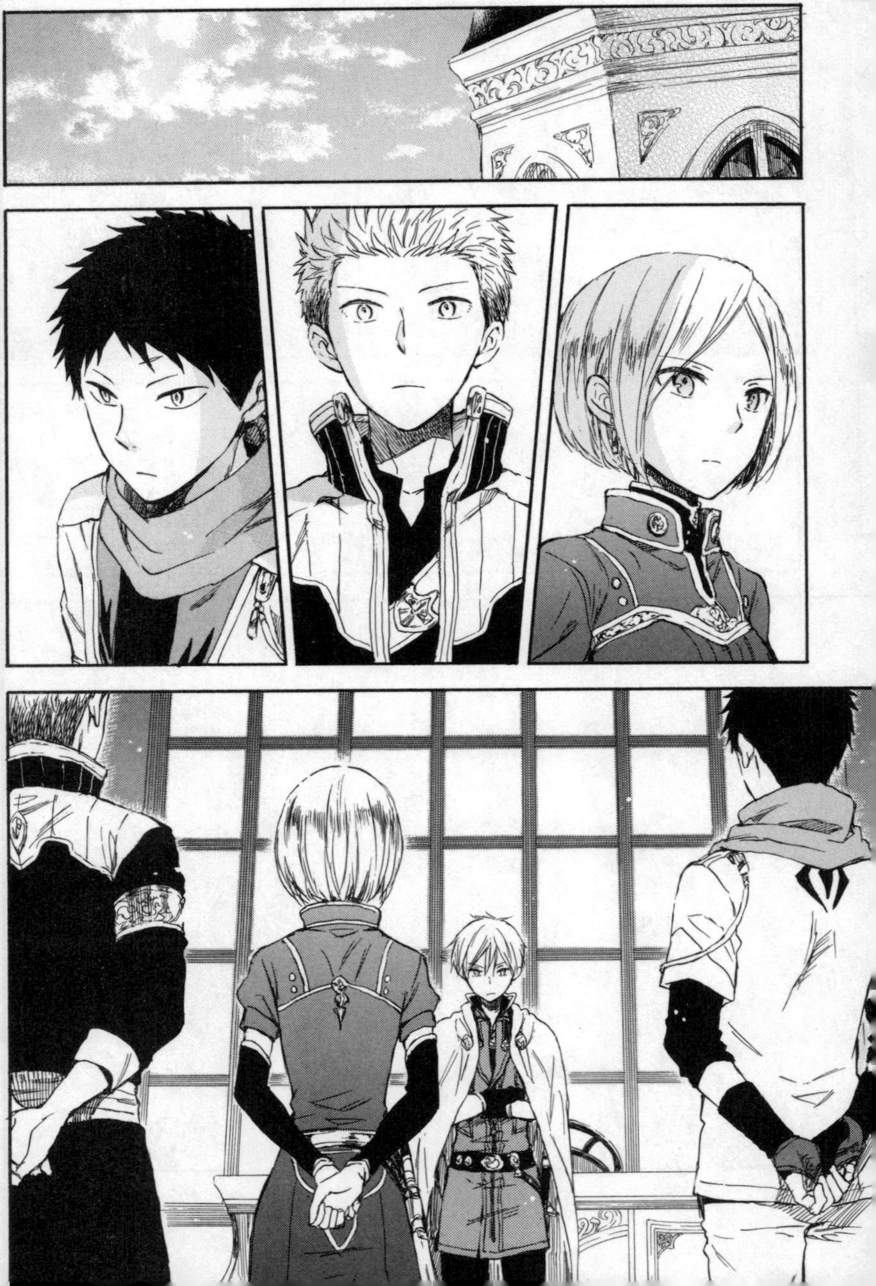

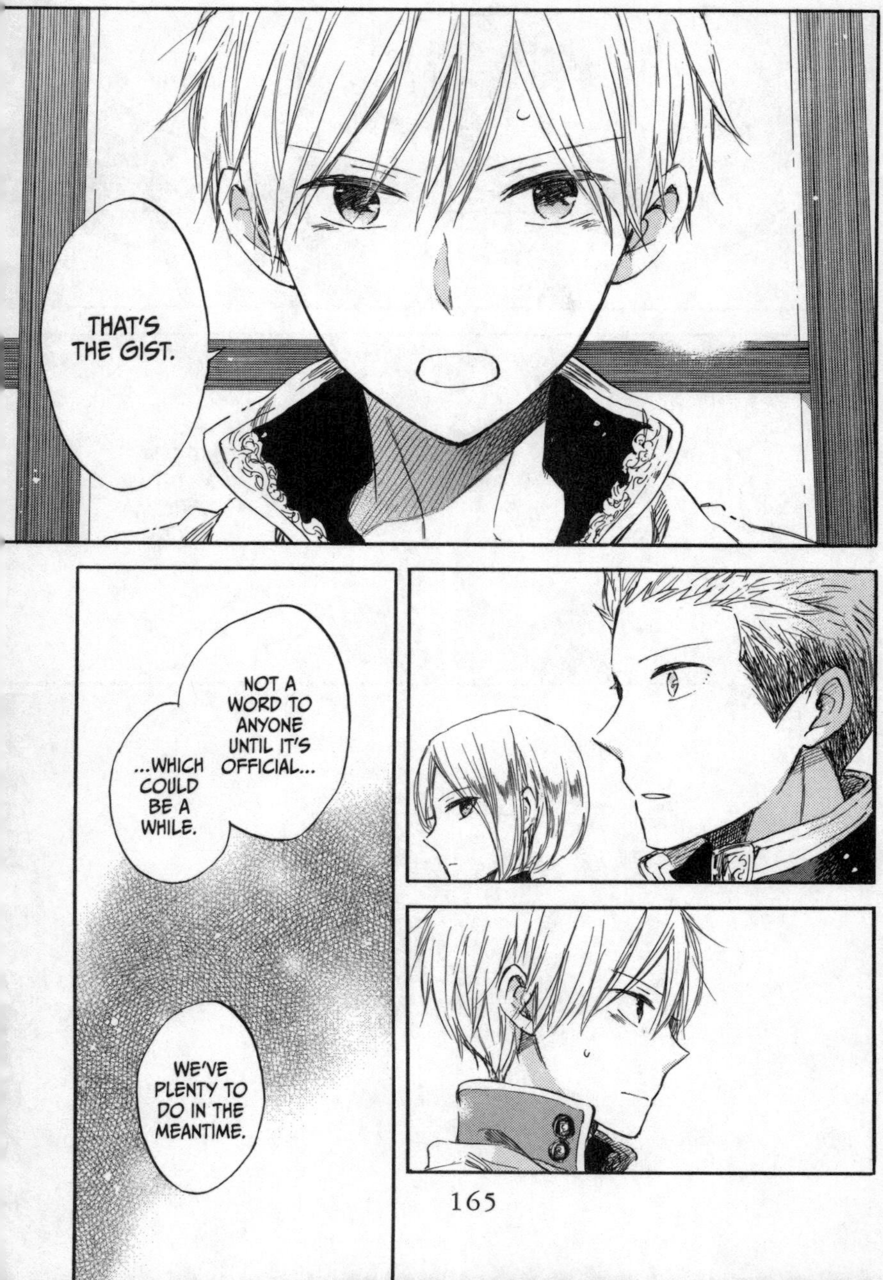
THAT'S THE GIST.
NOT A WORD TO ANYONE UNTIL IT'S OFFICIAL...
...WHICH COULD BE A WHILE.
WE'VE PLENTY TO DO IN THE MEANTIME.

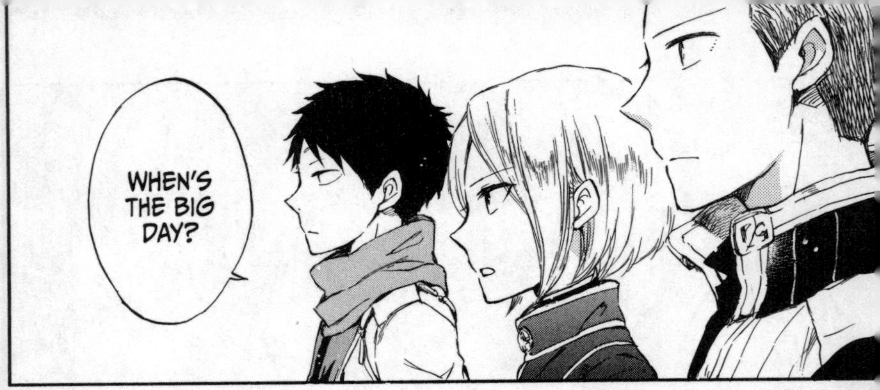
WHEN'S THE BIG DAY?

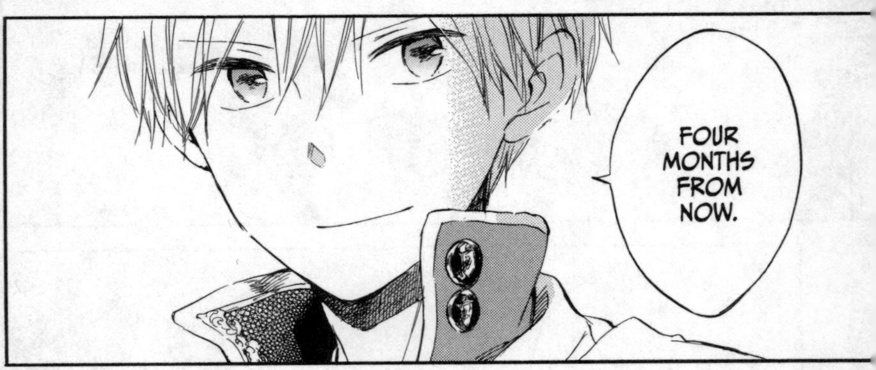
FOUR MONTHS FROM NOW.

HERE, IN THE CLARINES KINGDOM...

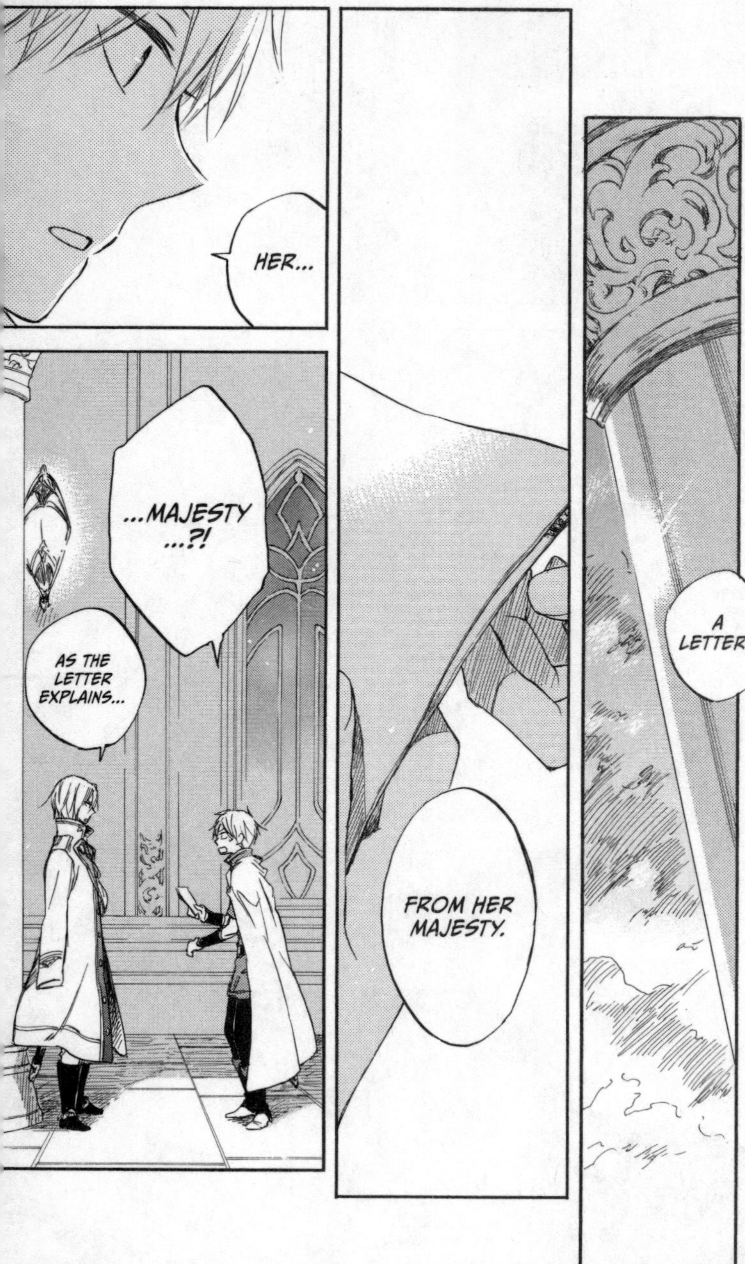
A LETTER?
FROM HER MAJESTY.
HER...
...MAJESTY ...?!
AS THE LETTER EXPLAINS...

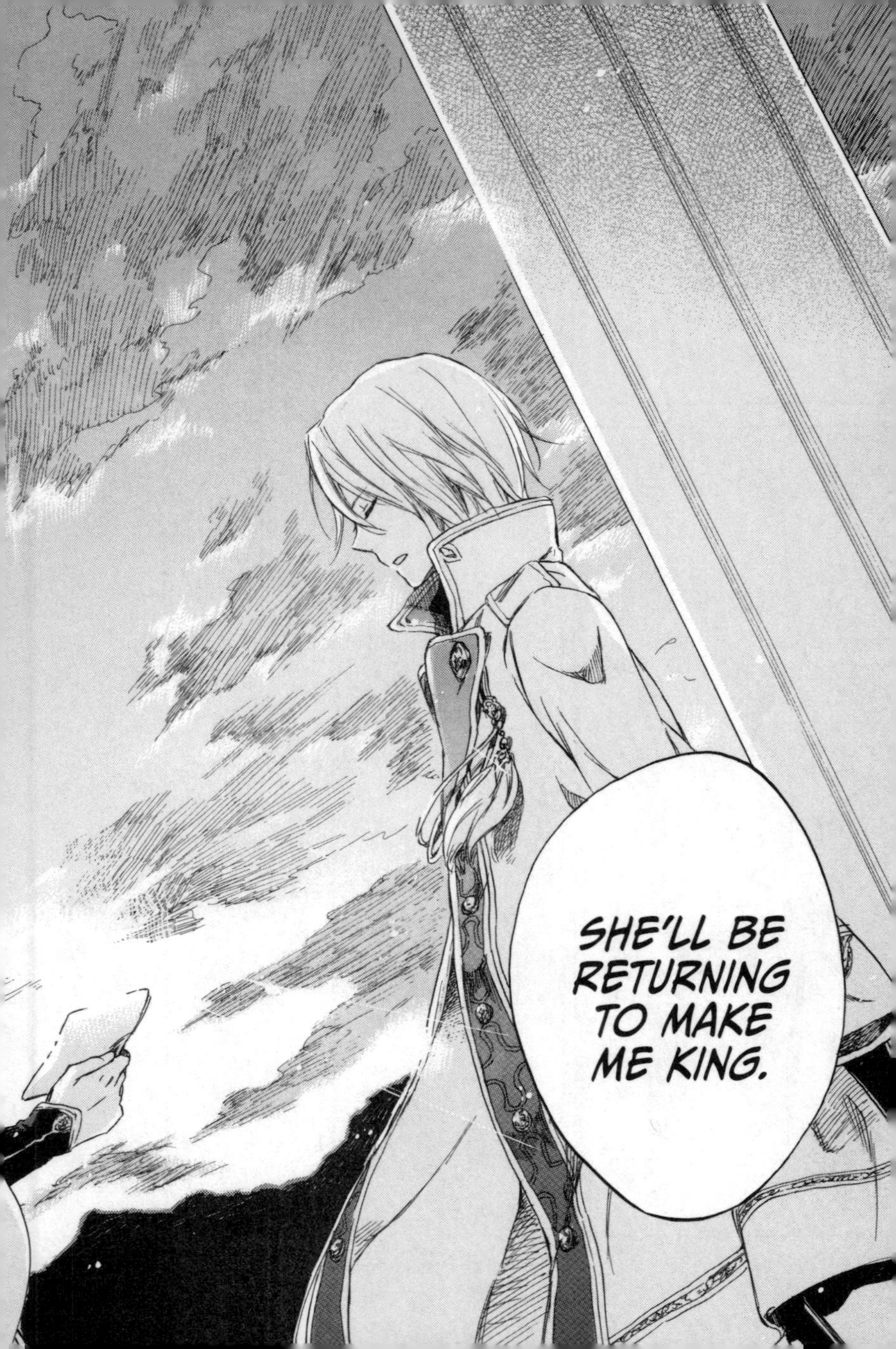
SHE'LL BE RETURNING TO MAKE ME KING.

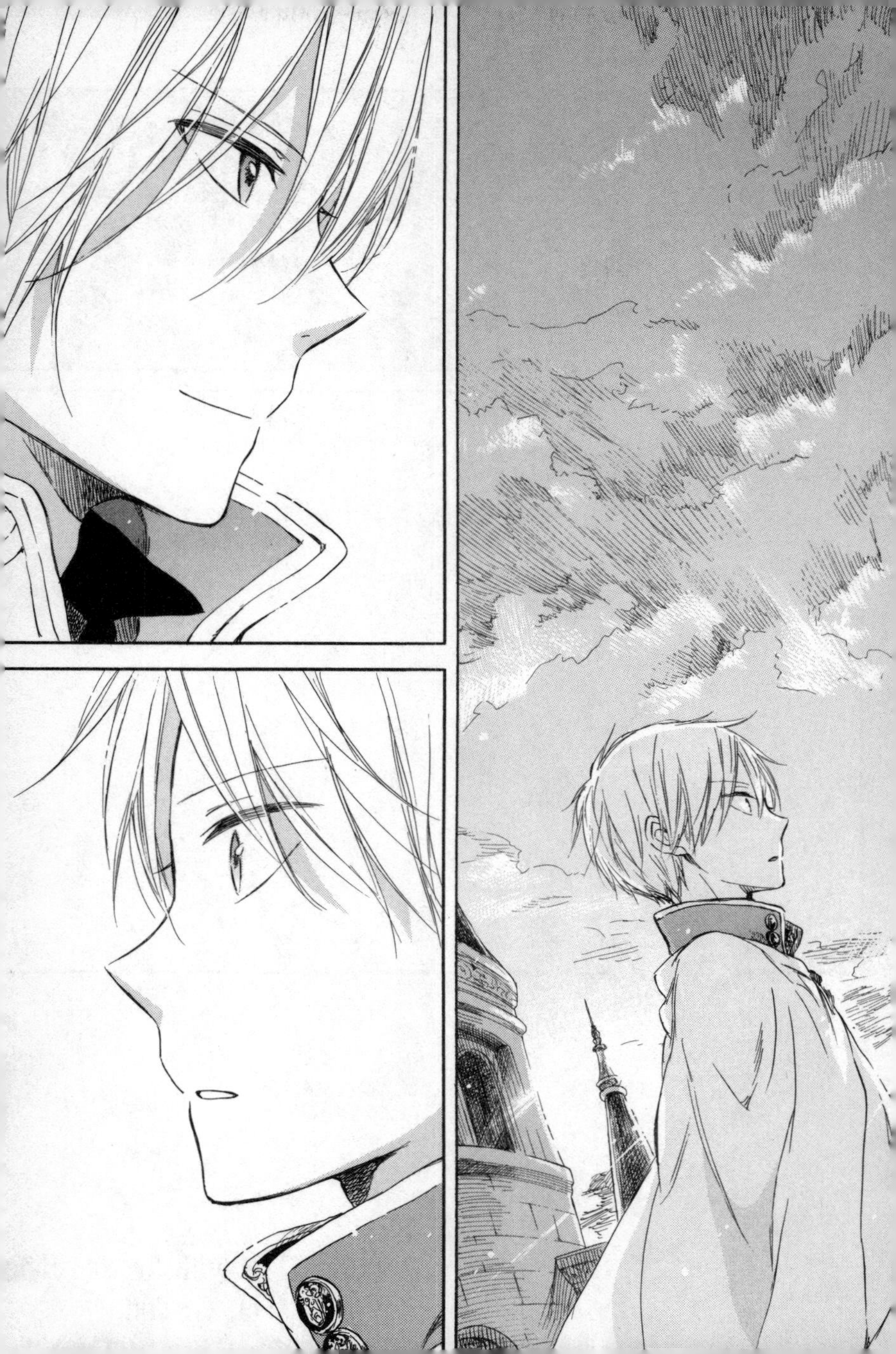

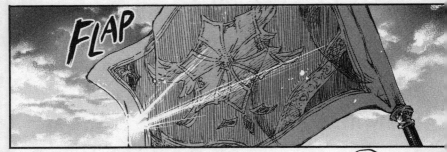

FLAP

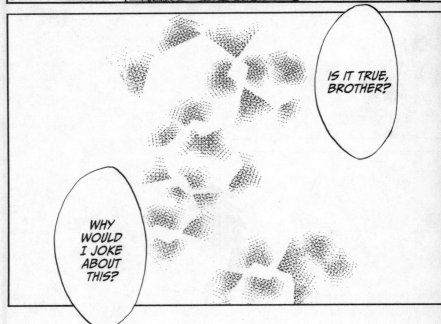

IS IT TRUE, BROTHER?

WHY WOULD I JOKE ABOUT THIS?

THE CORONATION CEREMONY...

...IS FOUR MONTHS AWAY.

Snow White with the Red Hair
Vol. 11: End

Snow White with the Red Hair

Chapter 49 Preview Image

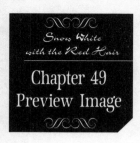

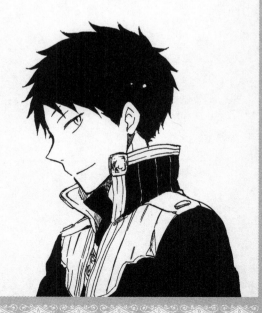

Bonus Chapter

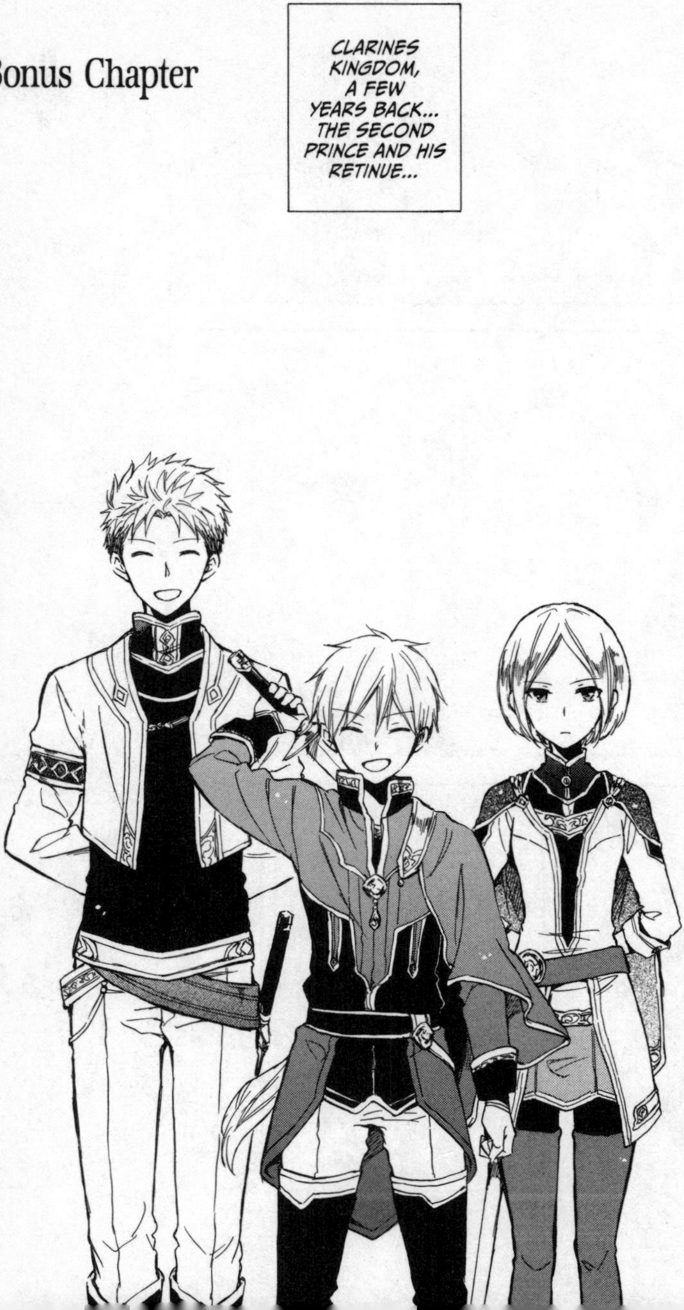
CLARINES KINGDOM, A FEW YEARS BACK... THE SECOND PRINCE AND HIS RETINUE...

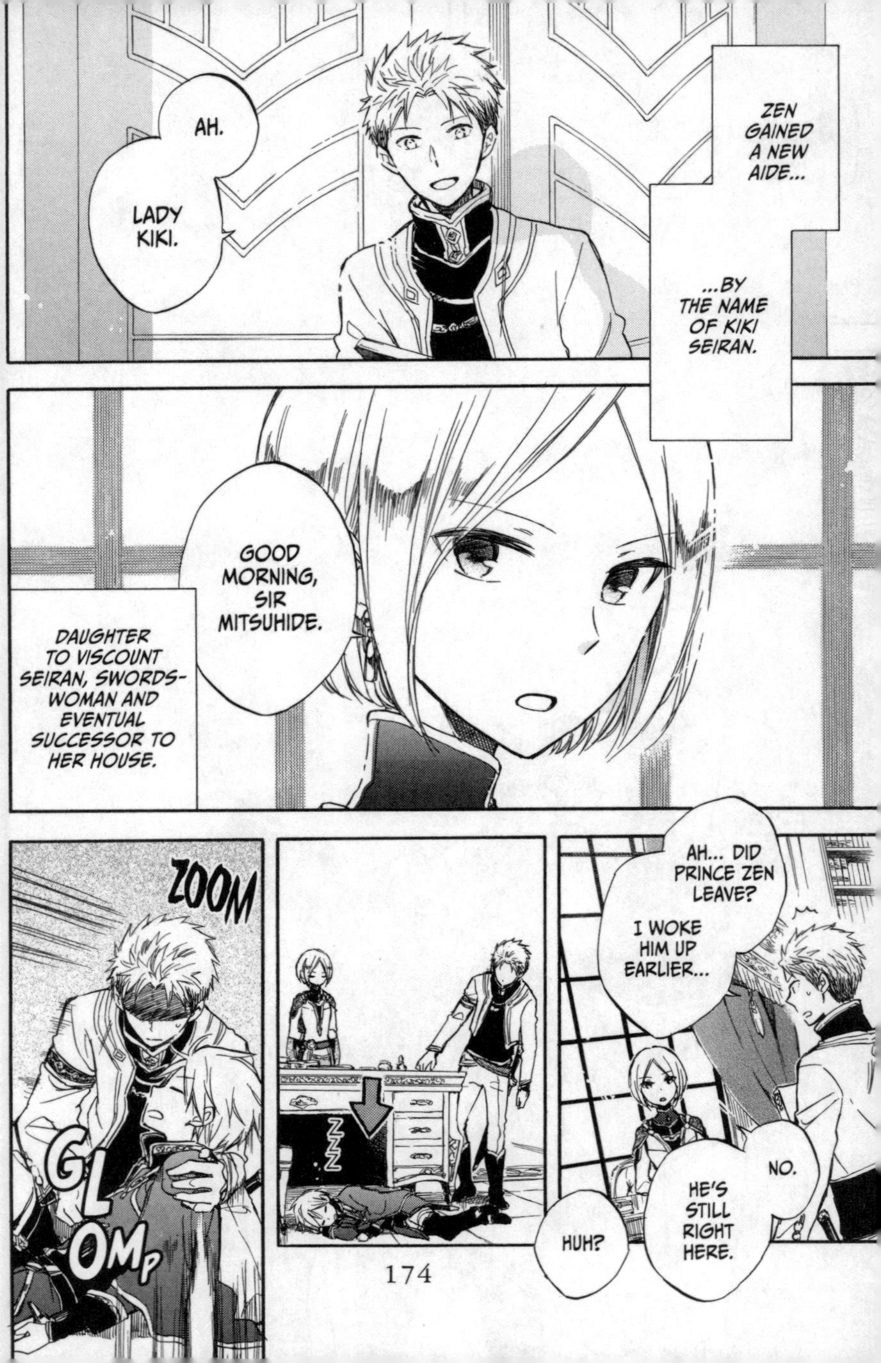
ZEN GAINED A NEW AIDE...
...BY THE NAME OF KIKI SEIRAN.
AH.
LADY KIKI.
GOOD MORNING, SIR MITSUHIDE.
DAUGHTER TO VISCOUNT SEIRAN, SWORDS-WOMAN AND EVENTUAL SUCCESSOR TO HER HOUSE.
AH... DID PRINCE ZEN LEAVE?
I WOKE HIM UP EARLIER...
NO.
HE'S STILL RIGHT HERE.
HUH?
ZZZ
ZOOM
GLOMP

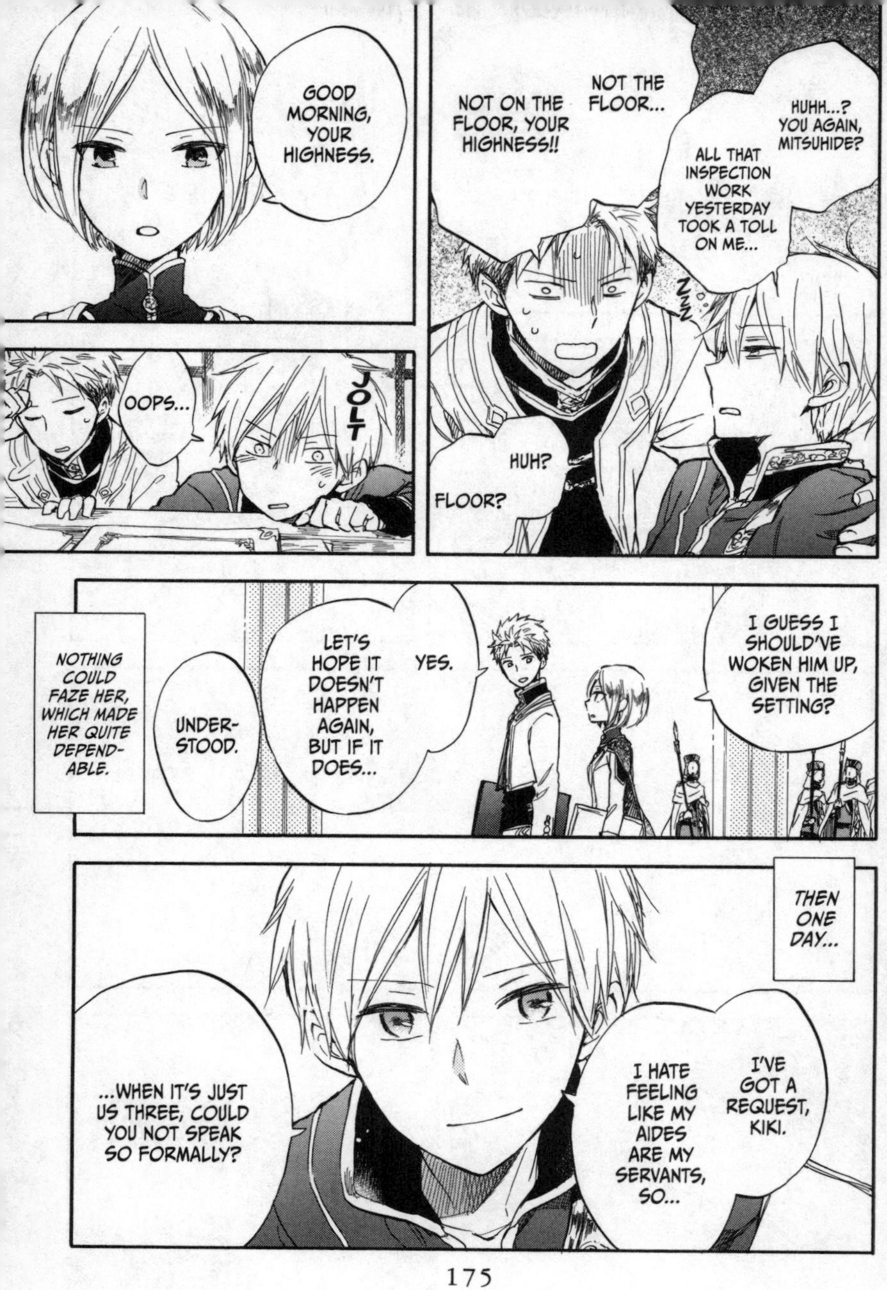
HUHH...? YOU AGAIN, MITSUHIDE?
ALL THAT INSPECTION WORK YESTERDAY TOOK A TOLL ON ME...
ZZZ
NOT THE FLOOR...
NOT ON THE FLOOR, YOUR HIGHNESS!!
HUH?
FLOOR?
GOOD MORNING, YOUR HIGHNESS.
JOLT
OOPS...
I GUESS I SHOULD'VE WOKEN HIM UP, GIVEN THE SETTING?
YES.
LET'S HOPE IT DOESN'T HAPPEN AGAIN, BUT IF IT DOES...
UNDER-STOOD.
NOTHING COULD FAZE HER, WHICH MADE HER QUITE DEPEND-ABLE.
THEN ONE DAY...
I'VE GOT A REQUEST, KIKI.
I HATE FEELING LIKE MY AIDES ARE MY SERVANTS, SO...
...WHEN IT'S JUST US THREE, COULD YOU NOT SPEAK SO FORMALLY?

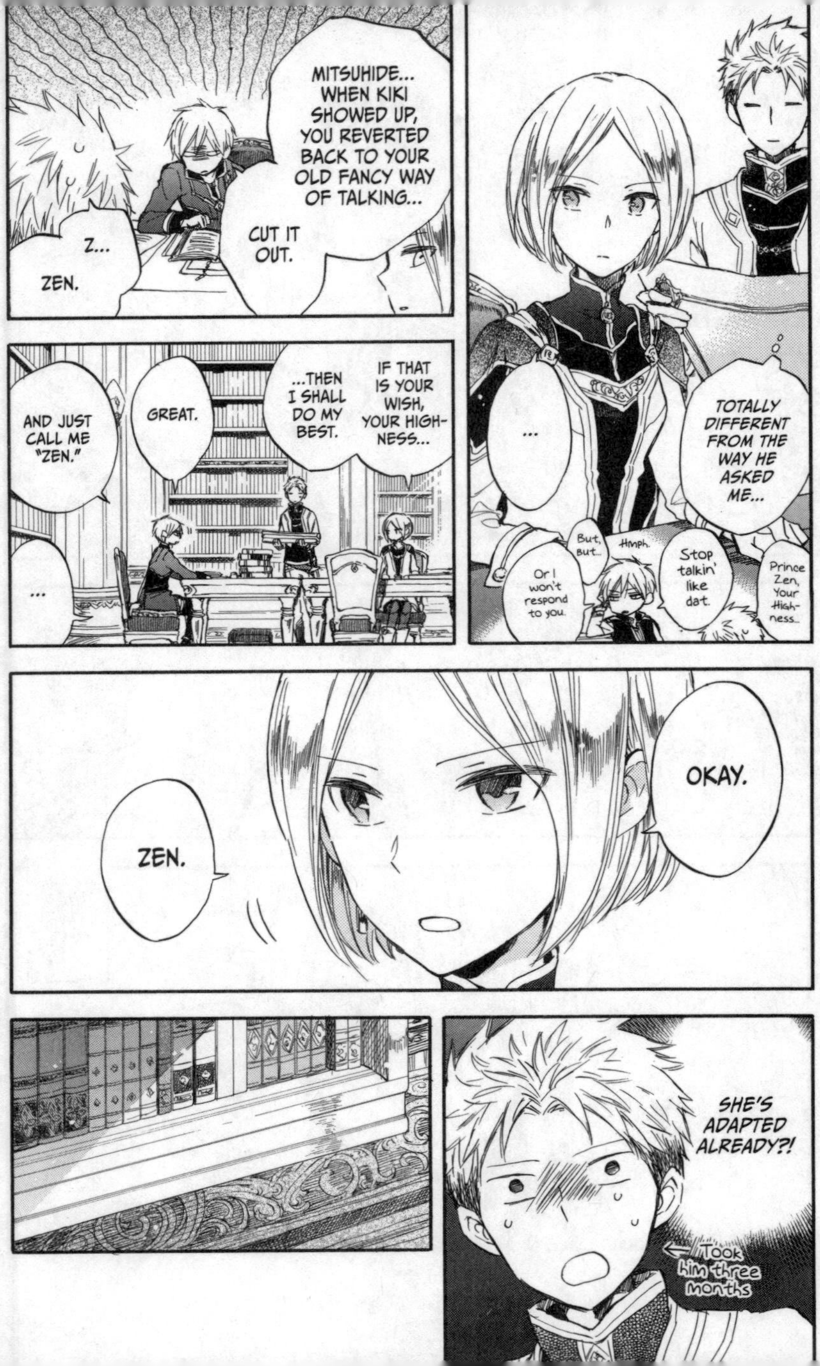
TOTALLY DIFFERENT FROM THE WAY HE ASKED ME...
...
Prince Zen, Your Highness...
Stop talkin' like dat.
Hmph.
But, but...
Or I won't respond to you.
MITSUHIDE... WHEN KIKI SHOWED UP, YOU REVERTED BACK TO YOUR OLD FANCY WAY OF TALKING...
CUT IT OUT.
Z...
ZEN.
IF THAT IS YOUR WISH, YOUR HIGHNESS...
...THEN I SHALL DO MY BEST.
GREAT.
AND JUST CALL ME "ZEN."
...
OKAY.
ZEN.
SHE'S ADAPTED ALREADY?!
← Took him three months

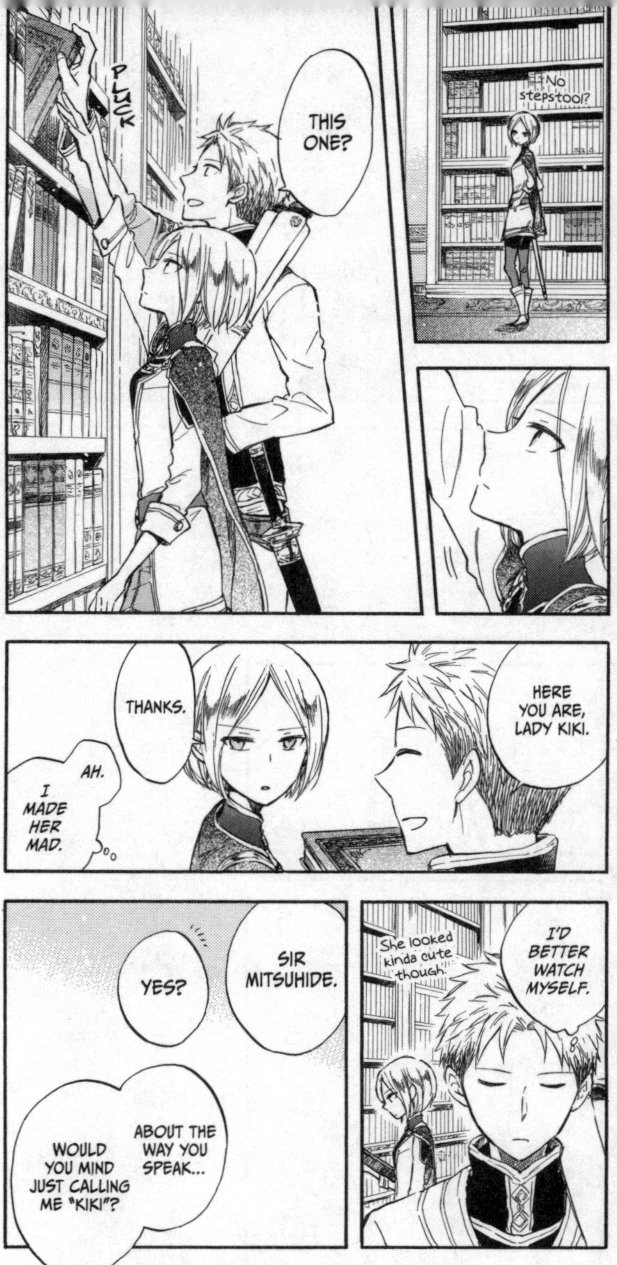
No stepstool?
THIS ONE?
PLUCK
HERE YOU ARE, LADY KIKI.
THANKS.
AH. I MADE HER MAD.
I'D BETTER WATCH MYSELF.
She looked kinda cute though!
SIR MITSUHIDE.
YES?
ABOUT THE WAY YOU SPEAK...
WOULD YOU MIND JUST CALLING ME "KIKI"?

END

So Shirayuki and the gang were basically inside the palace for the entirety of volume 11. Isn't that refreshing?

In chapter 49, Shirayuki froze up when she saw Obi's culinary skills firsthand, but she has more of a repertoire than he does.

Mitsuhide's specialty is big pots of food that feed about ten people, and Kiki is probably the same way.

Zen sometimes popped in to observe or lend a hand when Mitsuhide and Kiki were cooking over at Fort Laxdo or Sereg.

Mitsuhide's skills have dulled, so it takes longer for him to cook things.

And there you have it! Now, on to the end of the book!

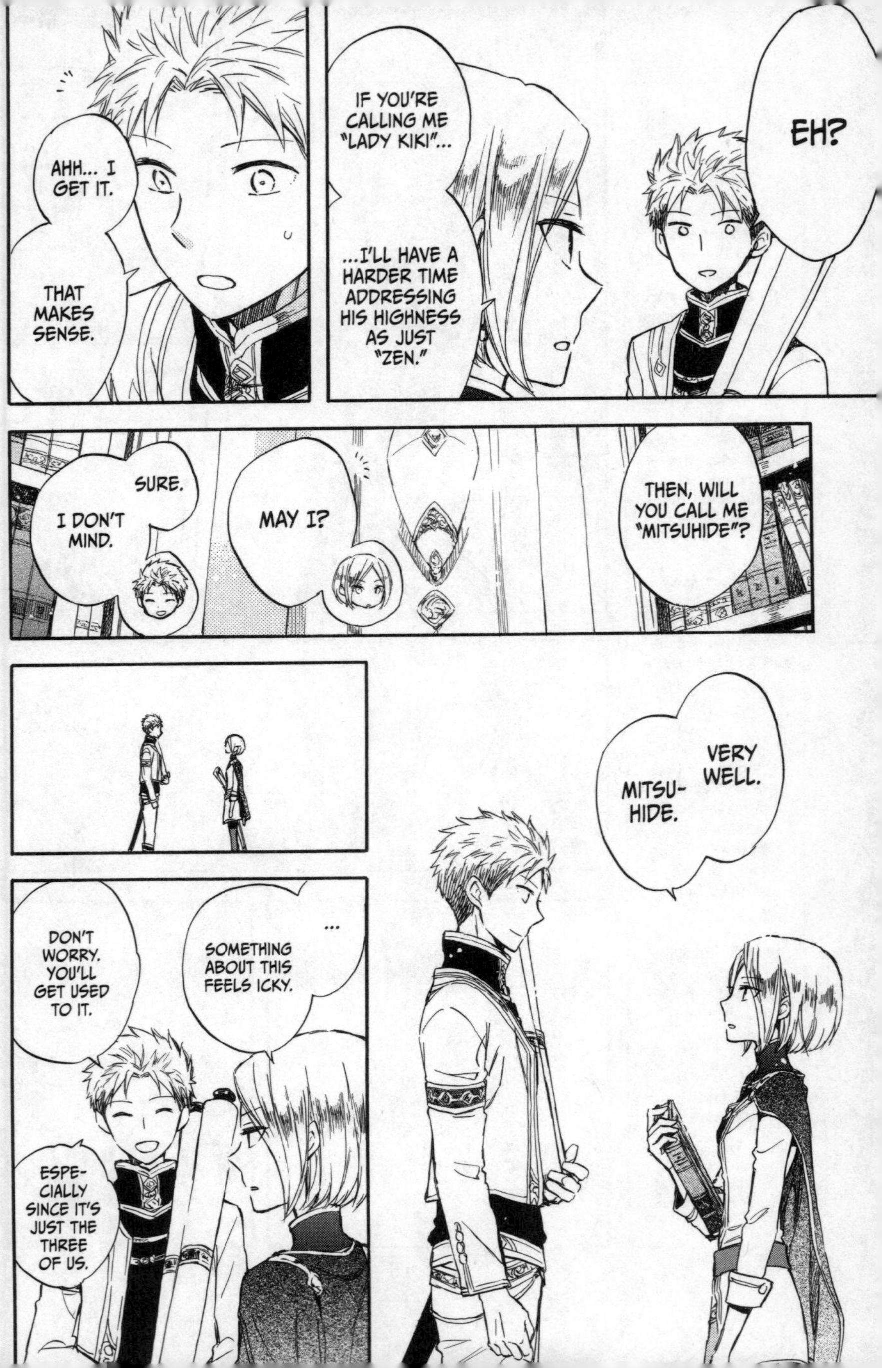
EH?
IF YOU'RE CALLING ME "LADY KIKI"...
...I'LL HAVE A HARDER TIME ADDRESSING HIS HIGHNESS AS JUST "ZEN."
AHH... I GET IT.
THAT MAKES SENSE.
THEN, WILL YOU CALL ME "MITSUHIDE"?
MAY I?
SURE.
I DON'T MIND.
VERY WELL.
MITSU-HIDE.
...
SOMETHING ABOUT THIS FEELS ICKY.
DON'T WORRY. YOU'LL GET USED TO IT.
ESPE-CIALLY SINCE IT'S JUST THE THREE OF US.

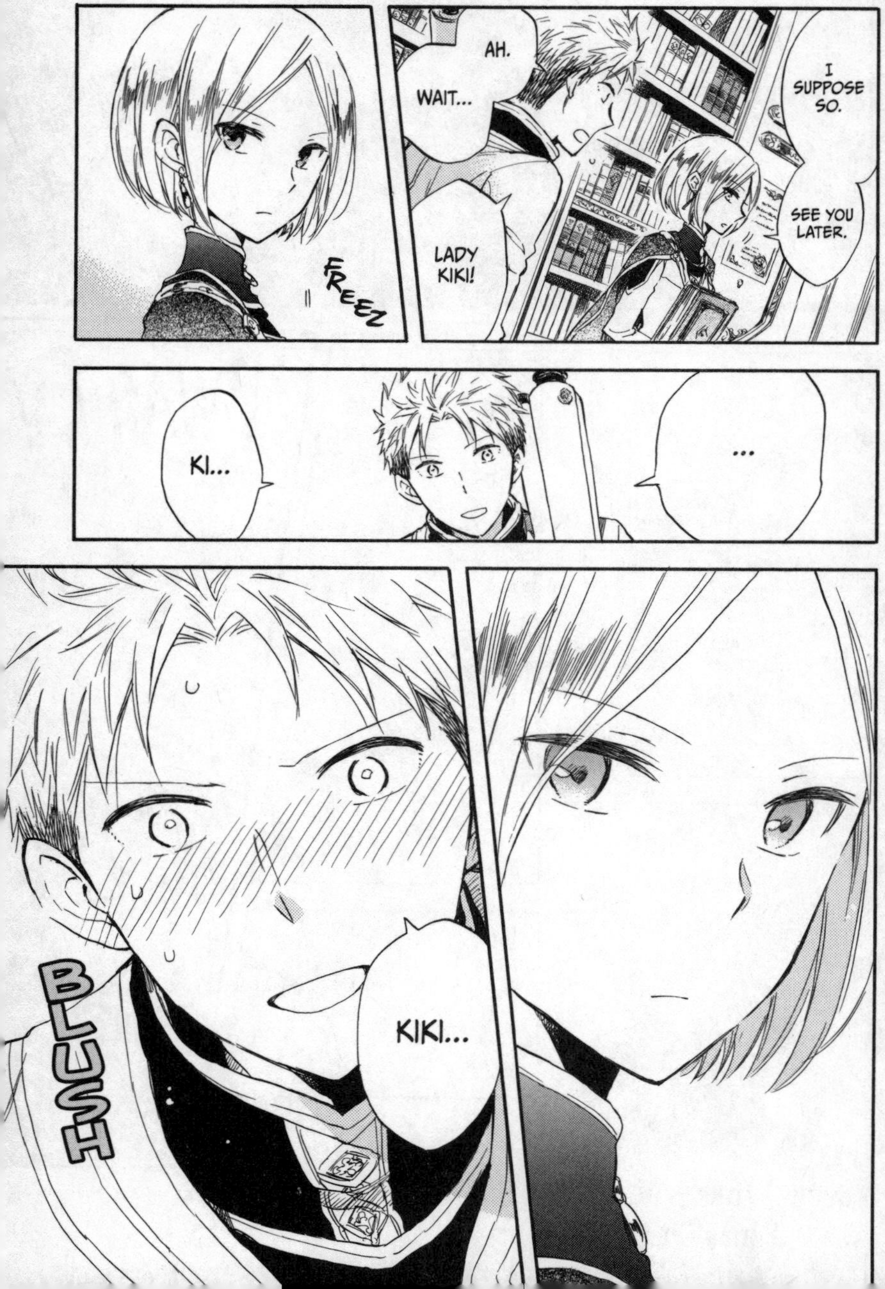
I SUPPOSE SO.
SEE YOU LATER.
AH.
WAIT...
LADY KIKI!
FREEZ
...
KI...
KIKI...
BLUSH

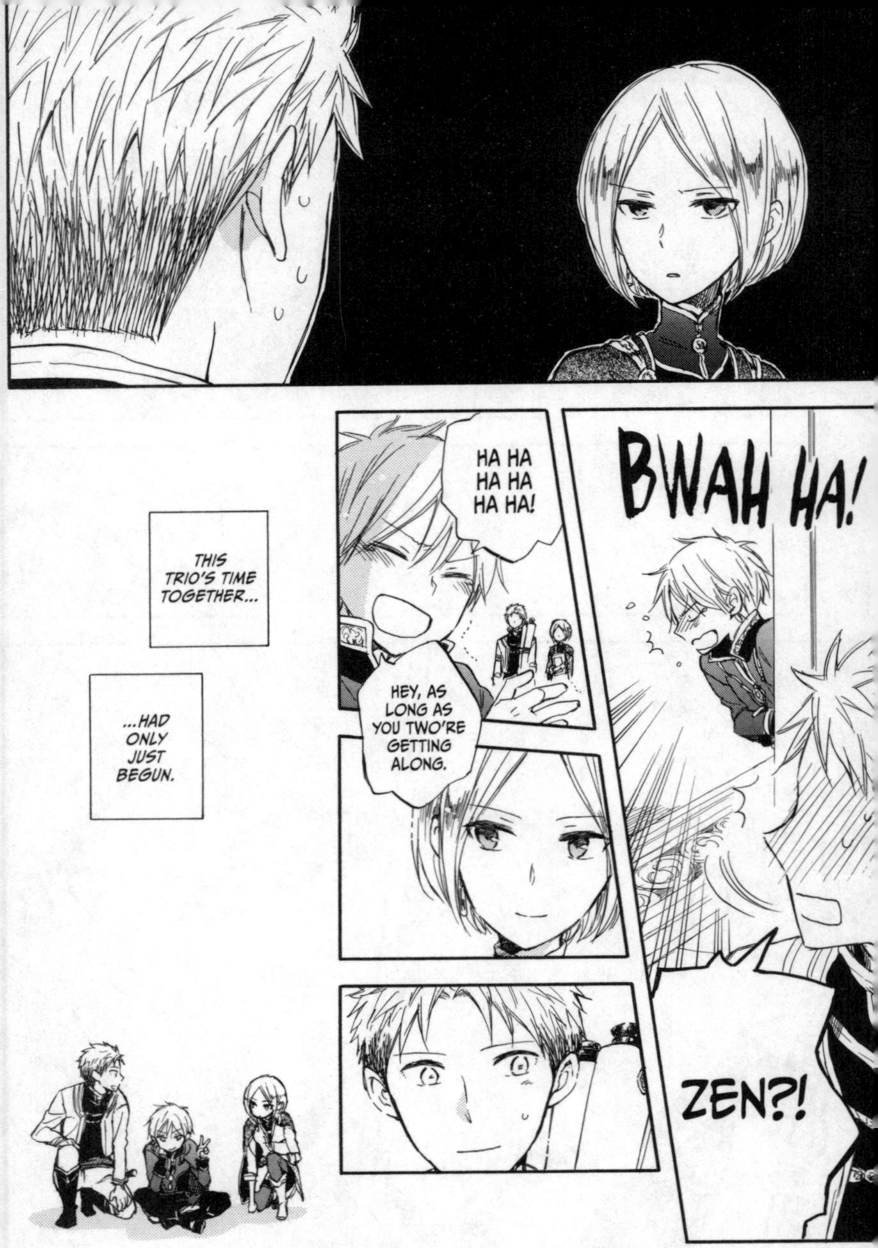
BWAH HA!
ZEN?!
HA HA HA HA HA HA!
HEY, AS LONG AS YOU TWO'RE GETTING ALONG.
THIS TRIO'S TIME TOGETHER...
...HAD ONLY JUST BEGUN.

Snow White with the Red Hair
Bonus Chapter: End

Big Thanks To:

-My editor

-The editorial staff at *LaLa*

-Everyone in Publishing/Sales

-Yamashita-sama

-Noro-sama

-Akatsuki-sama

-My mother, sister and father

-Everyone who sends me letters

-All the readers out there!

Sorata Akiduki

Yuzuri

Suzu

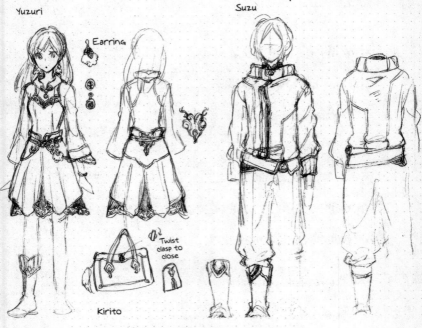

Earring

Twist
clasp to
close

Kirito

Diamond

The Lilias trio's
clothes during
their visit to
the palace

Night Off

How about the loser gets a punishment?
Nah.
Anything you've thought up can't be good, Obi.
C'mon. If I lose, I'll do anything you ask, but only once.
Okay, let's do it.
That was fast! Dying to make me do something specific?
And if one of you loses...
...you gotta pick the cutest thing you think Princess Kiki does—and tell her about it.
This game just got dangerous.

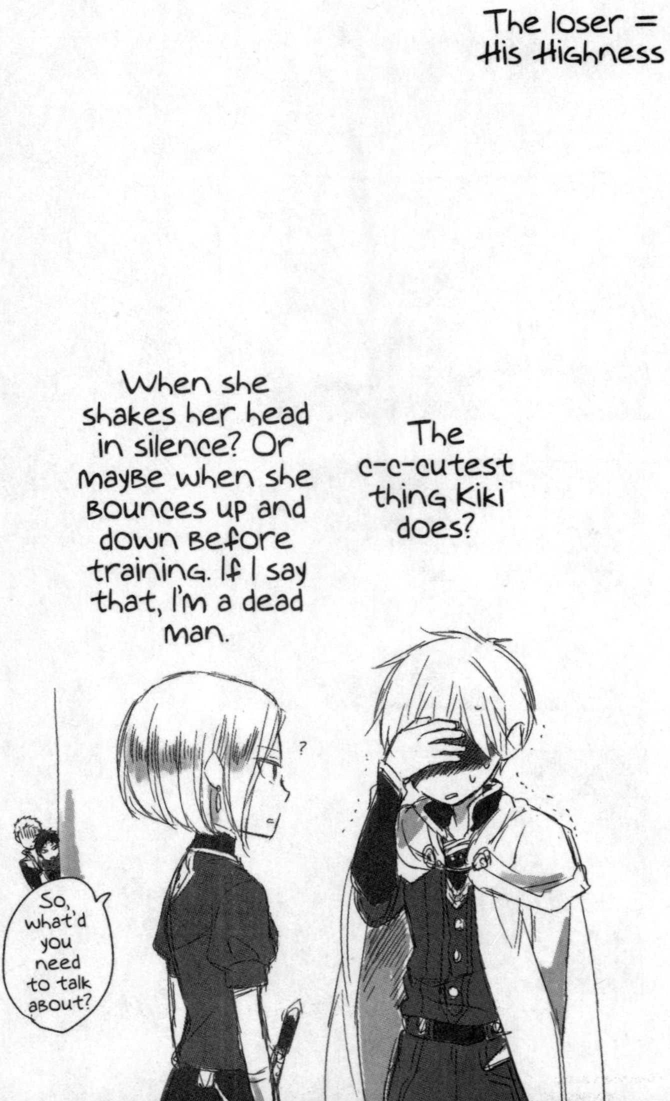
The loser = His Highness
The c-c-cutest thing Kiki does?
When she shakes her head in silence? Or maybe when she bounces up and down before training. If I say that, I'm a dead man.
?
So, what'd you need to talk about?

Sorata Akiduki was born on March 21 and is an accomplished shojo manga author. She made her debut in January 2002 with a one-shot titled "Utopia." Her previous works include *Vahlia no Hanamuko* (Vahlia's Bridegroom), *Seishun Kouryakuhon* (Youth Strategy Guide) and *Natsu Yasumi Zero Zero Nichime* (00 Days of Summer Vacation). *Snow White with the Red Hair* began serialization in August 2006 in *LaLa DX* in Japan and has since moved to *LaLa*.

Snow White with the Red Hair

11

SHOJO BEAT EDITION

STORY AND ART BY
Sorata Akiduki

TRANSLATION **Caleb Cook**
TOUCH-UP ART & LETTERING **Brandon Bovia**
DESIGN **Alice Lewis**
EDITOR **Karla Clark**

Akagami no Shirayukihime by Sorata Akiduki
© Sorata Akiduki 2014
All rights reserved.
First published in Japan in 2014 by HAKUSENSHA, Inc., Tokyo.
English language translation rights arranged with HAKUSENSHA, Inc., Tokyo.

The stories, characters and incidents mentioned
in this publication are entirely fictional.

Printed in the U.S.A.

Published by VIZ Media, LLC
P.O. Box 77010
San Francisco, CA 94107

10 9 8 7 6 5 4 3 2 1
First printing, January 2021

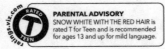

PARENTAL ADVISORY
SNOW WHITE WITH THE RED HAIR is
rated T for Teen and is recommended
for ages 13 and up for mild language.
ratings.viz.com

viz.com   shojobeat.com

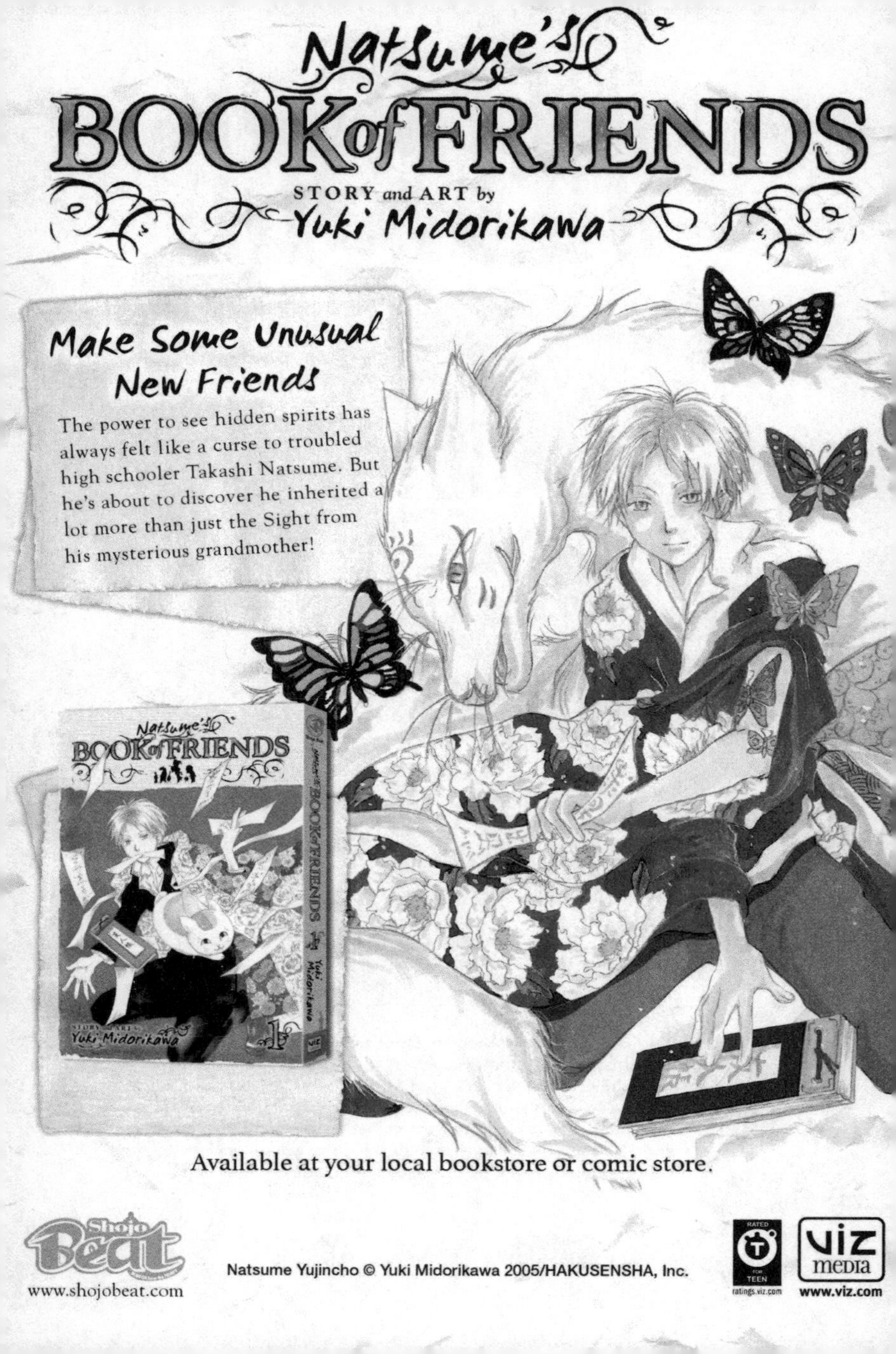
Natsume's
BOOK of FRIENDS
STORY and ART by
Yuki Midorikawa
Make Some Unusual New Friends
The power to see hidden spirits has always felt like a curse to troubled high schooler Takashi Natsume. But he's about to discover he inherited a lot more than just the Sight from his mysterious grandmother!
Available at your local bookstore or comic store.
Shojo Beat
www.shojobeat.com
Natsume Yujincho © Yuki Midorikawa 2005/HAKUSENSHA, Inc.
RATED T FOR TEEN
ratings.viz.com
VIZ MEDIA
www.viz.com

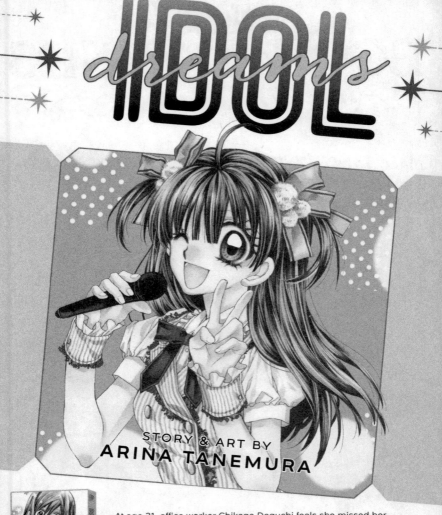

IDOL dreams

STORY & ART BY
ARINA TANEMURA

At age 31, office worker Chikage Deguchi feels she missed her chances at love and success. When word gets out that she's a virgin, Chikage is humiliated and wishes she could turn back time to when she was still young and popular. She takes an experimental drug that changes her appearance back to when she was 15. Now Chikage is determined to pursue everything she missed out on all those years ago—including becoming a star!

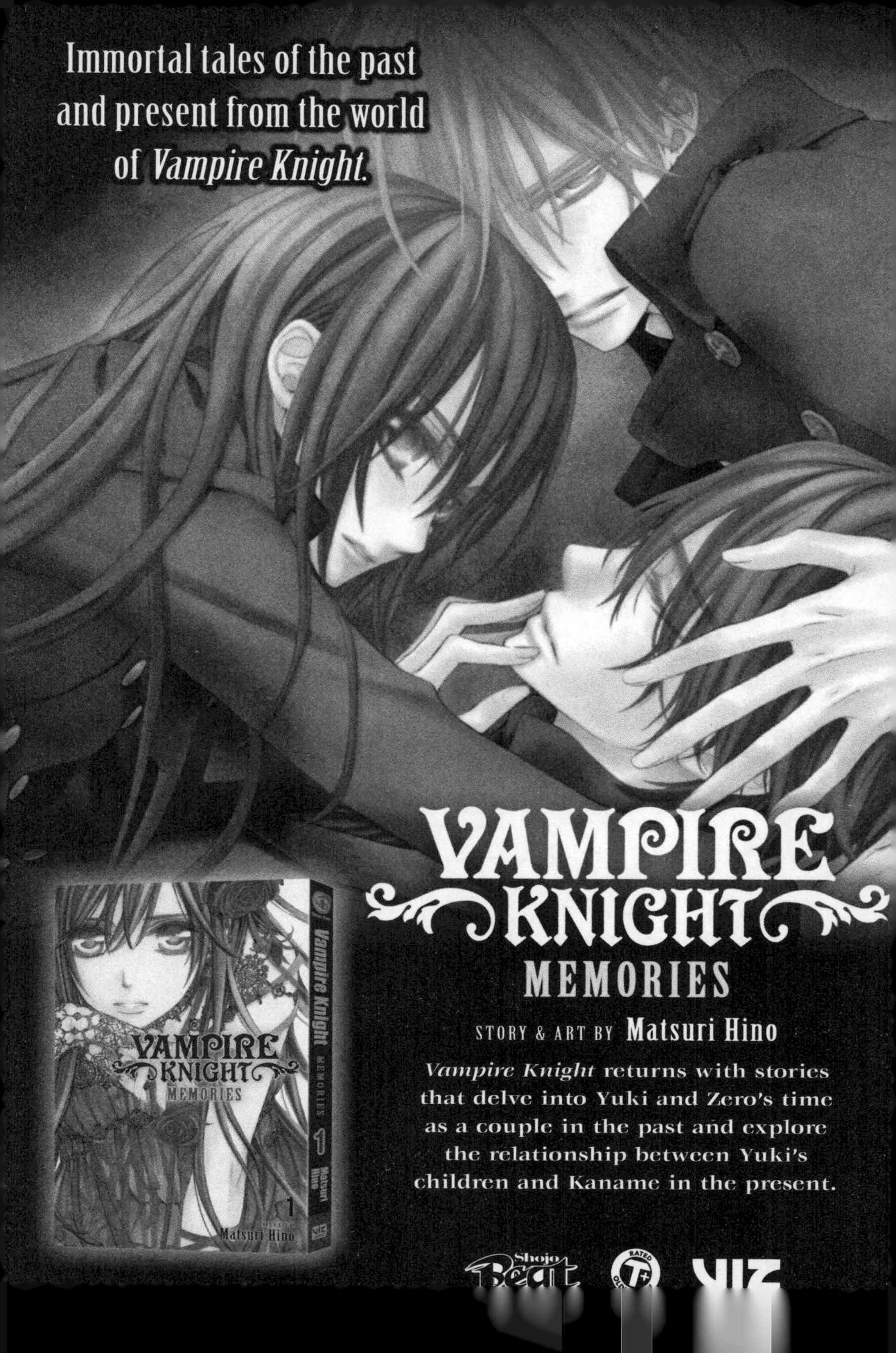
Immortal tales of the past and present from the world of Vampire Knight.
VAMPIRE KNIGHT
MEMORIES
STORY & ART BY Matsuri Hino
Vampire Knight returns with stories that delve into Yuki and Zero's time as a couple in the past and explore the relationship between Yuki's children and Kaname in the present.
VAMPIRE KNIGHT MEMORIES
1
Matsuri Hino
Vampire Knight MEMORIES 1 Matsuri Hino
Shojo Beat
RATED T+
VIZ